Instructional Technology and Media for Learning

Eleventh Edition

Instructional Technology and Media for Learning

Sharon E. Smaldino
Northern Illinois University

Deborah L. Lowther
University of Memphis

James D. Russell
Purdue University

Clif Mims
University of Memphis

PEARSON

Boston   Columbus   Indianapolis   New York   San Francisco   Upper Saddle River
Amsterdam   Cape Town   Dubai   London   Madrid   Milan   Munich   Paris   Montreal   Toronto
Delhi   Mexico City   São Paulo   Sydney   Hong Kong   Seoul   Singapore   Taipei   Tokyo

Vice President, Editor in Chief: Jeffery W. Johnston
Senior Acquisitions Editor: Meredith D. Fossel
Development Editor: Bryce Bell
Editorial Assistant: Maria Feliberty
Marketing Manager: Darcy Betts
Program Manager: Janet Domingo
Project Manager: Cynthia DeRocco
Editorial Production Service: Electronic Publishing Services Inc., NYC
Operations Specialist: Linda Sager
Electronic Composition: Jouve
Interior Design: Wanda Espana, Wee Designs
Cover Design: Wanda Espana, Wee Designs
Cover Image: Peathegee Inc/Blend Images/Getty Images

Credits and acknowledgments borrowed from other sources and reproduced, with permission, in this textbook appear on the appropriate page within text or on page 257.

Library of Congress Cataloging-in-Publication Data
Smaldino, Sharon E.
   Instructional technology and media for learning / Sharon E. Smaldino, Deborah L. Lowther, James D. Russell, Clif Mims. — Eleventh edition.
      pages   cm
   Includes bibliographical references and index.
   ISBN 978-0-13-356415-0
   1. Educational technology.   2. Audio-visual education.   I. Lowther, Deborah L.   II. Russell, James D.
III. Mims, Clif   IV. Title.
   LB1028.3.H45   2012
   371.33—dc23

                                                                                2013038898

10 9 8 7 6 5 4 3 2 1

PEARSON

ISBN 10: 0-13-356415-0
ISBN 13: 978-0-13-356415-0

About the Authors

Sharon E. Smaldino

Sharon holds the LD and Ruth G. Morgridge Endowed Chair for Teacher Education in the College of Education at Northern Illinois University (NIU). She has served as a professor of educational technology for many years. Sharon received her PhD from Southern Illinois University, Carbondale, with an emphasis on technology integration in education. She received an MA in elementary education from the University of Connecticut and served as a speech therapist and special educator in school districts from Florida to Minnesota. Sharon has taught courses in instructional development, technology integration, distance education, and professional standards and ethical practice. She has received several awards for her outstanding teaching. In her current role, she is focused on working with faculty and PK–12 teachers to integrate technology into the learning process. Presenting at state, national, and international conferences, Sharon has become an important voice on applications of technology in the classroom and in distance education. In addition to her teaching, Sharon has written articles for state and national journals on her primary research interest: effective technology integration in learning. She has worked on grants that are designed to support teachers to integrate technology into their teaching. She has served as a journal editor and president of the Association for Educational Communications and Technology (AECT).

Deborah L. Lowther

Deborah has been an educator for the past 30 years. For the first seven years of her career she taught middle school science and was highly engaged with providing professional development to teachers within and beyond her district. Because of her desire to work with teachers, she received her PhD in educational technology in 1994 and accepted a faculty position at the University of Memphis in 1995. At the University of Memphis, Deborah serves as Department Chair for Instruction and Curriculum Leadership (ICL). The ICL department offers eight initial teacher licensure programs as well as several MS and EdD options. Prior to accepting the chair position, Deborah served as the senior technology researcher for the Center for Research in Educational Policy, through which she investigates PK–12 technology integration issues. She has personally conducted observations in PK–12 classrooms and interviewed students, teachers, and principals in numerous schools across the country. She has used the knowledge and experiences gained through engagement in applied research to develop the iNtegrating Technology for inQuiry (NTeQ) Model with Dr. Gary Morrison. This model has been the foundational approach for several high-profile state-level technology initiatives. With regard to scholarship, Deborah has coauthored several books, chapters, and refereed journal articles; presented at numerous national and international conferences; and provided professional development to educational institutions across the nation.

James D. Russell

Jim is professor emeritus of Educational Technology at Purdue University, where he taught for 38 years. Jim also worked part time for Purdue's Center for Instructional Excellence, conducting workshops on teaching techniques and consulting on instructional improvement. During 14 spring semesters he was visiting professor of Educational Psychology and Learning Systems at Florida State University. There he also worked part time for the Center for Teaching and Learning. A former high school mathematics and physics teacher, Jim's teaching career spans 45 years. He has won numerous honors for his teaching at Purdue, including his department's Outstanding Teacher Award and the School of Education's Best Teacher Award. He is also the recipient of AECT's Diamond Mentor Award. He was selected as a member of Purdue's Teaching Academy and has been inducted into the Purdue Book of Great Teachers. His specialty areas, in which he has achieved national prominence through his writings and presentations, are presentation skills and using media and technology in classrooms. Through his teaching, workshops, consulting, and this textbook, Jim has made a significant impact on classroom teaching practice.

Clif Mims

Clif is a teacher, researcher, author, speaker, and educational consultant specializing in the effective integration of technology with teaching and learning. His teaching career began more than 20 years ago as an elementary and middle school teacher. He also coached basketball and math teams to numerous championships. While earning his doctorate in instructional technology at the University of Georgia, Clif began focusing on teacher education and professional development. He is a professor of instructional design and technology at the University of Memphis and is the founding executive director of the Martin Institute for Teaching Excellence. Clif is both a Project Zero Faculty Fellow and a Future of Learning Fellow at Harvard University. He and his wife have three children.

Award-Winning Book

Instructional Technology and Media for Learning has received the following recognition in past editions:

- **Outstanding Book in Educational Technology and Teacher Education** from the Association for Educational Communications and Technology (AECT) Teacher Education Division

- **The James Brown Award for the Best Non-Periodic Publication in the Field of Educational Technology** from AECT

- **The Outstanding Instructional Communication Award** from the International Society for Performance and Improvement (ISPI)

- **The Visual Design and Layout Award** from the Design Society of America

Brief Contents

Contents

10 Preparing for Tomorrow's Challenges   218

Appendix   Lesson Scenarios   231

Special Features

Instructional Technology and Media for Learning, 11th edition, shows how a complete range of technology and media formats can be integrated into classroom instruction using the ASSURE model for lesson planning. Written from the viewpoint of the teacher, the text shows specifically and realistically how technology and media fit into the daily life of the classroom. This book is intended for educators at all levels who place a high value on learning. Its purpose is to help educators incorporate technology and media into their repertoire—to use them as teaching tools and to guide students in using them as learning tools. We draw examples from elementary and secondary education because we know that instructors in these PK–12 settings have found previous editions of this book useful in their work.

This new edition is necessitated by the amazing pace of innovation in all aspects of technology, particularly in those related to computers and mobile technologies and the Internet. The text has been updated to reflect the accelerating trend toward digitizing information and school use of telecommunications resources, such as the Web. The 11th edition also addresses the interaction among the roles of teachers, technology coordinators, and school media specialists, all complementary and interdependent teams within the school.

New to This Edition

- Embedded video in the Pearson eText* enriches your experience with the text by allowing you to see real teachers in real classrooms, and shares their insights.
- Pop-up Selection Rubrics*, which are printable, aid in the process of selecting classroom technology materials.
- Web links at point-of-use help you further explore topics discussed.
- Revised chapters have updated information about designing instruction for 21st century learning, including the Common Core State Standards.
- Current technologies to support learning are identified and include overviews of how to use them with students of all ages.
- End-of-chapter activities guide the user through teacher performance assessment using the ISTE NETS as part of the process.
- Taking a Look at Technology Integration features are updated with examples of how actual classroom teachers use technology to support student learning. The examples place emphasis on integrating the 21st century skills and the Common Core Learning Standards.
- Increased focus is given to enhancing the use of classroom technology to meet the learning needs of all students. With the advent of Response to Intervention (RtI), classroom teachers are expected to meet the learning needs of their students. We have expanded the Technology for All Learners feature to help consider options that will be useful to facilitate learning experiences for all students in the classroom.

The Pearson eText* for this title is an affordable, interactive version of the print text that includes videos, pop-up content, and links to additional information. The play button appears where video is available, while hyperlinked words provide access to pop-ups and other related websites.

Go to **www.pearsonhighered.com/etextbooks** to learn more about the enhanced Pearson eText for *Instructional Technology and Media for Learning.*

*These enhancements are only available through the Pearson eText, and not other third-party eTexts such as CourseSmart or Kindle.

Our Approach

We share a number of convictions that underlie this edition. First, we believe in an *eclectic* approach to instruction. Advocates cite an abundance of theories and philosophies in support of different approaches to instruction—behaviorist, cognitivist, constructivist, and social-psychological. We view these theoretical positions as differing *perspectives*—different vantage points—from which to examine the complex world of teaching and learning. We value each of them and feel that each is reflected in the guidance we offer.

Second, we have a balanced posture regarding the role of technology in instruction. Because of this perspective, we consider each technology in light of its advantages, limitations, and range of applications. No technology can be described solely as being either "good" or "bad," so we strive to give a balanced treatment to a range of technologies and media resources.

Third, we believe that technology can best be integrated into instruction when viewed from a teacher's perspective. Therefore, throughout the book, we attempt to approach technology and media solutions in terms of a teacher's day-to-day challenges and to avoid technical jargon as much as possible. Our examples deal with everyday teaching issues in a range of content areas.

The ASSURE Model for Technology Integration

In this edition, the explanation of the ASSURE model has been revised to be more clear, practical, and focused on PK–12 teaching and learning. The text offers several chapter features (Classroom Case Study and Classroom Case Study Reflection) that show how teachers can effectively integrate technology and media into instruction, all in the context of each chapter's content. Chapters 3 through 9 open with a video feature that offers an example of how one teacher uses technology to augment the learning experiences of the students.

Focus on Professional Development

The "Professional Development" feature helps readers develop their ongoing professional knowledge and skills with regard to effectively using technology and media for learning.

The first section, "Demonstrate Professional Knowledge," poses questions based on the Knowledge Outcomes at the beginning of each chapter. In the next section, "Demonstrate Professional Skills," readers integrate their learning through activities that are aligned with the ISTE NETS for Teachers. The final section, "Build Your Professional Portfolio," includes three parts: Creating My Lesson, Enhancing My Lesson, and Reflecting on My Lesson. These are also linked to the ISTE NETS for Teachers.

- "Creating My Lesson" asks readers to select their own topics and settings for developing lessons that integrate the technology and media discussed in the chapter. Chapter-specific questions help readers make decisions to create their own lesson plan using appropriate instructional strategies, technology, and media.

- "Enhancing My Lesson" asks the reader to describe other strategies, technology, media, and materials that could enhance the lesson. The reader addresses how the lesson could be enhanced to meet the diverse needs of learners, including students who already possess the knowledge and skills targeted in the lesson plan.

- **Reflecting on My Lesson** prompts readers to reflect on their lesson, the process used to develop it, and different types of students who could benefit from it. Readers are also asked to reflect on what they learned about the process of matching audience, content, strategies, technology, media, and materials.

Special Features

The ASSURE Model for Technology Integration. Chapter opening "ASSURE Classroom Case Studies" (in Chapters 3 through 9) each presents a video clip of a specific classroom that will be revisited periodically throughout the chapter in the "ASSURE Case Study Reflections." These are brief notes and reflection questions that extend the opening case study by addressing the questions that a teacher may face when considering technology integration in the context of specific chapter content. At the end of the chapter, the "ASSURE Lesson Plan" provides a fuller version of the instructional or classroom situation outlined at the beginning of the chapter and offers a possible solution.

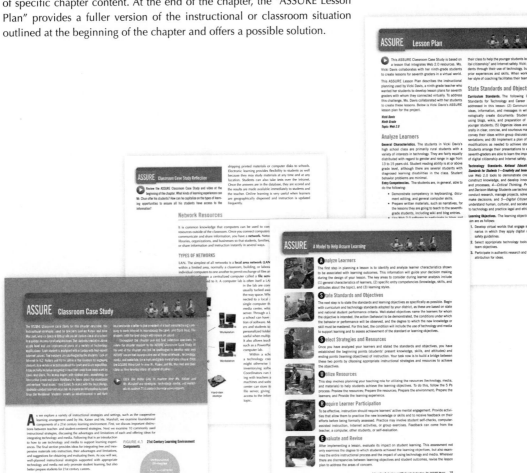

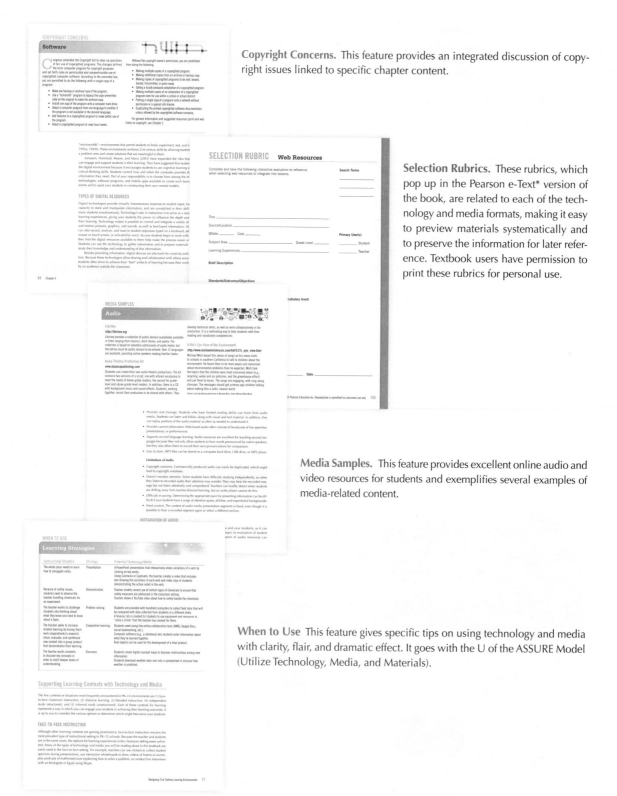

Copyright Concerns. This feature provides an integrated discussion of copyright issues linked to specific chapter content.

Selection Rubrics. These rubrics, which pop up in the Pearson e-Text* version of the book, are related to each of the technology and media formats, making it easy to preview materials systematically and to preserve the information for later reference. Textbook users have permission to print these rubrics for personal use.

Media Samples. This feature provides excellent online audio and video resources for students and exemplifies several examples of media-related content.

When to Use This feature gives specific tips on using technology and media with clarity, flair, and dramatic effect. It goes with the U of the ASSURE Model (Utilize Technology, Media, and Materials).

*Enhancements are only available in the Pearson eText, and not third-party eTexts such as CourseSmart or Kindle.

Technology for All Learners. This feature describes technology and media that can be used to meet the learning needs of diverse learners, ranging from those with learning disabilities to gifted and talented students.

Technology Resources. Because many schools have tight budgets, this feature offers a list of practical and valuable resources that are free or inexpensive. They also inform the reader how to obtain the resources. These are listed at the ends of chapters along with helpful web links.

Taking a Look at Technology Integration. These miniature case studies of technology and media applications demonstrate how teachers are using technology in a variety of settings. Like the ASSURE Classroom Case Study, they show technology and media use *in context*.

ISTE NETS-T Alignment. At the beginning of each chapter, the ISTE NETS-T are aligned with the chapter Knowledge Outcomes. At the end of each chapter, the professional skills activities reflect the ISTE NETS-T. For each end-of-chapter activity, at least one standard has been identified. Students who successfully complete the skills activities will demonstrate that they have accomplished the standards.

Instructor Resources

The following instructor resources support and reinforce the content presented throughout the text. They are available for download under the Educator tab at www.pearsonhighered.com. Simply enter the author, title, or ISBN, and then select this textbook. Click on the Resources tab to view and download the supplements detailed below.

For more information, contact your Pearson Education sales representative.

Instructor's Resource Manual and Test Bank. (0-13-356417-7) This guide provides chapter-by-chapter tools for use in class. Teaching strategies, in-class activities, student projects, key term definitions, and helpful resources will reinforce key concepts or applications and keep students engaged. A bank of test questions for each chapter provides multiple-choice and short answer items. Test items are designed to be flexible and adaptable to meet instructional needs.

TestGen. (0-13-356965-9) This powerful test generator is available exclusively from Pearson Education publishers. You install TestGen on your personal computer (Windows or Macintosh) and create your own tests for classroom use and for other specialized delivery options, such as over a local area network or on the Web. A test bank, which is also called a Test Item File (TIF), typically contains a large set of test items, organized by chapter and ready for your use in creating a test, based on the associated textbook material. Assessments—including equations, graphs, and scientific notation—may be created for both print or testing online.

PowerPoint® Presentations. (0-13-356416-9) Designed as an instructional tool, the presentations can be used to present and elaborate on chapter material. They are available for both students and instructors, and they reinforce key concepts and ideas presented throughout the text. These are available for download from the Instructor Resource Center.

Authors' Services. The authors are eager to assist you in putting together an outstanding course. We offer the following services to instructors who have adopted this book:

- *Online dialog.* The authors are available to "meet" with your students if you are using an online course delivery tool such as Blackboard or Moodle.

- *Telelectures and Videoconferences.* Contact any of the authors in advance to arrange a guest lecture in your class via telephone or video. Some instructors use this technology as a demonstration of the techniques described in Chapter 7. The authors' phone numbers, fax numbers, and email addresses are listed in the Instructor's Guide.

- *Workshops.* The authors have conducted workshops at the national convention of the Association for Educational Communications and Technology (AECT). This is a forum for exchanging ideas and networking among instructors of courses on technology and media. They are also available to provide a workshop in your area if you wish to arrange one.

- *Consulting.* The authors are available for consulting and conducting workshops at the local, state, and national levels. They are regular presenters and workshop facilitators across the country and around the world.

If you are a student or an instructor using this text and wish to share your comments with us, send them to Sharon Smaldino, Northern Illinois University, Gabel Hall 155, College of Education, DeKalb, IL 60115. She can also be reached at smaldinos@comcast.net.

Acknowledgments

Through each of the editions we have been fortunate to have guidance from the people who teach the courses for which this book is designed. In preparing this edition, we again surveyed a sample of adopters and other leaders in the field to elicit their advice about content and emphases. We also asked other well-respected colleagues in the field to critique the text. We thank all those who gave their time and expertise to help make this textbook what it is. In particular, we want to acknowledge those talented individuals who reviewed the previous edition and suggested improvements: Kathleen Bacer, Azusa Pacific University; Marjorie A. Mattis, Harrisburg Area Community College; John Mikulski, Medaille College; Elena Qureshi, Madonna University; Susan R. Sutton, St. Cloud State University; and David White, Texas Tech University.

We have been lucky to have Joe Sweeney, a University of Memphis graduate student, to serve as a photographer for this edition. We wish to thank him for assistance in updating and expanding the images included in this edition.

We offer an extended appreciation to the teachers for sharing their expertise and allowing us to record their technology integration lessons: Tiare Ahu, high school; Lindsay Kaiser and Jena Marshall, fifth grade; Kerry Bird, fourth grade; Vicki Davis, high school; Jimmy Chun, high school; Christine Edlund, art, and Mary Roman, third grade; Aina Akamu, high school; Scott James, fifth grade; and Phil Ekkers, first grade.

We would like to thank the editorial and production staff of Pearson Education, specifically Meredith Fossel, Bryce Bell, Maria Feliberty, and Cynthia DeRocco. We also want to thank our copy editor for valuable editing contributions and for assistance with the content related to computers. Fair Josey provided valuable assistance in updating the PowerPoint slides and preparing the Instructor's Guide and Test Bank. We have never had such intense and helpful support from any previous publication team.

We are grateful to our colleagues from our own universities—Northern Illinois University, the University of Memphis, and Purdue University—for their many and valuable forms of support over the years.

Finally, we thank our families for all they do to make this project possible. Their patience and support have been invaluable in helping us finish this project.

Sharon E. Smaldino
Deborah L. Lowther
James D. Russell
Clif Mims

ASSURE Learning in Action Video Clips

Chapter 3

Integrating Technology and Media into Instruction: The ASSURE Model

Tiare Ahu has her ninth-grade English students use computers, DreamWeaver, and iMovie software to create electronic portfolios as a way to improve their writing and comprehension skills.

Time: 10:20

Chapter 4

Designing 21st Century Learning Environments

Lindsay Kaiser and Jena Marshall co-teach fifth grade. To enhance their students' limited interest in social studies, they use a WebQuest to guide students' exploration of Lewis and Clark's famous expedition.

Time: 7:17

Chapter 5

Engaging Learners with Digital Devices

The students in Kerry Bird's fourth-grade class increase their understanding of the water cycle by using computers, PowerPoint software, and Internet resources to create individualized presentations of the water cycle.

Time: 6:57

Chapter 6

Learning with Web 2.0 and Social Media

Vicki Davis teaches a technology class comprising high school students who are interested in exploring new technology applications. The lesson involves students conducting a discussion about helping younger students learn online safety within a student-created virtual world. The students use online tools to record their discussions.

Time: 10:22

Chapter 7
Achieving Learning at a Distance

Jimmy Chun's high school social studies students from Hawaii use two-way audio/video distance education and Blackboard course management software to interact with students from New Hampshire.

Time: 12:23

Chapter 8
Enhancing Learning with Audio and Video

Scott James has his fifth-grade students use digital video, iMovie, and "green screens" to create student-scripted news broadcasts on natural disasters.

Time: 20:07

Chapter 9
Enhancing Learning with Text and Visuals

The third-grade students in Mary Roman's class work with the art teacher, Christine Edlund, to create an electronic art portfolio that demonstrates their understanding of mathematics concepts such as symmetry.

Time: 11:44

ASSURE Case Study videos embedded within chapters sometimes appear more than once when ASSURE Case Study Reflections provide instructions on specific, and different, details to watch for while viewing the clips. Watching the clip again, from these different viewpoints, can be very beneficial. Please note that these video clips are only available through the Pearson eText, and not third-party eTexts such as CourseSmart or Kindle.

Instructional Technology and Media for Learning

Exploring 21st Century Learning

Knowledge Outcomes

This chapter addresses ISTE NETS-T 3, 4, and 5:

1. Identify key components of the framework for 21st century learning.

2. Discuss the status of the technology and media in today's PK–12 schools.

3. Describe the roles of technology and media in learning.

4. Explain the roles of the typical 21st century teacher and the typical learner.

5. Discuss the framework for 21st century learning literacies.

6. Identify 21st century learning environments.

7. Explain the role of standards.

8. Describe the key concerns regarding copyright law for educational uses.

Goal

Learn about the uses of technology and media to ensure successful student learning in the 21st century.

This book offers a systematic approach for selecting and using technology and media to facilitate student learning in the 21st century. This approach is based on the ASSURE model, which helps teachers plan effective, integrated lessons by following a six-step process. Exploring both traditional technologies used in PK–12 classrooms today as well as innovative and cutting-edge approaches that may be commonplace in the future, we describe technology and media that teachers can use to promote learning both within and beyond the classroom. We describe how to select, use, and evaluate resources to ensure that learners emerge with the knowledge and skills needed for successful 21st century careers.

We begin by exploring the influence of technology and media within the 21st century learning process on the new roles of teachers to engage students in the classroom. No longer are teachers and textbooks the sources of all information. Instead, the teacher has become the facilitator of knowledge and skills acquisition. With a few keystrokes, students can explore the world using boundless online resources and a wide array of digital media to obtain the information they seek. Students can discuss their findings in real-time conversations with experts and with other students representing a global array of cultures and experiences.

These exciting innovations provide unlimited ways to expand educational opportunities for our students, but they also present new challenges to teachers. As a teacher, how will you go beyond the textbook? How will you select the "right" technology and media when so many choices are available? And more importantly, how will you create learning experiences that effectively use these tools and resources to ensure that your students gain new knowledge and skills?

Framework for 21st Century Learning: Technology and Media in Today's Schools

As we continue to move forward in the 21st century, it is critical that the foundational components of PK–12 education keep pace with evolving societal needs to prepare students for citizenship and successful careers. As a teacher today, you are challenged to help students achieve mastery of core subjects as well as gain 21st century knowledge and skills. Leaders from business and education, as well as other associations and institutions, are joining together to recommend new approaches and broader learning expectations for PK–12 students (ISTE, 2012; Partnership for 21st Century Learning, 2011). Foundational to 21st century knowledge and skills is the preparation of your students to meaningfully and purposefully use technology and media for creativity and innovation, communication, research, and problem solving. Themes based on global awareness, entrepreneurship, and lifelong learning skills, such as adaptability, leadership, and responsibility, are also recommended for inclusion within core subject area courses. This text will serve as a guide to assist you in integrating 21st century knowledge and skills into your instructional planning and practices.

INSTRUCTIONAL TECHNOLOGY

Currently, when most people hear the word *technology,* they think of products like computers, tablets, and mobile devices. In this text, we will be referring to **instructional technology,** which involves the integration of teacher and student use and knowledge of tools, resources, and techniques to improve student learning.

To promote student learning, you need to create an appropriate learning environment. Throughout the book we will describe the decision-making processes that you can use and the factors you must balance in your decisions. You will need to know the characteristics of your learners. The expected outcomes (objectives) must be specified. You will need to select the appropriate strategies and materials. The best available technology and media must be used properly to promote optimal learning. You will need to get your learners involved through appropriate practice and feedback. Throughout the process, you will be assessing student learning and evaluating the instructional experience, as well as its components, so you can revise as necessary. We have put all of these steps together in the ASSURE model.

Although some educators view technology as a classroom cure-all, it is important to note that technology resources don't automatically make teachers more capable. You will need to be versed in best practices for integrating technology into the curriculum. The ASSURE model provides a structure and easy-to-follow steps to guide teachers through the process of creating lessons that achieve the goals of effectively using technology. The model is applicable for all types of technology across all subject areas for different learning conditions.

Developed as a planning aid to help ensure that technology and media are used to their maximum advantage, not just as interchangeable substitutes for printed or oral messages, the ASSURE model provides a systematic process for creating learning experiences. Indeed, one of the most important roles of technology and media is to serve as a catalyst for change in the whole instructional environment.

TECHNOLOGY FOR ALL LEARNERS

Introduction

As a result of inclusion, the number of students with disabilities in the general classroom is increasing. Technology plays an important role in the education of students with exceptionalities. Adapted and specially designed technology and media can contribute enormously to effective instruction of all students and can help them achieve at their highest potential regardless of innate abilities.

Children with disabilities in particular need special instructional interventions. Children with mental disabilities have a greater opportunity to learn when presented with highly structured learning situations. Structure compensates for ill-structured prior knowledge that decreases students' abilities to incorporate messages into atypical mental constructs. These students benefit from having much more of the message placed within a familiar context.

Students with hearing or visual impairments require different kinds of learning materials. More emphasis should be placed on audio for students with visual impairments and on visuals for those with hearing problems. Adjusting instruction for all exceptional groups requires heavy reliance on technology and media, as well as the appropriate selection of these materials to fit specific purposes. Many teachers have found that these assistive strategies for students with disabilities have the added benefit of helping all students.

Assistive technologies can be classified as low tech, medium tech, or high tech. Low-tech devices do not use electricity (neither electricity nor batteries). For example, a magnifying glass to enlarge printed material for a visually impaired student would be a low-tech assistive technology. The medium-tech category includes electrical devices. A mini book light to increase illumination would be representative of medium-tech equipment. High-tech assistance

involves the use of a computer. The knfb Reader is an example of high-tech assistive technology.

Diverse learners also include gifted and talented students who, for example, could use newspapers, periodicals, DVDs, or archived documents to explore topics beyond or in addition to regular classroom assignments. They can also use the Internet to search for current information or to engage in a live chat with the author of a book the class is reading or a state senator who will vote on an environmental issue being studied. They can be asked to analyze the information they locate and to synthesize a presentation for the class, perhaps using PowerPoint, or they can post their findings on a class webpage.

For more information, see the Technology for All Learners features throughout this book.

A braille display is an example of an assistive technology.

Current technology offers several benefits for teachers. One is the ability to digitally store and access large amounts of information, whether as text, audio, visuals, games, or movies, in computer files, on CDs or DVDs, or in a cloud storage space. Another unique advantage of current technology is its adaptability to meet the varying needs of your students. As seen in the accompanying Technology for All Learners feature, you can differentiate instruction and access to learning experiences with a variety of technology tools. A third advantage of technology is that your students are no longer limited to the confines of the classroom. Through the school media center and computer networks such as the Internet, the world becomes each student's classroom.

Status of the Technology Gap. As you plan different technology integration activities, it is important to stay current on technology issues, such as the "digital divide," that may influence your instructional choices. The digital divide—or technology gap—in PK–12 schools continues to narrow. Students of all economic levels have greater access to high-speed Internet-connected computers at school. The current ratio of about one computer per every three students (Warschauer, 2010) helps bridge the gap for students who may not have home computers.

On the other hand, the technology gap varies when examining Internet usage by adults. Even though in 2011 approximately 80% of American adults used the Internet at home or work, disparities in Internet use still exist based on ethnic groups (Livingston, 2011). For example, 77% of white adults reported using the Internet at home, as compared to 66% of black and 65% of Latino adults. A similar pattern was seen for use of cell phones when focused on voice. Interestingly, the report revealed that nonvoice cell phone use was higher among all groups, with text messaging being the highest nonvoice use of the cell phone among all groups. So, when you are thinking about using the Internet to communicate with your students' families, remember that not all of them will have access to your webpages or emails.

Media Formats. Media, the plural of *medium,* are means of communication. Derived from the Latin *medium* ("between"), the term refers to anything that carries information between a source and a receiver. The purpose of media is to facilitate communication and learning.

Media are discussed in more detail in later chapters, but as an overview, let's look at the six basic types of media used in learning (Figure 1.1): text, audio, visuals, video, manipulatives (objects), and people. Text, the most commonly used medium, is composed of alphanumeric characters that may be displayed in any format—book, poster, whiteboard, computer screen, and so on. Audio, another medium commonly used in learning, includes anything you can hear—a person's voice, music, mechanical sounds (running car engine), noise, and so on. It may be live or recorded. Visuals are also regularly used to promote learning and include diagrams on a computer screen, drawings on a whiteboard, photographs, graphics in a book, cartoons, and so on. Video is a visual as well as audio medium that shows motion and can be stored on DVDs, streamed from the Internet, be in the form of computer animation, and so on. Although often not considered media, real objects and models are three-dimensional manipulatives that can be touched and handled by students. The sixth and final category of media is people. In fact, people are critical to learning. Students learn from teachers, other students, and adults.

There are many types of media in each category, which we will refer to as **media formats**—the physical forms in which messages are incorporated and displayed. Media formats include, for example, whiteboards and webpages (text and visuals), PowerPoint or Prezi slides (text and visuals), CDs (voice and music), DVDs (video and audio), and computer multimedia (audio, text, and video). Each has different strengths and limitations in terms of the types of messages that can be recorded and displayed. Choosing a media format can be a complex task, considering the vast array of media and technology available, the variety of learners, and the many objectives to be pursued (Table 1.1). When selecting media formats,

FIGURE 1.1   Six Basic Categories of Media

the instructional situation or setting (e.g., large group, small group, or self-instruction), learner variables (e.g., reader, nonreader, or auditory preference), and the nature of the objective (e.g., cognitive, affective, motor skill, or interpersonal) must be considered, as well as the presentational capabilities of each of the media formats (e.g., still visuals, video, printed words, or spoken words).

INSTRUCTIONAL MATERIALS

Once you determine the media format, such as a DVD, you must decide which of the appropriate DVDs you will use. The specific DVD becomes the instructional material.

TABLE 1.1	Examples of Media Formats and Instructional Materials	
Media	Media Formats	Instructional Materials Examples
Text	Printed book, computer software, e-book, webpages	A textbook StoryMaker software
Audio	CD, live presenter, podcast	State of the Union address on webcast
Visual	Drawing on interactive whiteboard Photo in a newspaper	Drawing of the musical scale Photo of local building
Video	DVD, IMAX documentary film, streamed video	*Lewis & Clark: Great Journey West* video
Manipulative	Real or virtual object	Algebra tiles
People	Teachers, subject-matter expert	The chief officer of NASA

Instructional materials are the specific items used within a lesson that influence student learning. For example, a middle school lesson may focus on adding polynomials with a computer software program that provides virtual manipulatives students use to create "concrete" examples of addition problems in order to reach solutions. The computer software offers feedback and opportunities to continue practicing. The specific math problems and feedback generated by this software are the instructional materials. Another example is this text that you are currently reading, which consists of the written information (text), visuals, and learning exercises found at the end of the chapter.

The design and use of instructional materials are critical, because it is the interaction of the students with those materials that generates and reinforces actual learning. If the materials are weak, improperly structured, or poorly sequenced, only limited learning will occur. On the other hand, powerful, well-designed instructional materials are experienced in such a way that they can be readily encoded, retained, recalled, and used in a variety of ways. Learners will remember these materials if they are created, integrated, and presented in a manner that allows them to have the needed impact.

Students can be actively involved individually, in small groups, or with a teacher.

ROLES OF TECHNOLOGY AND MEDIA IN LEARNING

Jonathan Bergmann and Aaron Sams (2012) coined the phase "the flipped classroom" to describe a model of instruction that mixes direct instruction with constructivist learning experiences. The idea merges technology-based instructional opportunities with teacher-guided learning. Students are able to gather information through video, online exploration, and audio formats outside the instructional setting that they then use in the classroom to extend their understanding of content with the teacher's guidance.

Technology and media play an important role in these types of learning experiences, either when you create them for your students to use or when your students explore new learning opportunities. The model provides you with the opportunity to bring technology more naturally into your classrooms and to explore more creative ways to engage your students in learning (Hertz, 2012).

The 21st Century Teacher

When instruction is teacher centered, technology and media are used to support the presentation of instruction. For example, you may use an electronic whiteboard to display variations of a bar graph as your students predict population growth over time. You may also use a pocket chart to show how the meaning of a sentence changes when word cards are rearranged. Projecting a live video feed from a zoo can facilitate a presentation on the feeding habits of birds. Certainly, properly designed instructional materials can enhance and promote learning. This book uses the ASSURE model to assist you in selecting and using instructional strategies, media, technology, and materials. However, the effectiveness of your choices depends on careful planning and selection of the appropriate resources, as seen in the next section.

THE DIGITAL TEACHER

Digital tools expand and enhance your capabilities to fulfill the numerous roles and responsibilities associated with being an educator. These tools better enable the "digital" teacher to plan for and provide interactive instruction while participating in a global community of practice with fellow educators. The following examples show the potential available in a well-equipped digital environment.

Interactive Instruction. A "digital" teacher's instruction includes presentations that are media rich and interactive. Live digital videoconferences bring historians, novelists, and content experts into your classroom. Notes and concept maps from brainstorming sessions are captured on electronic whiteboards and instantaneously emailed to your students. Instructional presentations seamlessly integrate streamed digital video and audio from Internet-based files that range from short clips demonstrating specific concepts to full-length documentaries. You instantaneously go to a specific section of a DVD and show a segment in slow or fast motion or as a still image to reinforce targeted outcomes for your students. PowerPoint or Prezi presentations integrate animations, sounds, and hyperlinks with digitized information.

Personal Response Systems (PRS). Digital teachers use handheld digital devices, such as **personal response systems** (PRS), to collect and graphically display student answers to teacher questions. The PRS, commonly called a "clicker," is a wireless keypad similar to a TV remote that transmits student responses. Because each PRS is assigned to a designated student, the PRS system can be used to take attendance. However, its main benefit is to allow you to know each of your student's responses in a variety of circumstances. Using PRS during instruction enhances learner–instructor interactivity in whole-class settings, which has been shown to produce better learning outcomes (Flynn & Russell, 2008). Educational uses of the PRS include measuring student understanding of concepts, comparing student attitudes about different ideas, predicting "What if" situations, and facilitating drill and practice of basic skills. The PRS graphs student responses to provide teachers and students immediate feedback. Teachers can use this information to guide the pace and direction of a discussion and to make instructional decisions to meet student learning needs.

Teachers can use technology to help students understand concepts.

Mobile Assessment Tools. Mobile computing resources enable teachers to record student assessment data directly into a mobile device that transfers the data to a computer for report generation. For example, mobile digital devices

Personal response systems provide teachers with immediate feedback from students.

are used to create running records of primary student reading ability or student performance data observed in presentations, lab experiments, or handwriting (Weinstein, 2005).

Elementary teachers are fast becoming large-scale users of mobile assessment tools to monitor and record the reading abilities of their students. Many use mCLASS: Reading by Wireless Generation, software that provides the text of a book the student is reading and a series of tools to let the teacher easily track performance while the student reads the book. The software also offers digital versions of leading reading assessment instruments, such as Dynamic Indicators of Basic Early Literacy Skills (DIBELS).

The mobile devices not only save you time, but the software also provides automatic timing and scoring of your student results. You can continually individualize instruction because of the availability of immediate results. Assessment data are easily downloaded to a secure, password-protected website that offers a variety of reporting options, from whole class to individual student.

Mobile devices allow you to gather information directly from your students. Ms. Unger, a fourth grade teacher, uses Quick Response (QR) Codes to gather information about her students as they enter her classroom every morning. She assigns her students homework that is a summary of what they learned and how they are feeling about school which they then transmit to her each morning. She uses the QR code system the school district installed as a quick way to gather the information. She scans through the student reports and adjusts her teaching to reflect her students' needs. While the data she gathers is informal, Ms. Unger feels that it helps her to ensure quality learning experiences for all her students.

Special education teachers often use a mobile device equipped with GoObserve software as a mobile assessment tool. The program can be customized to record designated activities in a student's Individual Education Plan. During an observation of your student performance or behavior, you use the stylus to record the observed strategies from a list of possible choices. As a teacher, you also can add written comments and notes to that student's record. After the observation, you can transfer the information to your computer to generate reports and graphs of student progress.

Community of Practice. Digital teachers participate in community of practice (CoP) activities, in which groups of educators with common goals from across the nation and around the world share ideas and resources. These Internet-based interactions allow teachers to collaborate and exchange ideas and materials. The Communities of Practice can include educators who are teaching the same subject area and grade level or educators with similar needs, such as technology integration, classroom management, or working with gifted and talented students.

Teachers interested in integrating technology into their instruction can utilize the resources and networks of experts, mentors, and new colleagues supported by a variety of web communities. An example is **TeacherFocus (www.teacherfocus.com),** a virtual community that offers you the opportunity to work collaboratively with teachers across the country and to learn about advances in best practice. TeacherFocus offers you topics of interest, event calendars, and focused discussions related to content and grade levels.

As members of the Virtual Math Teams (VMT) project at the Math Forum, math teachers can learn to enhance student use of technology in solving nonroutine, authentic problems requiring pre-algebra, algebra, or geometry knowledge and skills. Through the VMT, middle and high school teachers can work with peers in special Internet chat sessions with shared whiteboard software, which will then be used by their students.

The effective use of technology and media demands that teachers be better organized in advance, first thinking through their objectives, then altering the everyday classroom routine as needed, and finally evaluating to determine the impact of instruction on mental abilities, feelings, values, interpersonal skills, and motor skills. However, the shift to the 21st century and increased access to digital resources will change not only how you function as a teacher, but also student roles, as we discuss next.

NETS FOR TEACHERS

The National Educational Technology Standards for Teachers (NETS-T) provide five basic guidelines for becoming what we call a *digital teacher* (ISTE, 2012b). As seen in Table 1.2, the NETS-T describe classroom practices, lesson development, and professional expectations. Each chapter of this text includes a Professional Development section to help emphasize the importance of the NETS-T and to build your knowledge and skills through Demonstrating Professional Skills and Building My Professional Portfolio activities that are directly associated with NETS-T.

TABLE 1.2 National Educational Technology Standards for Teachers (NETS-T)	
Standard	Description
Facilitate and Inspire Student Learning and Creativity	Teachers use their knowledge of subject matter, teaching and learning, and technology to facilitate experiences that advance student learning, creativity, and innovation in both face-to-face and virtual environments.
Design and Develop Digital-Age Learning Experiences and Assessments	Teachers design, develop, and evaluate authentic learning experiences and assessment incorporating contemporary tools and resources to maximize content learning in context and to develop the knowledge, skills, and attitudes identified in the NETS-S.
Model Digital-Age Work and Learning	Teachers exhibit knowledge, skills, and work processes representative of an innovative professional in a global and digital society.
Promote and Model Digital Citizenship and Responsibility	Teachers understand local and global societal issues and responsibilities in an evolving digital culture and exhibit legal and ethical behavior in their professional practices.
Engage in Professional Growth and Leadership	Teachers continuously improve their professional practice, model lifelong learning, and exhibit leadership in their school and professional community by promoting and demonstrating the effective use of digital tools and resources.

Source: Reprinted with permission from *National Educational Technology Standards for Teachers and National Educational Technology Standards for Students.* Copyright (c) 2007, 2008 by ISTE (International Society for Technology in Education.) All rights reserved.

Carefully designed technology can make independent learning more effective.

21st Century Learner

When instruction is student centered, the primary users of technology and media are the students themselves. Student-centered activities allow teachers to spend more of their time assessing and directing student learning, consulting with individual students, and teaching one on one and in small groups. How much time you can spend on such activities will depend on the extent of the instructional role assigned to technology and media. Indeed, under certain circumstances, the entire instructional task can be left to technology and media. In fact, media are often "packaged" for this purpose—objectives are listed, guidance in achieving objectives is given, materials are assembled, and self-evaluation guidelines are provided. This is not to say, of course, that instructional technology can or should replace you as the teacher, but rather that technology and media can help you become a creative manager of the learning experience instead of a mere dispenser of information.

THE DIGITAL STUDENT

Digital students learn in classrooms where the technology is a seamless component of learning that expands the educational environment beyond the classroom walls. Devices and digital connections extend the existing capabilities of learners in many directions.

Students can gather information and study material prior to learning experiences in the "flipped" classroom.

Interactive Tools. The digital student uses mobile wireless devices in a variety of ways in and out of the school setting by taking technology where it is needed. For example, your students on the reading rug find Internet resources on wireless laptop computers or tablets. Students bring personal mobile devices (smart phones); handheld computers; or "netbooks," smaller and lighter computers, to the library to take notes from archived community newspaper articles. Student pairs use a digital camera to capture examples of symmetry found on the school campus. Elementary students with digital probes record the pH of six soil types used to grow radish plants. A high school student with a reading access barrier listens to an MP3, or compressed audio file, of Michael Chabon's "Inventing Sherlock Holmes," a homework reading assignment for the class (**www.assistivemedia .org**). These wireless devices extend and embellish the learning experience beyond anything nondigital methods can produce.

Interacting with Others. Never before have your students been so connected with each other as they are in today's wireless digital environments. Smart phones, tablets, and laptops are used to send video, voice, text, and animated messages; to listen to lessons, music, news, and sports; and to watch the latest music videos and movies. Students communicate with their digital devices through voice commands, written notes, or by using a touchscreen or mini keyboard. Documents with digitally embedded comments and edits are instantaneously exchanged between students and their teachers, among students, and with experts. Student learning communities extend around the globe through web-based interactive communication tools and social media sites such as **blogs** (publicly accessible personal journals), **wikis** (web information that can be edited by any registered user), and **podcasts** (Internet-distributed multimedia files formatted for direct download to mobile devices). For example, your students can create a blog on global warming in which they regularly exchange commentary and related hyperlinks with students located around the world. Middle school students use wikis to interact with college students who respond to their writing activities, while a high school American literature class uploads podcasts of interviews with authors to the class website.

These tools are becoming increasingly popular, as seen in a 2012 Nielsen report that shows continued increase in the use of technology and in the time spent on social media sites (Nielsen Company, 2012). Wikipedia is similarly popular, with over 3 million entries available in over 200 languages as of March 2013 (**http://en.wikipedia.org**). As with digital teachers, the digital students of today embrace and use technology to explore, inquire, and advance their personal learning, as well as contribute to the knowledge of others.

NETS FOR STUDENTS

The National Educational Technology Standards for Students (NETS-S) provide six critical skills students need to achieve success in school and in future careers (ISTE, 2012a). Notice in Table 1.3 that the NETS-S closely align with 21st century knowledge and skills. Also interesting is the placement of Technology Operations and Concepts as the last standard, a shift from the original arrangement that listed it as the first standard (ISTE, 1998). It is important that as a teacher you are familiar with the NETS-S and build your technology skills to match what is expected of your students. Throughout the text we provide multiple examples of how the NETS-S are integrated into ASSURE lesson plans.

TECHNOLOGY FOR INCLUSION

In today's classrooms, teachers will be working with students who have a variety of learning needs. Many students will have English as their second language. Other students will

TABLE 1.3 National Educational Technology Standards for Students (NETS-S)	
Standard	Description
Creativity and Innovation	Students demonstrate creative thinking, construct knowledge, and develop innovative products and processes using technology.
Communication and Collaboration	Students use digital media and environments to communicate and work collaboratively, including at a distance, to support individual learning and contribute to the learning of others.
Research and Information Fluency	Students apply digital tools to gather, evaluate, and use information.
Critical Thinking, Problem Solving, and Decision Making	Students use critical-thinking skills to plan and conduct research, manage projects, solve problems, and make informed decisions using appropriate digital tools and resources.
Digital Citizenship	Students understand human, cultural, and societal issues related to technology and practice legal and ethical behavior.
Technology Operations and Concepts	Students demonstrate a sound understanding of technology concepts, systems, and operations.

Source: Reprinted with permission from *National Educational Technology Standards for Teachers and National Educational Technology Standards for Students.* Copyright (c) 2007, 2008 by ISTE (International Society for Technology in Education.) All rights reserved.

have learning or physical challenges and will need assistance to be able to participate in classroom activities. Technology can provide the kinds of support these students need to be successful in their learning. Teachers will need to make choices and decisions about using technology to optimize learning for all the students in their classrooms. The ASSURE model can help you make technology decisions as you consider the learning needs of all your students.

Framework for 21st Century Learning Literacies

Classroom experiences must provide multiple opportunities for gaining new knowledge and skills that are encompassed in a critical set of literacies for 21st century learning. This text prepares you to embed key learning technologies that your students need to improve learning and achieve successful careers.

STUDENT OUTCOMES

Teachers need an understanding of the ability of a student to comprehend or decode information and to use, transform, and create new information. As you follow the ASSURE model to develop your lesson plans, always include opportunities for students to build general literacy knowledge and skills.

You will also want to consider the standards for learning and recognize how to support your students' learning experiences so that they can be successful. By recognizing your students as individuals with unique learning needs, you will be able to help them achieve the targeted learning outcomes.

SUPPORT SYSTEMS

As a classroom teacher you are not alone in helping your students achieve designated outcomes. There are many resources available to you, such as media specialists, technology coordinators, and area universities with courses and programs, that can help you gain additional knowledge about technology. Many of these support systems are focused on ensuring student engagement and learning. Their intent is to help you to make appropriate choices to meet your students' learning needs and to ensure you are able to use the resources successfully.

21st Century Learning Environments

The trend for today's teachers is a shift from traditional teaching strategies and tools to digital approaches that better meet the needs of 21st century students. However, the transition from traditional to digital classroom environments varies greatly from teacher to teacher and school to school. Prensky (2006) describes teachers in this variable process of technology adoption and adaptation as moving, whether slowly or quickly, through a four-phase process: (1) dabbling, (2) doing old things in old ways, (3) doing old things in new ways, and (4) doing new things in new ways (p. 43) (see Figure 1.2).

The process begins with Phase 1, "dabbling" with technology by randomly adding technology tools to a few learning situations. In Phase 2, technology is used to do old things in old ways, as when teachers display lecture notes in PowerPoint rather than using overhead transparencies. It is not until Phase 3, doing old things in new ways, that technology begins to shows its promise, such as when a teacher uses a virtual 3-D model to demonstrate the structure of a compound rather than drawing it on a chalkboard, or students use word processing and clip art rather than notebook paper and hand-drawn images to create a short story. Finally, Phase 4, doing new things in new ways, fully utilizes the power of technology and media, but it requires providing our students with "future-oriented content [to] develop their skills in programming, knowledge filtering, using their connectivity . . . with cutting edge, powerful, miniaturized, customizable, one-to-one technology" (Prensky, 2006, p. 45).

THE LEARNING CONTINUUM: TRADITIONAL TO DIGITAL

Many of today's classrooms have achieved Phase 4 by adopting and adapting their environments with digital tools that support and enhance "digital" teacher and student capabilities. For example, technology extends environments beyond the classroom walls by connecting students with other students, outside experts, and parents. Individual classroom websites provide access to homework calendars, assignment details, online resources, and often offer parents access to real-time reports of student progress.

Within these phases, three primary types of instruction are used: face-to-face instruction, distance learning, and blended learning. We have all experienced face-to-face instruction at school, at home, and during extracurricular activities. When done well, it is an excellent method of teaching that is prevalent in PK–12 schools. Distance learning occurs when the teacher and students are not in the same physical location during instruction. In 2011, nearly all of the states offered students options for taking middle or high school online virtual classes (Glass, Welner, & Bathon, 2011). Other schools are offering courses that combine face-to-face instruction with distance learning to create blended instruction, allowing students to see teacher demonstrations and work with other students during hands-on activities, such as labs, drama and musical arts performances, or building 3-D models. Many states are now adding a graduation requirement that all high school graduates must have completed at least one blended or totally online course.

THE CHANGING ROLE OF MEDIA CENTERS

Many school libraries have been merged into what are now called **media centers,** which offer traditional library reading resources but now also include a variety of information technology assets. Most media centers are equipped with multiple Internet-connected computers, often with subscriptions to PK–12 online resources such as libraries of digital books, reference materials, and educational software. The media centers also provide you with a variety of classroom support materials ranging from lab kits to subject-specific software and videos. The role of the media specialist is continually expanding to require increasing expertise in accessing the array of digital resources, as well as understanding basic computer technology to assist your students using the equipment in the center.

FIGURE 1.2 **Prensky's (2006) Technology Adoption and Adaptation Four-Phase Process**

PHASE 1	Dabbling
PHASE 2	Old things, old ways
PHASE 3	New things, old ways
PHASE 4	New things, new ways

A 21st century classroom representing Phase 4: doing new things in new ways.

The Role of Standards

COMMON CORE

The Common Core State Standards (CCSS) were developed over several years with an emphasis on higher-level learning (Calkins, Ehrenworth, & Lehman, 2012; CCSS, 2012). Students are expected to engage in reading and writing as an integral component of their learning within all content areas. The idea is that students can learn to read complex texts and then communicate their understanding of what they have read, whether the text is literature, mathematics, social science, or science. Also valued in the CCSS is the concept that learning is a process; thus, the standards are written so that each grade level's standards reflect what has been learned and what is to follow. Embedded in CCSS is the respect for the teacher's knowledge and skills in working with individual students to facilitate learning. The standards provide teachers with the flexibility to design instruction to meet their students' learning needs and to foster success in all aspects of their learning.

NATIONAL/STATE CURRICULUM STANDARDS

Even though the CCSS have become the focus of much of the implementation of standards throughout the United States, there is still the need to reflect individual learning needs within curricular areas. There are many common core content areas that have standards yet to be developed and some standards that will remain the domain of individual states. The state standards that are used to provide specific guidance for learning, for example, technology, are prominent at national and state levels.

Copyright Concerns: Copyright Law

To protect the financial interests of the creators, producers, and distributors of original works of information and art, nations adopt copyright laws. **Copyright** refers to the legal rights to an original work. These laws set the conditions under which anyone may copy, in whole or part, original works transmittable in any medium. Without copyright laws, writers, artists, and media producers would not receive the compensation they deserve for their creations. The flow of creative work would be reduced to a trickle, and we would all be the losers.

Technology, especially the Internet, has made it much easier to copy from a variety of digital materials—text, visuals, audio, and video. All material on the Internet is copyrighted unless stated otherwise. In 1998, the Conference on Fair Use issued a report (Lehman, 1998) that, despite not being a legal document, provides a consensus view (until tested in a court of law) on use of copyrighted material.

You have a legal and ethical responsibility to serve as a role model for your students; therefore, use all materials in a professional and ethical manner. We also recommend teaching relevant aspects of copyright laws to your students, even very young students. If you are unsure what to do, ask for your school's copyright guidelines. Librarians and media/technology specialists at your school may be able to help you interpret the national guidelines. Ignorance of the law is no excuse!

Please note that the copyright information presented here is *not* legal advice. It is based on what the authors have read in the literature and online. For more information on copyright, refer to the Print Resources at the end of this chapter.

EDUCATORS AND COPYRIGHT LAW

What happens if an educator knowingly and deliberately violates copyright law? The Copyright Act of 1976 contains both criminal and civil sanctions. Possible fines for copyright infringement are from $750 to $30,000 per infringement. If it can be proven that the law was broken by willful intent, the fine may be raised to $150,000. Willful infringement for private or commercial gain carries a possible fine of $250,000 and up to 5 years in prison. Copyright violation is a serious crime.

FAIR USE

Fair use provides an important copyright exception for teachers and students. Small portions of copyrighted works may be used in teaching, if properly cited and noted that they are copyrighted and by whom. Although there are no absolute guidelines for determining what constitutes fair use in an education setting, the law sets forth four basic criteria for determining what is fair use:

- *Purpose and character of the use, including whether such use is for nonprofit educational purposes rather than of a commercial nature.* Using a copyrighted work for an educational objective is more likely to be considered fair use than using it for commercial gain or entertainment.
- *Nature of the copyrighted work.* If the work is for a general readership, such as a magazine or periodical not specifically designed for education, it would tend to support fair use in the classroom. Works of an entertainment nature, such as movies or music, are less likely to be considered fair use. If the work itself is educational in nature, a judgment of fair use may not be supported because of potential impact on sales.
- *Amount and substantiality of the portion used in relation to the copyrighted work as a whole.* Using a smaller amount of the total work is more likely to be considered fair use than using a larger amount.
- *Effect of the use on the potential market for or value of the copyrighted work.* Use that negatively affects potential sales of the original work weighs against fair use.

Until the courts decide otherwise, teachers and media professionals can use the fair use criteria to decide when to copy materials that would otherwise be protected. For example, if the school media center subscribes to a journal or magazine to which you refer students and you make digital slides of several graphics to help students understand an article, this would be fair use based on the following criteria:

- The nature of the work is general, and its audience (and market) is not predominantly the educational community.
- The character of use is nonprofit.
- The amount copied is minimal.
- There is no intent to replace the original, only to make it more useful to students in conjunction with the copyrighted words.

SEEKING PERMISSION TO USE COPYRIGHTED MATERIALS

Aside from staying within the guidelines that limit but recognize our legal right to free use of copyrighted materials, what else can we do to ensure students have access to these materials? We can, obviously, seek permission from copyright owners and, if requested, pay a fee for their use. Certain requests will ordinarily be granted without payment of fee—transcripts for the blind, for example, or material to be tried out once in an experimental program. Permission is not needed for use of materials in the public domain—materials on which copyright protection has run out or materials produced by federal government employees in the course of their regular work.

In seeking permission to use copyrighted materials, it is generally best to contact the distributor or publisher of the material rather than its creator. Whether or not the creator is the holder of the copyright, the distributor or publisher generally handles permission requests and sets fees. If the address of the publisher is not given on the material, you can usually find it on the Internet.

When seeking permission:

- Be as specific as possible. For printed materials, give the page numbers and exact amount of print material you wish to copy. If possible, send along a photocopy of the material. Fully describe nonprint material. State how you intend to use the material, where you intend to use it, and the number of copies you wish to make.

- Remember that fees for reproduction of copyrighted materials are sometimes negotiable. If the fee is beyond your budget, do not hesitate to ask whether it can be lowered.

- If for any reason you decide not to use the requested material, make this fact known to the publisher or producer. Without this formal notice, it is likely to be assumed that you have in fact used it as requested and you may be charged a fee you do not in fact owe.

- Keep copies of *all* your correspondence and records of *all* other contacts that you make relevant to seeking permission to use copyrighted instructional materials.

Another solution is to obtain "royalty free" collections of media. Many vendors now sell CDs that contain collections of images and sounds that can be used in presentations or other products without payment of royalties. Be sure to read the fine print. What "royalty free" means varies from one collection to the next. In one case, there may be almost no restrictions on the use of the materials; in another, you may not be allowed to use the materials in any kind of electronic product.

TERM OF PROTECTION

The term, or duration, of copyright was changed by the Sonny Bono Copyright Term Extension Act of 1998. For an individual author, the copyright term continues for 70 years after his or her death. If a work is made for hire (i.e., by an employee or by someone commissioned to do the work), the term is 100 years from the year of creation or 75 years from the date of first publication or distribution, whichever comes first. Works copyrighted prior to January 1, 1978, are protected for 28 years and then may have their copyright renewed. The renewal protects them for a term of 75 years after their original copyright date.

CHANGING THE MATERIAL'S FORMAT

Even though you (or your school) have the capability to convert analog materials to a digital format, it is usually a violation of copyright laws and guidelines. The originators of copyrighted material are granted the sole right to make derivatives of their original work. For example, it is illegal to purchase an analog VHS video and convert it to a digital format. Likewise, you cannot convert copyrighted printed materials into a digital format.

Copyright law protects the format in which ideas are expressed (Becker, 2003). Teachers cannot make audio recordings of library books or textbooks for student use. One exception in the law permits the audio recording of books for use by students who are legally blind.

STUDENTS WITH DISABILITIES

For PK–12 students with disabilities, the National Instructional Materials Accessibility Standard (NIMAS) guides the production and electronic distribution of digital versions of textbooks and other instructional materials so they can be more easily converted to accessible formats, including Braille and text-to-speech.

There are many school resources available for students who have physical or learning challenges. With the addition of **Response to Intervention** (RtI), a program of assessment and appropriate instructional assistance in schools, challenged students are recognized earlier and their needs are more quickly met. Often these challenged students who are in the regular classroom setting are provided with technology resources that aid their ability to be successful in the classroom. As a teacher, you need to seek the assistance of school specialists to ensure that your students have access to the appropriate technology for their learning needs.

UNIVERSAL DESIGN

Additional guidelines include the concept of universal design for learning (UDL), which was created to expand learning opportunities for all individuals, especially those with disabilities (Center for Applied Special Technology [CAST], 2013). The UDL framework consists of three primary principles:

- *Multiple means of representation,* to give diverse learners options for acquiring information and knowledge
- *Multiple means of action and expression,* to provide learners options for demonstrating what they know
- *Multiple means of engagement,* to tap into learners' interests, offer appropriate challenges, and increase motivation (CAST, 2013)

Summary

In this chapter you read about the foundations that will be important in your study of technology and media as they affect your students' learning. We presented information about the roles of technology and media in learning from both your perspective as the teacher and your students' perspectives. The idea of using technology as a learning tool prior to participating in classroom activities was introduced. Both you and your students were identified within the context of the 21st century setting. Key 21st century literacies needed to achieve effective learning were introduced, as well as the variety of learning settings now available based on access to technological tools. An overview of copyright was presented, which will be further discussed in later chapters as it relates to specific technology and media.

Professional Development

DEMONSTRATING PROFESSIONAL KNOWLEDGE

1. What are the key components of the framework for 21st century learning?
2. How would you describe the status of the technology use in today's PK–12 schools?
3. What are ways technology and media can be used in learning?
4. What are the six basic categories of media and the key features of each?

5. In what ways are teacher and student uses of technology and media different?
6. Why is it important to consider 21st century learning outcomes?

7. How would you describe the three types of instruction (face to face, distance, and blended) as they relate to the classroom continuum?
8. What are the key concerns regarding copyright law for educational uses?

DEMONSTRATING PROFESSIONAL SKILLS

1. Prepare a 10-minute presentation on your reaction to the framework for 21st century learning (ISTE NETS-T 5.C).
2. Analyze an instructional situation (either real or hypothetical) and identify the standards (Common Core, state, national) being reinforced in the lesson (ISTE NETS-T 2.C).

3. Prepare a concept map that depicts the benefits and concerns of the three types of instruction (face to face, distance, or blended) presented in this chapter (ISTE NETS-T 5.C).
4. Create a one-page guide about copyright that will assist you in following copyright laws for educational uses (ISTE NETS-T 5.C).

BUILDING YOUR PROFESSIONAL PORTFOLIO

- *Enhancing My Portfolio.* Select a technology integration lesson from the Web. After citing the source of the lesson, analyze it according to topics discussed in this chapter. Specifically, take note of how or if the lesson addresses the following: (1) use of technology and media, (2) types of media used, (3) types of learning standards identified, (4) type(s) of instruction, (5) teacher use of technology, (6) student use of technology, and (7) areas where copyright laws will need to be followed. Reflect on this lesson

analysis, providing strengths, weaknesses, and recommendations for using technology and media to enhance student learning (ISTE NETS-T 5.C).
- *Reflecting on My Learning.* Reflect on the 21st century knowledge and skills as compared to the knowledge and skills required for your own PK–12 educational experiences. What are the primary differences? What do you see as the greatest benefits and as your most difficult challenges in ensuring that your students build 21st century knowledge and skills (ISTE NETS-T 2.B)?

Suggested Resources

PRINT RESOURCES

Ashburn, E., & Floden, R. (2006). *Meaningful learning using technology: What educators need to know and do.* New York, NY: Teachers College Press.

Becker, G. H. (2003). *Copyright: A guide to information and resources* (3rd ed.). Lake Mary, FL: Gary H. Becker.

Bielfefeld, A., & Cheeseman, L. (2006). *Technology and copyright law: A guidebook for the library, research, and teaching professions* (2nd ed.). New York, NY: Neal-Schuman.

Bottertbush, H. R. (1996). *Copyright in the age of new technology.* Bloomington, IN: Phi Delta Kappa Educational Foundation.

Brooks-Young, S. J. (2009). *Making technology standards work for you* (2nd ed.). Washington, DC: International Society for Technology in Education.

Brown, J. M. (2002). Enhancing on-line learning for individuals with disabilities. *New Directions for Teaching and Learning, 91,* 61–68.

Burke, J. J. (2006). *Library technology companion: A basic guide for library staff* (2nd ed.). New York, NY: Neal-Schuman.

Clyde, W., & Delohery, A. (2005). *Using technology in teaching.* New Haven, CT: Yale University Press.

Cummins, J., Brown, K., & Sayers, D. (2006). *Literacy, technology, and diversity: Teaching for success in changing times.* Boston, MA: Allyn & Bacon.

Lamb, A. (2006). *Building treehouses for learning: Technology in today's classroom* (4th ed.). Emporia, KS: Vision to Action.

Male, M. (2002). *Technology for inclusion: Meeting the special needs of all students* (4th ed.). Boston, MA: Allyn & Bacon.

Scherer, M. J. (2003). *Connecting to learn: Educational and assistive technology for people with disabilities.* Washington, DC: American Psychological Association.

WEB RESOURCES

Edutopia
www.edutopia.org
Edutopia is sponsored by the George Lucas Foundation and provides teachers current and archived access to special reports, blogs, and videos.

eSchool News
www.eschoolnews.com
eSchool News is a convenient way to keep up to date electronically with what is going on in schools.

Sophia
www.sophia.org
Sophia is a source for tutorials, teacher tools, and professional development. The site holds many resources for teachers and students directed at helping students learn.

AECT.org
www.aect.org
AECT Copyright Committee blog disseminates committee presentations, news, and announcements.

Gary Becker's Copyright Information Site
www.beckercopyright.com
Gary Becker's copyright information site provides you with a quick reference to copyright issues.

Fair Use Guidelines for Educational Multimedia
www.uspto.gov/web/offices/dcom/olia/confu/confurep.pdf

Technology, Education, and Copyright Harmonization (TEACH) Act (2002)
http://www.ala.org/ala/issuesadvocacy/copyright/teachact

U. S. Copyright Office
www.copyright.gov The U.S. Copyright Office offers expert and impartial information about copyright law. The website offers a variety of information and services related to the law.

CHAPTER 2

Designing and Assessing 21st Century Learning

Knowledge Outcomes

This chapter addresses ISTE NETS-T standards 2, 4, and 5.

1. Describe the similarities and differences in learning theories.

2. List the eight principles of effective instruction for 21st century learners.

3. Describe the similarities and differences in the principles of effective technology and media utilization.

4. Describe the similarities and differences between the types of effective learning assessment.

Goal

Understand how to design and assess 21st century learning.

Learning is the development of new knowledge, skills, or attitudes as an individual interacts with information and the environment. Learning doesn't happen by magic. Rather, teachers must make important decisions to ensure learning, especially when integrating technology and media into a lesson. Foundational learning theories, the principles of effective instruction that integrate technology and media, and effective assessment of learning are all elements of designing and assessing 21st centruy learning.

The resources available to students today offer them many opportunities for learning.

Technology and media can be valuable resources to integrate into the assessment of learning. Learners in the 21st centrury need to be better educated to assume the challenges of continually evolving knowledge and skill requirements for the future (Partnership for 21st Century Skills, n.d.). What students are learning today needs to prepare them for an uncertain tomorrow, and lifelong learning is a cornerstone to guiding students toward understanding how to approach the shifting knowledge and skills of their future. By creating seamless access to the global community and opening new avenues for addressing how and what to learn, technology and media have become essential interfaces for learners as they move forward in their education.

Even as students are entering the classroom with greater understanding of worldwide issues, other learning challenges prevail. Many come into school speaking more than one language, and it is predicted that by 2025, nearly half of all classrooms will have students who do not speak English as their first language (Partnership for 21st Century Skills, n.d.). Students also have greater fluency with technology and media and have greater opportunities for exposure to different points of view and cultures. Even before today's children enter school, many have experience with technology as a learning tool through television programs designed to instruct young children. Many also understand how computers can be used for learning and for communicating. Another medium for communication and interactivity, the cell phone, has become the great equalizer for all students regardless of their social and ethnic backgrounds. How teachers view the role of technology and media in the classroom depends very much on their beliefs about how people learn.

Learning Theories

Even at an early age, children learn to use technology to expand their learning opportunities.

Over the past half-century there have been several dominant theories of learning. Each has implications for instruction in general and for the use of technology and media in particular. We briefly survey each of the major perspectives on learning and discuss their implications. Driscoll (2005) discusses learning theories and their impact on teaching decisions in greater detail.

BEHAVIORIST PERSPECTIVE

In the 1950s, B. F. Skinner, a psychologist at Harvard University and a proponent of **behaviorism,** conducted scientific studies of observable behavior. He was interested in voluntary behavior, such as learning new skills, rather than reflexive behavior, as illustrated by Pavlov's famous salivating dog. He demonstrated that reinforcing, or rewarding desired responses, could

Learning is sometimes done best by the individual student working alone.

shape the behavior patterns of an organism. Skinner based his learning theory, known as *reinforcement theory,* on a series of experiments with pigeons. He noted that when the pigeons were given a reward for a desired behavior, they tended to repeat it. When the pigeons did not receive any reinforcer, they tended to stop a particular behavor. Skinner reasoned that the same procedures could be used with humans. The result was the foundation for computer-assisted instruction. Unlike earlier learning research, Skinner's work was logical and precise, leading directly to improved instruction and learning.

Behaviorists refuse to speculate on what goes on internally when learning takes place. They rely solely on observable behaviors. As a result, they are more comfortable explaining relatively simple learning tasks. Because of this posture, behaviorism has limited applications in teaching higher-level skills. For example, behaviorists are reluctant to make inferences about how learners process information. Although most would argue that, in the 21st century, behavioral concepts are not necessarily applicable to the types of learners you are encountering in your classrooms, you may determine that some basic knowledge or skills require a behaviorist approach to instruction. For example, you might have a student who would benefit from completing a math program that guides him through a series of incremental steps to learning multiplication, with reinforcements integrated throughout, until he has mastered the multiplication table. The student will not be finished with the program until his work is considered to be acceptable and he can demonstrate his ability to complete multiplication facts.

COGNITIVIST PERSPECTIVE

In the latter half of the twentieth century, cognitivists made new contributions to learning theory by creating models of how learners receive, process, and manipulate information. **Cognitivism,** based on the work of Swiss psychologist Jean Piaget (1977), explores the mental processes individuals use in responding to their environment—that is, how people think, solve problems, and make decisions. For example, behaviorists simply state that practice strengthens the response to a stimulus. Cognitivists, on the other hand, create a mental model of short-term and long-term memory. New information is stored in short-term memory, where it is rehearsed until ready to be stored in long-term memory. If the information is not rehearsed, it fades from short-term memory. Learners then combine the information and skills in long-term memory to develop cognitive strategies, or skills for dealing with complex tasks.

Cognitivists have a broader perception of learning than that held by behaviorists. Students are less dependent on the guiding hand of the teacher and rely more on their own cognitive strategies in using available learning resources. Many would suggest that the cognitivist approach to instruction is a good compromise between required **benchmarks,** those standards against which students are tested, and **metacognition,** thinking about one's own learning.

CONSTRUCTIVIST PERSPECTIVE

Constructivism is a movement that extends beyond the ideas of cognitivism, considering the engagement of students in meaningful experiences as the essence of experiential learning. Shifting from passive transfer of information to active problem solving and discovery, constructivists emphasize that learners create their own interpretations of the world of information. They argue that students situate the learning experience within their own experiences and that the goal of instruction is not to teach information but to create conditions in which students can interpret information for their own understanding. The role of constructivist instruction is to provide students with ways to assemble knowledge rather than to dispense facts. Constructivists believe that learning occurs most effectively when students are engaged in authentic tasks that relate to meaningful contexts (i.e., learning by doing). The ultimate measure of learning is therefore the ability of the student to use knowledge to facilitate thinking in real life. This approach fits with the needs of 21st century learners who must solve problems that not only capitalize on their existing knowledge, but also require them to seek additional information or skills in finding effective solutions.

SOCIAL-PSYCHOLOGICAL PERSPECTIVE

Teachers can help guide the 21st century learner explore new information.

Social psychology is another well-established approach to the study of instruction and learning. Social psychologists look at how the social organization of the classroom affects learning. For example, what is the group structure of the classroom—independent study, small groups, or the class as a whole? What is the authority structure—how much control do students have over their activities? What is the reward structure—is cooperation rather than competition fostered?

Researchers such as Robert Slavin (1990) have taken the position that cooperative learning is both more effective and more socially beneficial than competitive and individualistic learning. Slavin developed a set of cooperative learning techniques embodying the principles of small-group collaboration, learner-controlled instruction, and rewards based on group achievement.

The 21st century learner enters your classroom with many skills developed from technology-based social networking. The ideas fostered in the social psychology perspective address such interdependent collaborative abilities that 21st century learners need to use as part of their learning.

Teachers need to develop an eclectic attitude toward the various schools of learning psychology. You are not obliged to swear allegiance to a particular learning theory. You want to use what works. If you find that a particular learning situation is suited to a behaviorist approach, then you should use behaviorist techniques. Conversely, if the situation seems to call for cognitivist or constructivist strategies, those are what you should use. When guiding the 21st century learners in your classroom, consider which learning theory best applies to the particular type of learning task at hand.

Together, a group of students can collaborate on their learning.

Principles of Effective Instruction for 21st Century Learners

As a classroom teacher, your role is to establish learning experiences that foster the defined learner outcomes. At times those outcomes may be based on specific state or national learning standards; at other times they may be based on negotiated outcomes with individual learners. Whichever direction you take, you need to think about how to engage students in the learning process.

As an educator seeking ways to improve your practice, it is important to consider how to engage learners in their learning.

Because one common feature across all classroom settings is the variety of learning levels and needs among students, it is also critical to determine the best ways to meet the needs of all students by becoming skilled at differentiating instruction to ensure that all learners are adequately and appropriately challenged in their learning. For example, you may offer in-depth reading materials for students who are reading above grade level for extended learning experiences, and worksheets with hints and answer keys for those who are struggling to understand the concepts of the topic.

Research-based classroom practices to engage learners have evolved over time. These principles of effective instruction offer ways to engage your learners regardless of their ability levels:

- *Assess prior knowledge.* Before you can properly provide instruction, you should gather relevant information about each student's knowledge and skill level. You need to know what knowledge your students already have learned. To learn from most materials and activities, students must possess prerequisite knowledge and skills (Newby, Stepich, Lehman, & Russell, 2010).

- *Consider individual differences.* Learners vary in terms of personality, general aptitude, knowledge of a subject, and many other factors. Be aware of the multiple learning needs of your students—for example, whether a language other than English is spoken in a child's home. You need to consider the technology and media experiences your students have had and what resources are essential to help your students learn. Effective instruction allows individuals to progress at different rates, cover different materials, and even participate in different activities (Cooper & Varma, 1997).

- *State objectives.* For you and your students to know where instruction is going and what is to be accomplished, the goals must be specified. Learning objectives must match expected outcomes or standards (Mager, 1997).

- *Develop metacognitive skills.* The skills of selective monitoring, evaluating, and adjusting their approaches enhance students' learning and help to make them lifelong learners. Learners need assistance in understanding how they learn and what resources help in that process (Nelson, 1992).

- *Provide social interaction.* Teachers and peers serving as tutors or group members can provide a number of pedagogical as well as social supports. Learners gain experience and expertise when collaborating with others in and beyond the classroom (Jonassen, Howland, Marra, & Crismond, 2008).

- *Incorporate realistic contexts.* Learners are most likely to remember and to apply authentic knowledge presented in a real-world context. Rote learning leads to "inert knowledge"; that is, learners know something but cannot apply it to real life. Students benefit from understanding how their knowledge and skills fit into the world around them (Bransford, Brown, & Cocking, 2000).

- *Engage students in relevant practice.* The most effective learning experiences are those requiring learners to practice skills that build toward the desired outcome. Learner participation increases the probability of learning. Practice, especially in varying contexts, improves retention rate and the ability to apply the new knowledge, skill, or attitude. Practice promotes deeper, longer lasting learning (Morrison & Lowther, 2010).

- *Offer frequent, timely, and constructive feedback.* Student learning requires accurate information on misconceptions, misunderstandings, and weaknesses. Learners need to know if their thinking is on track. Feedback may come from a teacher, a tutor, electronic messages from a computer, the scoring system of a game, or oneself. In addition to knowing that responses are incorrect, students need to know why they have been unsuccessful and how they can improve their performance. Further, knowing details about their correct responses in terms of how and why they are accurate helps students understand more about what they have learned (Black & William, 1998).

INFORMATION VERSUS INSTRUCTION

As educators, it is important to distinguish between information and instruction. **Information** is knowledge, facts, news, comments, and content. Information can be presented in a memo, in the classroom, in a textbook, or on the Web. Often the presentation, whether it is live, printed, or on the Internet, is general in content and its purpose is to give an overview of ideas or subject matter—to generate interest, to provide background information, or to give procedural details.

Learners should not be expected to be responsible for the retention or use of information they have only seen or heard. The information provided by a job aid (a short guide to help the user), like a phone book, is not meant to be memorized. It is assumed that you will look up the information when needed. With computers, it has become possible to give ever more rapid and detailed information in specific situations, to the point that the computer could be said to be helping or "coaching" the individual. Although with frequent use of a job aid or a computer help system a person might gradually internalize information, remembering more and more of the information provided, the learning is not an intentional part of the system, whose aim is only to provide just-in-time assistance or specific information.

Instruction, on the other hand, refers to any intentional effort to stimulate learning by the deliberate arrangement of experiences to help learners achieve a desirable change in capability. Instruction is meant to lead to learning. Active engagement with the information—questioning it, discussing it, applying it to practice situations—is the critical component of instruction. Meaningful understanding, retention, and application require instructional activities, including practice with feedback. Instruction, therefore, has as its goal a lasting change in the capability of the learner. This is a crucial point in distinguishing instruction from just providing information.

Instruction is also the arrangement of information and the environment to facilitate learning. By *environment* we mean not only where instruction takes place, but also the strategies, technology, and media needed to convey information and guide learning. The learner or the instructor may do this. Gagné (1985) describes instruction as a set of events external to the learner designed to support the internal process of learning.

Preparing the instructional environment is another critical role for teachers. As a teacher responsible for creating learning opportunities for your students, you will need to help them work within learning communities. By using collaborative learning tools such as classroom blogs, wikis, social networking resources, and learning management systems, you can help your 21st century learners move through the various levels of learning appropriate to their goals, the state learning standards, and expected outcomes.

BLOOM'S DIGITAL TAXONOMY AND 21ST CENTURY 4 CS

Benjamin Bloom developed a learning taxonomy that he described as stages focused on cognitive learning skills ranging from knowledge through evaluation (Bloom and Krathwohl, 1984). His idea was that students progressed in an orderly fashion from simple to complex mental abilities. He suggested that students started at the knowledge stage by recalling specific content (e.g., reciting a poem from memory). Students then progressed to the comprehension stage, in which they would be able to paraphrase or summarize the content (e.g., using your own words, describe what the author meant in her poem). He assumed if students could understand meaning, then they were ready for the next step, application. At the application step, students could use the ideas or information in a meaningful way (e.g., using the author's ideas in her poem, relate those ideas to a similar topic). Finally, Bloom felt that when the student had progressed through these prior steps, it was now time to generate a new idea or example (e.g., using a similar poetry style, write your own poem about a similar topic). He called this highest step evaluation.

Over time, Bloom's Taxonomy has been revised and modified. While best known for his original work in the cognitive domain, Bloom added the psychomotor (manipulative or physical skills) and affective (attitudes or feelings) domains, which followed a similar pattern in a taxonomy. Bloom further expanded his cognitive taxonomy and divided it into lower-order thinking skills, such as requiring the ability to recall specific facts, and higher-order thinking skills, such as applying the facts to a unique task. His idea was that students needed the lower-order skills in order to be successful at the higher-order skills. In addition, he advocated that all students were to be guided through the steps into higher-order thinking. For example, a teacher would require students to learn multiplication tables, explain relationships between the number facts, use multiplication to solve a specific story problem, and finally to use their multiplication knowledge in a unique and different way, such as in an art project in which they discussed how they repeated certain design elements as a means to demonstrate their understanding of multiplication concepts.

The most recent modification to Bloom's original steps has been termed Bloom's Digital Taxonomy (Churches, 2008). What is significantly different about the new taxonomy is that it is not focused on only cognitive skills, but rather integrates action and resources into the stages. In the Digital Taxonomy, the interplay of use of resources with the cognitive process is an essential element to understanding how students learn. The premise of moving through each stage is not emphasized, but rather the intent is to capitalize on where the student is and what approaches will best help the student to learn the information and use it in meaningful ways. Also critical to the new taxonomy is a focus on collaboration and scaffolding of ideas. In the Digital Taxonomy, the teacher's role as a learning guide is emphasized, as is the idea that technology and media are essential tools to facilitate student learning. Now the teacher does not need to require prior knowledge of multiplication skills in order for students to gain that knowledge as they apply multiplication skills to a problems they generated as part of their explorations of a local problem to be resolved.

Fast forward several years, and the Partnership for 21st Century Skills (**www.p21.org**) identified skills that every student needs to have to be a successful learner (Figure 2.1). The focus is on those higher-order thinking skills that Bloom and Churches identified as critical to quality learning experiences. The Partnership identified four skills as the means by which children can acquire their academic knowledge: critical thinking, communication, collaboration, and creativity. Each of these skills requires that students have knowledge or can locate the information they need in order to be successful in the implementation of the knowledge as part of their active learning experiences. As a teacher, you would work with groups of students who share their knowledge and understanding to gain further knowledge as they resolve a creative and unique problem that has significant impact on a local setting.

Closely aligned to the four 21st century skills are cross-cultural understandings through which students have opportunities to view their learning experiences in a global context. For the classroom teacher, these new views of Bloom's Taxonomy and the 21st century skills suggest new approaches of facilitating learning using media and technology outside the regular classroom to facilitate preparation of classroom activities. You can guide your students to work on larger issues across a greater span and learn more from students outside the classroom setting. The GlobalSchoolNet (**www .globalschoolnet.org**) offers teachers opportunities to collaborate, plan, and

FIGURE 2.1   21st Century Student Outcomes and Support Systems

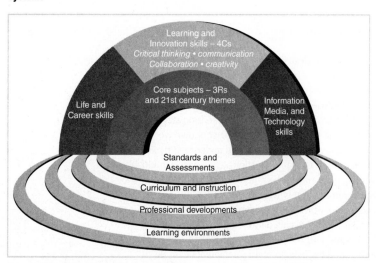

Source: Reprinted with permission of the Partnership for 21st Century Skills.

TAKING A LOOK AT TECHNOLOGY INTEGRATION

New Tech Network

Started in California, the New Tech Network is a national initiative to develop innovative high schools. It is an outgrowth of the philosophy that empowering students through an alternative instructional approach will help them to become creators, leaders, and tomorrow's productive citizens. New Tech Network advocates learning environments that provide student-centered settings in which

- Problem-based learning engages learners
- Students and teachers have ownership of their learning experiences
- Technology is integrated throughout the entire learning experiences

The goal is to provide students with an integrated curriculum that focuses on critical thinking, collaboration, and problem solving as vehicles to learning. They have the data to demonstrate that their ideas are working, with graduation rates that are significantly higher than the national averages. Also, more of the graduates from

New Tech high schools pursue careers in mathematics, science, and engineering than their regular high school peers.

Technology and media are good sources for gathering information prior to classroom activities.

conduct joint learning projects that engage students from varied locations in working together to solve a common problem. Teachers can also participate in topical discussions with groups focused on key educational issues. Other possibilities include the opportunity to manage or attend online courses, mentor other educators, or try out new ideas in a safe, supportive environment.

The teacher is no longer the source of knowledge, standing and delivering as in earlier school models. Rather, the teacher designs learning situations that focus on engaging learners in active learning experiences while developing their knowledge, understanding, and ability to use knowledge to generate new ideas. As a teacher, you will design lessons, considering the NETS-T (**www.iste.org/standards/nets-for-teachers**) and NETS-S standards (**www.iste .org/standards/nets-for-students**) and the resources available to students in order to facilitate moving students toward critical thinking, collaboration, and creativity. Technology and media provide the valuable resources that teachers and students can use to achieve the learning outcomes while engaging in those higher-order thinking arenas. In other words, you can "flip" your classroom by having your students explore the content through media and technology prior to coming to the classroom where you can engage them in applying that knowledge to real-world situations.

Teachers guide students in their effective use of technology to support learning.

MEETING LEARNER NEEDS

Your students are the focus of your instruction; everything you do in the classroom is designed to help your students meet the intended learning outcomes. The more you understand their levels of learning and their interests, the easier it will be for you to address ways to help them learn. When making instructional decisions your goal is to find ways to ensure success. Decide on the strategy or strategies you will use, the technology and media that will offer the best support, and how you will assess students' learning progress.

It is important for teachers to be aware of the multiple types of student intelligences when planning lessons. Howard Gardner (2011), who was dissatisfied with the concept of IQ and its unitary view of intelligence, developed the concept of **multiple intelligences.** Noting that not everyone has the same abilities nor do they learn in the same way, he identified nine aspects of intelligence:

- Verbal/linguistic (language)
- Logical/mathematical (scientific/quantitative)
- Visual/spatial (imagining objects in space/navigating)
- Musical/rhythmic (listening/movement)
- Bodily/kinesthetic (dancing/athletics)
- Interpersonal (understanding other people)
- Intrapersonal (understanding oneself)
- Naturalist (relating to one's surroundings)
- Existentialist (ability to reflect)

Gardner's theory implies that effective teachers need to consider the different learning abilities of their students, recognizing that students vary widely in terms of strengths and weaknesses in each of these areas. The best way to do this is by designing lessons that actively address the range of learning abilities, considering students' perceptual preferences and strengths, information processing habits, motivational factors, and physiological traits that influence their ability to learn. Your 21st century learners come into your classroom with abilities in varying states of development. Your responsibility is to determine how best to address their learning needs while also attending to their individual approaches to acquiring knowledge and skills.

Most lessons can include a variety of technology and media that address the wide range of student abilities. For example, your lessons can include writing activities for students with verbal/linguistic strengths, use of graphics for visual/spatial abilities, or out-of-seat activities for students who prefer bodily/kinesthetic learning. Using Storymaker software allows your students to blend images with text and gives them the opportunity to practice both their verbal/linguistic and their visual/spatial intelligences.

Principles of Effective Technology Utilization

The National Education Technology Plan sets clear expectations for today's teachers to be competent in the use of technology in their teaching (U.S. Department of Education, 2010). This is especially true when working with 21st century learners and addressing the skills outlined for them. Teachers not only need to use technology effectively in their teaching, but they also need to guide students in using those tools to enhance their learning (Bowes, D'Onofrio, & Marker, 2006). The advent of newer technologies requires critical decisions related to the best tools to integrate into teaching. We will be addressing many of these newer technology resources throughout the remaining chapters of this textbook.

The **National Education Technology Standards for Students** (NETS-S), noted in the following list, specifically outline expectations for student use of technology to guide their learning (International Society for Technology in Education [ISTE], 2007).

- Creativity and Innovation
- Communication and Collaboration
- Research and Information Fluency
- Critical Thinking, Problem Solving, and Decision Making

- Digital Citizenship
- Technology Operations and Concepts[*]

Many of these standards address the essential elements for success in acquiring 21st century knowledge and skills. As a teacher you will be expected to enhance students' abilities to engage in the use of technology to support their learning and address these six areas of competency, also known as **technology literacy** skills. In addition you are expected to enhance learning by engaging students in the 21st century skills of critical thinking, collaboration, communication, and creativity and innovation. What you can note in looking at the two lists of skills to emphasize is that they are very similar and are not something to be considered as "add ons," but rather they can be integrated into the learning experiences you arrange for your students.

Information can be learned from materials beyond the classroom.

You should combine knowledge and skills related to content areas and information literacy skills by using technology in ways that help students learn information and communicate knowledge. For example, in a science lesson on weather, you can present a problem to your students that will require them to search websites for data or information, use communication tools to collaborate with outside experts, generate solutions to the problem collaboratively, and present their ideas to classmates using creative resources. By approaching your instruction in that manner, you have addressed many of the standards by which your students will be measured and will have given them guided practice in developing their knowledge and skills.

Principles of Effective Media Utilization

Learning from multiple sources of media provides us with information and challenges our thinking. As users of these sources we need **media literacy** skills to know how to access them, how to understand and analyze the content, and how to create new media messages (Stansbury, 2009).

Text, television, video, and a host of other media sources covered within this textbook are all valid and vital sources of information. Your role is to guide your students to use these media as sources for their learning in ways that are wise, safe, and productive. For example, students need to learn to find multiple sources to verify facts they may have heard on the news or read in the newspaper. They need to learn to be critical users of these resources to ensure that they are well informed and their conclusions are accurate. As mentioned earlier, the NETS-S and 21st century skills address many of the abilities learners need to be successful consumers of the media resources surrounding them.

Furthermore, your teaching approach should provide students with opportunities to explore how to use these media resources to communicate their knowledge. Later in this textbook you will see examples of how teachers guide their students to use a variety of media to express their knowledge and skills.

Principles of Effective Learning Assessment

The method of assessing achievement depends on the nature of the objective. Some learning objectives call for relatively simple cognitive skills—for example, stating Ohm's Law, distinguishing adjectives from adverbs, or summarizing the principles of the Declaration of Independence. Learning objectives such as these lend themselves to more traditional written tests.

[*]*Source:* Reprinted with permission from *National Educational Technology Standards for Teachers and National Educational Technology Standards for Students.* Copyright (c) 2007, 2008 by ISTE (International Society for Technology in Education.) All rights reserved.

Other objectives may call for process-type behaviors (e.g., diagramming a sentence, solving quadratic equations, or classifying animals), the creation of products (e.g., a sculpture, a written composition, a PowerPoint presentation, or a portfolio), or to exhibit attitudes (e.g., choosing to read during free-time activities, placing used paper in the recycle bin, or eating healthy snacks). This type of learning objective requires a more comprehensive, **authentic assessment**, such as a performance-based evaluation of a student's demonstration of learning in a natural context.

AUTHENTIC ASSESSMENT

Rising interest in authentic assessment of students is driven by commitment to a constructivist perspective. Authentic assessments require students to use processes appropriate to the content and skills being learned and to how they are used in the real world. It is the difference between learning science facts and doing what scientists do. How many people take paper-and-pencil tests as part of their occupation?

Authentic assessments can be applied to most performance or products that students develop to demonstrate their knowledge or understanding of the content. The most commonly used rating scales for authentic assessments include performance checklists, attitude scales, product-rating checklists, and rubrics.

When assessing basic process skills, a performance checklist can be an effective, objective way of recording student performances. Figure 2.2 shows a primary-grade checklist for using an audio storybook. Notice the simple yes or no recording system.

Although attitudes are admittedly difficult to assess, measurement tools have been devised, such as attitude scales (see the biology example in Figure 2.3). The five-point scale (strongly agree to strongly disagree) offers the opportunity to capture a range of attitudes. A number

FIGURE 2.2   Performance Checklist: Using an Audio Storybook

Performance Checklist: Using an Audio Storybook

Name _____ Class _____

Indicate Yes or No with an "X" in the appropriate column.

Did the Student	Yes	No
1. Locate the assigned audio storybook?	____	____
2. Complete the Material Checkout Form for the storybook?	____	____
3. Select the appropriate CD player?	____	____
4. Select the appropriate headphones?	____	____
5. Correctly insert the storybook CD?	____	____
6. Correctly connect the headphones?	____	____
7. Play the CD and follow along as the storybook was read?	____	____
8. Remove the CD and headphones when the story was finished?	____	____
9. Return the audio storybook, CD player, and headphones to the proper location?	____	____
10. Complete the Materials Return Form?	____	____

Teacher Name _____ Date _____

FIGURE 2.3   Attitude Scale: Biology

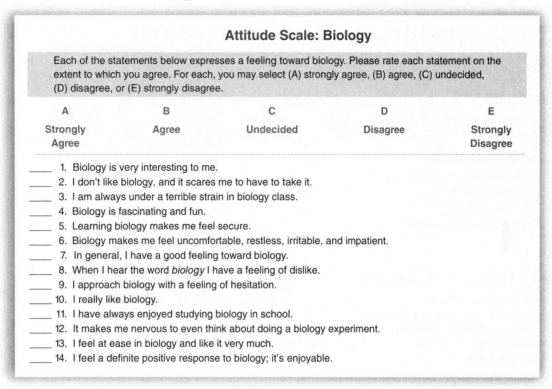

Attitude Scale: Biology

Each of the statements below expresses a feeling toward biology. Please rate each statement on the extent to which you agree. For each, you may select (A) strongly agree, (B) agree, (C) undecided, (D) disagree, or (E) strongly disagree.

A	B	C	D	E
Strongly Agree	Agree	Undecided	Disagree	Strongly Disagree

_____ 1. Biology is very interesting to me.

_____ 2. I don't like biology, and it scares me to have to take it.

_____ 3. I am always under a terrible strain in biology class.

_____ 4. Biology is fascinating and fun.

_____ 5. Learning biology makes me feel secure.

_____ 6. Biology makes me feel uncomfortable, restless, irritable, and impatient.

_____ 7. In general, I have a good feeling toward biology.

_____ 8. When I hear the word _biology_ I have a feeling of dislike.

_____ 9. I approach biology with a feeling of hesitation.

_____ 10. I really like biology.

_____ 11. I have always enjoyed studying biology in school.

_____ 12. It makes me nervous to even think about doing a biology experiment.

_____ 13. I feel at ease in biology and like it very much.

_____ 14. I feel a definite positive response to biology; it's enjoyable.

of other suggestions for attitude measurement can be found in Robert Mager's _How to Turn Learners On . . . without Turning Them Off_ (see this chapter's Suggested Resources).

For product skills, a product-rating checklist can guide your evaluation of critical subskills and make qualitative judgments more objective, as in the rating form in Figure 2.4 for a student-created digital concept map. This checklist provides more detailed information regarding student performance because each product component is rated from poor to excellent rather than on a yes/no scale.

Used to provide a more comprehensive assessment of student performance, a rubric is a set of assessment criteria for appraising or judging student products or performances. A rubric typically consists of a rating scale for performance criteria based on level-of-performance descriptors. The performance criteria are the key area of focus for the performance or the product (e.g., problem presentation, supporting graphics, appropriate labels). Rating scales to measure achievement of performance criteria normally range from three to six levels designated by names and/or numbers. A three-point scale might be shown as (1) needs work, (2) okay, (3) good. An example of a four-point scale might show the following levels: (1) beginning, (2) developing, (3) accomplished, and (4) exemplary. The descriptors for the levels of performance describe the student performance or product at each level. By comparing an actual student product or performance to the descriptors, a teacher can give a numerical score. An example rubric for a multimedia product is presented in Figure 2.5. See "Technology Resources: Rubrics" for rubric resources.

FIGURE 2.4   Product Evaluation Checklist: Digital Concept Map

Product Evaluation Checklist: Digital Concept Map

Name _____ Date _____

Rate the digital concept map on the basis of content and layout by checking the appropriate box.

Content	Poor	Fair	Good	Very Good	Excellent
• Key ideas are represented	☐	☐	☐	☐	☐
• Supporting ideas are logical	☐	☐	☐	☐	☐
• Information is accurate	☐	☐	☐	☐	☐
• Paraphrasing is appropriate	☐	☐	☐	☐	☐

Comments about the content:

Layout					
• Main idea shapes are appropriate	☐	☐	☐	☐	☐
• Supporting idea shapes are appropriate	☐	☐	☐	☐	☐
• Connecting lines are meaningful	☐	☐	☐	☐	☐
• Graphics support concepts	☐	☐	☐	☐	☐
• Use of colors is appropriate	☐	☐	☐	☐	☐
• Font is clear and easy to read	☐	☐	☐	☐	☐

Comments about the layout:

Overall Evaluation:

_____ Poor
_____ Fair
_____ Good
_____ Very Good
_____ Excellent

Overall Comments:

Portfolio Assessment. If your assessment plan involves determining the overall individual performance of each student, traditional or electronic portfolio assessments can help achieve your goal. Portfolios are used to assess tangible products that exemplify student accomplishments in terms of analysis, synthesis, and evaluation. A key component of portfolios is their requirement for students to self-reflect on their own learning as demonstrated in the portfolio products. For example, students are asked to select a piece of work that demonstrates achievement of a learning objective and then to explain why they chose the piece and how it shows the target knowledge and skills. The reflections can be extended to develop metacognitive skills by asking the students to describe what they would do differently to improve their learning.

To use portfolios, begin by deciding between traditional or electronic formats. Then identify the types of artifacts that will demonstrate student achievement of the standards and objectives and select or develop an appropriate rating scale (previously described). The rubrics should be given to students before they begin working on the products. The types of artifacts that a portfolio might contain include the following:

- Written documents such as poems, stories, or research papers
- Audio recordings of debates, panel discussions, or oral presentations
- Video recordings of skits, lab experiments, or 3-D models
- Computer multimedia projects such as animated timelines, podcasts, or WebQuests

Traditional versus Electronic Portfolios. Traditional portfolios are physical collections of student work, whereas electronic portfolios contain digital work. Traditional portfolios consist of paper documents, photos, video and audio recordings, or perhaps 3-D models. The portfolios

FIGURE 2.5 **Multimedia Product Rubric**

Multimedia Product Rubric

Student's Name _____ Date _____

Category	4	3	2	1
Content	Covers topics in-depth with details and examples. Subject knowledge is excellent.	Includes essential knowledge about the topic. Subject knowledge appears to be good.	Includes essential information about the topic but there are 1–2 factual errors.	Content is minimal OR there are several factual errors.
Sources	Source information collected for all graphics, facts, and quotes. All documented in desired format.	Source information collected for all graphics, facts, and quotes. Most documented in desired format.	Source information collected for all graphics, facts, and quotes, but not documented in desired format.	Very little or no source information was collected.
Organization	Content is well organized, uses headings or bulleted lists to group related material.	Uses headings or bulleted lists to organize, but the overall organization of topics appears flawed.	Content is logically organized for the most part.	There was no clear or logical organizational structure, just lots of facts.
Requirements	All requirements are met and exceeded.	All requirements are met.	One requirement was not completely met.	More than one requirement was not completely met.
Originality	Product shows a large amount of original thought. Ideas are creative and inventive.	Product shows some original thought. Work shows new ideas and insights.	Uses other people's ideas (giving them credit), but there is little evidence of original thinking.	Uses other people's ideas, but does not give them credit.

Rubrics

Rubistar

http://rubistar.4teachers.org

Rubistar is a free online tool designed to assist teachers in creating a variety of rubrics. The website has numerous examples of rubrics that can be accessed through keyword searches. If you are new to rubrics, the site offers a rubric tutorial. When you are ready to try it out, Rubistar provides an easy-to-use template to create and print rubrics. If you complete the registration, you can save and edit rubrics online.

Assessment Focus

www.assessmentfocus.com/rubrics-rubric-makers.php

Assessment Focus offers a number of links to sites that will help you generate rubrics. The site includes links for ready-made rubrics, as well as sites that will allow you to build your own rubrics.

Teach-nology

www.teach-nology.com/web_tools

The Teach-nology site offers a variety of rubric resources for teachers. Both samples and templates are available to use. The rubrics are developed for grades K–12 to include social studies, math, science, and reading and language arts.

---

are often kept in large three-ring binders and storage boxes, which are moved from teacher to teacher as the student progresses through school. As can be imagined, over time the portfolios can become quite large and hard to manage and store.

Electronic portfolios (called **e-portfolios**), on the other hand, store all the student work as digital files. For example, any computer-generated products, such as spreadsheets, word-processed reports, or WebQuests, can be directly added to the portfolio. Student work created on paper, such as drawings, handwritten poems, or illustrated stories, can be converted to digital format with a scanner. For capturing actual student performances, digital audio and video are also important components of an electronic portfolio, including readings, skits or presentations, student-created 3-D models, or lab experiments conducted by students. The digital format also allows students to add their self-reflections as text or audio narration.

An e-portfolio provides the opportunity for a student to use artifacts in multiple ways. For example if a student writes a paper on how the Mississippi River influenced the economy of the bordering communities that he feels is a good example of his language arts skills, he would place it in the e-portfolio for that purpose. If later, that student realizes that the paper would also serve to demonstrate his insights into social studies knowledge, he can connect that same artifact to another aspect of his e-portfolio. The ability to move or connect the artifacts within the e-portfolio offers students more options in how they capitalize on the ways to demonstrate their success in learning outcomes.

Electronic portfolios can be created with specialized portfolio software, at online sites, or with combinations of basic software such as PowerPoint. Drawbacks for electronic portfolios include availability of equipment and time, as well as questions of access to the tools. Moreover, creating e-portfolios is initially time-consuming because teachers and students need to learn how to scan, save, and format documents in a useful and appealing manner. However, once the process is mastered, e-portfolios take less time to maintain and obviously require less storage space than traditional portfolios. Security is a concern when deciding who will have access to the files among parents, principals, counselors, teachers, and other students. For some practical tips on using Google Docs as an open source software solution for e-portfolios, visit Dr. Helen Barrett's ePortfolios website, http://electronicportfolios.org.

TRADITIONAL ASSESSMENT

There are times when, as a teacher, you need to verify that students have specific knowledge or skills. Often, more traditional measures are used to demonstrate levels of knowledge. Such things as multiple-choice, fill-in-the-blank, true/false, or short-answer tests are ways to identify students who have mastered particular facts and to determine which students may need additional instruction (Waugh & Gronlund, 2012). Traditional tests tend to be used to measure lower-order learning, which is sometimes essential to ensuring students are meeting state and local learning standards.

Teachers can design traditional tests using learning objectives as their guide. Many instructional materials, such as textbook series, include tests as part of their teacher resource package. Teachers can use these types of tests as quick measures to determine which students need additional instructional assistance or to check on student progress on a particular topic or skill. Traditional tests can serve as a way to identify where students are in their knowledge about a topic prior to designing instruction; thus, you will not repeat content that students have already mastered.

In addition, each state is required to annually report the progress of students' learning. State-wide **standardized tests,** which are administered in a consistent manner and use the same scoring procedures, are a type of traditional assessment measure. In this instance, the tests are scheduled for a specific date across the state and the procedures are carefully orchestrated so that student learning is measured in the same way. Currently, state standardized tests are used to identify student learning that is meeting or exceeding state standards and to determine where there is a need for improvement.

Summary

In this chapter we discussed the major theories of learning and how teachers need to consider them when working with a variety of students. Teachers need to design instruction to meet the needs of 21st century learners. As a teacher, you will want to be prepared to engage your students with technology and media to motivate them and help them to gain the types of knowledge and skills they need to be successful learners. In addition, we addressed several ways to assess student learning.

Professional Development

DEMONSTRATING PROFESSIONAL KNOWLEDGE

1. Describe the similarities and differences in the learning theories discussed in this chapter.
2. What are the eight principles of effective instruction for the 21st century learner?
3. Describe the similarities and differences in the principles of effective technology and media utilization.
4. Describe similarities and differences in the different types of effective assessments presented in this chapter.

DEMONSTRATING PROFESSIONAL SKILLS

1. Prepare a 10-minute presentation on your reaction to a topic of interest in this chapter (ISTE NETS-T 5.C).
2. Analyze an instructional situation (either real or hypothetical) and identify the psychological perspective on learning and the technology and media used (ISTE NETS-T 5.C).

3. Prepare a position paper on the roles of technology and media in learning (ISTE NETS-T 5.C).

4. Describe different instances in which you would use the types of assessment described in this chapter (ISTE NETS-T 2.D).

BUILDING YOUR PROFESSIONAL PORTFOLIO

- *Enhancing My Portfolio*. Select a lesson from a source on the Web. Indicate how specific portions of the lesson illustrate, if present, the psychological perspectives addressed in this chapter (behaviorist, cognitivist, constructivist, and social psychology). Identify the assessment that is used to measure student learning. Discuss the value of the assessment being used. Cite the source of the lesson. Reflect on this analysis, providing strengths, weaknesses, and recommendations for teaching this lesson to a specific group of students (ISTE NETS-T 2.C).

- *Reflecting on My Learning*. Reflect on the different assessment processes described in the chapter. Discuss how these assessment strategies measure student learning and where they best fit into an instructional situation. Comment on the types of teacher feedback that might contribute to student understanding of the assessment results (ISTE NETS-T 5.C).

Suggested Resources

PRINT RESOURCES

Anderson, R., Grant, M., & Speck, B. (2008). *Technology to teach literacy: A resource for K–8 teachers* (2nd ed.). Boston, MA: Allyn & Bacon.

Callison, D. (2003). *Key words, concepts and methods for information age instruction: A guide to teaching information inquiry.* Englewood, CO: Libraries Unlimited.

Del, A., Newton, D., & Petroff, J. (2007). *Assistive technology in the classroom: Enhancing the school experiences of students with disabilities.* Upper Saddle River, NJ: Prentice Hall.

Erben, T., Ban, R., & Castanda, M. (2008). *Teaching English language learners through technology.* New York, NY: Routledge.

Jonassen, D. H., Howland, J., Moore, J., & Marra, R. M. (2002). *Learning to solve problems with technology: A constructivist perspective* (2nd ed.). Upper Saddle River, NJ: Merrill/Prentice Hall.

Mager, R. (1997), *How to turn learners on . . . without turning them off.* Atlanta, GA: CEP Press.

O'Bannon, B., & Puckett, K. (2010). *Preparing to use technology: A practical guide to curriculum integration* (2nd ed.). Boston, MA: Allyn & Bacon.

Roblyer, M., & Doering, A. (2010). *Integrating educational technology into teaching* (5th ed.). Boston, MA: Allyn & Bacon.

WEB RESOURCES

International Society for Technology in Education

www.iste.org

ISTE is an association focused on improving education through the use of technology in learning, teaching, and administration. ISTE members include teachers, administrators, computer coordinators, information resource managers, and educational technology specialists.

eSchool News

www.eschoolnews.com

This site offers a convenient way to keep up to date electronically with what is going on with technology in schools.

Partnership for 21st Century Skills

www.p21.org

The Partnership for 21st Century Skills advocates for infusing 21st century skills into education. Working with leaders in business, education, and policy, the organization's goal is to work with schools to infuse 21st century skills into education and provides tools and resources to help facilitate and drive change.

Learning Styles Inventory

http://www.learning-styles-online.com/inventory/questions .php?cookieset=y

The Learning styles inventory has 70 questions that assess dominant and secondary learning styles concerning the following areas: aural, verbal, physical, logical, social, and solitary.

Learning Styles Inventory for Students with Learning Disabilities

www.ldpride.net/learning_style.html

This website offers an inventory to identify the preferred learning styles of students with learning disabilities. The inventory results provide educators and parents with a better understanding of students' learning preferences. This information will assist in adapting learning environments to better meet the needs of individual learners.

Integrating Technology and Media into Instruction: The ASSURE Model

Knowledge Outcomes

This chapter addresses ISTE NETS-T 2, 4, and 5.

1 State the three primary types of information used to analyze learners and describe the role of the information in the systematic planning process for learning.

2 Demonstrate how to go from national standards to learning objectives that include the audience, behavior, conditions, and degree of mastery.

3 Outline the procedures for selecting, modifying, and designing instructional strategies and resources.

4 Create examples of the five basic steps in utilizing resources (e.g., technology, media, and materials).

5 Describe and justify methods for eliciting student participation when using technology and media during instruction.

6 Compare and contrast the techniques for evaluating student achievement, strategies, and resources and for making data-based revisions.

Goal

Use the ASSURE model to systematically plan lessons that effectively integrate classroom use of technology and media.

The ASSURE model consists of six steps designed to help teachers plan lessons that effectively integrate use of technology and media for learning. To illustrate how to use the model, we provide you with an easy-to-understand description and a classroom case study to demonstrate implementation of each step. These steps taken together constitute a sample ASSURE lesson plan that describes the instructional planning of actual classroom teachers highlighted in the classroom case study.

Ninth-Grade English

This ASSURE classroom case study describes the instructional planning used by Tiare Ahu, a high school English teacher who wants to increase student learning and communication skills through the use of electronic portfolios, often referred to as *e-portfolios*. Tiare feels that her ninth-grade students often lack interest in improving their writing and oral communication skills. Her students typically complete each class assignment without reflecting on past learning experiences, thus inhibiting their ability to grow and improve. She first addresses the concern by having students create paper-based portfolios of their writing. However, it proves difficult for students to revise and improve an existing paper-based assignment and equally difficult to add reflective comments without detracting from the original documents. Her solution is to use e-portfolios that allow students to easily update, modify, and add written or video reflections to their assignments. Throughout the chapter you can follow Tiare's use of the ASSURE model to design a lesson that integrates the use of electronic portfolios.

▶ *This ASSURE Classroom Case Study was created by Tiare Ahu. Watch Ms. Ahu's ninth-grade English class working on their electronic portfolios.*

Today's teachers have exciting opportunities, using technology and media to guide students' 21st century learning experiences. This chapter introduces you to the ASSURE model, which uses a step-by-step process to create lessons that effectively integrate the use of technology and media to improve student learning. Lessons created with the ASSURE model directly align with the Common Core State Standards, the National Education Technology Standards for Teachers (ISTE, 2008) and students (ISTE, 2007) (hereafter referred to as NETS-T and NETS-S, respectively), as well as curriculum standards from the local to the national level. In addition, the ASSURE model utilizes a standard research-based approach to lesson design that easily aligns with school or district lesson plan templates.

The ASSURE Model

All effective instruction requires careful planning. Teaching with instructional technology and media is certainly no exception. This chapter examines how to plan systematically for the effective use of technology and media. We have constructed a procedural model to which we have given the acronym ASSURE—it is intended to *assure* effective instruction.

Some aspects of teaching and learning have stayed consistent over the years, such as the progressive stages or "events of instruction" that occur (Gagné, 1985). Research has shown that well-designed lessons begin with the arousal of students' interest and then move on to present new material, involve students in practice with feedback, assess their understanding, and provide relevant follow-up activities. The ASSURE model incorporates all these events of instruction, beginning with the analysis of learners.

Analyze Learners

The first step in planning a lesson is to identify and analyze learner characteristics shown to be associated with learning outcomes. This information will guide your decision making during the design of your lesson. The key areas to consider during learner analysis include (1) general characteristics of learners, (2) specific entry competencies (knowledge, skills, and attitudes about the topic), and (3) learning styles.

State Standards and Objectives

The next step is to state the standards and learning objectives as specifically as possible. Begin with curriculum and technology standards adopted by your district, as these are based on state and national student performance criteria. Well-stated objectives name the learners for whom the objective is intended, the action (behavior) to be demonstrated, the conditions under which the behavior or performance will be observed, and the degree to which the new knowledge or skill must be mastered. For this text, the condition will include the use of technology and media to support learning and to assess achievement of the standard or learning objectives.

Select Strategies and Resources

Once you have analyzed your learners and stated the standards and objectives, you have established the beginning points (students' present knowledge, skills, and attitudes) and ending points (learning objectives) of instruction. Your task now is to build a bridge between these two points by choosing appropriate instructional strategies and resources to achieve the objectives.

Utilize Resources

This step involves planning your teaching role for utilizing the resources (technology, media, and materials) to help students achieve the learning objectives. To do this, follow the 5 Ps process: Preview the resources; Prepare the resources; Prepare the environment; Prepare the learners; and Provide the learning experience.

Require Learner Participation

To be effective, instruction should require learners' active mental engagement. Provide activities that allow them to practice the new knowledge or skills and to receive feedback on their efforts before being formally assessed. Practice may involve student self-checks, computer-assisted instruction, Internet activities, or group exercises. Feedback can come from the teacher, a computer, other students, or self-evaluation.

Evaluate and Revise

After implementing a lesson, evaluate its impact on student learning. This assessment not only examines the degree to which students achieved the learning objectives, but also examines the entire instructional process and the impact of using technology and media. Wherever there are discrepancies between learning objectives and student outcomes, revise the lesson plan to address the areas of concern.

Analyze Learners

The ASSURE model provides you with a systematic approach for analyzing learner characteristics that impact their ability to learn. The analysis information is used to plan lessons tailored to meet the needs of your students. The learner analysis examines three types of information: general characteristics, specific entry competencies, and learning styles.

GENERAL CHARACTERISTICS

It is critical to understand the general characteristics that may influence student learning. These characteristics range from constant variables, such as gender and ethnicity, to those that vary on a regular basis, such as attitudes and interest.

Review student records to identify the age differences of your students to better understand behavioral patterns or ability to focus during learning activities. When planning group work, consider gender differences that may impact student attention and willingness to participate. For example, mixed-gender groups may work well in early elementary classes but inhibit student learning for some middle school students. When students represent multiple ethnic groups, select instructional materials and examples that give high priority to cultural identity and values. For example, select photos and clip art with children of the same ethnicity as your students to increase their connection to the lesson topic. Once you have this background understanding of your students' general characteristics, couple it with your observations of student attitudes and interest to design and implement meaningful lessons that address the unique needs of each student.

SPECIFIC ENTRY COMPETENCIES

Research reveals that students' prior knowledge of a particular subject influences how and what they learn more than does any psychological trait (Dick, Carey, & Carey, 2014). Therefore, a critical component of designing lessons is to identify the specific entry competencies of your students. You can do this informally (such as through in-class questioning) or by more formal means (such as reviewing standardized test results or giving teacher-made tests and assessments). **Entry tests** are assessments that determine whether students possess the necessary **prerequisites**, or competencies, to benefit from instruction. For example, if you are going to teach students to calculate the area of geometric shapes, the entry test would focus on multiplication skills to identify students who need remediation prior to the lesson. An important prerequisite skill for many lessons is reading ability. Therefore, you may want to test or arrange to have your students' reading abilities determined.

Once specific entry competencies are identified, list them in your lesson and include an entry **pretest** to identify students who need remediation prior to lesson implementation and also to identify those who have already mastered what you plan to teach.

LEARNING STYLES

Learning style refers to the following psychological traits that determine how an individual perceives, interacts with, and responds emotionally to learning environments: multiple intelligences, perceptual preferences and strengths, information processing habits, motivation, and physiological factors.

The information you learn from analyzing the general characteristics, specific entry competencies, and learning styles of your students will guide your decision-making process as you design your ASSURE lesson (see the ASSURE case study for an example of the process).

Analyze Learners

Ninth-Grade English

General Characteristics

Tiare Ahu is teaching the basic ninth-grade English course geared toward the average learner. The students are 14 and 15 years old. Several students have learning disabilities, whereas others are above-average readers and writers. Her students come from primarily moderate- to low-income socioeconomic environments and represent an ethnic population common to an urban setting. Generally, the students are well behaved. However, some show lack of interest and apathy toward learning when activities are textbook and paper-and-pencil oriented.

Entry Competencies

The students in general are able to do the following:

- Create and save word processed documents
- Navigate the Internet
- Create and save digital video
- Respond via written and verbal communication that ranges from below to above grade-level proficiency

Learning Styles

Tiare has found that her students appear to learn best from activities that incorporate technology and media. Using computers provides intrinsic motivation through the creation of personalized work and the careful reflection of learning. Her students vary in their preferred forms of expression; some favor inputting their thoughts as written text, others choose to capture them with digital video, and still others prefer audio recordings. Tiare has also discovered that most of her students have difficulty working in a completely silent atmosphere and therefore she allows the option of listening to music on MP3 players when they work on their digital portfolios.

 Review the ASSURE video, paying particular attention to how Tiare Ahu addressed the learner analysis of her ninth-grade students.

State Standards and Objectives

The second step in the ASSURE model is to state the standards and learning objectives for the lesson. What new capability should learners possess at the completion of instruction? The learning objectives are derived from curriculum and technology standards—descriptions of expected student performance outcomes established at the school district, state, or national level. For this text, we focus on NETS-S, Common Core State Standards, and other national curriculum standards. As seen in Table 3.1, curriculum and technology standards provide general descriptions of expected student performance, whereas learning objectives, typically written by the teacher or school district, identify very specific outcomes. It is important to note that a learning objective is a statement of what each learner will achieve, not how the lesson will be taught.

IMPORTANCE OF STANDARDS AND OBJECTIVES

It is important to state the standards and learning objectives for each lesson because they serve as the basis for three critical components of the ASSURE lesson plan. The three components are described in more detail in subsequent sections of this chapter.

TABLE 3.1 Going from Standards to Learning Objectives: PK–4 and 9–12 Examples

Grades PK–4 Examples

Common Core State Standards (CCSS) and National Curriculum Standards	National Educational Technology Standards for Students (NETS-S) (www.cnets.iste.org)	Learning Objective Aligned to National Standards
CCSS English Language Arts (www.corestandards.org/ELA-Literacy/RI/4) **RI.4.9** *Reading—Informational Text:* Integrate information from two texts on the same topic in order to write or speak about the subject knowledgeably **National Center for History in the Schools (NCHS)** (http://nchs.ucla.ed) **K–4 Content Standards:** *Topic 2:* The History of the Students' Own State or Region *Standard 3A:* The student understands the history of indigenous peoples who first lived in his or her state or region. **Grades 3 and 4** Therefore the student is able to compare and contrast how Native American or Hawaiian life today differs from the life of these same groups over 100 years ago.	**NETS-S Standards:** 1. **Creativity and Innovation** Students demonstrate creative thinking, construct knowledge, and develop innovative products and processes using technology. 2. **Communication and Collaboration** Students use digital media and environments to communicate and work collaboratively, including at a distance, to support individual learning and contribute to the learning of others. 6. **Technology Operations and Concepts** Students demonstrate a sound understanding of technology concepts, systems, and operations **NETS-S Grades PK–4** Performance Indicator 4: In a collaborative work group, use a variety of technologies to produce a digital presentation or product in a curriculum area. (1,2,6)	Given different storybooks that describe the lifestyles of Southwest Native Americans over the past 100 years, the third-grade students select two texts from which they will create a six-slide PowerPoint presentation for Parent Night that compares and contrasts the housing, diets, traditions, and work of today's Southwest Native Americans with those from 100 years earlier.

Grades 9–12 Examples

Common Core State Standards (CCSS) and National Curriculum Standards	National Educational Technology Standards for Students (NETS-S) (www.cnets.iste.org)	Learning Objective Aligned to National Standards
CCSS English Language Arts (www.corestandards.org/ELA-Literacy/W/9-10) **W.9-10.1** *Writing - Text Types and Purposes:* Write arguments to support claims in an analysis of substantive topics or texts, using valid reasoning and relevant and sufficient evidence. **National Standards for Arts Education (NSAE)** (see http://artsedge.kennedy-center.org/teach/standards.cfm) **Grades 9–12: Visual Arts** *Content Standard 1:* Understanding and applying media, techniques, and processes *Achievement Standard:* Students conceive and create works of visual art that demonstrate an understanding of how the communication of their ideas relates to the media, techniques, and processes they use.	**NETS-S Standards:** 1. **Creativity and Innovation** Students demonstrate creative thinking, construct knowledge, and develop innovative products and processes using technology. 2. **Communication and Collaboration** Students use digital media and environments to communicate and work collaboratively, including at a distance, to support individual learning and contribute to the learning of others. **NETS-S Grades 9–12** Create and publish an online art gallery with examples and commentary that demonstrate an understanding of different historical periods, cultures, and countries. (1,2)	Given a digital camera, computer, and Photoshop software, the tenth-grade student will (1) create a visual art product that includes at least three digital photos and two descriptive words to represent the concept of freedom, and (2) provide a written argument/rationale that supports their choice of media, techniques, and processes to demonstrate an understanding of freedom.

Source: Common Core State Standard Initiative reprinted with permission from the National Governors Association Center for Best Practices (NGA Center) and the Council of Chief State School Officers (CCSSO), Washington, DC. Reprinted with permission from National Educational Technology Standards for Teachers and National Educational Technology Standards for Students. Copyright © 2007, 2008 by ISTE (International Society for Technology in Education.) All rights reserved.

Basis for Strategies, Technology, and Media Selection. When you have clear statements of what students will know and be able to do at the conclusion of the lesson, you are better able to carefully select the strategies, technology, and media that will ensure learning.

Basis for Assessment. Stating standards and learning objectives also helps ensure accurate assessment of student learning. The explicitly stated student outcomes serve as a guide when creating assessments to measure the targeted knowledge and skills that are directly aligned with standardized tests.

Basis for Student Learning Expectations. Your students are better able to prepare for and participate in learning activities when they know the expected outcomes. The learning objectives may be viewed as a type of contract between teacher and learner: "My responsibility as the teacher is to provide learning activities suitable for your attaining the objective. Your responsibility as the learner is to participate conscientiously in those learning activities."

THE ABCDs OF WELL-STATED LEARNING OBJECTIVES

The ABCDs of well-stated objectives provide an easy-to-follow process for writing learning objectives: Specify the *Audience* for whom the objective is intended, the *Behavior* to be demonstrated, the *Conditions* under which the behavior will be observed, and the *Degree* to which the new knowledge or skill must be mastered.

Audience. Because learning objectives focus on what learners will know and be able to do after the lesson, it is important to clearly identify the targeted learners—for example, second-grade students. For students you will be teaching all year, you may choose the common audience identifier "The learner will . . . ," which is often abbreviated as TLW. For students who have individual education plans, the objectives will be targeted to students by name.

Behavior. The heart of the objective is the verb describing the new capability that learners will have *after* instruction. This verb is stated as an observable behavior, such as *define, categorize,* or *demonstrate*. Vague terms such as *know, understand,* and *appreciate* do not communicate observable performance. The Helpful Hundred list in Table 3.2 offers verbs that highlight the behavior or performance.

Strive to solicit student behavior or performance that reflects deep understanding and real-world capability. In other words, rather than having students "select the correct answers on a test about water conservation," have them "compare and contrast two water conservation systems to identify which is most eco-friendly." Or rather than selecting names of geometric shapes on a worksheet, have students identify shapes used in the Golden Gate Bridge.

Conditions. Learning objectives should include the conditions under which the performance is to be assessed. In other words, what materials or tools will students be allowed or not allowed for use in demonstrating mastery of the objective? Thus, an objective might state, "Given a list of earthquake occurrences over the past 100 years, the student will generate a line graph to demonstrate trends over time." A language arts objective might say, "Without using reference materials, the student will write a 300-word essay on the relationship of nutrition to learning."

Degree. The final requirement of a well-stated objective is the degree of accuracy or proficiency by which minimally acceptable performance will be judged. Certainly students can exceed the stated expectations. A high school chemistry objective may read, "Given six unknown substances and testing equipment, students will identify five of the six unknown substances." When stating the degree or criterion for assessing student products that are more comprehensive in

TABLE 3.2 The Helpful Hundred

Suggested Behavior Terms

Add	Compute	Draw	Label	Predict	State
Alphabetize	Conduct	Estimate	Locate	Prepare	Subtract
Analyze	Construct	Evaluate	Make	Present	Suggest
Apply	Contrast	Explain	Manipulate	Produce	Swing
Arrange	Convert	Extrapolate	Match	Pronounce	Tabulate
Assemble	Correct	Finish	Measure	Read	Throw
Attend	Cut	Fit	Modify	Reconstruct	Time
Bisect	Deduce	Generate	Multiply	Reduce	Translate
Build	Defend	Graph	Name	Remove	Type
Categorize	Define	Group	Operate	Revise	Underline
Change	Demonstrate	Hit	Order	Select	Verbalize
Choose	Derive	Hold	Organize	Sketch	Verify
Classify	Describe	Identify	Outline	Solve	Weave
Color	Design	Illustrate	Pack	Spell	Weigh
Compare	Designate	Indicate	Paint	Sort	Write
Complete	Diagram	Install	Plot	Specify	
Compose	Distinguish	Kick	Position	Square	

scope, a rubric rating scale that assesses several components of the product is appropriate. An average of the combined rubric scores can be used to provide an overall proficiency rating. For example, proficiency on a student product may be stated as follows: "Students are to achieve an overall rubric rating of 3 (on a four-point scale, where 4 = Exceeds Expectations)." Details on creating rubrics are presented in Chapter 2, "Designing and Assessing 21st Century Learning."

ABCD OBJECTIVES CHECKLIST

Use the ABCD Objectives Checklist (Figure 3.1) to assess the degree to which your objectives communicate the intent of the learning. Further guidelines for writing objectives are discussed in Gronlund's (2009) *Writing Instructional Objectives for Teaching and Assessment*.

You will find that learning objectives appearing in curriculum standards, textbooks, online lessons, and other instructional materials are written in a general format that often lacks one or more of the ABCD components. Teachers can modify such objectives to meet the specific learning needs of their students; for example, a district standard may state: "The learner will be able to divide fractions." If you have students who struggle with math, you could adapt the objective by adding the following condition: "Given manipulatives, the learner will be able to divide fractions." The same objective for more advanced students would not include manipulatives.

Many curriculum standards also lack the use of technology to assist students in achieving the learning objective. This concern can be addressed by adding the appropriate NETS-S (ISTE, 2007) to lessons. Include technology in the Condition component of the objective, as in the following examples:

- *Given spreadsheet software and data on population growth, natural resources, and global warming,* sixth-grade science students will use a spreadsheet to estimate the impact of population growth on natural resources from at least three perspectives.

FIGURE 3.1 ABCD Objectives

ABCD Objectives Checklist			
	Appropriately Stated	Partly Stated	Missing
Audience			
Specifies the learner(s) for whom the objective is intended	☐	☐	☐
Behavior (action verb)			
Describes the capability expected of the learner following instruction • Stated as a learner performance • Stated as observable behavior • Describes a real-world skill (versus mere test performance)	☐	☐	☐
Conditions (materials and/or environment)			
Describes the conditions under which the performance is to be demonstrated • Equipment, tools, aids, or references the learner may or may not use • Special environmental conditions in which the learner has to perform	☐	☐	☐
Degree (criterion)			
States, where applicable, the standard for acceptable performance • Time limit • Range of accuracy • Proportion of correct responses required • Qualitative standards	☐	☐	☐

- *Given clip art and PowerPoint software,* first-grade students will construct a four-slide presentation with one student-selected clip art image per slide to demonstrate four student moods: happy, sad, angry, and bored.

- *Given access to word processing software and web-based resources on American wars,* American history high school students will generate *a word-processed table* that shows 25 similarities of and differences between World War I and World War II.

- *Given a list of randomly grouped words and Inspiration software,* seventh-grade language arts students will create a concept map that arranges the words into six parts-of-speech groups.

LEARNING OBJECTIVES AND INDIVIDUAL DIFFERENCES

It is important to adapt learning objectives to the abilities of individual learners (Figure 3.2). The stated philosophy of most schools is to help students achieve their full potential. In a physical education class with students of mixed ability, for instance, the midsemester goal might be for all students to complete a 100-meter run, with time standards that vary to show similarity of achievement. For a few, 12 seconds might be attainable; for many others, 16 seconds is doable; and for some, 20 seconds might be realistic. For a student with physical disabilities, it might be a major victory to move 10 meters in one minute.

Learning objectives are not intended to limit what students learn, but rather are intended to provide a minimum level of expected achievement. Serendipitous or incidental learning should be expected to occur (and should be encouraged) because learning takes different forms with

FIGURE 3.2 Assistive software helps meet the individual needs of students.

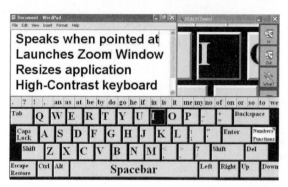

Source: High Contrast REACH Key Band–Yellow. Reprinted with permission of Applied Human Factors.

different students. Class discussions and other kinds of student involvement in the instructional situation, therefore, should rarely be rigidly limited to a specific objective. Indeed, to foster incidental learning and provide for individual differences, it is sometimes advisable to have students specify some of their own learning objectives. (See a set of standards and learning objectives in the ASSURE case study.)

Select Strategies and Resources

The next step in creating effective lessons that support learning through the appropriate use of technology and media is the systematic selection of instructional strategies and resources, which include technology and media, and lesson materials. The following guidelines discuss the selection process.

SELECT STRATEGIES

All instructional strategies, whether teacher- or student-centered, should engage students in active learning. When identifying instructional strategies for a lesson, first consider where teacher-centered approaches should be used and where student-centered strategies might be more appropriate. The teacher strategies involve your own teaching activities, as when you present a concept by showing a video or reading a story, or when you use the interactive white-board to engage students in demonstrating how to conjugate a verb. The student-centered strategies are those in which the teacher acts as a facilitator. Examples of student-centered learning include small groups discussing the pros and cons of a topic, pairs of students conducting an Internet search or taking digital photos of a process, or individuals listening to podcasts on a current news story. Most lessons include several teacher and student strategies.

Marzano and Heflebower (2012) propose that today's teachers need to implement instructional strategies that engage students in activities that build both cognitive and conative skills. The cognitive skills prepare students to (1) analyze and use information, (2) address complex problems and issues, and (3) create patterns and mental models. On the other hand, the conative skills prepare students to (1) understand and control themselves, and (2) understand and interact with others (p. 11). These types of activities prepare students for future careers requiring similar application of knowledge and skills.

Another key consideration for selecting instructional strategies is keeping students motivated to learn. In other words, the strategies should be designed to encourage students to believe they have the *competence* to succeed and enough *control/autonomy* to make choices

State Standards and Objectives

Ninth-Grade English

Standards

- Curriculum—*National Council of Teachers of English Standard 4:* Students adjust their use of spoken, written, and visual language (e.g., conventions, style, vocabulary) to communicate effectively with a variety of audiences and for different purposes. *Common Core State Standards, ELA Literacy.SL.9-10.4:* Present information, findings, and supporting evidence clearly, concisely, and logically such that listeners can follow the line of reasoning and the organization, development, substance, and style are appropriate to purpose, audience, and task.
- Technology—*National Educational Technology Standards for Students 3 (Technology Productivity Tools):* Students use technology tools to enhance learning, increase productivity, and promote creativity.

Lesson Objectives

1. Given the following questions, the ninth-grade English student will demonstrate ability to express reflective thinking by answering the following questions in a written or video reflection that meets the "Final Year Reflections" criteria listed on the assignment sheet.
   - What did I learn about myself, reading, writing, learning, and overall during the past year?
   - What do I hope to accomplish in these areas next year when I am a sophomore?

2. Using DreamWeaver software, the ninth-grade English student will create a new page titled "Final Year Reflections" that meets the formatting criteria for being included in the electronic portfolio reflections folder.

3. Using files of previously completed work, the ninth-grade student will be able to add the written reflection or upload a video reflection in an accessible format to the "Final Year Reflections" page in the electronic portfolio folder.

▶ *Review the ASSURE video to observe Tiare Ahu as she discusses the curriculum and technology standards and objectives for the English lesson.*

during the learning process. It is also important to provide students opportunities to interact with and receive recognition from teachers, family, and others of social importance to them (Usher & Kober, 2012).

SELECT RESOURCES

When selecting resources for ASSURE lessons, decisions are made regarding the technology and media and the types of support materials needed to achieve the lesson outcomes. In addition to selecting support materials, teachers often need to modify existing materials or design new materials to meet specific needs. Guidelines and tools for making these decisions follow.

Technology and Media. Selecting appropriate technology and media can be a complex task, considering the vast array of available resources, the diversity of your learners, and the specific learning objectives to be pursued. Videos, for example, raise the issue of presentation pace, which varies for individual learners. In examining educational games, look for relevant practice and feedback. When selecting an audio storybook, look for functions such as embedded definitions and ease of returning to previously read sections. To help with this process, selection rubrics are provided for key technology and media presented in selected chapters, as noted in the Special Features of this text.

Selection Rubrics. The selection rubrics provide a systematic procedure for assessing the qualities of specific technology and media. Each rubric includes a set of consistent selection criteria (as shown here) as well as criteria for the designated technology or media (e.g., computer software, audio). You need to decide which criteria are most important for your students' achieving the stated learning objectives.

Selection Rubric Criteria

- Alignment with standards, outcomes, and objectives
- Accurate and current information
- Age-appropriate language
- Interest level and engagement
- Technical quality
- Ease of use (for student or teacher)
- Bias free
- User guide and directions

The selection rubrics are templates with separate fields to enter the media title, source, and a brief description along with a predefined rating scale to assess the technology/media being reviewed.

SELECTING, MODIFYING, OR DESIGNING MATERIALS

When you have selected your strategies and the type of technology and media needed for your lesson, you are ready to select the materials to support lesson implementation. This step involves three general options: (1) selecting available materials, (2) modifying existing materials, or (3) designing new materials.

Selecting Available Materials. The majority of instructional materials used by teachers are "off the shelf"— that is, ready made and available from school, district, or other easily accessible sources. Many of these resources are free or inexpensive. Among many offerings, how do you go about making appropriate choices from available materials?

Involving the Technology/Media Specialist. You may want to begin by meeting with your technology/media specialist and discussing your learning objectives, instructional strategies, and desired media format(s). As the specialist gains a better idea of your needs, arrangements can be made to check out the appropriate materials from your school's library/media center or other media collections (public, academic, or regional).

Joining Other Teachers. Because evaluation of materials is time consuming and complex, it may be useful to involve other teachers, especially experienced teachers whose years of work with media and material alternatives have involved a lot of critical analysis about education resources. Working with other teachers allows a pool of shared ideas for using materials and a collective strength that may make it easier to acquire materials from museums or organizations.

Surveying Media Resource Guides. Media resource guides survey and review free and inexpensive materials. For example, the Gateway to 21st Century Skills (**www.thegateway.org**)

delivers over 1 million resources to educators worldwide on an annual basis. These resources include lesson plans, thematic units, student materials, and much more provided by some of the country's best museums, universities, and government programs, including NASA, the Smithsonian Institution, the National Science Foundation, and the Exploratorium in San Francisco. You can search the Gateway database by subject area, grade level, and keyword. In addition, the Gateway requires each resource to be reviewed and meet specified standards before being added to the collection.

Kathy Schrock's Guide to Everything includes links to an alphabetized list of technology resource support sites such as iPads in the Classroom, Literacy in the Digital Age, and Twitter for Teachers. Also included are links to Apps for That, Authentic Learning, Video of the Month, and DEN Blog: Kathy's Katch **(www.schrockguide.net)**.

Modifying Existing Materials. As you strive to meet the diverse needs of your students, you will find that "off-the-shelf" materials often need modifications to more closely align with your learning objectives. Technology provides several options for modifying existing materials.

Encouragingly, many educational resources are provided as copyright-free digital files or as paper copies. Digital materials are typically found on educational websites that provide downloadable resources. Example resources include lesson handouts, teacher PowerPoint presentations, and Excel spreadsheets formatted for easy data entry.

However, when materials are only available in PDF or paper format, modifications can be accomplished with digital scanning or creative use of a copy machine. For example, materials can be scanned and modified with editing software. Another approach is to modify a paper original and then make copies of the revised resource. For instance, if you want students to label 20 grasshopper features but have a handout based on 50, you can carefully cover the 30 unwanted features and then make copies.

A word of caution about using and modifying commercially produced materials is to be sure not to violate copyright laws and restrictions. If in doubt, check with your school media specialist, administrator, or legal adviser. General copyright guidelines were discussed in Chapter 1.

Designing New Materials. When ready-made materials are not available or existing materials cannot be easily modified, you need to design your own lesson materials, which can range from hand printing a flip chart to using your computer to create handouts, presentations, or an online WebQuest. The remaining chapters provide guidance for developing meaningful materials involving a variety of technology and media. Remember to keep learner needs and learning objectives as the key considerations when designing your lesson materials (as in the ASSURE classroom case study).

Utilize Resources

This step involves planning your role as a teacher for utilizing the lesson resources (e.g., technology, media, and materials). Follow the 5 Ps process: Preview and Prepare the resources; Prepare the environment; Prepare the learners; and Provide the learning experience.

PREVIEW RESOURCES

During the selection process you identified lesson resources appropriate for your learners. At this stage you need to preview the selected technology and media resources in relation to the learning objectives. The goal is to select the portions that directly align with your lesson. For example, if your lesson is on correct use of prepositions, preview several language arts software

ASSURE Classroom Case Study

Select Strategies and Resources

Ninth-Grade English

Select Strategies

Tiare Ahu selects teacher- and student-centered strategies for the electronic portfolio lesson. Teacher-centered strategies are chosen for reviewing the overall goals of using an electronic portfolio and to introduce student guidelines for completing the final reflections. The student-centered strategies are used for students' written or video reflections of their learning that are added to electronic portfolios. Tiare addresses student motivation by using the ARCS model (Keller, 2010) to consider how electronic portfolios gain student *attention*. To achieve *relevance*, students reflect on their personal growth over the year and set goals for next year. Their *confidence* is reinforced by the lesson's use of skills previously mastered in other electronic portfolio activities. Students gain *satisfaction* through personalizing their reflections with digital media such as colors, clip art, and photos.

Select Resources

Technology and Media. This lesson involves the continued use of Blackboard course management software and DreamWeaver software to create web-based portfolios. The lesson also calls for a digital video camera to record student reflections and the use of iMovie to edit the video reflections. The following guidelines help Tiare assess the appropriateness of her technology and media selections:

- *Alignment with standards, outcomes, and objectives.* The software provides the necessary tools for her students to meet the learning objectives.

- *Accurate and current information.* Not applicable for the chosen technology and media.
- *Age-appropriate language.* The software applications are written at a level appropriate for ninth-grade students.
- *Interest level and engagement.* The software applications provide features that enable the students to personalize their electronic portfolios.
- *Technical quality.* The software applications have superior technical quality.
- *Ease of use.* The applications require initial training and periodic review of functions for students to easily use the features.
- *Bias free.* The software applications are bias free.
- *User guide and directions.* The online help features of the software are moderately easy to use. Students most frequently ask each other, the teacher, or the technology assistant for help with technical difficulties.

Select Materials

This lesson includes a teacher-produced student assignment sheet that explains the details of creating and adding the final reflections to the electronic portfolio. Tiare was not able to use available materials or modify existing materials because the assignment sheet requires details very specific to the lesson.

 Review the ASSURE video to observe the strategies and resources used by Tiare Ahu in her ninth-grade English class.

programs to find drill-and-practice activities that match your objectives. Then, design your lesson to include just the preposition sections of the software rather than the entire sequence. Similarly, if using a DVD video documentary, identify the segments that directly align with your lesson.

Although your decision may have already involved published reviews, distributor's blurbs, and colleagues' appraisals, you should *insist* on previewing the materials yourself before using them. Not only will a thorough review enable you to use resources to their full potential, it will ensure that students are not exposed to inappropriate content or language found in some computer games, videos, and online or printed periodicals.

Carefully preview multiple resources when planning your lesson.

Prepare the resources to support attainment of lesson objectives.

Prepare the environment by arranging the facilities to ensure proper use of resources.

Carefully prepare learners to fully participate in the lesson activities.

PREPARE RESOURCES

Next, you need to prepare the resources that will support your instructional activities. The first step is to gather all the equipment you will need. Determine the sequence for using the materials and what you will do with each one. For example, you may want to change how an instructional game is used by preparing a new set of questions at a different level of difficulty or even on a new topic. Or, if the audio portion of a video doesn't align with the needs of your students, you can turn off the sound and provide the narration yourself.

Keep a list of the materials and equipment needed for each lesson and an outline of the presentation sequence of the activities. Finally, practice using the resources before implementing the lesson.

PREPARE THE ENVIRONMENT

Wherever the learning is to take place—in the classroom, in a laboratory, at the media center—the facilities will have to be arranged for effective use of the resources. Some media require

When providing the learning experience, remember that both teacher-centered and student-centered activities may be utilized.

a darkened room, a convenient power source, and access to light switches. You should check that the equipment is in working order. Arrange the facilities so that all students can see and hear properly. Arrange the seating so students can see and hear each other when cooperative learning is included.

PREPARE THE LEARNERS

Foundational research on learning tells us that what is learned from an activity depends highly on how learners are prepared for the lesson (Gagné, Wager, Golas, & Keller, 2004). We know that in show business entertainers are passionate about having the audience properly warmed up. Effective instruction also requires a proper warmup, which can include one or more of the following:

• An introduction giving a broad overview of the lesson content

• A rationale telling how the content relates to real-world applications

• A motivating statement that creates a need to know the content

• Cues directing attention to specific aspects of the lesson

In most cases, you will also want to inform students of the learning objectives, introduce unfamiliar vocabulary, and review prerequisite skills needed for the lesson, including any new skills needed to use technology and media.

PROVIDE THE LEARNING EXPERIENCE

Now you are ready to provide the instructional experience. A teacher-centered learning experience often involves a presentation, demonstration, drill and practice, or a tutorial. The provision of these learning experiences may require the use of various resources. (See the ASSURE case study for Tiare Ahu's approach to the stage of utilizing resources.)

Require Learner Participation

As predicted by Bloom, Engelhart, Furst, Hill, and Krathwohl (1956) over 50 years ago, today's global economy will require students to have experience and practice applying, analyzing, synthesizing, and evaluating rather than just knowing and comprehending information. This follows constructivist views that learning is an active mental process built from relevant authentic experiences or **practice** for which students receive informative **feedback,** a response that lets them know the degree to which they have achieved the objective and how to improve their performance. The NETS-S support this level of student participation through the use of a variety of technology and media (ISTE, 2007).

PRACTICE

The objectives for your lesson explicitly state what students are expected to know and do after instruction. Thus, it is critical to require learner participation through explicit practice with

Utilize Resources

Ninth-Grade English

Preview Resources

Tiare Ahu previews the site map and selection properties of DreamWeaver and how to use the digital video camera and iMovie software.

Prepare Resources

Tiare creates a handout that explains what students should do to complete their "Final Year Reflections" in written or video formats. She also adds a "Final Year Reflection" to her sample electronic portfolio.

Prepare the Environment

The lesson will take place in the computer lab and in the video recording studio. Each computer in the computer lab needs to be checked to ensure that DreamWeaver and iMovie software programs are functional and that all computers can save to the server and print. The studio needs to be arranged for recording student video reflections by setting up the tripod for the digital video camera and arranging the seating in a location with an appropriate background. Tiare also needs to check that the digital media storage device has enough space to store the student video reflections.

Prepare the Learners

To prepare the students, Tiare introduces the lesson and reviews the learning objectives. Students receive a handout about completing the "Final Year Reflection" for their electronic portfolios. In addition, the handout also includes the evaluation criteria for the reflection.

Provide the Learning Experience

Tiare guides student learning by reviewing how to add reflections to their electronic portfolios and by monitoring students as they create their written or video work.

 Review the ASSURE video to see how Tiare Ahu utilizes her lesson resources for the e-portfolio lesson.

---

the new knowledge and skills. The NETS-S have direct applicability when planning student participation activities, in which students use a variety of technology and media to support learning.

Creativity and Innovation. One common way of requiring learner participation is through the student use of technology to "construct knowledge and develop innovative products and processes" (NETS-S 1) (ISTE, 2007). For example, in early childhood experiences learning vocabulary words, word meanings can be enhanced when students use KidPix to find images representing new words and then must explain their choices. Another example involves middle school students creating PowerPoint presentations depicting trends in American folk music over the past 100 years. The activity requires summarizing key ideas from historical documents, choosing the best photos and sound clips, and sequencing content in a meaningful way. At the high school level, social studies students can use spreadsheets to examine national population trends and make growth predictions for the next 50 years.

Communication and Collaboration. The NETS-S consider how students can use "digital media and environments to communicate and work collaboratively, including at a distance, to support individual learning and contribute to the learning of others" (NETS-S 2) (ISTE, 2007). For example, when using projected still pictures of students living in Alaska, you can engage students in a lively discussion in which they compare themselves with the students in the photos. Students can then exchange emails with Alaskan students to gain firsthand knowledge of life in Alaska. As another example, if the outcome is to increase student awareness of their right and responsibility to express opinions, student groups could write and submit their ideas to a public opinion section of a local news website.

Research and Information Fluency. The Internet provides students with instant access to limitless resources. Therefore, they can readily "apply digital tools to gather, evaluate, and use information" (NETS-S 3) (ISTE, 2007). As a teacher, it is critical for you to plan activities that actively engage students in processing information and reporting results that are meaningful for the assigned task. Student research should also include information from books, periodicals, and people, because multiple resources will better ensure that students do not merely cut and paste web-based information into their work. For instance, if your students are to create a concept map of events influencing the rights of women, you want to set expectations for using multiple digital and nondigital resources, paraphrasing content, and providing appropriate citations.

Critical Thinking, Problem Solving, and Decision Making. "Students use critical thinking skills to plan and conduct research, manage projects, solve problems, and make informed decisions using appropriate digital tools and resources" (NETS-S 4) (ISTE, 2007). Never before have students had access to such vast amounts of data and information. Students of all ages can more closely examine information than any previous generation through tools such as electronic devices (e.g., science probes and microscopes), digital audio and video equipment (e.g., cameras and whiteboards), and software in general (e.g., spreadsheets and databases). If students were addressing the question "Does the person with the most popular votes win a presidential election?" they could download election results into a spreadsheet to compare electoral votes to popular vote totals. To determine whether artificial ponds are as safe for fish as natural ponds, students could gather water samples and use a variety of electronic probes to collect data to compare in a spreadsheet. Young students learning colors could solve the following problem: "Can you find a rainbow in our room?" Student pairs would use a digital camera to photograph items matching each color of the rainbow for a "Rainbows in Our Room" activity book.

Technological tools specifically designed to engage students in problem solving include computer games and simulations. Games use competition, intrigue, and inquisitiveness as vehicles for students to gain content knowledge. An excellent example is Math Blaster, award-winning software that engages students in fast-action games to learn standards-based math content. Simulations use the same features, yet allow learners great flexibility in making choices that affect outcomes in the games. SimCity is a well-known simulation game in which students design and manage a variety of systems (e.g., power, water, taxes, education) for one or more cities. The design addresses a variety of systems required to support the citizens, for example power, water, taxes, education, transportation, hospitals, and police. The planning also needs to include identification of different zones within the city, such as residential, business, recreational and industrial, while keeping in mind environmental and safety factors. The overall goal is to create a self-sustaining city with a balanced budget.

Using Educational Software for Practice. In addition to NETS-S activities, educational software provides excellent resources for engaging students with diverse abilities in individualized learning activities focused toward core content knowledge and skills. The programs allow students of lower-than-average abilities to move at their own pace and provide immediate feedback and remediation. Other students can try more challenging activities after demonstrating mastery of previous skills.

Using Other Media for Practice. Discussions, short quizzes, and application exercises can provide opportunities for practice and feedback during instruction. Teacher guides and manuals often suggest techniques and activities for eliciting and reinforcing student responses. However, many of these resources do not integrate the use of technology and media. Therefore, you will

Require Learner Participation

Ninth-Grade English

Student Practice Activities

Students individually write responses to the reflection question, "What did I learn this year about myself; about reading, writing, and learning; and about life generally?" Students have the option of using written or video reflections.

The students use computers and DreamWeaver software as a production tool to add reflection pages to their personal electronic portfolios. Students who choose to write their reflections add them directly to the page. Those choosing video meet with Tiare to record their reflections with a digital camera. The file is then transferred to students' computers for editing with iMovie before uploading to their electronic portfolios.

Feedback

Tiare uses the assignment criteria to review each student's electronic portfolio. She adds individualized comments to each student's file in the gradebook section of Blackboard for the electronic portfolio assignment.

▶ *Review the ASSURE video to observe various levels of student participation required to create electronic portfolios as well as scenes showing Tiare Ahu providing feedback to students about their work.*

need to use applicable components of the ASSURE model to decide where student use of these tools is appropriate.

FEEDBACK

In all cases, learners should receive feedback on the correctness of their responses. The feedback may come from the teacher, or students may work in small groups and give one another feedback. Feedback may also be part of a self-check activity done independently or with a mentor, often using the computer. Regardless of the source, the important thing is that students receive helpful feedback (as in the ASSURE case study).

Evaluate and Revise

The final component of the ASSURE model, Evaluate and Revise, is essential to the development of quality instruction, yet this component of lesson design is often neglected. Without this step, it is often impossible to know whether instruction is successful or how to revise unsuccessful strategies. It also makes it difficult to judge the efficacy of different types of technology and media without taking the time to evaluate their use.

EVALUATE IMPACT ON STUDENT LEARNING

The ultimate question regarding instruction is whether students have learned what they were supposed to learn. Can they demonstrate the capabilities specified in the stated standards and objectives? The first step in answering this question was taken near the beginning of the ASSURE model, when you formulated your learning objectives, including a criterion of acceptable performance. The next step is to develop assessment tasks that require students to demonstrate the behavior stated in the objective.

As seen in Chapter 2, the method of assessing achievement depends on the nature of the objective. Some learning objectives call for relatively simple cognitive skills—for example, stating Ohm's law, distinguishing adjectives from adverbs, or summarizing the principles of the Declaration of Independence. Learning objectives such as these lend themselves to conventional written tests.

Other objectives may call for process-type behaviors (e.g., diagramming a sentence, solving quadratic equations, or classifying animals), the creation of products (e.g., a sculpture, a written composition, a PowerPoint presentation, or a portfolio), or an exhibit of attitudes (e.g., choosing to read during free-time activities, placing used paper in the recycle bin, or eating healthy snacks). This type of learning objective requires a more comprehensive, **authentic assessment,** such as a performance-based evaluation of a student's demonstration of learning in a natural context.

EVALUATE AND REVISE STRATEGIES AND RESOURCES

Evaluation also includes assessment of your instructional strategies and the resources used to support the lesson. Were the instructional strategies effective? Could they be improved? Did the technology and media resources assist students in meeting the learning objectives? Were they effective in arousing student interest? Did they support meaningful student participation? A key component to the evaluation and revision of a lesson is learner input. You may solicit learner input on the effectiveness of specific media, such as a video, an activity, or on the entire lesson. A student survey similar to Figure 3.3 can be used to collect learner comments.

You can also obtain student feedback regarding your instructional strategies and use of technology and media through discussions and interviews. For example, you may learn that students would have preferred independent study to your choice of group presentation. Or perhaps students didn't like your selection of online resources and feel they would have learned more from watching a video. Your students also may let you know, subtly or not so subtly, that your own performance left something to be desired.

Evaluation of Teaching. Although evaluation of your teaching may evoke some apprehension, the resulting information will provide excellent feedback for addressing areas of needed improvement—and for celebrating areas of high-quality teaching. There are four basic types of teacher evaluation: self, student, peer, and administrator.

For self-evaluation, you can create an audio or video recording of your instruction that you then listen to or view at a later time while using an evaluation form such as Figure 3.4.

Students, even in early grades, can provide valuable feedback through age-appropriate surveys. Students may be reluctant to "evaluate" their teacher in open-class discussions, but might share ideas in a group or submit comments anonymously.

You may ask a colleague, usually another teacher, to sit in the back of the room and observe your teaching skills. Feedback could be given in an open-ended evaluation (blank sheet of paper) or you may design a form that addresses areas for which you would like to receive feedback.

In most schools, administrators visit teachers on a scheduled sequence, often annually or semiannually. You may ask an administrator to visit more frequently on an "unofficial" basis. Many schools have a standard form that administrators use to observe teachers and provide feedback to them. You may also inform your administrator of other characteristics you would like her to observe.

FIGURE 3.3 **Sample Form Used by Students to Evaluate Their Teachers**

Student Rating Form for Classroom Teaching	Your Reaction
1. I could easily understand the teacher.	☺ 😐 ☹
2. I could always hear the teacher.	☺ 😐 ☹
3. I paid attention.	☺ 😐 ☹
4. I felt involved.	☺ 😐 ☹
5. The teacher looked at me.	☺ 😐 ☹
6. Overall, I would grade the presentation	A B C D F

Completed forms to be collected by a student

Presentation Evaluation Form

Teacher _____   Evaluator _____   Date _____

SA = Strongly Agree   A = Agree   D = Disagree   SD = Strongly Disagree

1. Presenter appeared nervous.   SA   A   D   SD
   Comment ....

2. Content was delivered well.   SA   A   D   SD
   Comment ....

3. Movement enhanced presentation.   SA   A   D   SD
   Comment ....

4. Voice was natural and conversational.   SA   A   D   SD
   Comment ....

5. Vocal variety was used.   SA   A   D   SD
   Comment ....

6. Presenter could be easily heard.   SA   A   D   SD
   Comment ....

7. There were no distracting mannerisms.   SA   A   D   SD
   Comment ....

8. Eye contact was established and maintained.   SA   A   D   SD
   Comment ....

9. Natural gestures were used.   SA   A   D   SD
   Comment ....

10. Overall, presentation was well done.   SA   A   D   SD
    Comment ....

Strengths of presenter
....
....

Weaknesses of presenter
....
....

Overall comments
....
....

Evaluate and Revise

Ninth-Grade English

Assessment of Learner Achievement

Tiare Ahu uses the following rating form to evaluate students' Final Year Reflections:

Reflection Rating Scale

1 = Response is minimal, primarily states facts
2 = Response is adequate, reveals moderate reflection
3 = Detailed response that demonstrates meaningful reflection

- At what level did the student write reflections for each item in question 1, "What did I learn about the following?"
  - Myself
  - Reading
  - Writing
  - Learning
  - Overall
- At what level did the student write a reflection for question 2, "What do I hope to accomplish in these areas next year when I am a sophomore?"

Technology Rating Scale

1 = Did not complete task as described
2 = Completed task as described

- Did the student use DreamWeaver software to create a new page titled "Final Year Reflections" in his or her electronic portfolio folder?
- Did the student add a written or video reflection to the "Final Year Reflections" page in his or her DreamWeaver electronic portfolio folder?

Evaluation of Strategies and Resources

To evaluate the strategies and resources utilized, Tiare conducts debriefing activities with the students. In addition, she talks informally with students during the entire process. Tiare invites comments that address the importance of using an electronic portfolio to assess learning over time. The primary purpose of this debriefing session is to determine whether the students think creating electronic portfolios is worthwhile. In addition, they are asked to write their ideas for improving the lesson.

Revision

The students and Tiare complete a teacher-developed form for an overall evaluation of learner achievement, strategies, and resources. Tiare compares the student responses and overall average rating with her own perceptions. For items that appear discrepant, she will address the need for revision in her choice of learning activities, resource selections, and evaluation materials.

 Review the ASSURE video to observe ideas and strategies for evaluating ninth-grade students' electronic portfolios.

REVISION OF STRATEGIES AND RESOURCES

The final step of the instructional cycle is to sit back and look at your assessment and evaluation data. Examine discrepancies between your intentions and what actually happened. Did student achievement fall short on one or more of the learning objectives? How did students react to the instructional strategies and lesson resources? Are you satisfied with the value of the materials you selected?

Reflect on the lesson and each component of it. Make notes immediately following completion of the lesson, and refer to them before you implement the lesson again. If your evaluation data indicate shortcomings, now is the time to go back to the faulty part of the plan and revise it. The model works, but only if you constantly use it to upgrade the quality of your instruction (as in the ASSURE case study).

Summary

This chapter introduced you to the ASSURE model and demonstrated how it can be used to plan lessons that effectively use technology and media to support and enhance student learning. The model incorporates six critical aspects of instructional planning, as seen in the following ASSURE Lesson Template.

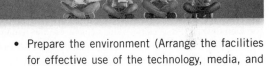

ASSURE Lesson Plan Template

Analyze Learners

- Describe general characteristics of the class as a whole—age, grade, and so forth.
- Describe entry competencies or types of knowledge expected of the learners before instruction.
- Describe the learning style preferences of individual students.

State Standards and Objectives

- List curriculum and technology standards to be achieved.
- Describe the learning objectives using the ABCD format.

Select Strategies and Resources

- Describe the strategies and resources (e.g., technology, media, and materials) that are essential to the lesson.
- Provide a rationale for each selection.
- Use selection rubrics to evaluate resource that best helps students meet the intended outcomes.

Utilize Resources

- Preview resources (It is essential to know the technology, media, and materials prior to teaching with them.)
- Prepare resources (Practice using the technology, media, and materials prior to the lesson.)

- Prepare the environment (Arrange the facilities for effective use of the technology, media, and materials.)
- Prepare the learners (Knowing what is expected of them helps ensure learner involvement in the learning.)
- Provide the learning experience (Provide teacher-centered and student-centered learning experiences.)

Require Learner Participation

- Require active mental engagement by learners.
- Engage learners in practice of new knowledge or skills.
- Support learning with technology and media.
- Provide performance feedback prior to formal assessment.

Evaluate and Revise

- Use traditional and authentic assessments to determine learner achievement of stated standards and objectives.
- Examine the entire instructional process and the impact of using technology and media.
- If discrepancies between learning objectives and student outcomes are identified, revise the lesson plan to address the areas of concern.

DEMONSTRATING PROFESSIONAL KNOWLEDGE

1. What are the primary types of criteria used to analyze learners and how is this information used to design lessons?
2. Describe how to go from a national standard to a learning objective that includes the audience, behavior, conditions, and degree of mastery.
3. List and describe the procedures for selecting, modifying, and designing instructional strategies and resources.

4. What are the five basic steps for utilizing resources (e.g., technology, media, and materials)?
5. Describe methods of eliciting student participation and providing feedback during student educational use of technology and media.
6. In what ways are the techniques for evaluating student achievement, technology, media, strategies, and instruction similar and different?

DEMONSTRATING PROFESSIONAL SKILLS

The Demonstrate Professional Skills activities in the remaining chapters are designed to address many of the NETS-T (ISTE, 2008). Items aligned to NETS-T are noted with the standard number in parentheses.

1. Write a learner analysis of your students or those you plan to teach. Describe their general characteristics, note their specific entry competencies for a topic of your choice, and discuss their learning styles. If you are not yet a teacher, you may need to do some research on students in the grade level you plan to teach.

2. Write at least five learning objectives for a lesson you might teach and assess each objective with the Objectives Checklist (Figure 3.1).
3. Select a topic you might teach that would incorporate student use of technology and develop a set of learning strategies, resources, and associated assessment instruments (including traditional and authentic assessments) (NETS-T 2.A, 2.C, and 2.D).
4. Locate a lesson, perhaps using the Internet, that does *not* provide learner practice and feedback. Design activities for the lesson that provide those elements.

BUILDING YOUR PROFESSIONAL PORTFOLIO

An important component for continuing your professional development is the creation of a professional portfolio to demonstrate the knowledge and skills gained from this text. Following the model shown in this section of each chapter you will have the opportunity to create, enhance, and reflect on lessons developed for each chapter.

- *Creating My Lesson.* Using the ASSURE model, design a lesson for a scenario from the table in Appendix A, from an example in the chapter, or use a scenario of your own design. You can do this by selecting a content area standard or topic you plan to teach. Be sure to include information about the learners, the learning objectives, and all other elements of the ASSURE model. When you have finished, reflect on the process you used and what you have learned about matching learners, content, strategies, technology, media, and materials.
- *Enhancing My Lesson.* Enhance the lesson plan you created by describing how you would meet the diverse needs of learners in your class. Specifically, describe

strategies you would include for students who already possess the knowledge and skills targeted in your lesson plan. Also describe strategies, technology, and media you could integrate to assist students who have not met the lesson prerequisites or who have disabilities that impact their ability to learn. For example, how would you meet the needs of students with visual or hearing limitations, or the needs of students who are reading below or above grade level?

Describe other types of technology and media that can be integrated into your instructional strategies for the lesson. If the lesson requires word processed reports, you might consider having students take photos with a digital camera and make interactive presentations of their reports. Or if students use drill-and-practice software to learn multiplication facts, you could have them create their own PowerPoint electronic flashcard practice set (NETS-T 2.A, 2.B, 2.C, 3.B, and 4.B).

- *Reflecting on My Lesson.* Reflect on the lesson you created for this chapter and on how you enhanced the lesson. Address the following in your reflections: How did use of the ASSURE model strengthen the lesson?

What aspect of the ASSURE model do you consider the most critical for the lesson you created? How could your ASSURE lesson be improved? (NETS-T 4.B and 5.C)

Suggested Resources

PRINT RESOURCES

Ambrose, S. A., Bridges, M. W., DiPietro, M., Lovett, M. C., & Norman, M. K. (2010). *How learning works: 7 research-based principles for smart teaching.* San Francisco, CA: Jossey-Bass.

Bailey, G., & Ribble, M. (2007). *Digital citizenship in schools.* Washington, DC: International Society for Technology in Education.

Baker, F. W. (2012). *Media literacy in the K-12 classroom.* Washington, DC: International Society for Technology in Education.

Bray, M., Brown, A. H., & Green, T. D. (2005). *Technology and the diverse learner: A guide to classroom practice.* Thousand Oaks, CA: Corwin.

Brooks-Young, S. J. (2009). *Making technology standards work for you* (2nd ed.). Washington, DC: International Society for Technology in Education.

Carr-Chellman, A. A. (2010). *Instructional design for teachers.* New York, NY: Routledge.

Chapman, C., & King, R. S. (2006). *Differentiated reading and writing strategies for middle and high school classrooms: A multimedia kit for professional development.* Thousand Oaks, CA: Corwin.

Greenstein, L. M. (2012). *Assessing 21st century skills: A guide to evaluating mastery and authentic learning.* Thousand Oaks, CA: Corwin.

O'Donoghue, J. (2006). *Technology supported learning and teaching: A staff perspective.* Hershey, PA: Information Science.

Stiggins, R. J., & Chappuis, J. (2012). *An introduction to student-involved assessment for learning* (6th ed.). Boston, MA: Pearson Education.

Walker-Tileston, D. E. (2006). *Teaching strategies for active learning: Five essentials for your teaching plan.* Thousand Oaks, CA: Corwin.

WEB RESOURCES

ISTE Wikispaces: NETS-S 2007 Implementation Wiki
http://nets-implementation.iste.wikispaces.net
This wiki hosts discussions on how to implement the 2007 NETS-S into classroom instruction. The site provides opportunities to participate in surveys about technology integration practices and policies.

Writing Educational Goals and Objectives
www.personal.psu.edu/staff/b/x/bxb11/Objectives/index.htm
Teaching and Learning with Technology, a website hosted by Penn State, provides teachers easy-to-follow guidelines for writing educational goals and objectives. The site also includes multiple examples of goals and objectives for various subject areas and grade levels.

Electronic Materials for Children and Young Adults
www.eduscapes.com
This site offers links to educational materials for a range of learners on multiple topics areas and grade levels.

21st Century Educational Technology and Learning
http://21centuryedtech.wordpress.com
Michael Gorman hosts this site as an "advocate for teachers and students while concentrating efforts at transforming education and bringing 21st Century Skills to every classroom." Mike Gorman received the Top 50 Education Innovator Award and hosts this site, which is rated among the Top 40 Most Trusted Education Blogs.

Designing 21st Century Learning Environments

Knowledge Outcomes

This chapter addresses ISTE NETS-T 1, 2, 3, and 5.

1. Describe 10 learning strategies in the classroom.

2. Differentiate between types of learning contexts.

3. Discuss how to support learning with technology and media.

4. Describe the value of integrating free and inexpensive materials into instruction.

Goal

Understand how to select and use appropriate learning strategies, technology, media, and materials to achieve 21st century learning in different PK–12 environments.

they advise that in order to advance learning, it is essential to ensure that all learners are taught the essential content they need using an active presentation format. They advocate that a presentation should contain several attributes: presentation, practice, assessment, and monitoring and feedback. They contend that a presentation should guide learners to understanding the content in meaningful ways.

Technology can play a major role during a presentation, such as including a live Internet broadcast from the International Space Station, a podcast of an author reading her poetry, or a concept map of bird migration that students build on an interactive whiteboard. However, classroom presentations can also involve nontechnological support strategies, such as reading a book or giving a lecture.

Advantages

- *Present once.* You only have to present the information once for all the students.
- *Note-taking strategies.* Students can use a number of different note-taking strategies to capture the information presented.
- *Information sources.* Technology and media resources can serve as quality sources for the most current information.
- *Student presentations.* Students can present information they have learned to the whole class or a small group.

Limitations

- *Difficult for some students.* Not all students respond well to a presentation format to learn information; therefore, the lesson will need to include more than one way of presenting content (e.g., reading, listening, or viewing a video).
- *Potentially boring.* Without interaction, a presentation can be very boring. It is important to include ways to keep students interactive through questions and answers, check sheets to complete, or dialog.
- *Note-taking difficulty.* Students may need to learn how to take notes to benefit from a presentation. One solution is to provide a partially completed notes sheet to assist with note-taking skills.
- *Age appropriateness.* Younger students may have difficulty sitting for lengthy presentations, so it is important to adjust presentation time based on student age and attention level.

Integration. There are a number of technology resources that can enhance presentation of information. For example, you or your students can use an interactive whiteboard to seamlessly move from a video to a spreadsheet chart to notes recorded from student comments. PowerPoint or Prezi slides are another very common way of presenting information that can include hyperlinks to Internet information or animated diagrams to illustrate a concept, along with summarized content and related images. Just ensure that you and your students follow copyright guidelines when adding information to presentations. Student "clickers" are technology tools that can enhance presentations by immediately displaying student responses to questions. Another way to integrate technology into a presentation is through the use of document cameras, which project printed materials and small 3-D objects. Examples include closely examining an old photo of a landmark, displaying a storybook as it is read, or watching the metamorphosis of a caterpillar into a butterfly.

Presentation is a core instructional strategy that has been successfully used for many generations. Today's teachers have the advantage of expanding on tried-and-true strategies by integrating technology resources to further engage students in deep-level thinking and processing to yield even higher levels of meaningful learning. In addition, a presentation is something that can last as long as necessary to help convey the information to students. As you think about using this strategy, you may want your presentation to be very short with your questions as the

Interactive whiteboards provide teachers with multiple ways to engage students during presentation of information.

guide to engaging your students in a more student-centered activity for the rest of the classroom learning experience. Remember that a presentation can be an effective strategy if you do not overuse it and if you consider how to keep your students actively engaged during the presentation.

DEMONSTRATION

In a demonstration, learners view an exhibition of a skill or procedure to be learned. Demonstrations can be used with a whole class, a small group, or an individual who needs a little extra explanation on how to do a task. With younger students, you can demonstrate basic procedures such as how to print letters, use a digital camera, or pronounce a word. When working with older students, you might demonstrate more complicated processes, such as how to solve an alge-bra problem, read tables of historical data, create interactive websites, or understand the way something works.

The purpose of the demonstration may be for your learn-ers to imitate a physical performance, such as using a digital wind gauge, or to adopt the attitudes exemplified when you serve as a role model, such as how to ask questions when working in cooperative groups. In some cases, the point is simply to illustrate how something works, such as the effect of heat on a bimetallic strip. Just-in-time peer demonstrations often take the form of one-on-one sessions, with an experi-enced student showing a peer how to perform a procedure, such as using the copy/paste function in a word processing program. Demonstration allows your students to ask ques-tions that you can answer during active learning experiences.

Advantages

- *Seeing before doing.* Students benefit by seeing something done before having to do it themselves.
- *Task guidance.* A teacher can simultaneously guide a large group of students to complete a task.
- *Economy of supplies.* Only a limited number of supplies are necessary because not every-one will be handling all materials.
- *Safety.* A demonstration allows the teacher to control the potential danger to students when using caustic materials or dangerous equipment.

Limitations

- *Not hands-on.* Students do not get direct hands-on experience unless they are following along as the teacher demonstrates steps or skills.
- *Limited view.* Every student may not have an equal view of the demonstration, thus possibly missing some aspect of the experience. A technological solution involves using a document camera to project the demonstration.
- *Nonflexible pacing.* Not all students may be able to follow the demonstration's pace of pre-sentation. Recording the procedure on video will allow students to review the demonstra-tion as needed.

Integration. Demonstrations can be enhanced with the use of technological equipment such as digital cameras. Digital video cameras can be used to record a demonstration during or before class. The recording can be viewed with the class to further examine various aspects of the demonstration or used by small groups or individuals to review the process. Students can be assigned as videographers. If more than one camera is available to record the demonstration, the videos can be merged with iMovie or MovieMaker. Creating videos is particularly effective with complex procedures or messy projects using actual objects for the demonstration.

Other types of digital equipment used during demonstrations include devices that record specific phenomena, such as wind, temperature, moisture, speed, and pH, as well as magnification devices, such as digital microscopes. These devices are primarily useful in mathematics and science demonstrations in which the results are projected for whole-class or small-group viewing.

Another option involves integrating demonstrations with digital video from online sources such as YouTube or TeacherTube. These demonstrations might include the basics of using an abacus app on an iPhone, how to divide integers, or how to test the pH of pond water. As expected, multiple examples emerge when searching for online videos, so review carefully before using them in class and remember to follow all copyright guidelines.

DRILL-AND-PRACTICE

In **drill-and-practice,** learners complete practice exercises to refresh or increase fluency in content knowledge and skills, most commonly in mathematics and language arts. Use of this strategy assumes that your learners have received some instruction on the concept, principle, or procedure they are practicing. To be effective, the drill-and-practice exercises should include feedback to reinforce correct responses and to remediate errors learners might make along the way.

Advantages

- *Corrective feedback.* Students receive feedback on their responses.
- *Information chunking.* Information is presented in small chunks, allowing students to review the material in small bits.
- *Built-in practice.* Practice is built into the small chunks of information, giving immediate opportunities to try out the new knowledge in some positive way.

Limitations

- *Repetitive.* Not all students respond well to the repetitive nature of drill-and-practice. It is important to limit the time spent or number of exercises to prevent monotony.

- *Potentially boring.* Some drill-and-practice materials have too many items, which can lead to boredom. A solution is to review the content and only assign material that is relevant.

Many software programs lend themselves to helping a student practice skills.

- *Nonadaptive.* If a student is making repeated errors, continued use of drill-and-practice material does not help the student learn. Keep track of student progress and use a different intervention if learning doesn't improve.

Integration. Many computer applications offer students opportunities to review information and practice their knowledge or skill while enjoying a game-like experience. Other drill-and-practice software titles follow more traditional approaches, such as online flashcards and interactive worksheets. Digital versions of drill-and-practice are available as stand-alone software packages, like Math Blaster and Reader

Rabbit, and as free interactive online programs, like the Magic School Bus series. There are also many nondigital drill-and-practice resources with years of proven effectiveness that offer a tactile alternative to working on the computer. Most popular are items that your students can use individually or in pairs, such as flashcards, word cards, and worksheets in spelling, mathematics, and language instruction.

TUTORIAL

Tutorials involve learners working with an agent—in the form of a person, computer software, or special printed materials—that presents the content, poses questions or problems, requests the learner's responses, analyzes the responses, supplies appropriate feedback, and provides practice until the learner demonstrates a predetermined level of competency. Your students often work independently or with a partner as they are provided chunks of information designed to build knowledge. Students learn through practice with feedback after each small section. The difference between a tutorial and drill-and-practice is that the tutorial introduces and teaches new material, whereas the drill-and-practice focuses on content previously taught in another type of lesson (e.g., presentation).

Advantages

- *Independent work.* Students can work independently on new material and receive feedback about their progress.

- *Self-paced.* Students can work at their own pace, repeating information if they need to review it before moving on to the next section of the material.

- *Individualization.* Computer-based tutorials respond to students' input by directing their study to new topics when content is mastered or to remediation activities when review is needed.

Limitations

- *Potentially boring.* The repetition can become boring if the tutorial follows a single pattern that lacks variation.

- *Possibly frustrating.* Students can become frustrated if they do not seem to be making progress while working on the tutorial. Care needs to be taken to assign students to tutorials that are aligned with their abilities.

- *Potential lack of guidance.* The lack of a teacher's guidance can mean that a student does not move through the material effectively. To avoid this, teachers must carefully select and provide ongoing support when tutorials are used.

Integration. Tutorial arrangements include instructor-to-learner (e.g., Socratic dialog), learner-to-learner (e.g., peer-tutoring), computer-to-learner (e.g., computer-assisted tutorial software), and print-to-learner (e.g., workbook) pairings. Tutorials are often helpful for students who have difficulty working in large-group situations or who need extra assistance as they learn new material.

As a teacher providing instructor-to-learner tutoring, you can work with an individual or a small group of students, guiding them carefully at their pace through the material being presented. Learner-to-learner tutoring needs oversight from you as a guide to ensure the students have clear instructions for the one-to-one sessions. Computer-to-learner tutoring is very popular in PK–12 classrooms due to the immediate, individualized feedback such programs can provide in a patient and consistent manner. For example, **integrated learning systems (ILS),** such as SuccessMaker, NovaNet, and Plato Learning, offer computer- or Internet-based instruction. Your student is required to follow a **log-on** procedure, entering the specific name and password you have provided, to begin a new tutoring session or continue with a previously started session. Student progression through the tutorial is based on mastery of content. Because ILS systems can be expensive, they are typically purchased at the district rather than the school level.

Your **school media center** is an excellent source of tutorials. Most centers have a wide variety of tutorial formats, including computer software, audio recordings, and printed materials that you can check out to use with your students.

DISCUSSION

As a strategy, **discussion** involves the exchange of ideas and opinions among students or among students and the teacher. Available at any time during instruction in small or large groups, it is a useful way of assessing the knowledge, skills, and attitudes of a group of students before determining instructional objectives, particularly when introducing a new topic or at the beginning of the school year when the teacher is less familiar with the students. Discussion can help you establish the kind of rapport within the group that fosters collaborative and cooperative learning.

Discussions can be an effective way to introduce a new topic or to delve more deeply into foundational concepts. You can lead discussions by introducing questions to elicit student responses or assign discussion topics to student groups. You may need to prepare your students for a discussion strategy when they are not familiar with the expectations for their participation. Be sure to focus questions on what you wish to have students learn. Also, use higher-level questions involving "What if . . . ?" and "How would . . . ?" to give students the opportunity to think about the topic or issue (Marzano, Pickering, & Heflebower, 2011). When asking higher-level questions, you will want to provide ample wait-time for your students to generate responses. To encourage everyone to participate, you might wish to pair students to share their ideas. When you approach a discussion this way, the shy students will be more comfortable in sharing their ideas with a peer. In addition, you will allow your students to generate more ideas or responses that can contribute to a broader understanding of the concepts or issues.

Advantages

- *Interesting.* Often more interesting for students than sitting and listening to someone tell them facts.
- *Challenging.* Can challenge students to think about the topic and apply what they already know.
- *Inclusive.* Provides opportunities for all students to speak, rather than only a few answering teacher questions.
- *Opportunity for new ideas.* Can be a way to bring in new ideas to the information presentation.

Limitations

- *Potential for limited participation.* Not all students participate, making it important for the teacher to be certain that everyone has a chance to talk.
- *Sometimes unchallenging.* Sometimes students don't learn beyond what they already know and are not challenged to extend their knowledge.
- *Difficulty level.* Some questions asked to elicit a discussion may be too difficult for students to consider based on their level of knowledge.
- *Age appropriateness.* May not be an effective strategy to use with younger students without teacher direction.

Students enjoy educational opportunities to exchange ideas with children at a distance.

Integration. Technology-supported discussions are becoming more popular in today's classrooms as a method to extend the conversation beyond the classroom. Video conferencing with software such as Skype or FaceTime allows students from two or more locations to see and hear each other during discussions. For example, students at Amersfort School of Social Awareness in New York use video conferencing to engage in one of their regular conversations with students in the Netherlands. Students can also engage in online discussions that may allow others beyond the classroom to join in at certain times. These discussions can incorporate video, audio, and/or text as part of the exchange of ideas. Technology and media can also be used to support an in-class discussion. For example, concept-mapping software can help record key ideas and issues raised during the conversation to guide further input and archive the session. As you and your students develop a concept map during the discussion, you are guiding them to consider options and ideas that they might not have otherwise identified. A discussion that incorporates your students' questions is a very effective way to engage them in higher-order thinking.

COOPERATIVE LEARNING

Cooperative learning is a grouping strategy in which students work together to assist each other's learning. Research supports the claim that students learn from each other when they work on projects as a team (Johnson & Johnson, 1999; Slavin, 1989–1990). Two or three students at a computer terminal learn more as they work through the assigned problem together than they would working individually.

Johnson and Johnson (1999) suggest the following conditions need to be present for successful cooperative learning groups:

- Members who view their role as part of a whole team
- Interactive engagement among the members of the group
- Both individual and group accountability
- Interpersonal and leadership skills
- The ability to reflect on personal learning and group function

You can create formal cooperative groups designed to ensure that specific learning outcomes will be accomplished (Marzano et al., 2011). As a teacher you may wish to assign specific roles to each member of the group, such as secretary, time keeper, task director, and so on.

Cooperative learning experiences can be informal as well. Students may determine their own learning needs and work with others to enhance their learning experiences. Informal groups will need to be monitored to ensure that all students in the group benefit from the interactions.

Many educators have criticized the competitive atmosphere that dominates many classrooms and interferes with students' learning from each other. To instead allow students to gain knowledge from each other, you can engage them in cooperative learning situations. Cooperative learning has the additional benefit of equipping your students with the skills required for success in the 21st century world of work.

Advantages

- *Learning benefits.* Mixing the ability levels of students within a group leads to learning benefits for all.
- *Formal or informal.* Groups can be informal or formal based on the learning requirements.

- *Learning opportunity.* Long-term groups can be developed, creating multiple learning opportunities.
- *Content areas.* Cooperative learning can be used with all content areas.

Limitations

- *Size limitation.* Groups need to be kept small (three to five students) to ensure equal participation.
- *Potential overuse.* If the strategy is overused, it can lose its effectiveness. Choose cooperative learning when student learning will be enhanced from discussion and sharing ideas.
- *Group member limitation.* Grouping members of the same ability level does not enhance learning opportunities for all students. Form groups carefully to ensure that multiple levels of ability are represented.

Integration. Students can learn cooperatively not only by discussing text material and viewing media, but also by producing media. For example, students can design and produce a podcast, video, or PowerPoint or Prezi presentation. You will want to be a working partner with the students in such learning situations to serve as a guide in their learning.

Collaboration gives students opportunities to help each other in learning.

If your classroom has a single computer, it is possible to establish cooperative groups to allow all students access. A team of students can easily use programs like World Hunger—Food Force. Such software programs can accommodate cooperative grouping because of the **collaborative** or sharing nature of the experience.

You can have groups prepare presentations on topics for the rest of the class. Thus, each group becomes an expert on a portion of the total content. Preparing presentations requires students to achieve a higher level of mastery than can be derived from studying (see "Taking a Look at Technology Integration: Westward Movement").

PROBLEM-BASED LEARNING

Lifelike problems can provide the starting point for learning. In the process of grappling with real-world challenges, your students acquire the knowledge and skills needed for success in the 21st century. Through the use of **problem-based learning** your students actively seek solutions to structured or ill-structured problems situated in the real world.

TAKING A LOOK AT TECHNOLOGY INTEGRATION

Westward Movement

Connie Courbat, a third-grade teacher, was aware of the various ability levels of her students and wanted them all to have a positive experience studying the westward movement of the 1800s. The lesson objectives were focused on helping students gain a better understanding of the impact of historical events on lifestyle choices. She introduced the topic by forming cooperative groups that used the Oregon Trail software on the one computer in her classroom to experience the adventures of a pioneer traveling the Oregon Trail. She grouped the students to ensure that all ability levels were represented within each group, thus allowing all students to benefit from the experience. Ms. Courbat was careful to establish roles for each member of the group, such as team leader, recorder, and materials manager. She moved among the groups as they worked together, helping them to address questions and ensuring that they were accomplishing the tasks. Each group gave a presentation of their travels westward, explaining their successes and failures in achieving the goal of reaching Oregon.

Structured problems present students with a clear sense of what might constitute an appropriate response. For example, math word problems are often structured applications of math computation skills students already possess. On the other hand, ill-structured problems can be solved in more than one way. For example, if your students are asked to propose solutions to increase student participation in school recycling, multiple responses will be submitted. Because there is more than one correct way to solve the problem, tools such as rubrics will be needed to assess whether your students have attained the stated objectives. See the accompanying feature box on the Ebola Problem for an excellent example of problem-based learning in which technology is used to reach a solution.

Jonassen, Howland, Marra, and Crismond (2008) suggest that technology becomes an "intellectual partner" with students by engaging and supporting them during problem-based learning. The technology provides the environment and tools students use to access, manipulate, and display information. The processes require students to use cognitive learning strategies and critical-thinking skills.

Advantages

- *Engaging.* Students are actively engaged in real-world learning experiences.
- *Context for learning.* The relationship between knowledge and skill becomes apparent as students work toward a problem solution.
- *Levels of complexity.* Introducing additional problem issues over time can control the level of problem complexity.

Limitations

- *Difficult to create.* Creating quality problems for learning can be difficult. It can help to develop problem-based lessons with other teachers and use web resources.
- *Age appropriateness.* Age and experience levels of students may may mean that the teacher will need to adjust a problem to ensure that students will have a successful experience.
- *Time consuming.* Creating and using problem-solving lessons can be very time consuming. Use the ASSURE evaluation step to refine and reuse lessons.

TAKING A LOOK AT TECHNOLOGY INTEGRATION

The Ebola Problem

Some high school students walked into class recently and found this memo on their desks: You are a United Nations doctor stationed in Brazzaville, Congo. When you arrived at your office this morning a message marked "Urgent" was on your desk from a tribal chieftain in a village 100 miles west of your clinic.

The message read: "Come quickly! This village has been stricken with something no one has seen before. Twenty villagers have terrible fevers, diarrhea, and have become demented. Four have already died a terrible death. The other 16 sick people have been placed in a hut where we will keep them until you get here. Please help!"

After forming hypotheses about the possible illness and designing a data-gathering plan, students used their mobile devices to create an initial spreadsheet with the known data. Next, the students left their classroom and walked to a darkened room, the village hut, where they found 14 paper cutouts of people on the floor. (Yes, the discrepancy in numbers was the first problem to solve. An additional death had occurred and another person had left the hut to rejoin the general population.) On each cutout was a card that listed that person's symptoms, which were entered into the spreadsheet. With help from online medical diagnosis sites, such as http://virtualmedicalcentre.com, the students examined the spreadsheet information to determine what the villagers might be facing and how far the outbreak had progressed. The class reached a consensus that the village was facing an outbreak of Ebola and a case of malaria that had been mistakenly grouped with the other sick villagers. The students then developed a written proposal of next steps to treat the afflicted and to prevent the outbreak from spreading.

Source: Stepien, W. J. (1999). Consortium for problem based learning - Northern Illinois University. [Ebola Problem no longer available]. Accessed June 6, 2010 from http://ed.fnal.gov/trc_new/tutorial/

Integration. Many computer applications are available to support problem-based learning. Software packages like The Factory Deluxe provide specific pattern design problems that start out relatively easy but gain complexity as students progress. Cognitive mapping software such as Inspiration provides tools to graphically represent information, with links between concepts to depict relationships needed to solve problems. Database and spreadsheet software such as Access or Excel permits students to develop and explore data sets for answers. For example, students could create a database of U.S. presidents to provide information for the following problem statement: "What are the most common traits of U.S. presidents?" Or, they can look at an Excel file to calculate how changes in income or expenses can affect a budget.

WebQuests are structured problems that include specific steps for students to follow, identify online resources, and provide instructions for students to prepare a report or presentation on their solution. Numerous teacher-developed WebQuests are available on the Web, as is software for teachers who want to create their own WebQuests. Topics for WebQuests cover an array of subject areas including social studies, science, math, and the fine arts. While an effective tool to use with children to guide them to discover the information, your will want to be selective in how often you use this type of resource with your students and how complex you make your WebQuests.

GAMES

Educational gaming provides a competitive environment in which learners follow prescribed rules as they strive to attain a challenging goal. Involving from one to several learners, games are highly motivating, especially for tedious and repetitive content. Games often require learners to use **problem-solving skills** in figuring out solutions or to demonstrate mastery of specific content demanding a high degree of accuracy and efficiency.

By playing games, your students begin to recognize patterns found in particular situations, take on participant roles within a game, and become immersed in the decision-making process as they search for solutions (Smutny & von Fremd, 2009). For example, young children playing a game of concentration will learn to match patterns and increase their memory recall. Older students can learn French, German, Italian, or Spanish with Leonardo's Language Bridge game, in which students are taken on a fun adventure requiring use of the new language to build virtual bridges over a variety of obstacles. An online stock market game engages your students in determining how best to invest an imaginary sum of money. They need to make choices for their investments, deciding the best way to raise additional funds. Along the way, they also reinforce math and literacy skills and help students develop an understanding of financial responsibility.

Challenging and fun to play, computer and traditional games add variety to learning experiences and offer opportunities to practice skills. Students like to play games and benefit by extending their learning experiences into challenging environments.

Students take turns playing a computer game.

Advantages

- *Engaging.* Students are quickly engaged in learning through games.
- *Match to outcomes.* Games can be adapted to match learning outcomes.
- *Variety of settings.* Games can be used in a variety of classroom settings, from whole-class to individual activities.
- *Gain attention.* Most games are colorful, interactive, and competitive, helping to gain student attention for learning specific topics or skills.

Limitations

- *Competition concerns.* Because of the orientation to winning, games can become too competitive unless caution is used.
- *Levels of difficulty.* Less able students may find the game structure too fast or difficult. Provide alternate games to match student ability levels.
- *Expense.* Games, such as computer games, can be expensive to purchase. Often a similar game is available for free on the Web.
- *Misdirection of intention.* The learning outcomes may be lost because of the interest in winning rather than learning. Make sure to clearly state learning objectives before students use games.

Integration. The variety of games used for educational purposes includes digital or paper-based crossword puzzles, Sudoku, jigsaw puzzles, and logic puzzles (sometimes called *brainteasers*). Puzzles can be used to practice information such as spelling words or state capitals. Students can build problem-solving and logic skills with Sudoku games, or strengthen thinking skills with jigsaw puzzles.

One common type of instructional game involves learning about business. In K–8 classrooms, students practice buying and selling products in a store. At middle school and high school levels, students may prepare a product, which they then market and sell to demonstrate their understanding of the world of business, as in the computer game Hot Dog Stand: The Works. The team with the highest corporate profits is the winner.

The Web offers a multitude of free games for students of all ages across core content areas from highly reputable sources. Example providers include NASA's Space Place (**http://spaceplace.nasa.gov/en/kids/games.shtml**), Smithsonian Education, The Environmental Protection Agency's Environmental Kids Club Game Room, and PBS KIDS GO! from the Public Broadcasting Service. Teachers should carefully review games prior to use to ensure that the activity supports achievement of the stated standards and objectives. Also note that students should only complete the game activities that are directly associated with the lesson.

The Stock Market Game, offered by the Simfa Foundation, is very effective in helping your students gain financial skills. This online, multiuser game requires that your students invest their online $100,000 portfolio, tracking their investments and working toward the goal of developing the highest performing portfolio among those who are participating. They work in teams, assuming leadership roles and building skills in cooperation and collaboration as they learn about investing. The game also provides your students with opportunities to practice their language arts and math skills as they work through their investment strategies.

Role-playing is an effective strategy for engaging students in learning.

SIMULATIONS

Simulation allows learners to confront a scaled-down version of a real-life situation. It permits realistic practice without the expense or risks otherwise involved. With the advent of newer technology, 3-D simulations are readily available on the Web or as educational software. Simulation may also involve participant dialog and manipulation of materials and equipment.

Simulations can be used as whole-class or small-group activities, offering experiences that might not otherwise be possible in the real world. For example, your students can learn about the various aspects of voting by engaging in a class election process. They can create campaign information, determine voter registration guidelines, set up voting booths, and elect a counting commission to record and report the results.

Beyond role-playing, simulations can represent situations that may be too large or too complex to bring into your classroom. For example, in a science lesson about internal combustion, you can use two types of simulation resources. For direct hands-on experience, you can use a small color-coded automobile engine model that your students can manipulate to learn about internal combustion. Then your students can watch a 3-D simulation of an engine, such as the 4-Stroke Engine Simulator, to see it in action. By using the model engine and viewing the 3-D simulation, your students are able to get the inside look they need to help them understand the concepts being presented, while being protected from the hazards of operating a real engine.

Online simulations such as The Whole Frog Project (and other suggested websites at the end of this chapter) provide another type of simulated learning experience. The Whole Frog Project engages high school students in a complex study of frogs using technology such as MRI imaging to reveal digital images of internal organs they would not have access to in their classroom, allowing them to gather information about the frog's circulatory, digestive, and muscular systems.

Advantages

- *Safety.* Provides a safe way to engage in a learning experience.
- *Recreate history.* May be the only way to engage in the situation (e.g., role-playing ancient Roman history).
- *Hands-on.* Offers opportunities for hands-on experience.
- *Variety of ability levels.* Students of all ability levels can be included in the experience.

Limitations

- *Questionable representation.* May not be truly representative of the actual event when the simulation is an artist's rendering rather than video or photos of an event.
- *Complexity.* May become too complex or intense for the classroom setting. Review all simulations before use and only integrate relevant sections.
- *Time factor.* May require too much time to complete. Search for a model that demonstrates the concepts in a shorter time frame.

Integration. Interpersonal skills and laboratory experiments in the physical sciences are popular subjects for simulations. In some simulations, learners manipulate mathematical models to determine the effect of changing certain variables, such as controlling the speed of a skier by changing the degree of incline.

Role-playing is another common form of simulation. Software such as Tom Snyder's Decisions, Decisions provides roles for each member of a group, a real-life situation that needs to be resolved, and information to help members as they move along in the process. The sample topics in Decisions, Decisions include Ancient Empires, The Constitution, Violence in Media, and The Cold War. This software has the additional benefit of requiring only one computer in the classroom for use with a whole class.

You can simulate an event that occurred locally or a major event that occurred a century ago, like the sinking of the *Titanic*. One teacher engages her students in understanding the impact of the decisions made that eventful night on the ocean by assigning roles to her students to reenact the evening of the encounter with the iceberg. Her students are given the name of an actual passenger. While they are participating in the "onboard" activities, such as playing card games, dancing, eating a meal, or taking a stroll along the deck of the boat, she guides the "crew" to begin their scurry to deal with the accident. Before the experience is over, she identifies who must leave the area because they have drowned. Her children quickly understand how devastating the event was because so many of their classmates are escorted out of the room. She guides them in understanding the implications of how an event such as this affects family members and what can be done to prevent such catastrophes.

DISCOVERY

The **discovery** strategy uses an inductive, or inquiry, approach to learning that fosters a deeper understanding of the content through the learner's involvement with it. A common approach to discovery is the scientific method, which involves creating a hypothesis or question, trying out a possible solution, and analyzing the information learned to determine whether the approach worked. Various software applications, such as spreadsheets, databases, and concept-mapping applications, and digital devices, such as science probes and microscopes, assist students in organizing, analyzing, and reporting data and information needed to discover the answer to a question.

When using the ASSURE model or other lesson plans to design discovery lessons, ensure that the selected strategies include sufficient guidance and support when students are utilizing technology, media, and materials to solve the problem. This will involve a carefully planned **scaffold** approach, building on prior knowledge as students progress through the learning experience. For instance, you will need to consider what supports will be needed if students fail to complete a step along the way as they move through the experience.

Advantages

- *Engaging.* Very engaging for students at all levels of learning.
- *Repeated steps.* Can use procedures or steps that have been taught previously.
- *Student control of learning.* Allows students the feeling of control over their own learning.

Limitations

- *Time factor.* Time consuming for design and implementation. An option is to adapt web-based discovery lessons.
- *Preparation is critical.* Requires teacher to think through all the possible issues that students might encounter. This becomes easier with practice.
- *Misunderstanding.* Can lead to misunderstandings about a content area. Make sure to debrief students after a lesson.

Integration. There are a variety of ways that instructional technology and media can help promote discovery or inquiry. For instance, your students can set up a digital camera to take time-lapse photos of a plant during the day to discover that plants follow the sun, or they can examine a series of GPS images of the same location on a river to discover how landscapes change over time. Your students can use word processing tools to discover the reading level of well-known documents, such as the Bill of Rights and the Preamble to the Constitution, or to compare excerpts from classic books to discover whether fiction is easier to read than historical biographies.

Digital video may be used for discovery teaching in the sciences by allowing you to stop, enlarge, or slow down naturally occurring events to allow the development of curiosity and student questions. You will guide students by asking questions or having them tell you what they have "discovered" or learned.

ASSURE Classroom Case Study Reflection

Review the ASSURE Classroom Case Study and video at the beginning of the chapter. What learning strategy could Ms. Kaiser and Ms. Marshall integrate into a social studies lesson that would achieve the goal of increasing student interest in U.S. history while being exciting and fun? How could this strategy assist in achieving this goal?

Learning Strategies

Instructional Situation	Strategy	Potential Technology/Media
The whole class needs to learn how to conjugate verbs.	Presentation	A PowerPoint presentation that interactively shows variations of a verb by clicking on key words. Using Camtasia or Captivate, the teacher creates a video that includes text showing the variations of each verb and video clips of students demonstrating the action noted in the verb.
Because of safety issues, students need to observe the teacher handling chemicals for an experiment.	Demonstration	Teacher models correct use of certain types of chemicals to ensure that safety measures are addressed in the classroom setting. Teacher shows a YouTube video about how to safely handle the chemicals.
The teacher wants to challenge students into thinking about what they know and need to know about a topic.	Problem solving	Students are provided with handheld computers to collect field data that will be compared with data collected from students in a different state. A forensic lab is created for students to use equipment and resources to "solve a crime" that the teacher has created for them.
The teacher seeks to increase student learning by having them work cooperatively to research, share, evaluate, and synthesize new content into a group product that demonstrates their learning.	Cooperative learning	Students meet using free online collaboration tools (NING, Google Docs, social bookmarking, etc.). Computer software (e.g., a database) lets students enter information about what they've learned together. Real objects can be used for the development of a final product.
The teacher wants students to discover key concepts in order to instill deeper levels of understanding.	Discovery	Students create digital concept maps to discover relationships among new information. Students download weather data sets into a spreadsheet to discover how weather is predicted.

Supporting Learning Contexts with Technology and Media

The five contexts or situations most frequently encountered in PK–12 environments are (1) face-to-face classroom instruction, (2) distance learning, (3) blended instruction, (4) independent study (structured), and (5) informal study (unstructured). Each of these contexts for learning represents a way in which you can engage your students in achieving their learning outcomes. It is up to you to consider the various options to determine which might best serve your students.

FACE-TO-FACE INSTRUCTION

Although other learning contexts are gaining prominence, face-to-face instruction remains the most prevalent type of instructional setting in PK–12 schools. Because the teacher and students are in the same room, the options for learning experiences in the classroom setting seem unlimited. Many of the types of technology and media you will be reading about in this textbook are easily used in the face-to-face setting. For example, teachers can use clickers to collect student opinions during presentations, use interactive whiteboards to show videos of historical events, play podcasts of mathematicians explaining how to solve a problem, or conduct live interviews with archeologists in Egypt using Skype.

As the teacher, you might assign a media-based task to be completed prior to the face-to-face learning experience. You would provide an instructional resource to your students to learn the content prior to your classroom exerience, which might be a hands-on activity that guides your students as they apply that knowledge. By "flipping the classroom," you are giving your students more responsibility for their own learning while you are guiding them to the desired outcomes. For example, you might have your students review a video about the solar system as their evening assignment and then have them construct a model of the solar system as part of their classroom activity in a collaborative group. While they are busy with their model construction, you are providing them with hints and suggestions of ways to draw upon the knowledge they gained from viewing the video.

Combining instructional materials into a **learning center,** a self-contained environment designed to promote individual or small-group learning, helps focus students to learn about a specific topic. A learning center may be as simple as some chairs and a table in an area where there might be an activity with audio instructions or a desktop computer with a specific software game. You may set up the learning center as a way of breaking the class into small groups so they can complete a set of tasks. Or, you could establish a series of learning centers that provide your students with a mix of learning activities throughout the day. In your design of the learning center, you will want to encourage active participation by your students. You will want to also be sure that your learning center is partially enclosed to reduce distractions while groups of your students are engaged in the center's learning activities.

Learning centers can take several forms. An interest center might be a way for you to stimulate new interests or encourage creativity. You might set up a center on an upcoming topic, like a unit on insects, to generate your students' curiosity. You could consider the possibility of a remedial center to help specific students who might benefit from additional assistance with a particular topic or skill. This could be a "safe place" for your students to practice their math computation skills. You can be creative in designing this type of center and be sure to include fun-to-do activities, computer time, and other types of assistive resources for your students. An enrichment center could offer stimulating learning experiences for those students who have completed their required work. You might, for example, allow students who have finished their geometry activities to go to a video center and view a DVD showing geometric shapes in bridges.

When working with your students in the face-to-face setting, you might find it appropriate for your learners to use objects as part of their learning experiences. **Manipulatives** are the objects that can be viewed and handled by students. Manipulatives come in a variety of sizes and shapes and are generally categorized into three groups: real objects, models, and mock-ups.

Real objects, such as coins, tools, artifacts, plants, and animals, are some of the most accessible, intriguing, and engaging materials used in education. Gerbils can draw a crowd of young children, the terrarium can help middle schoolers understand the concept of ecology, and a collection of colonial-era coins displayed in a high school social studies class are just a few examples of the potential of real objects that help students with obscure ideas or help stimulate their imaginations.

Models are three-dimentional representitons of real objects. A model can be larger, smaller, or the same size as the object it represents. It can be complete in detail or simplified for instructional purposes. Indeed, models can provide learning experiences that real objects cannot offer. For example, important details can be accented with color, or the model can be constructed to provide interior views that would not be possible with the real object. Models can be of almost anything and are often found in school

A learning center is an effective way to help students achieve.

media centers because of their size or costs to the school. You also can borrow models and artifacts from regional media centers and museums.

Mock-ups are simplified representations of complex devices. By highlighting essential elements and eliminating distracting details, mock-ups help to clarify the complex. They are sometimes constructed as working models to demonstrate basic operations of the real device, allowing your students to manipulate the mock-up so they can comprehend how it operates. For example, a mock-up of a laptop computer might have the internal components labeled and spread out in a large container with a printed circuit diagram on a board. Your students' task is to put the components onto the diagram to "assemble" the internal workings of the computer. The most sophisticated type of mock-up, the simulator, is a device that allows learners to experience the improtant aspects of a real-life activity without undue costs or risk. Many young aviators learn about the complexities of flying by first experiencing how to fly in a simulator.

Also of value in your fact-to-face instructional situation is providing your learners with experiences seeing things. **Exhibits** are collections of various objects designed to form an integrated whole for instructional purposes. Any display surface can contribute to an exhibit. A **display** is an array of visuals and printed materials, often including real objects, with discriptive information included. For a lesson on your local region, a display could include a road map of the area, some pamphets about points of interest, and some miniatures of types of vehicles that might be used for traveling around the region. A **diorama** is a static display consisting of a 3-D recreation of real scenes. Dioramas are usually designed to reproduce scenes and events from the past or present or to depict future scenarios. Your students can design their own dioramas as a follow-up activity from a lesson.

DISTANCE LEARNING

Although distance learning has been around for over 100 years, starting with correspondence study using the post office to exchange materials and assignments, recent technology innovations have made it more convenient and dynamic. Students can be in one location while other members of the class and the teacher can be at other locations. You and a colleague may combine your classes at a distance to enhance their learning opportunities. For example, you might work with a teacher in California who has a class near the San Andreas fault line while your students are studying geology and causes of earthquakes. The California students could take your students on a field trip to the fault line without your students leaving their own seats.

If you are invited to teach at a distance, you will need to think about the classroom as if it were divided into many little parts. When you think of it this way, you can begin to consider ways to teach in such a setting. Your students will not be in the classroom with you and will be unable to see you if your only connection is using audio. Video conferencing using the computer and classroom cameras is becoming more cost efficient and makes it possible to both see and hear your students at a distance. The instructional choices you make will depend on the technology resources available for getting materials to and from your students efficiently and effectively.

Your students might be able to benefit from learning at a distance. For example, if you have a small group of students who have a particular learning need and can benefit from additional tutoring, you might be able to arrange with a nearby college for individual tutoring opportunities. Your students can use **video conferencing** to meet regularly with a tutor who can provide them with additional help. The convenience of having the extra help without the hassle of trying to arrange transportation or locations makes it possible for your students to benefit from additional expertise.

Another way your students might benefit from a distance learning opportunity is when only a handful of students want to study a particular topic. If there are not enough students interested in a particular topic to form a whole class in your school building, you can use online learning options to form a class group across several schools. One teacher, or several teachers working together, could offer the course of study for credit. It could be a way for your students to participate in advanced placement or college-credit courses if they are eligible for this level of study. In this way, your students would be able to extend their learning opportunities.

Of recent interest to educators is the fact that many states already offer online schools, mostly at the high school level, but a few are even offering course work to middle school learners. Some states have initiated the requirement that all seniors must have completed at least one distance or online course prior to graduation. Distance education is becoming an integral component of many school experiences for your students.

BLENDED INSTRUCTION

Another way to use distance learning experiences is through **blended instruction,** a mix of **synchronous settings** (e.g., face-to-face classroom or real-time video conferencing) and **asynchronous settings,** in which the teacher and students are not together at the same time. For example, high school students enrolled in a blended instruction Algebra 1 course might meet in a face-to-face classroom on Mondays and Wednesdays every other week. When not meeting in class, students use online courseware to work on assignments at times convenient for them. Students follow a schedule of due dates for uploading completed student products. The teacher would work with individuals and groups of students throughout the entire time, but the experiences would be varied.

As you design blended learning experiences, you want to be sure you know your students' content knowledge and their experiences with blended online learning settings. You may wish to start with your class having more synchronous meetings, such as in your classroom, or scheduled online video meetings before you move to more asynchronous types of experiences. You will be providing your students with the opportunity to become comfortable with the mixed schedule of class meetings and independent work time. If you find your students are familiar with a blended learning class, you will have more flexibility in arranging the course schedule.

STRUCTURED INDEPENDENT STUDY

Structured independent study is based on the idea your students can learn information and acquire skills without the teacher's direct instruction. However, you will have to prepare the independent study context, using materials you have selected or developed yourself. The Web provides unlimited access to current and archived information that extends content covered in the text. Students will be able to work at their own pace and come to class ready to apply the knowledge.

Independent study can also occur during class through the use of learning centers. You can use a variety of technology, media, and materials, such as web resources, text, audio, video, and computer software. Or you can develop remedial materials for students who are having difficulty with the topic being taught in class.

NONSTRUCTURED INFORMAL STUDY

Students today have many opportunities to learn from their experiences outside of the classroom. You can prepare your students to successfully engage in informal study through the application of information and communication technology (ICT) literacy skills during class activities. At the same time, you can use techniques to help instill in them a love for learning and demonstrate through your own enthusiasm how to be a lifelong learner.

The nature of the study is what makes it informal. Many students seek information on the Internet and challenge themselves to learn about topics that might not be part of their in-class study. For example, student self-study may involve online discussions on how to "go green," searching for information about the history of pandas after visiting the zoo, or examination of sites about earthquakes to discover why they occur. Another example of informal learning occurs when students watch television shows on the History Channel, the National Geographic Channel, or the Public Broadcasting System. These experiences increase general knowledge without your directed instruction.

Integrating Free and Inexpensive Materials

ASSURE Classroom Case Study Reflection

▶ Review the ASSURE Classroom Case Study and video at the beginning of the chapter. What learning contexts would best support the learning experiences Ms. Kaiser and Ms. Marshall would like to integrate into their social studies lesson? Why do you consider these learning contexts to be the most appropriate choices?

With the ever-increasing costs of instructional materials, teachers should be aware of the variety of materials they may obtain for classroom use at little or no cost. The types of free and inexpensive materials available online are almost endless. Of key importance to schools with limited technology budgets are **open source** websites that offer free productivity suites (e.g., word processing, spreadsheets, presentation software) similar to Microsoft Office and Apple iWorks. Among the most popular are Google Docs and Oracle's OpenOffice.

In addition, by connecting to websites around the world, teachers and students can acquire digital video, audio, photos, and documents, such as books and news articles. The Web also offers free collaboration tools to facilitate cooperative learning and connections with classrooms around the globe. Many teachers post lesson ideas, media, and instructional materials, such as worksheets, for an array of subjects on the Web.

Free and inexpensive materials include all the types of media. Commonly available items include posters, games, pamphlets, brochures, reports, charts, maps, books, CDs, audio, video, multimedia kits, and actual objects. The more costly items are usually sent only on a free-loan basis and must be returned to the supplier after use. In some instances, single copies of computer software, audio and video files, or DVDs will be donated to your school media center to be shared among many users.

Advantages

- *Up to date.* Free and inexpensive materials from online resources can provide current information not found in textbooks or other media.

- *In-depth treatment.* Subject-specific materials typically provide in-depth information on a topic.

- *Variety of uses.* Students can access open source applications outside of school. Audiovisual materials can be used for self-study or for presentation to the class. Posters, charts, and maps can be combined to create topical displays.

- *Student manipulation.* Materials that are expendable have the extra advantage of allowing learners to get actively involved with them. They can also scan printed information and visuals to import into digital products.

Limitations

- *Bias or advertising.* Many free and inexpensive materials are produced and distributed by particular organizations. These organizations, whether private corporations, nonprofit associations, or government agencies, often have a message to convey. Carefully preview materials to ensure they are appropriate for classroom use.

- *Promotion of special interests.* Some materials do not contain advertising but do promote a special interest in a less obvious way. Soliciting materials on a topic from a variety of sources can help provide different points of view.

- *Limited quantities.* With the increasing expense of producing and shipping printed materials, your supplier may limit the quantities available at one time. You may not be able to obtain a copy for every student in the class.

Integration. The materials that you obtain through free and inexpensive sources can be used just like you would use any classroom resource. Many times you will find that the types of materials you obtain can best fit into learning centers because they often have a distinct focus on a topic. Or you might find it better to use the materials in a presentation to the whole class at one time. For example, if a local fishing shop sends a video about fishing on a regional river, you might wish to show it one time to all your students.

When a vendor sends you items, you will need to be vigilant about what is appropriate for your students to handle and what might not be. You might obtain materials from the American Red Cross about caring for a cut or scratch. It might be ideal to have childen work in small groups and use the materials to learn the steps involved. But, there may be some things included that are too mature for your students, so you can decide not to use them. Some of the materials sent might be fragile or subject to wear and tear, so you might display them but keep your students from handling them.

SOURCES FOR FREE AND INEXPENSIVE MATERIALS

There are local, state, national, and international sources for free and inexpensive materials, and many of these are now available online. Table 4.1 lists many popular sources of free educational materials.

TABLE 4.1 Sources of Free and Inexpensive Materials	
Source	Types/Topics of Materials
Business organizations and chambers of commerce	Guest speakers and materials on entrepreneurship, investing, budgeting, and so on
Community organizations	Brochures on special interest topics (American Red Cross, the League of Women Voters, etc.)
Federal publications	Posters, charts, brochures, and books (see figure 4.2) from the U.S. Government Printing Office (www.gpoaccess.gov) and the National Technical Information Services (www.ntis.gov)
Foreign governments	Posters, maps, travel booklets, and videos on a free-loan basis
Government agencies	Classroom materials on topics related to each service—Cooperative Extension Services (e.g., agriculture, animals, biotechnology, environment, technology), Department of Public Health (speakers, reports, brochures on health issues, public readiness for emergencies), and National Park Service (speakers, field trip planning)
Medical societies	Health resources, such as booklets or guest speaker podcasts, and information from the National Medical Association, including Tox Town audio, video, brochures, handouts, slide shows, and clip art (see figure 4.3)
Museums	PDF copies of booklets on culture, art, how to visit a museum, lesson plans—Smithsonian, Natural History Museum, National Gallery of Art (teaching packets with image CDs, DVDs, videos, online interactive, etc.)
News broadcasters	Interview videos/audio podcasts, articles
Police and fire departments	Safety presentations and materials
Public broadcasting	Handouts, online activities, videos/audio on history, social studies, health, environment, and so on
Public libraries	Videos, prints, software, books, speakers
Utility companies	Classroom materials to teach energy conservation, going green, and safety
Weather stations	Guest speakers and materials on severe weather, the difference between climate and weather, and so on

FIGURE 4.2   Government Printing Office

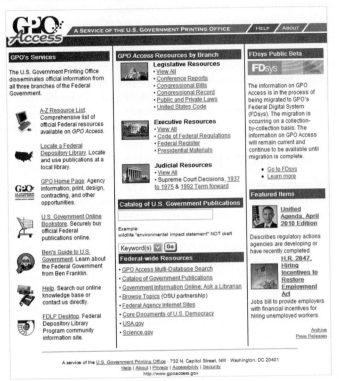

Numerous resources are available from the Government Printing Office.

Source: www.gpoaccess.gov

FIGURE 4.3   Tox Town

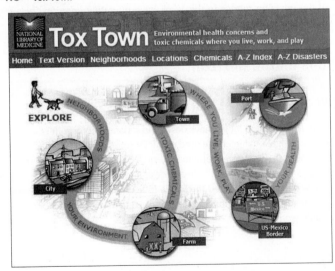

The National Medical Association's Tox Town provides an interactive experience to learn about toxic chemicals and environmental health risks, as well as a suite of teacher resources (audio, video, brochures, handouts, slide shows, clip art, etc.).

Source: http://toxtown.nlm.nih.gov/index.php

There are a number of websites that serve as repositories for open source materials, the online products that are available for sharing. Among the websites are Curriki (http://curriki.org) and Gooru (http://goorulearning.org), which are educator communities for sharing educational resources. Teachers, students, and families can use these sources for lessons or practice on specific topics or share ones they've designed themselves. Gooru uses a media-based format and actually includes the lesson's media, such as videos, as part of the lesson resources. Illustrative Mathematics (http://intmath.com) is another website that provides games and activities to practice math concepts for grades 7 through 12. The Illustrative Mathematics author has years of experience teaching mathematics and offers many ideas for helping young people learn math concepts while enjoying the learning experiences.

OBTAINING FREE AND INEXPENSIVE MATERIALS

Most classroom materials are available in a format that can easily be downloaded from the provider's website. For those resources that are not available online, you can submit your request via email, phone, fax, or mail. Some agencies may require the request to be submitted on school letterhead and signed by your principal, such as scheduling a police officer for a guest presentation. Any student requests should include your endorsement. When ordering hard copies of materials, please ask for a preview copy before requesting multiple copies and, when appropriate, share the resources with other teachers. When obtaining online resources from sites with feedback options, respond with descriptions of how the materials were used along with student reactions. Be courteous, but be honest! Many suppliers attempt to improve free and inexpensive materials on the basis of user comments. When online feedback isn't possible, send a thank you note.

EVALUATING FREE AND INEXPENSIVE MATERIALS

As with all types of materials, evaluate the educational value of free and inexpensive materials critically. Some are very "slick" (technically well presented) but not educationally sound. Use the appropriate selection rubric for the type of media (web resources, video, etc.) you are evaluating. All the selection rubrics in this book have the rating criterion "bias free." Use it judiciously when reviewing free and inexpensive materials.

Innovations on the Horizon

INTERACTIVE MULTI-TOUCH DESKS

Classrooms of the future will no longer have desks and separate laptops. Interactive multi-touch desks resemble the navigational interface used in the TV series *Star Trek*. The screen serves as an individual workspace, an interactive whiteboard, and a collaboration tool for several students. Students use fingers or pens to interact with the desk and can define their own space with an icon or avatar. The desks are connected through a fully interactive classroom system, which is monitored with a teacher's console that can also be used to view student work on every screen or display example work.

Summary

In this chapter we explored the differences between teacher-centered and student-centered instruction and discussed in detail 10 commonly used instructional strategies. We included advantages and disadvantages of each and provided multiple examples for integrating the strategies into your classroom. We also emphasized how to include specific technology, media, and materials to enhance student learning. We examined five contexts for learning commonly found in PK–12 education: face-to-face classroom instruction, distance learning, blended instruction, structured independent study, and nonstructured informal study. The chapter ended with a discussion of the types and sources of free and expensive materials.

ASSURE Lesson Plan

This ASSURE Classroom Case Study is based on Lindsay Kaiser and Jena Marshall implementing a Lewis and Clark lesson in which fifth-grade students complete a WebQuest and design a Lewis and Clark boat.

Analyze Learners

General Characteristics. Ms. Kaiser and Ms. Marshall's fifth-grade students are of mixed ethnicities and from middle-income homes. They are fairly equally distributed with regard to gender and are all either 10 or 11 years old. All students are reading at or above grade level. Student behavior problems are minimal.

Entry Competencies. The fifth-grade students are, in general, able to do the following tasks required to complete the lesson activities:

- Conduct an Internet search
- Create and save word processing documents
- Create and save documents with publishing software (e.g., Microsoft Publisher)
- Use graph paper to draw images to scale

Learning Styles. The fifth-grade students learn best when engaged in hands-on activities that are interesting and challenging. The students' level of interest and motivation increases when working as a team to win a competition. The students vary in the style with which they prefer to demonstrate their learning. For example, when creating the boat advertisement, some students prefer to write the content, whereas others choose to select and arrange photos and images to express their ideas.

Standards and Objectives

Curriculum Standards. National Center for History in the Schools, United States Grades 5–12 Standards, Era 4 Expansion and Reform (1801–1861): Standard 1: United States territorial expansion between 1801 and 1861, and how it affected relations with external powers and Native Americans; Standard 1A: The student understands the international background and consequences of the Louisiana Purchase.

Technology Standards. *National Educational Technology Standards for Students 3.B—Research and Information Fluency:* Locate, organize, analyze, evaluate, synthesize, and ethically use information from a variety of sources and media.

Learning Objectives

1. Given Internet resources and drawing materials, pairs of fifth-grade students will design a boat appropriate for the challenges faced by Lewis and Clark during their expedition (e.g., able to withstand rough currents while portable enough for carrying across rugged terrain).

2. Using the student-created boat design, pairs of students will create an advertisement for their Lewis and Clark boat that clearly defines the reasons why it fulfills the requirements of suitability for the Lewis and Clark expedition.

3. Using the student-created boat design, pairs of students will write a persuasive letter to the president of a boat manufacturing company about why their Lewis and Clark boat should be produced by the company.

Select Strategies, Technology, Media, and Materials

Select Strategies. Ms. Kaiser and Ms. Marshall select four student-centered strategies: discussion, problem solving, discovery, and cooperative learning. Examples include working in cooperative pairs to complete a WebQuest, conducting Internet searches for information on boats used by Lewis and Clark, designing the boat, creating an advertisement to sell the boat, and writing a letter to the president of a boat manufacturing company.

Select Technology and Media. This lesson involves student use of Internet-connected computers, the Lewis and Clark WebQuest, an Internet browser to locate information about boats, publishing software to create the advertisement, library resources, and word processing tools to write the letters. Students might also need access to a scanner to copy paper-based photos for their advertisements.

- *Align to standards, outcomes, objectives.* The WebQuest, Internet and library resources, and production software (publishing and word processing) provide the necessary tools for students to meet the learning objectives.
- *Accurate and current information.* Students will access multiple resources of Lewis and Clark information, which will allow the students to cross-check content accuracy. Current information may be used for new ideas on building handmade boats with tools available at the time.
- *Age-appropriate language.* The WebQuest is written at an appropriate level for fifth-grade students. The teacher may need to assist with interpretation of some web-based resources.
- *Interest level and engagement.* The combined use of the WebQuest, the boat design, and the advertisement competition will keep student interest and engagement at a high level.
- *Technical quality.* The WebQuest and production software used by the students are of high technical quality.
- *Ease of use.* The WebQuest is designed for fifth-grade students. Students can easily use word processing software; however, the publishing application may require initial training and support.
- *Bias free.* The WebQuest and production software are bias free.
- *User guide and directions.* The online help features of the WebQuest and production software are fairly easy for fifth-grade students to use. However, students most frequently will ask each other, Ms. Kaiser, or Ms. Marshall for assistance with technical difficulties.

Select Materials. Ms. Kaiser and Ms. Marshall selected the WebQuest on Lewis and Clark because it provides information needed for students to achieve the learning objectives. They met with the media specialist to create a special collection of relevant resources and preselected example websites that provide grade-appropriate Lewis and Clark information.

Utilize Technology, Media, and Materials

Preview the Technology, Media, and Materials. Ms. Kaiser and Ms. Marshall preview the WebQuest and an online bookmarking site to list relevant Internet resources.

Prepare the Technology, Media, and Materials. Ms. Kaiser and Ms. Marshall prepare the lesson instructions and rubrics for the boat design, letter, and advertisement. They add the WebQuest link and Internet resources links to Lewis and Clark information on the class webpage.

Prepare the Environment. Ms. Kaiser and Ms. Marshall check the classroom laptops to ensure the Internet connections are functional and that the publisher software is loaded on all machines. They retrieve the library cart with Lewis and Clark material and set out all instruction sheets and rubrics for the lesson.

Prepare the Learners. Ms. Kaiser and Ms. Marshall provide a brief overview of U.S. history studied up to the 1800s to provide a context for learning about the Lewis and Clark expedition. They also ask students to share personal boating experiences and projects in which they designed or built a model.

Provide the Learning Experience. Ms. Kaiser and Ms. Marshall begin the class by presenting a brief introduction to Lewis and Clark and the historical background of the time. They then present the boat competition challenge and explain how the lesson activities are structured.

Require Learner Participation

Student Practice Activities. The students in Ms. Kaiser and Ms. Marshall's class use computers, the Internet, and word processing and publishing software to complete their work assignments. Each student individually completes the Lewis and Clark WebQuest. Students then join their partners and conduct research using the Internet and resources from the library cart. The goal is to locate additional information about the Lewis and Clark boats and boat construction. This research allows students to cross-check information learned in the WebQuest. The students use the information to design their boat, create the advertisement, and write their letter. All the activities provide opportunities for the students to engage in practice and relearning of Lewis and Clark information.

Feedback. Ms. Kaiser and Ms. Marshall provide ongoing feedback to students as they conduct Internet and library information searches, draft beginning boat designs, and write the first drafts of their letters to the boat manufacturer. Students use the rubrics (see next section) for these three products to check progress and focus of the work.

Evaluate and Revise

Assessment of Learner Achievement. Ms. Kaiser and Ms. Marshall use the rubrics to assess each team's final boat design, advertisement, and letter. The rubrics assess demonstration of content knowledge, as seen in the students' advertisements and letters and in their technology skills. Ms. Kaiser and Ms. Marshall assess these skills by evaluating the final student advertisements and letters according to the assignment criteria.

Evaluation of Strategies, Technology, and Media Ms. Kaiser and Ms. Marshall evaluate the strategies, technology,

and media. Evaluation of the lesson strategies involves reviewing the students' final products to determine the degree to which students have met the learning objectives. They also engage in continuous communication with the students to learn what is working and identify areas of needed improvement. Ms. Kaiser and Ms. Marshall regularly communicate with the school's technology support staff regarding technology upkeep and problems.

Revision. Ms. Kaiser and Ms. Marshall review the information collected from evaluation of the lesson strategies, technology, and media. The evaluation shows that the Lewis and Clark WebQuest was an excellent source of information to guide the remaining boat design activities. However, students struggled with writing the persuasive letter. Ms. Kaiser and Ms. Marshall revised the lesson to include a review and practice for writing persuasive letters.

Professional Development

DEMONSTRATING PROFESSIONAL KNOWLEDGE

1. Differentiate between teacher-centered and student-centered learning strategies.
2. Differentiate between the types of learning strategies described in this chapter.
3. Discuss how to support learning with technology and media.
4. Explain the value of integrating free and inexpensive materials into instruction.

DEMONSTRATING PROFESSIONAL SKILLS

1. Develop a table that lists the 10 types of instructional strategies in the first column. In the second column, write a brief description of how you could use each strategy in an ASSURE lesson (ISTE NETS-T 2.A and B).
2. Using the table developed for Item 1, add a third column that describes how technology can be used to support each of the 10 learning experiences (ISTE NETS-T 2.A and B).
3. Design an ASSURE lesson for one of the learning contexts and settings (ISTE NETS-T 2.A and B).
4. Using the district or state curriculum guide from the grade level and subject area that you teach or plan to teach, create an annotated list of free and inexpensive resources you could integrate into your teaching and describe how you could use the resources (ISTE NETS-T 5.C).

BUILDING YOUR PROFESSIONAL PORTFOLIO

- *Creating My Lesson.* Using the ASSURE model, design a lesson for one of the case studies presented in Appendix A or use a scenario of your own design. Incorporate into your lesson one or more of the instructional strategies and technology and media ideas described in this chapter. Choose a learning context appropriate for your lesson. Carefully describe the audience, the objectives, and all other elements

of the ASSURE model. Be certain to match your intended outcomes to state or national curriculum and technology standards for your content area.
- *Enhancing My Lesson.* Using the lesson you created in the previous activity, consider how to meet the needs of students with varying abilities. What adaptations are needed to keep advanced learners actively engaged while helping students who struggle with reading? What

changes are needed to ensure that students transfer knowledge and skills to other learning situations? You might look for free and inexpensive resources to enhance the lesson. How can you integrate additional use of technology and media into the lesson?

- *Reflecting on My Lesson.* Reflect on the process you have used in the design of your lesson and your efforts

at enhancing that lesson to meet student needs within your class. How did information from this chapter about instructional strategies, learning contexts, and free and inexpensive materials influence your lesson-designing decisions? In what ways did the technology and media you selected for your lesson enhance the learning opportunities for your students?

Suggested Resources

PRINT RESOURCES

Conklin, W. (2007). *Instructional strategies for diverse learners.* Huntington Beach, CA: Teacher Created Materials.

Herr, N. (2008). *The sourcebook for teaching science, grades 6–12: Strategies, activities, and instructional resources.* San Francisco, CA: Jossey-Bass/Wiley.

Hoffner, H. (2007). *The elementary teacher's digital toolbox.* Upper Saddle River, NJ: Merrill/Prentice Hall.

Lengel, J. G., & Lengel, K. M. (2006). *Integrating technology: A practical guide.* Boston, MA: Allyn & Bacon.

Nehmer, K. (2007). *Elementary teachers guide to free curriculum materials* (67th ed.). (2010). Randolph, WI: Educators Progress Service.

Nehmer, K. (2010). *Middle school teachers guide to free curriculum materials* (12th ed.). Randolph, WI: Educators Progress Service.

Nehmer, K. (2012). *Secondary teachers guide to free curriculum materials* (119th ed.). Randolph, WI: Educators Progress Service.

Nash, R. (2009). *The active classroom: Practical strategies for involving students in the learning process.* Thousand Oaks, CA: Corwin.

SchifferDanoff, V. (2008). *Easy ways to reach and teach English language learners: Strategies, lessons, and tips for success with ELLs in the mainstream classroom.* New York, NY: Scholastic.

WEB RESOURCES

The Federal Reserve Board
http://www.federalreserveeducation.org
The Federal Reserve Board created a web page designed for students aged 11 to 14 to learn more about its role, why it was created, and its primary responsibilities. The site includes a built-in assessment.

Leon M. Lederman Science Education Teacher Resource Center
http://ed.fnal.gov/home/educators.shtml
The U.S. Department of Energy collaborated with Fermi National Accelerator Laboratory to develop a teacher resource center. Teachers can explore a variety of mathematics and science materials developed to enhance K–12 education.

The Whole Frog Project
http://froggy.lbl.gov
The U.S. Department of Commerce collaborated with a variety of publicly supported science labs across the United States to prepare instructional materials for teachers and students in science areas such as astronomy, biology, earth science, and environmental control.

Resources to Help ELL Students
www.mcsk12.net/SCHOOLS/peabody.es/ell.htm
This page, created by Judie Haynes, provides suggested strategies for using online activities and games to assist ELL students in increasing their understanding of English and improving their language skills each time they visit a site.

Dan Meyer's Three-Act Math Tasks
www.livebinders.com/play/play_or_edit?id=330579
Dan Meyer has generated a spreadsheet with lists of math activities that many people have added to over time. The activities are designed in three parts and they are linked to Common Core State Standards. Each activity includes questions you can use with your students as they complete the activity.

Creative Commons
http://creativecommons.org
Creative Commons is a resource for you to "license" your own work using the open source options that are available. Creative Commons provides you with instruction about open source materials, gives you directions for assigning a license to your own work, and helps you locate other materials you might like to use.

SELECTION RUBRIC   Simulations and Games

Complete and save the following interactive evaluation to reference when selecting simulations and games to integrate into lessons.

Search Terms

_____

_____

_____

Title _____

Source/Location _____

©Date _____   Cost _____

Subject Area _____ Grade Level _____

Learning Experiences _____

Primary Format

_____ Simulation

_____ Game

Primary User(s)

_____ Student

_____ Teacher

Brief Description

Standards/Outcomes/Objectives

Prerequisites (e.g., prior knowledge, reading ability, vocabulary level)

Strengths

Limitations

Special Features

Name _____   **Date**_____

Rating Area	High Quality	Medium Quality	Low Quality
Alignment with standards, outcomes, and objectives	Standards/outcomes/objectives addressed and use of simulation or game should enhance student learning.	Standards/outcomes/ objectives partially addressed and use of simulation or game may enhance student learning.	Standards/outcomes/objectives not addressed and use of simulation or game will likely not enhance student learning.
Accurate and current information	Information is correct and does not contain material that is out of date.	Information is correct, but does contain material that is out of date.	Information is not correct and contains material that is out of date.
Age-appropriate language	Language used is age appropriate and vocabulary is understandable.	Language used is nearly age appropriate and some vocabulary is above/below student age.	Language used is not age appropriate and vocabulary is clearly inappropriate for student age.
Interest level and engagement	Topic is presented so that students are likely to be interested and actively engaged in learning.	Topic is presented to interest students most of the time and engage most students in learning.	Topic presented so as not to interest students and not engage them in learning.
Technical quality	The material represents the best technology and media.	The material represents technology and media that are good quality, although they may not be best available.	The material represents technology and media that are not well prepared and are of very poor quality.
Ease of use (student or teacher)	Material follows easy-to-use patterns with nothing to confuse the user.	Material follows patterns that are easy to follow most of the time, with a few things to confuse the user.	Material follows no patterns and most of the time the user is very confused.
Bias free	There is no evidence of objectionable bias or advertising.	There is little evidence of bias or advertising.	There is much evidence of bias or advertising.
User guide and directions	The user guide is an excellent resource for use in a lesson. Directions should help teachers and students use the material.	The user guide is a good resource for use in a lesson. Directions may help teachers and students use the material.	The user guide is a poor resource for use in a lesson. Directions do not help teachers and students use the material.
Practice of relevant skills	Much valuable practice of skills to be learned.	Some practice of skills to be learned.	Little or no practice of skills to be learned.
Game: winning depends on player actions	The actions of players determine their success in the game.	Success in the game is determined by both player actions and chance.	Winning or losing the game is determined by chance.
Simulation: realistic, accurate depiction of reality	The simulation is an accurate representation of actual situations.	There is some relationship between the simulation and actual situations.	There is little or no correlation between the simulation and the actual situations.
Clear descriptions for debriefing	The debriefing directions are clearly stated and easy for users to understand.	The debriefing directions are confusing for users at some points.	The debriefing directions are poorly stated and difficult for users to understand.

Recommended for Classroom Use: _____ Yes   _____ No

Ideas for Classroom Use: _____

_____

Engaging Learners with Digital Devices

Knowledge Outcomes

This chapter addresses ISTE NETS-T 1, 2, and 3.

1. Describe strategies for and examples of integrating digital devices into the curriculum.

2. Describe five types of software that might be used in the classroom.

3. Discuss the advantages and limitations of using technology in learning.

4. Discuss the differences among a single-device classroom, a multiple-device classroom, technology carts, and technology laboratories in terms of setups and uses.

5. Describe an appropriate instructional situation for using technology to support student learning. Include the setting, topic, audience, objectives, content of the materials, and rationale for using this media format.

Goal

Select and integrate computer resources into instruction to promote learning.

ASSURE Classroom Case Study

The Chapter 5 ASSURE Classroom Case Study describes the instructional planning of Kerry Bird, an elementary teacher for nearly 30 years, and one of the first in his school to embrace new technology. Kerry, who views the advent of computers as one of the biggest changes in education during his career, is currently teaching fourth grade, where he strives to integrate a variety of computer projects into instruction. He has found that student motivation and learning increase during active hands-on engagement with computers. As one of his projects, he is considering how to upgrade his presentation of the water cycle, a concept with which his students have struggled. He currently teaches this process by having students create water cycle posters. He would like his students to use computers to demonstrate their understanding of the water cycle, but is not sure of the best approach.

The Chapter 5 ASSURE Classroom Case Study Video explores how Mr. Bird develops a lesson about the water cycle. View the video to explore how he selects the activities and instructional strategies, and chooses the materials, multimedia, and technology that will promote 21st century learning. Throughout the chapter you will find reflection questions to relate the chapter content to the ASSURE Classroom Case Study. At the end of the chapter you will be challenged to develop your own ASSURE lesson that incorporates use of these strategies and resources for a topic and grade level of your choice.

 Watch Mr. Bird and his class as they explore the water cycle.

Computers have become one of the key instructional technologies in education, especially in light of what we know about the 21st century learner. The computer plays multiple roles within the curriculum, ranging from tutor to student creativity resource. Teachers can use the computer as an aid to collect student performance data, as well as to manage classroom activities. To make informed choices on computer use, you need to be familiar with the various computer applications—word processing, graphics, and presentation software; games and simulations; tutorials; and teacher resources. It is extremely important to develop critical skills for appraising instructional software because there are so many available programs. The hardware, too, becomes much less intimidating when you know some of the basic technology. Whether you teach with a single computer in the classroom or a room full of them, you can learn to make optimal use of the computer to support student learning. This chapter focuses on the types of computer resources available for the classroom, as well as how to go about selecting software to support student learning. To help understand how computers operate, there is information on the components of the computer, as well as classroom setup options to optimize computer use.

Using Digital Devices in the Classroom

When the International Society for Technology in Education (ISTE) first developed standards for students, they started their list of knowledge and skills with the ability to operate the equipment. In 2007, ISTE reordered the list for students and changed the importance of computer operations and concepts from the first skill to the last (ISTE, 2009). Although determining that it was still important for students to know about and be able to operate the computer efficiently, ISTE decided that knowing how to use tools to support learning was more important than being able to label the parts of a computer or select and use applications.

ISTE also developed a set of standards for teachers that parallel those for the students. The teacher standards also do not place much emphasis on the operations of the tools but rather emphasize the ability to create learning opportunities for students with computers and technology. Teachers are expected to model appropriate use of the resources and to guide students as part of their learning experiences. The decisions teachers make about using digital tools to support learning are considered more important than knowledge of basic operations. Digital literacy helps teachers understand how the integration of technology can enhance instructional practice and increase student performance.

Educating 21st century students has shifted from providing information to opening doors for them to explore topics and create meaningful learning experiences for themselves.

STRATEGIES AND APPROACHES

Educating 21st century students has shifted from providing information to opening doors for them to explore topics and create meaningful learning experiences for themselves. Technology has been incorporated as a central feature of this process. The implication is that educators are moving away from the idea of school as a place to *get knowledge* to the view that school is a place to *learn how to learn*. The challenge for you as a teacher is to provide opportunities for all students to use technology in meaningful ways to accomplish learning tasks. This may mean selecting specific software for individual students—for example, to practice math skills or to search online databases. This may mean changing your entire approach to a lesson. Student projects, such as working on an ecology report, are not new within the school curriculum, but the approach certainly can be.

You should be a model user of technology for your students. Students will quickly notice if the teacher makes illegal copies of programs and apps and doesn't follow copyright guidelines. Remember, actions speak louder than words. Check with your technology coordinator, library media specialist, or principal for the specific guidelines and licensing agreements that you should follow.

Students can interact directly with various technologies as part of their instructional activities in a variety of ways, from working with material presented by the computer or mobile device in a controlled sequence, such as a drill-and-practice program, to a student-initiated creative activity, such as a digitally published book of student poems. Learners may take tests on the computer or a mobile device or input information into personal e-portfolios. Students can use the e-portfolio to demonstrate specific learning or to create a catalog of their work over time to record their educational progress. The technology can help both the teacher and students in maintaining information about their learning and in guiding instruction. That is, the digital device can organize and store easily retrievable information about each student and about relevant instructional materials. Many programs and apps can generate reports and graphs detailing the progress of an individual student or an entire class. Many computer programs and mobile apps can also diagnose the learning needs of students and prescribe optimal sequences of instruction for each student.

Traditionally, computers were used to reinforce classroom instruction. Software was designed to provide direct instruction or practice for students, often programmed to branch to other segments of the lesson based on student responses. Many of these designs are still in use today. Based on the constructivist view of learning, current instructional strategies try to engage students in ways that allow them to develop, or construct, their own mental structure in a particular area of study. To engage students in this type of learning, the environment must provide them with materials that allow them to explore. Early research by Papert serves as the foundation for digital

©COPYRIGHT CONCERNS

Software

Congress amended the Copyright Act to clear up questions of fair use of copyrighted programs. The changes defined the term *computer program* for copyright purposes and set forth rules on permissible and nonpermissible use of copyrighted computer software. According to the amended law, you are permitted to do the following with a single copy of a program:

- Make one backup or archival copy of the program.
- Use a "locksmith" program to bypass the copy-prevention code on the original to make the archival copy.
- Install one copy of the program onto a computer hard drive.
- Adapt a computer program from one language to another if the program is not available in the desired language.
- Add features to a copyrighted program to make better use of the program.
- Adapt a copyrighted program to meet local needs.

Without the copyright owner's permission, you are prohibited from doing the following:

- Making multiple copies of a copyrighted program.
- Making additional copies from an archival or backup copy.
- Making copies of copyrighted programs to be sold, leased, loaned, transmitted, or given away.
- Selling a locally produced adaptation of a copyrighted program.
- Making multiple copies of an adaptation of a copyrighted program even for use within a school or school district.
- Putting a single copy of a program onto a network without permission or a special site license.
- Duplicating the printed copyrighted software documentation unless allowed by the copyrighted software company.

For general information and suggested resources (print and web links) on copyright, see Chapter 1.

"microworlds"—environments that permit students to freely experiment, test, and invent (Papert, 1993a, 1993b). These environments reinforce 21st century skills by allowing students to focus on a problem area and create solutions that are meaningful to them.

Jonassen, Howland, Moore, and Marra (2003) have expanded the idea that technology can engage and support students in their learning. They have suggested that students learn from the digital environment because it encourages students to use cognitive learning strategies and critical-thinking skills. Students control how and when the computer provides them with the information they need. Part of your responsibility is to choose from among the many possible technologies, software programs, and mobile apps available to create such learning environments and to assist your students in constructing their own mental models.

TYPES OF DIGITAL RESOURCES

Digital technologies provide virtually instantaneous response to student input, have extensive capacity to store and manipulate information, and are unmatched in their abilities to serve many students simultaneously. Technology's role in instruction is to serve as a resource for rich learning experiences, giving your students the power to influence the depth and direction of their learning. Technology makes it possible to control and integrate a variety of media—still and motion pictures, graphics, and sounds, as well as text-based information. Digital devices can also record, analyze, and react to student responses typed on a keyboard, selected with a mouse or touch screen, or activated by voice. As your students begin to work with information, they find the digital resources available to them help make the process easier and more fun. Students can use the technology to gather information and to prepare materials that demonstrate their knowledge and understanding of that information.

Besides providing information, digital devices are also tools for creativity and communication. Because these technologies allow sharing and collaboration with others around the world, students often strive to achieve their "best" artifacts of learning because their work can be seen by an audience outside the classroom.

Computers and mobile devices can be used for word processing and desktop publishing. Most students have access to word processing programs to produce papers and assignments. Some students create multimedia projects, integrating graphics, sound, and video for presentations to their classmates or other groups. Presentation software, which can be connected to a digital projector, allows students to share and discuss their work.

Word Processing and Desktop Publishing. Using concept-mapping software and mobile apps such as Inspiration and SimpleMind+, students can gather their ideas into concept maps. They can then begin to develop those ideas into connected text from outlines generated by the concept-mapping programs. These outlines can be imported into a word processing program, which makes it easy for students to edit their work. The word processor makes it possible for students to work with their ideas and to quickly make changes as they explore various ways to present them. Spelling and grammar checking are available to assist your students in identifying and correcting errors in draft versions of their papers. In many programs, an integrated thesaurus helps students find the right word for a specific situation. Editing, a process children are not prone to enjoy, suddenly becomes easier. Students are more willing to make changes when editing is simplified.

Students enjoy putting their ideas onto paper. They especially enjoy seeing their work in finished copy. Desktop publishing allows students to design layouts that are creative and enjoyable to read. Using a desktop publishing program, students can add graphics to their pages. They can see how the pages will look before they print them or publish them on the Web. Students of all ages like to produce their writings in formal documents, such as small books and newsletters. Class newsletters are also very popular, as students work together to produce a document they are proud to share with family and friends.

Calculators and Spreadsheets. Most computers and mobile devices include calculators as one of the basic tools built into the operating system, with newer equipment offering graphing calculators as a more robust option. Learners can use these calculators to solve complex mathematical problems. Students can also learn to use a spreadsheet program to prepare sets of data collected as part of a project. The technology can also facilitate data gathering when connected to laboratory equipment. The collected data are downloaded to a spreadsheet program for analysis and to prepare tables or graphic displays of the results. These opportunities can also be combined with live spreadsheets, as presented in Chapter 6.

Text-Based Communications. Today's students frequently communicate via email, text messaging, or online chatting. This can be accomplished from a computer, mobile phone, tablet, or through online platforms such as Google+, Edmodo, and Facebook. This type of message format is quick and easy to use. In the classroom, you may wish to engage students with email messages as a means for connecting with classmates or students from a distant location (e-pals). As communications through these technologies continue to increase, you may want to take some time to teach your students when it is appropriate to use formal (traditional) versus informal (textspeak and shorthand) writing techniques.

Audio- and Video-Based Communications. Communication in your class is not limited to text-based communications. You can encourage students to incorporate audio files they create to enhance their communication with others. Many types of audio resources are available for learners to create exciting representations of their learning. For example, students can add narration, music, and sound effects for a presentation, create an audio podcast in which they reflect on global warming, or practice their diction and articulation as they learn a foreign language. Students who enjoy music or have musical talent can create interesting vocal and instrumental music with programs like GarageBand and incorporate their music into slideshows and multimedia presentations.

Students are very creative and can use images captured on their mobile devices or digital cameras to enhance their messages or as substitutes for words. In addition, you and your students can interact with each other, as well as experts around the world, using teleconferencing tools such as Skype and Google+ Hangouts.

Graphics. Drawing and creating graphics is a fun activity for students. Computer software such as KidPix 3D and mobile apps such as Doodle Buddy can make drawing even more pleasurable. These programs and apps provide a variety of engaging effects, with special tools such as a rubber stamp that makes noise as it marks on the screen or a path animation tool that makes characters come to life with walking, running, and flying. It is also possible to import a photo and then customizing it by drawing on it, editing it, or adding special effects and filters to it. Computer technology thus changes the dynamics of art for children.

As students gain skill with drawing software, they can learn more complex drawing and drafting programs. High school students can use computer-aided design (CAD) and graphics programs to prepare complex visuals. Many of the skills associated with these types of software are easy for students to learn. As another example, an art program such as Photo Deluxe allows your students to develop complex projects with an array of tools ranging from basic drawing tools for lines and shapes to advanced tools for editing and redesigning. They may create their own pictures or begin with commercially designed clip art available from many suppliers. A simple picture can be developed into a very artistic piece with only a few keystrokes.

Presentations. Presentations have become a popular format for teachers and students. With the computer connected to a digital projector, it is possible to share information and ideas using colorful slides and animations. Many students enjoy preparing presentations for their classmates using programs and online services such as PowerPoint, Keynote, and Prezi. These programs can also be used to create other forms of media, such as e-portfolios, digital storybooks, and interactive games that allow students to demonstrate their understanding or to challenge other learners. You should supervise your students carefully; they can be distracted by the "bells and whistles" and spend more time deciding the color scheme, the transitions, or the font style than they do thinking about and preparing the content of the presentation.

Games and Simulations. Games and simulations are instructional tools that support students in learning knowledge and skills and involve the use of problem-solving strategies and techniques. Computer games, mobile apps, and electronic simulations incorporate many important learning principles, such as interactivity, challenge, problem solving, systems thinking, distributed knowledge, and performance related to competency (Gee, 2005). In short, games and simulations provide learners with multiple opportunities to practice solving structured or ill-structured problems, engaging students in complex, higher-order thinking. Students are asked to analyze a task, determine the conditions needed to address that task, identify cues, and engage in self-monitoring and evaluation. Problems can be introduced to students as a way to have them practice skills in practical applications. Providing students with rich and varied problems challenges them to integrate knowledge and skills into their learning strategies while they are engaged in a meaningful activity within a virtual world (Shaffer, Shaffer, Squire, & Gee, 2005).

Computer-Assisted Instruction. Students benefit from practice on basic skills or knowledge. **Computer-assisted instruction (CAI)** helps students learn specific knowledge and skills. Technology can be used to reinforce classroom instruction. The variety of instructional tools across all content areas is vast. Possibilities range from basic drill-and-practice and tutorials to more extended and complex learning problems. For students who need review or practice, drill-and-practice programs can help them acquire the specific steps needed to complete a task. For example, Math Blaster's computer games and mobile apps assist students in learning math facts (addition, subtraction, multiplication, and division) through drill-and-practice using an arcade game format, giving students the opportunity to practice what they have learned. You will want to use caution not to overuse the drill-and-practice types of activities when using computer resources with your students. It is important to provide them with a wide spectrum of learning opportunities.

Software is capable of providing students with complex tasks that engage them in real-world problems. Programs such as Neighborhood MapMachine engage students in activities related to geography in which they create and navigate maps of their own neighborhoods and other communities while learning challenging navigation concepts, such as using scale to determine the distance between places on maps. Video technologies can easily be incorporated, focusing attention on tangible examples of geographic distances and how they impact travel, trade, and more. Word processing, graphics, and a host of computer software programs help students organize and communicate their ideas.

Computer-Managed Instruction. Computer-managed instruction (CMI) is a label for a broad category of applications designed to assist in the management of the instructional process. CMI aids you in the management of instruction without actually doing the teaching. CMI can provide you with learning objectives, learning resources, and assessment of learner performance. For example, you can use a mobile device to collect information on how students are completing tasks. You can also use the computer to assist you in preparing instructional materials such as handouts or presentations.

Advantages

- *Learner Participation.* The R of the ASSURE model is achieved with digital materials because they require learners to engage in activities. These materials help to maintain students' attention.

- *Individualization.* Digital resources allow students control over the rate and sequence of their learning, giving them more control over outcomes. High-speed personalized responses to learner actions yield immediate feedback and reinforcement.

- *Special needs.* Digital technologies are effective with special learners, gifted and at-risk students, and students with diverse physical or demographic backgrounds. Their special needs can be accommodated to ensure that instruction proceeds at an appropriate pace.

- *Monitoring.* The recordkeeping ability of the software, mobile apps, and online services makes instruction more individualized; you can prepare individual lessons for all your students and monitor their progress.

- *Information management.* Electronic resources can cover a growing knowledge base associated with the information explosion. They can manage all types of information—text, graphic, audio, and video. More information is easily accessible by you and your students so they can monitor their own progress as well.

- *Multisensory experiences.* Digital devices provide diverse learning experiences. These can employ a variety of instructional strategies that use audio, visual, and tactile approaches at the level of basic instruction, remediation, or enrichment.

Limitations

- *Copyright.* The ease with which software and other digital information can be duplicated without permission has inhibited some commercial publishers and private entrepreneurs from producing and marketing high-quality instructional software. For additional information regarding copyright, refer to "Copyright Concerns: Copyright Law" in Chapter 1.

- *High expectations.* You and your students may have unrealistic expectations for technology. Many view computers and mobile devices as magical and expect learning to happen with little or no effort, but in reality users derive benefits proportional to their investments.

- *Complex.* More advanced programs may be difficult to use, especially for student production, because they require the ability to use complex skills.
- *Lack of structure.* Students whose learning preferences require more structured guidance may become frustrated. Students may also make poor decisions about how much information to explore.

Integrating Technology with Learning

The ultimate value of technology in education depends on how fully and seamlessly it is integrated into the curriculum. Technological devices in the classroom are not additional "things" that you must include, but rather are integral to the support and extension of learning for all your students (ISTE, 2009). You need a framework for using technology that covers a variety of learning styles and accommodates varied teaching strategies. Most important, results need to be measurable to align with a clear set of objectives—the second step in the ASSURE model. In classrooms where technology is integrated successfully, students use it with the same ease with which they use pencils, books, rulers, and maps. In technology-rich classrooms, you and your students engage in problem solving, cultivate creativity, collaborate globally, and discover the value of lifelong learning.

With increasing ease of use, technology is becoming more natural to use in problem-solving and cooperative learning strategies. Software, telecommunications, and social media can provide students with experiences in working together to solve complex problems. Often, students incorporate several different types of applications to explore a problem situation. For example, when assigned to prepare a report on ecology, a group of your students might use computer databases to search for information resources to include in their report. They might connect with people in different locations around the world through email, texting, teleconferencing, or social media to request information. They might use spreadsheet programs to store, sort, analyze, and share their information.

The use of multimedia can be helpful for information and tasks that must be shown rather than simply told. Printed material and lecture alone cannot adequately present some instruction. Your students who want to interact with the instruction may need to find an appropriate software choice. Many newer versions of software now come with interactive media demonstrations. For example, The Ellis Island Experience is an interactive documentary with a wealth of information about the role this primary immigration station played in U.S. history from 1892 to 1954. Designed for middle-level and high school students, the software lets them explore five modules filled with images, audio, and video to learn more about the experiences of immigrants as they entered the United States. An artifact viewer resource lets students look at images, memorabilia, and documents in detail.

TAKING A LOOK AT TECHNOLOGY INTEGRATION

Testing the Waters

A school in Ann Arbor, Michigan, was being bothered by an odor from a stream in a small park next to its property. A trio of science teachers decided to integrate their classes and present students with the problem of the smelly stream. They introduced the scientific inquiry model and provided an array of technologies that could help students analyze and hypothesize.

Groups worked together to investigate the source of the problem and initiated community action to alleviate it. Reorganizing the science classes and integrating technologies to successfully solve real problems demonstrated to the administration that problem-based learning is a constructive and beneficial way for students to learn.

Source: Hi-C Research Group, University of Michigan (http://sitemaker.umich.edu/hice/home)

Technology

Use when student learning will be enhanced by . . .

Guidelines	Examples
Practicing what they have just studied in class	Students who need extra help with a skill or task can play a drill-and-practice game to practice skills or reinforce their understanding.
Learning independently	Technology can be part of a kindergarten classroom learning center. Young students can complete learning tasks by using digital tutorials from software, mobile apps, or multimedia to advance their knowledge.
Creating learning opportunities for gifted students	Gifted students can be challenged to expand or enhance their learning by using more complex programs and apps or by extending classroom activities with challenging problems.
Working collaboratively with other students	Students can work together to navigate through instructional materials to help each other understand the information.
Reaching a student who is having difficulty in learning	Students can use the material in personally meaningful ways, navigating through the material as appropriate to their style of learning.
Challenging students to present information in a new way	Students can create their own materials to share their knowledge with others in the class or school.

Software Selection

NOTE: For the purposes of this discussion, the term *software* includes computer software, mobile apps, and online services. Therefore, PowerPoint, Creationary, and Google Docs would all be considered software in this context.

There are several factors associated with selecting software (see **Selection Rubric: Software**). It is very important to examine the software within the context of learning outcomes. Other factors that should be considered include how the software stimulates creativity, fosters collaboration, and provides feedback. You should also consider your **operating system,** which is the computer's underlying system software, such as Mac OS, Windows, or Unix, that functions as the computer's interface with the user. Specific software programs, also called **applications,** are written to run on different operating systems, which determine precisely how the user, computer, and application interact to produce the desired results. You must ensure that software you select is designed to run on your available operating system and that it will function properly with your specific hardware configuration.

When you are evaluating instructional software, you should consider how information is presented to be certain it is done in a clear and logical manner to ensure learning (see **Selection Rubric: Software**). You need to examine the intent of the lesson and its relation to your intended outcomes, the curriculum, and the pertinent achievement standards. The information needs to be presented in a manner designed to maintain student interest and involvement in the learning tasks. Additional aspects to consider are accuracy, age appropriateness, and ease of use.

Software and Apps

Computer software and mobile apps can help with a variety of learning needs. The following examples demonstrate ways that learners can use technology to help with specific learning difficulties.

Students can work on improving their problem-solving abilities with **The Factory Deluxe**, software that highlights different strategies for problem solving, such as working backward, analyzing a process, and determining a sequence. Learners are given a square on the computer and four types of machines to shape it as they work through a series of levels that build their knowledge of geometric attributes in order to prepare a product. The "rotator" machine can be programmed to rotate the square from 30 to 180 degrees. The "puncher" machine can punch square or triangular holes in the square. The "striper" machine paints thin, medium, or thick stripes of various colors. And the "cutter" cuts off and discards parts that are not needed. Learners must apply problem-solving strategies in order to successfully manufacture a product with the machines.

For students with visual impairments who need to use computer software, email, or the Internet, adaptive software programs called *screen readers* use speech synthesizers to read aloud the text and names of icons. Learners can navigate using the keyboard, hitting the tab button to move from icon to icon. Nontext items, such as graphics and photos, are labeled with alternative textual descriptions, called *alt-tags,* which allow learners with visual impairments to hear descriptions of these items. These software programs are available on both PC and Mac operating systems in the settings of the operating software called "universal access." Some learners with visual impairments may be able to avoid the necessity for screen readers by using increased font sizes and modified display settings that provide higher contrast. These modifications can be made in the operating system's general settings under "universal access."

Students with advanced learning skills can be challenged to put on their thinking caps and create interesting solutions by completing complex puzzles. Puzzles are an interactive way to engage students in finding alternative ways to examine an issue or problem. For example, using inquiry and imagination, students link their knowledge of facts to the resolution of the puzzles presented in the **Jewel Quest** game. Students are given clues along the way to help them find the golden path. In the process, students learn some information about archeology. Jewel Quest is only one of many types of puzzle-based games available to challenge students.

ASSURE Classroom Case Study Reflection

▶ Review the ASSURE Classroom Case Study video and consider which software would be appropriate for Kerry Bird's fourth-grade students to create a product that will demonstrate knowledge of the water cycle. What would be a good way for students to share materials with each other?

It is important that instructional software follows sound educational techniques and principles and also provides your students with **feedback** on their efforts. In a drill-and-practice program, it is important that students have frequent informative feedback in order to improve their skills. When using software designed to challenge higher-order thinking, students will need feedback to determine the quality of their choices. If your goal is to provide students with collaborative learning opportunities, many programs are designed so that groups of students can work together to achieve the intended outcomes. Several of these types of programs are designed with the one-computer classroom in mind (see "Media Examples: Software").

Sometimes software has special effects or features that may be essential for effective learning. Often, however, special effects are only window dressing that adds no value to the learning. In fact, they may interfere with learning. Color, graphics, animation, and sound should be a part of quality software only if they contribute to student learning. Text should be presented in a consistent manner, using size, color, and location to reduce the cognitive burden of deciphering meaning. Keystroking and mousing techniques should be intuitive for students. The manner in which students interact with software needs to be transparent, allowing them to focus on content.

Hardware

NOTE: For the purposes of this discussion, the term *computer* refers to all computing devices, including computers, laptops, smart phones, and tablets.

Regardless of type of computer or complexity of the system, computing devices have a number of standard components. The physical equipment that makes up the computer is referred to as the **hardware.** A computer's specific combination of hardware components is called its **configuration**. The basic hardware components are diagrammed in Figure 5.1.

Input devices transmit information to the computer; **output devices** display the information to the user. The most commonly used input device is the keyboard. Others include the mouse, stylus, joystick, graphics tablet, probe, scanner, microphone, and camera. Both students and teachers can use graphics tablets to incorporate drawings into their programs. Science laboratory monitoring devices, such as temperature probes, can also be connected directly to a computer with the proper interface device.

Monitors are the standard output device. Another output device, which allows large-group viewing, is the digital projector. Connected to the computer, the digital projector can be used as part of class instruction, such as in a PowerPoint display or to show slides outlining steps for students to follow when using specific software in a computer lab. Other output devices include speakers, printers, and peripherals, such as Lego Mindstorms, remote controlled vehicles, and flying drones.

The **central processing unit (CPU)** is the core element, or "brain," that carries out all the calculations and controls the total system. In a personal computer, the CPU is one (or more) small chips (microprocessors) inside the machine.

The computer's memory stores information for manipulation by the CPU. The memory contains what is termed the *control function*—that is, the programs written to tell the CPU what to do and in what order. In computers, control instructions and sets of data are stored in two types of memory:

- *Read-only memory (ROM).* The control instructions that have been "wired" permanently into the computer's memory make up the ROM, which the computer needs constantly to read programming language and perform internal monitoring functions.

- *Random access memory (RAM).* The more flexible part of the memory makes up the RAM. The particular program or set of data being manipulated by the user is temporarily stored in RAM, only to be erased or transferred to storage after use to make way for the next program.

A computer's memory size is usually described in terms of how many bytes it can store at one time. A **byte** is the number of bits required to represent and store one character (letter or number) of text. A **bit** is a single unit of data, coded in binary form as either 0 (off) or 1 (on). A byte is usually made up of 8 bits of various combinations of 0s and 1s (Figure 5.2) A **kilobyte (KB)** refers to approximately 1,000 bytes (1,024 to be exact), a **megabyte (MB** or "meg") indicates 1,000 KB or approximately a million bytes, and a **gigabyte (GB** or "gig") is equal to 1,000 MB or approximately one billion bytes. Megabytes are the units used to measure the RAM storage capacity of a computer. Thus, if a computer can process 1,024,000 bytes, it is said to have 1 "meg" of memory capacity. We now talk about RAM storage in terms of **terabytes (TB),** which is a million megabytes or a trillion bytes. More powerful machines are capable of processing more bytes simultaneously, thus having more computing capacity.

FIGURE 5.1 **Basic Elements of a Desktop or Laptop Computer**

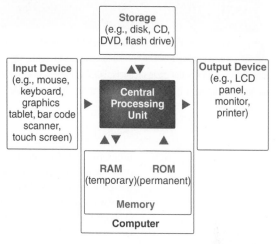

FIGURE 5.2

Representation of the Letter *A* in ASCII (American Standard Code for Information Interchange)

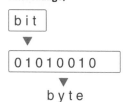

A computer's memory is one of its limiting factors. You need to be sure that the computer has enough memory to run the software you will be using. If you plan to use more than one application at a time, it is recommended you have a minimum of 1 GB. Although 1 MB of memory can hold approximately 2,000 single-spaced pages of text, many graphics and animations require several megabytes to display properly. The computer's operating system, application programs, and data files are usually stored on the computer hard drive, which is inside the computer. The hard drive provides a "permanent" place within the computer for these types of programs and documents to reside. But a hard drive is vulnerable and can crash, so it is often best to keep backups of programs and data files separately from the CPU. Portable flash drives (discussed further in the following paragraph) and external hard drives are common ways to store programs, and recordable DVDs are also available on most machines. Storage capacity (measured in MB or GB) has expanded to keep pace with the rapidly growing memory demands of today's software and the ever-increasing size of graphics- and animation-laden data files.

High-capacity removable media devices serve as the portable storage format of choice. Generally termed **removable storage devices,** they are small, portable, and used primarily for backing up and archiving data files. **USB** (universal serial bus) is a hardware interface technology that allows the user to connect a device without having to restart the computer. A USB mini-drive, more commonly called a **flash drive** (or jump drive), is a form of removable storage device that lets you store files in a portable unit. The capacity of a flash drive can range from a few megabytes to a gigabyte or more. Some mini-drives have removable flash memory cards, allowing the user to increase the memory capacity of the mini-drive by changing the memory chip. This same memory chip might also fit into a digital camera or a hand-held device, thus making the interchange of visual and text information very flexible. The USB mini-drive does not require any special wiring and can fit into your pocket. One additional feature is its suitability for either Windows or Mac computers, permitting users to switch between platforms with ease. Removable storage devices have many uses, including:

- Archiving old files that you don't use anymore but may want to access someday
- Storing unusually large files, such as graphic images, that you need infrequently
- Exchanging large files with someone
- Moving your files from one computer to another, perhaps from your desktop to your laptop computer or from your home computer to a classroom computer
- Keeping certain files separate from files on your hard disk (e.g., old test files)

The Digital Classroom

There has been a trend in schools toward the multiple-device classroom, in particular toward the use of laptop carts and carts of mobile devices. In earlier days, when schools had a limited number of computers, they often resided in a computer laboratory. As more computers became available, single computers were assigned to individual classrooms. Teachers soon discovered how to successfully use multiple computers in their classrooms. Some schools, therefore, dismantled the laboratories and distributed the computers to individual classrooms, thereby increasing the number of classrooms with multiple computers.

SINGLE-DEVICE CLASSROOM

In some schools, access to technology is still limited. Often there is just a single technology lab where you can take your whole class of students to work on computers or mobile devices as part of a lesson (see "Taking a Look at Technology Integration: Single Device with a Large Group"). However, increased interest by many teachers in incorporating technology into lessons limits the availability of the technology lab. One solution has been to place a single computer or mobile device in each classroom that the teacher and students can use throughout the day.

It is possible for you to use a single computer or mobile device in creative ways with a whole class of students. Although some software is intended to be used by single students for work on specific tasks, other software is designed for group activities. For example, with the series Decisions, Decisions, groups of students interact with the technology to get specific information before they can proceed with their group activity. Your students do not need to work on the device during the entire lesson. While one group interacts with the computer or mobile device, the remaining groups are working at their desks.

The single-device classroom allows several formats for use of the equipment:

- *Large group.* With a digital projector, you can demonstrate to a whole class how to use a particular software program or how to manage a particular set of data.

- *Small group.* A small group of students can work together on the computer or mobile device. Each group has a turn using the software to gather or present data and then returns to their seats, allowing the next group to have their turn.

- *Learning center.* Individual students or small groups can go to a learning center anchored by the computer or mobile device. By integrating a specific software program, you create an interactive learning center on that subject.

- *Personal secretary.* The computer or mobile device can assist you with maintaining grades, communicating with parents, and preparing instructional materials.

MULTI-DEVICE CLASSROOM

Many classrooms have several computers and/or mobile devices available. This can be helpful when groups of students need to use the same software simultaneously (Figures 5.3 through 5.5). Student groups of two or three can share one device. You may also have a projector to display information for your students on one screen.

TECHNOLOGY CARTS IN THE CLASSROOM

A popular variation of the multi-device classroom is the mobile technology cart. Many schools provide a laptop cart or a cart of mobile devices as a way to offer devices for the classroom without

FIGURE 5.3 **Elementary Classroom with Four Computers Used for Individual and Small-Group Study**

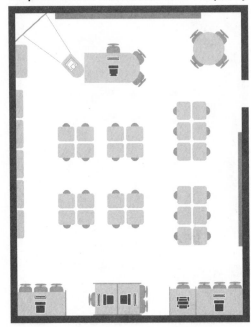

Source: Plan developed by Interactive Learning Systems, Inc., Cincinnati, OH.

FIGURE 5.4 **High School Classroom with 12 Computers and 2 Printers Used Individually**

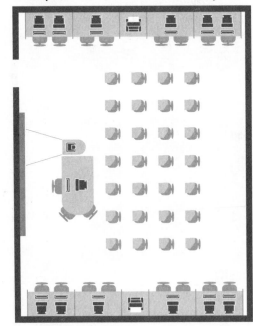

Source: Plan developed by Interactive Learning Systems, Inc., Cincinnati, OH.

FIGURE 5.5   Middle School Classroom with Chairs Arranged at Computers for Collaborative Learning

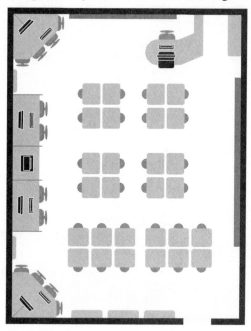

Source: Plan developed by Interactive Learning Systems, Inc., Cincinnati, OH.

FIGURE 5.6   Computer Lab

Computers around the wall in a laboratory allow one teacher to monitor all student activity.

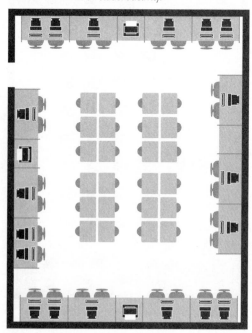

the major expense of permanent installations. The carts allow you access to a set of computing devices when needed. You share the cart with other teachers and benefit from technology in classroom settings when you need it, rather than having to leave the classroom to go to a technology laboratory, which might not be available at a time you wish to use it. In addition, the carts take advantage of wireless technology, thus providing access to the Internet or to software available on the central school server. Most schools have wireless available throughout the building for easy access to the Internet.

TECHNOLOGY LAB

When you want each of your students to be working on a computer or mobile device during a lesson, it may be necessary for the whole class to have access to technology simultaneously. Schools often place 20 to 30 networked computers or mobile devices together in a single room shared by all. The technology laboratory or "lab" is appropriate if you want your students to be working independently or in small groups on different programs and different activities. To monitor student activity and keep them on task, as well as to prevent students from viewing inappropriate or irrelevant material, the devices can be arranged around the walls of the computer lab with the monitors facing the center of the room (see Figure 5.6), allowing you to quickly see what each student is doing and respond to student questions individually. In some networks, the teacher can control and monitor what is shown on each student computer.

There are advantages to using a technology lab. A group of students can be taught the same lesson simultaneously, which might be more efficient for you. Also, software can be located in one place conveniently. Supervision and security are often easier when all the computers are located in a single room. Labs are often structured to facilitate ease of use by putting all the computers on one network, sharing software stored on a central server. This allows connected computers to be placed throughout the school building so students can connect to the network from the technology lab, their classrooms, or the media center.

The foremost limitation with the technology lab is access. If there are no other computers or mobile devices available to students outside the lab, then students will have to wait until the lab is not scheduled to use the facilities. If one class is scheduled to use the lab, the other classes will have to wait. Also, because of scheduling problems, some classes may not have access to the lab at all. Creative use of school-wide networks can ease some of the congestion problems so that classroom computers and mobile cart devices can be connected to the resources. Thus, if the lab is not available, then the students can use the classroom technology to do what they needed to do in the lab.

Innovations on the Horizon

DIGITAL FABRICATOR: A PRINTER FOR REAL OBJECTS

Three-dimensional printers or rapid prototyping machines, also known as "fabbers" (short for fabricators), are a relatively new form of computer output device that can build 3-D objects by carefully depositing materials drop by drop, layer by layer. Using a geometric blueprint from a CAD program and the proper type of fast-setting liquid, you can create complex objects that would normally take special tools and skills when using conventional manufacturing techniques. A fabber can allow you to explore new designs, email physical objects to other fabber owners, and most importantly, set your ideas free.

Traditional 3-D printers are room-sized and cost thousands of dollars. The Fab@Home digital fabricator printer is designed to be the size of a desktop printer and cost about the same as a home computer system. It uses common materials to create the 3-D objects. Silicon caulk, fast-drying liquid resin, and even Cheez Whiz work well in the fabricator. The one thing the printer cannot print is paper! If you can imagine it, you can build it on your fabricator.

These printers are appearing in schools around the world where students are learning to use CAD programs. Now students can design their ideas with the CAD program and than actually print or "fab" them on the spot. They can hold the object and view it from all directions, permitting 21st century learners to move literally into new dimensions of learning.

ASSURE Classroom Case Study Reflection

▶ Review the ASSURE Classroom Case Study video and consider which type of computer access would be appropriate for Kerry Bird's fourth-grade students as they work on their product. Describe the advantages and limitations of each of his choices.

Summary

Computing devices (computer and mobile technologies) are the most common and important form of instructional technology used in education. Students can use them for active, hands-on learning experiences. The teacher can use the computer or mobile device to help in collecting information about student progress and for preparing and presenting instructional materials. Whether you have one or a few computing devices in your classroom, you can effectively integrate them into student learning. Many schools have technology labs; however, the trend is to make mobile carts available so that any classroom can be converted into a lab setting.

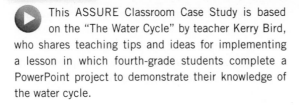

ASSURE Lesson Plan

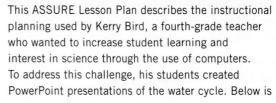

▶ This ASSURE Classroom Case Study is based on the "The Water Cycle" by teacher Kerry Bird, who shares teaching tips and ideas for implementing a lesson in which fourth-grade students complete a PowerPoint project to demonstrate their knowledge of the water cycle.

This ASSURE Lesson Plan describes the instructional planning used by Kerry Bird, a fourth-grade teacher who wanted to increase student learning and interest in science through the use of computers. To address this challenge, his students created PowerPoint presentations of the water cycle. Below is

Kerry Bird's ASSURE lesson plan for the water cycle project.

Kerry Bird
Fourth Grade
Topic: Water Cycle

Analyze Learners

General Characteristics. The students in Kerry Bird's class are of mixed ethnicities and from low- to middle-income homes. They are fairly equally distributed by gender and all are 9 or 10 years old. The majority of the students are reading at grade level, with four reading above grade level and three struggling with reading. Generally, the students are well behaved, but tend to become restless when required to complete traditional seatwork.

Entry Competencies. The students are, in general, able to do the following:

- Create and save PowerPoint presentations
- Locate and download digital files from the server
- Insert graphics into presentations
- Enter and edit presentation text

Learning Styles. Kerry's students learn best when engaged in hands-on activities. Their level of motivation increases when using computers because they can personalize their work. Some students prefer to express their creativity through written narratives or drawn images, whereas some choose to create or find existing images to express their ideas. Students' learning styles also vary in their preference for working independently or with other students.

State Standards and Objectives

Curriculum Standards. *National Science Education Standards—Content Standard D:* As a result of their activities in grades K–4, all students should develop an understanding of changes in earth and sky.

Technology Standards. *National Educational Technology Standards for Students 3—Technology Productivity Tools:* Students use technology tools to enhance learning, increase productivity, and promote creativity.

Learning Objectives. The learning objectives for this lesson are as follows:

1. The students will illustrate and accurately label the four stages of the water cycle in a hand-drawn storyboard.
2. The students will create a PowerPoint presentation meeting the following criteria: contains five slides, with first slide as title slide; each slide includes a graphic, text, and sound; transitions are used between each slide; and the presentation uses a design template that supports the water cycle theme. The PowerPoint presentation illustrates and provides an accurate text explanation of each of the four phases of the water cycle.
3. The students will verbally describe each of the four phases during their PowerPoint presentations of the water cycle.

Select Strategies

Kerry Bird selects teacher- and student-centered strategies. The teacher-centered strategies involve a review of the water cycle process by the use of a wall poster and a student question-and-answer session. Kerry also guides students through the beginning stages of producing their water cycle storyboards to ensure they understand the process. The student-centered strategies occur in three stages. First, students complete their water cycle storyboards by writing descriptions of each phase and sketching images to illustrate the concepts. Next, students go to the computer lab to create PowerPoint presentations of the water cycle. The final strategy involves how students present their water cycle projects.

Select Resources

This lesson involves student use of computers and PowerPoint software to create water cycle presentations. Kerry uses the computer lab for the lesson because each student is required to create an individual PowerPoint presentation. The lab also has a digital projector and screen for the student presentations. Students download digital photos of local areas and insert audio files of weather sounds and music to their PowerPoint presentations. Kerry uses the following guidelines to assess the appropriateness of his technology and media selections:

- *Alignment with standards, outcomes, and objectives.* PowerPoint provides the necessary tools for students to meet the learning objectives.
- *Accurate and current information.* Not applicable for the chosen technology and media.

- *Age-appropriate language.* PowerPoint is written at a somewhat advanced level for fourth-grade students; however, the icons assist with understanding.
- *Interest level and engagement.* PowerPoint provides features, such as inserting graphics and sound and personalizing backgrounds and color, that increase student interest level and engagement.
- *Technical quality.* PowerPoint has superior technical quality.
- *Ease of use.* Use of PowerPoint requires initial training and support when using some features, such as inserting graphics from a server or the Web.
- *Bias free.* PowerPoint is bias free.
- *User guide and directions.* The online help features of PowerPoint are difficult for fourth-grade students to use. Students most frequently ask each other or the teacher for assistance with technical difficulties.

Utilize Resources

Preview Resources. Kerry previews the PowerPoint software to ensure it has the features needed for the lesson. He previews the water cycle poster to ensure it has content that matches the lesson standards and objectives. He also previews the digital photos saved on the school server to ensure that images accurately reflect water cycle stages.

Prepare Resources. Kerry prepares two sets of materials for the lesson. The first is a hand-drawn storyboard of the water cycle that will serve as a model for the student products. The second is a PowerPoint presentation of the water cycle that not only serves as a model for the students, but also ensures that the planned activities are workable. In other words, students will be able to access and download files from the server, students will be able to insert and listen to audio files, and the presentations will be viewable with the digital projector.

Prepare the Environment. The lesson takes place in the classroom and the computer lab. Computers in the lab should be checked to ensure that PowerPoint software is functional and that all computers have access and can save to the school server. The projector needs to be tested to ensure that it projects clear images, is properly connected to the appropriate computer, and displays PowerPoint presentations with full functionality.

Prepare the Learners. To prepare the students, Kerry introduces the lesson and reviews the learning objectives. When in the computer lab, he reviews the basics of using PowerPoint software, downloading files from the server, and operating the digital projector.

Provide the Learning Experience. The learning experience occurs in the classroom and the computer lab. It involves both teacher-centered and student-centered activities and the use of computers to produce and present student-created PowerPoint presentations of the water cycle.

Require Learner Participation

Large-Group Activities. Kerry introduces the lesson, reviews the learning objectives, and asks students questions about the water cycle as he completes the first two stages of a "class-size" storyboard. Kerry uses the questions to check for student understanding of previously learned content.

Independent Student Activities. Following the large-group activity, the students individually complete their water cycle storyboards. Taking the storyboards to the computer lab, the students use computers and PowerPoint software to create water cycle presentations. Students produce the basic five-slide presentation and add text to each slide as it is written on their storyboards. They then review images saved on the server and select one or more for each water cycle stage. When the text and images are in place, students can add audio, change the backgrounds and color schemes, and add transitions between slides. For the final activity, students present their water cycle PowerPoint products to the class.

Evaluate and Revise

Assessment of Learner Achievement. Kerry assesses learner achievement in two ways. He first assesses demonstration of content knowledge from the information in students' PowerPoint displays and in their oral narrations during the presentations. The second part of his assessment considers the technology skills shown, which Kerry assesses by evaluating the final student presentations according to the assignment criteria stated in the learning objectives: five slides, the first of which is the title slide; each slide containing a graphic, text, and sound; transitions used between each slide; presentation based on a design template that supports the water cycle theme.

Evaluation of Strategies and Resources. Kerry evaluates the water cycle lesson strategies, technology, and media by continually checking with students during lesson implementation and by also conducting a whole-class discussion of the process at the conclusion of the lesson. His goal is to determine student impressions of this use of technology and to solicit their ideas for improving the process. Also, because Kerry keeps notes for each lesson,

he can review past water cycle lessons and compare the current lesson to identify strengths and weaknesses.

Revision. The evaluation reveals that the students really enjoyed creating the PowerPoint presentations but were uncomfortable presenting them to the class, primarily due to feeling unprepared and from lack of student interest in the presentations. Kerry revises the lesson by providing instruction on how to give an oral presentation. He also introduces the use of a peer evaluation form that includes student ideas about what an "excellent" presentation would include.

Professional Development

DEMONSTRATING PROFESSIONAL KNOWLEDGE

1. Describe strategies for and examples of integrating digital devices into the curriculum.
2. Describe five types of software that might be used in the classroom.
3. Discuss the advantages and limitations of using technology in learning.
4. Discuss the differences among a single-device classroom, a multiple-device classroom, technology carts, and technology laboratories in terms of setups and uses.
5. Describe an appropriate instructional situation for using technology to support student learning. Include the setting, topic, audience, objectives, content of the materials, and rationale for using this media format.

DEMONSTRATING PROFESSIONAL SKILLS

1. Create a list of topics you would include if you were to conduct a one-day computer implementation workshop for teachers in your content area (ISTE NETS-T 5.D).
2. Describe how you can use a computer resource as a learning tool within your content area (ISTE NETS-T 2.A and B).
3. Select at least five computer programs suitable for your content area. Critique each program using the Selection Rubric: **Software** found later in this chapter (ISTE NETS-T 2.A).
4. Select a topic or standard that can be used in a classroom setting of your choice. Describe three ways to use computer software to address the diverse learning needs of students and three ways to develop students' higher-order thinking skills and creativity (ISTE NETS-T 2.A, B, and C).

BUILDING YOUR PROFESSIONAL PORTFOLIO

- *Creating My Lesson.* Using the ASSURE model, design a lesson for one of the case studies presented in Appendix A or use a scenario of your own design. Incorporate into your lesson one or more of the instructional strategies and technology and media ideas described in this chapter. Be sure to include information about the audience, the objectives, and all other elements of the ASSURE model. Be certain to match your intended outcomes to state or national learning standards for your content area (ISTE NETS-T 2.A).
- *Enhancing My Lesson.* Using the lesson you have just designed, consider your audience again. Assume that some of your students have special needs, such as physical or learning impediments. Also assume that several students are identified as gifted. How will you adapt or change your lesson design to ensure that

these students are recognized and supported, to allow them to succeed in your lesson (ISTE NETS-T 4.B)?

- *Reflecting on My Lesson.* Reflect on the process you have used in the design of your lesson and your efforts at enhancing that lesson to meet student needs within your class. What have you learned about

matching audience, content, instructional strategy, and materials? What could you have done to develop your students' higher-order thinking or creativity skills? In what ways did the materials you selected for your lesson enhance the learning opportunities for your students (ISTE NETS-T 5.C)?

Suggested Resources

PRINT RESOURCES

Cook, A., & Hussey, S. (2007). *Assistive technologies: Principles and practice* (3rd ed.). St. Louis, MO: Mosby.

Counts, E. L. (2003). *Multimedia design and production for students and teachers.* Boston, MA: Allyn & Bacon.

Gura, M. (2005). *Recapturing technology for education: Keeping tomorrow in today's classrooms.* Latham, MD: Scarecrow Education.

Ivers, K. S., & Barron, A. E. (2005). *Multimedia projects in education: Designing, producing, and assessing* (3rd ed.). Westport, CT: Libraries Unlimited.

O'Bannon, B., & Puckett, K. (2010). *Preparing to use technology: A practical guide to curriculum integration* (2nd ed.). Boston, MA: Allyn & Bacon.

Roblyer, M., & Doering, A. (2010). *Integrating educational technology into teaching* (5th ed.). Boston, MA: Allyn & Bacon.

WEB RESOURCES

Kathy Schrock's Guide

www.schrockguide.net

This directory of educational resources offers classroom teachers an array of links, lesson plans, and professional development suggestions.

Awesome Library

www.awesomelibrary.org

A resource for technology use in the classroom at all levels and for helping schools with technology decisions.

Education World

www.education-world.com

Lesson plans, school resources, and new technology ideas are all included in Education World's site.

InTime

www.intime.uni.edu

Watching teachers use technology in their teaching and following along as they describe what they do, InTime

provides many different types of examples of using technology in learning.

Technology in the Classroom Center

www.education-world.com

This site contains many resources relating to integrating technology in the classroom. Some professional development resources and tutorials are on the site as well.

Best Kids Apps

www.bestkidsapps.com

This website provides reviews of educational apps for Apple and Android mobile devices.

SELECTION RUBRIC   Software

NOTE: For the purposes of this discussion, the term *software* includes computer software, mobile apps, and online services.

Complete and save the following interactive evaluation to reference when selecting software to integrate with learning.

Search Terms

_____

_____

_____

Teacher

_____

Title _____

Hardware Required _____

Source/Location _____

©Date _____ Cost _____ Length _____ Minutes _____

Primary User(s) _____

Subject Area _____ Grade Level _____

Instructional Strategies _____

Brief Description

Standards/Outcomes/Objectives

Prerequisites (e.g., prior knowledge, reading ability, vocabulary level)

Strengths

Limitations

Special Features

Name _____ **Date** _____

Rating Area	High Quality	Medium Quality	Low Quality
Alignment with standards, outcomes, and objectives	Standard/outcome/objective addressed and use of technology should enhance student learning.	Standard/outcome/objective partially addressed and use of technology may enhance student learning.	Standard/outcome/objective not addressed and use of technology will likely not enhance student learning.
Accurate and current information	Information correct and does not contain material that is out of date.	Information correct but does contain material that is out of date.	Information is not correct and does contain material that is out of date.
Age-appropriate language	Language used is age appropriate and vocabulary is understandable.	Language used is nearly age appropriate and some vocabulary is above/below student age.	Language used is not age appropriate and vocabulary is clearly inappropriate for student age.
Interest level and engagement	Topic presented so that students are likely to be interested and actively engaged in learning.	Topic presented to interest students most of the time and engage most in learning.	Topic presented so as not to interest students and not engage them in learning.
Technical quality	The material represents best available technology and media.	The material represents technology and media that are good quality, although there are some problems.	The material represents technology and media that are not well prepared and are of very poor quality.
Ease of use (user may be student or teacher)	Material follows easy-to-use patterns with nothing to confuse the user.	Material follows patterns that are easy to follow most of the time, with a few things to confuse the user.	Material follows no patterns and most of the time the user is very confused.
Bias free	There is no evidence of objectionable bias or advertising.	There is little evidence of bias or advertising.	There is much evidence of bias or advertising.
Stimulates creativity	Most students can use the software to create original pieces that represent learning.	Some students can use the software to start original pieces that begin to show their learning.	Most students cannot use the software to create original pieces that represent their learning.
Fosters collaboration	Students are able to work in collaborative groups when using the software with little problem.	Students are able to work in collaborative groups when using the software most of the time.	Students are not able to work in collaborative groups when using the software.
Practice and feedback	Software provides students with skill or knowledge practice and information that helps them complete their learning tasks.	Software provides students with some skill or knowledge practice and information that sometimes helps them complete their learning tasks.	Software does not provide students with skill or knowledge practice, nor information that helps them with their learning tasks.

Recommended for Classroom Use: _____ Yes _____ No

Ideas for Classroom Use: _____

_____

Learning with Web 2.0 and Social Media

Knowledge Outcomes

This chapter addresses ISTE NETS-S 1, 3, and 4.

1. Define cyberlearning and provide an example of a classroom application.

2. Identify three Web 2.0 and social media resources and describe an example of how they might assist learning.

3. Explain why social networking issues are important for the classroom.

4. Identify two social-ethical issues and why they are important in working with students.

Goal

Understand the use of Web 2.0 resources and social media to facilitate learning.

Vicki Davis is a high school technology teacher who incorporates Web 2.0 tools into her teaching. The ASSURE Classroom Case Study for this chapter describes the planning process she uses to create a lesson. Her primary goals are to engage her students to organize their thoughts, to communicate clearly, and to plan for the implementation of their project.

The ASSURE Classroom Case Study video for this chapter explores how Ms. Davis develops instruction to lead students through their discussion and sharing of ideas. View the video to explore how she selects the activities and instructional strategies and chooses the materials, multimedia, and technology that will promote 21st century learning. Throughout the chapter you will find reflection questions that relate the chapter content to the ASSURE Classroom Case Study. At the end of the chapter, you will be challenged to develop your own ASSURE lesson that incorporates strategies, technology, media, and materials for a topic of your choice.

 Watch Ms. Davis and her class as they engage in this technology-rich lesson.

Schools of the 21st century are changing. No longer are they limited to the existing structure or resources of the building. It is possible to reach beyond the traditional school setting to design learning opportunities with global reach to engage today's learners. **Cyberlearning** is the use of networked computing and communication technologies to support learning. By dynamically integrating the Internet and social media into instruction, cyberlearning is transforming learning opportunities while requiring new perspectives on teaching.

Using Web 2.0 and Social Media

The term **Web 2.0** refers to websites that are more than static webpages, or Web 1.0 resources. A Web 2.0 site may allow users to interact with and publish data and information, while a Web 1.0 website limits users to passively viewing content. Blogs, wikis, web applications, and websites dedicated to social bookmarking, pin boarding, audio, video, social networking, and mashups are examples of Web 2.0 sites. Connections are driven by content.

Social media are mobile and web-based applications that enable users to interact, collaborate, co-create, share, and publish information, ideas, and multimedia. Social media connects people and is built on the foundations of Web 2.0.

A **web application,** also referred to as a *web app,* uses a browser technology as a client to accomplish one or more tasks over a network. Common web applications include webmail, wikis, and office productivity tools such as Google Docs, Slides, and Sheets.

With Web 2.0 resources and social media, students can connect to share ideas, engage in inquiry, and search for additional information. Sometimes called **learning communities,** collaboration among students and teachers expands educational possibilities through electronic connectedness. Wagner's (2008) suggestions for improving learning opportunities outline many types of strategies that can effectively integrate technology with learning.

Wagner's ideas that learners need to be engaged in experiences that frame their thinking can be facilitated by current Web 2.0 resources and social media. Students can now engage in critical thinking and problem solving while collaborating and communicating with others and by using curiosity and imagination to explore new ideas. The Web 2.0 tools and social media

Students can now engage in critical thinking and problem solving while collaborating and communicating with others.

described in this chapter target those skills and provide students with many types of learning opportunities beyond simple information access.

STRATEGIES AND APPROACHES

Mobile Learning. Mobile learning can be defined by two characteristics. One characteristic is that learning can occur anywhere and is not reliant on the student being at a specific location, such as a classroom. The second characteristic is that learning takes advantage of mobile technologies, such as mobile phones and iPads. Educational opportunities are considered mobile learning when either or both of these characteristics are present.

Informal Learning. On the one hand, instructional settings can include formal, organized learning experiences for which teachers are responsible. On the other hand, **informal learning** gives students opportunities to learn from experiences outside of the classroom setting. For example, students can surf, or explore, websites on the Internet and find information that may be important for their formal classroom study. Because you do not assign this activity, this exploration becomes an informal learning experience. For instance, when students study a region of the country in social studies they can access the Internet to find a website describing the region or email someone living in that area.

Even students lacking an Internet connection at home may have access to Internet-connected computers in school media centers and libraries. And the majority of students have access to mobile technology resources through their cell phones (Johnson et al., 2013). As the cell phone becomes more ubiquitous, even students from families with limited incomes generally have a cell phone available to them. Students learn how to informally seek information and will challenge themselves to learn about topics that might not be part of their in-class study because they find value in that type of experience.

Web 2.0 and Social Media Resources

Online resources that enhance student learning include blogs, wikis, web apps, social bookmarks, pin boards, audio and video, social networks, mashups, and mobile technologies. These types of Web 2.0 tools and social media provide learners different ways of accessing information and sharing their thinking and understanding. As their teacher, you can integrate these resources into your lessons to ensure students are able to communicate and share their knowledge and creativity with others.

Most of the resources available as Web 2.0 tools and social media are the products of the open source concept, meaning that software is unrestricted and free for anyone's use (Pfaffman, 2007). Open source resources are designed to foster collaboration and allow access to tools that make work easier. As a teacher, you need to determine when it is appropriate to use these types of tools in your lessons. There may be times when you determine that using Web 2.0 resources and social media may not facilitate the types of learning experiences you want for your students.

ASSURE Classroom Case Study Reflection

Consider the use of Web 2.0 tools in helping students organize their thoughts and communicate their ideas. How does Ms. Davis support learning through the discussion and her guidance in expressing ideas clearly? In what way is she using Web 2.0 tools and social media to facilitate students' learning experiences?

Open source Web 2.0 resources and social media include programs such as word processing, database, and image software that are freely available to educators for use in classrooms. However, because the software is free and thus not purchased and licensed, you have little control over the quality and stability of the software. You could plan to use a particular application, only to find that it is no longer available or is now only usable if you pay a fee.

One emerging direction for open source tools is called **cloud computing,** in which files and applications can be synced to and used on multiple devices across a network. Cloud-based resources can be free or very low cost and include substantial capabilities for sharing files and information with others across the Web. The software and files are not stored on individual computers but rather are stored in the cloud, or network of computers supporting the software application being used.

BLOGS

Blogs, short for *web logs,* were initially designed to be a set of personal commentaries about a specific topic. Many teachers have adapted blogs and use them for class websites, weekly newsletters to parents, daily homework communication, writing journals, and much more. Blogs can contain text, visuals, multimedia, and links to websites, and they allow learners to share information with each other, with the teacher, and with the world. A blog can also be a dialog with a group of people around the world that share an interest in a common topic or issue (Figure 6.1). The structure of a blog is arranged so that the most recent posting is first, allowing easy access to the most recent comments. Any reader who wishes, however, can easily scan through the blog postings to see earlier entries.

Content experts such as scientists often write blogs, giving students a chance to be informed about a topic with the most up-to-date information. However, although content may be current, it may not necessarily be accurate. You should guide your students in their search for credible sources, as many blogs may be highly subjective in nature, written by individuals as a way to express their ideas to an audience. When teaching students writing skills, a blog is a great way to offer them an audience that can comment on their ideas or their writing. You may wish to start with a class blog, giving your students a chance to learn how to use good writing skills successfully in a blogging environment before you engage them with their own personal blogs or having them visit public blogs.

As an educator, you can create your own blog using a site such as Wordpress.com or Blogger.com. You can invite other professionals in your building or district to join you in exploring topics of interest and developing new ideas to use in your teaching. As part of your exchange with other educators, you can build in professional development opportunities. You can include special guests who can provide insights that may prompt additional discussion among your colleagues. There are national blogs that include a larger community of educators such as TeacherLingo.com, which invites teachers to share ideas and exchange resources. By exploring your educational endeavors through a blog, you are providing opportunities for other educators to advance their ideas and to share in improving educational options for students.

FIGURE 6.1   Teachers' Websites

Well, I'm happy to report that I've managed to acquire 5 iPads in the Computer Lab. These are, as I'm sure you've guessed, a big hit. Students learned how to take care of and treat the machines with respect a few weeks ago, and everyone has the routines down. The iPads are perfect for a Center station and offer a myriad of learning opportunities, able to engage students at different learning styles.

Presently, the Grades 1 and 2 have been using them for *reading non-fiction books* (primarily the app, "Lulu in the Amazon"(https://itunes.apple.com/us/app/lulu-in-the-amazon/id571916239?mt=8). Grades 3 and 4 started off with a challenging Math game called, "SubtractionTop-It" (https://itunes.apple.com/us/app/everyday-mathematics-subtraction/id425203268?mt=8) which makes use of solving for the difference between two numbers *mentally* instead of on paper (with "regrouping" or "borrowing" as we used to call it).

It can be very interesting to read about other teachers' successful use of technology in the classroom.
Source: Reprinted by permission of Bob Sprankle.

FIGURE 6.2 Wikipedia

Similar to an encyclopedia, Wikipedia provides a current source about a vast array of topics.

Source: http://www.wikipedia.org

WIKIS

Wikis are web-based resources that let users engage in collaborative writing and editing. A wiki is a webpage that permits users to interact with a document that others have written or edited. Wikis allow users to write new information or edit the information that is posted on a collaborative site. Content can change whenever a user interacts with the page. A group of teachers or students can work together on a paper or project, providing immediate feedback for ideas as they are entered in the document. Wikis provide teachers and learners with a tool for sharing information and media with others. Wikipedia, a collaborative encyclopedia, is a well-known type of wiki (Figure 6.2). The content on Wikipedia can be updated or changed by users to keep it current, unlike a large printed encyclopedia that is updated only every 10 years.

Wikis are good tools for students working on collaborative writing projects. Students can access a Wiki using any computer and any web browser. In addition, students do not need to be in the same location, but can work together while one student is at home and the other is in a nearby library. Wiki spaces, such as Google Docs, are often free to educators, making them even more useful for teachers to provide guidance for students as they write collaboratively with others.

WORD CLOUDS

A **word cloud,** also called a *tag cloud,* is a visual representation of text-based data. Single pieces of data in the word cloud are called *tags.* The importance or frequency of tags is conveyed through font size or color. Word clouds can be used to convey concepts, key vocabulary, significant events, ideas from brainstorming, and much more.

Wordle.net is one of the most commonly used web applications for creating word clouds. Students can use Wordle to practice vocabulary or to produce visuals that help them see the relationships among words (Figure 6.3). Students can create their own wordles to express their ideas or, as their teacher, you can help them see the relationships among ideas through the visual you prepare in advance or as part of a group brainstorming activity. A wordle is also a handy way for students to see how they may have overused a particular word in their writing. A fun site for students is **Guess the Wordle,** which features daily wordle puzzles that become more complex through the week.

ONLINE PRODUCTIVITY TOOLS

Online **productivity tools,** also known as online office tools, are web applications that are becoming more commonly used as alternatives to traditional software suites such as Microsoft Office. Examples include web apps for word processing, slideshows and presentations, spreadsheets, note taking, concept maps, and calendars. These types of productivity tools allow users to create and edit documents online while collaborating in real time with other users.

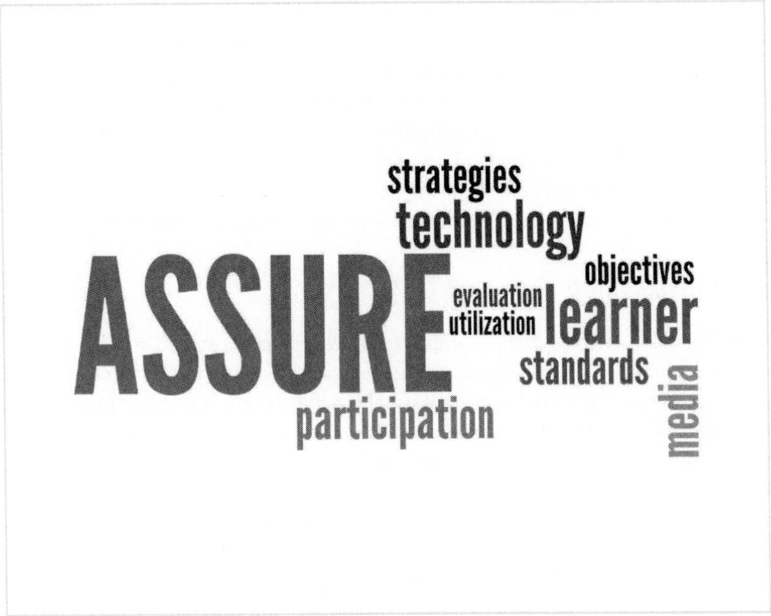

FIGURE 6.3

Wordle

A wordle can be used to visualize a concept or to reinforce vocabulary.

Source: www.wordle.net

These technologies can support thinking and support student engagement and social interaction. Files are saved on the website's server, making them available across any device with an Internet connection. Many of these tools make it possible to save the files to the local computer or mobile device using a variety of common file formats. Most of these online productivity tools are free or far less expensive than their competitors. It is common for schools and districts to choose to use these web applications as alternatives to the expensive traditional software suites.

Google offers a suite of online productivity tools consisting of a number of web apps, including Google Docs for word processing and Google Sheets for spreadsheets, calculations,

WHEN TO USE

Web 2.0 and Social Media

Use when student learning will be enhanced by ...	Examples
Reading and writing about shared learning experiences	Middle school students post information on a classroom blog site.
Practicing English as a second language	High school English learners listen to podcasts to help them with their classroom studies.
Sharing information with classmates	Elementary students post their digital stories on Storybird to share both their visual and written stories with others.
Exchanging information about a carbon footprint class project	Middle school students post video captured on their cell phones to a classroom blog site and write about what they have seen.

and forms. These web apps enable teachers to collaboratively develop instructional materials online, make it possible for students to enter data from a chemistry experiment into a shared live spreadsheet, and facilitate the possibility for paperless assignments.

Prezi is an online productivity tool that is commonly used for presentations and storytelling. Ideas, information, and media are organized on the *canvas,* and the presentation interface allows users to navigate by zooming in on and out of the presentation content. Prezi can be used collaboratively, with multiple users having the ability to edit presentations. Prezi enables students to construct and present their thinking and understanding in creative ways.

SOCIAL BOOKMARKING

Social bookmarking enables users to organize, store, manage, and search for bookmarked resources online. Social bookmarks provide users with links to online resources they want to remember and share. These bookmarks are usually public, but it is possible to save them privately, or share them with only specified people or groups. Typically, bookmarks can be viewed chronologically, by category or tags, or found using the bookmarking service's search engine. As these services have grown, additional features have been included. These include the addition of ratings, commenting, importing and exporting bookmarks from browsers, emailing of bookmarks, and other social networking features. One of the most robust social bookmarking tools is Diigo. In addition to bookmarking useful web resources, Diigo users can also highlight and annotate webpages. These additional features make it a useful research tool when writing research papers or preparing reports in social studies and science.

PIN BOARDS

Online **pin boards** enable users to organize photos, videos, and other information onto digital boards by lesson, unit, grade-level, or subject area. A team of fifth-grade teachers in Grenada, Mississippi, have setup boards for each of the units they teach throughout the year. Collaboratively, they "pin" new ideas and resources to the corresponding boards and then use these resources as they develop their lessons and materials during team planning. Mr. Charsky, a tenth-grade social studies teacher, used Learni.st to organize a board that he used as an instructional module about global warming that the students were able to complete independently.

It is important that you and your students are mindful when using images that do not belong to you. Be sure that you and your students use these images with attribution and in accordance with each image's copyright or creative commons license. A creative commons license will provide you with specifics as to how the resource can be used and what types of attribution will be necessary.

ONLINE AUDIO AND VIDEO

Learning can be enhanced through the integration of audio and video resources. The use of multimedia can foster an atmosphere of excitement, motivation, and learning by engaging students and capturing their attention. The use of audio and video prompts can also help learners generate cognitive connections through the process of linking new ideas to existing schema, resulting in the development of new memory. Students can also use these production tools to demonstrate their thinking and depth of understanding beyond written text.

MASHUPS

Data **mashups** are websites that bring together content from a variety of resources, creating resources that are new and different from the original sources. For example, online news media sites combine text, video, audio, and real-time information updated about every 15 minutes.

This combination of information gives you and your students current data to use in reports or as part of classroom activities.

Your students can take advantage of mashup sites to learn more about geography or mapping skills. They can use a mashup site that combines mapping and satellite information to identify specific locations in cities around the world. The assignment might be to locate particular types of buildings or specific monuments using a site like Google Maps, in which students can easily pinpoint specific places, get directions, or view the maps to identify the location's proximity to surrounding areas. You can have them plan an imaginary trip to a city, such as Washington, DC, making sure they organize the easiest route through the city as they "visit" targeted historical sites.

Students can also create digital posters and timelines that are comprised of information and multimedia from a variety of sources. Websites such as **Glogster** make it possible for students to combine photos, audio and video clips, slideshows, text-based information, links to other websites, and animations into online posters. These learning artifacts can be media rich and provide opportunities for students to engage multiple learning modalities.

Students can communicate their thinking and understanding through a variety of modalities using multimedia in mashups.

MOBILE TECHNOLOGIES

Although not new, **mobile technologies** (smart phones, portable music players, tablet computers, e-readers, and other handheld technologies) offer expanded tools and applications. **Mobile apps,** software applications designed for mobile devices, enable many of these devices to take photos and short video, email, surf the Web, play games, provide location-based services (GPS), and use calendars and other personal management tools.

Mobile technology has been dubbed the great social equalizer (Paine, 2009). Today, the majority of school-age children have cell phones and learn their applications with little trouble. Although phones for younger children, often purchased for child safety reasons, may only be able to call a parent's cell phone, many older students have phones with greater access to online resources.

As educators, we need to begin thinking of ways to apply these extended mobile capabilities as learning tools. Examples include field-based learning experiences where students can take photos of events or phenomena, such as demonstrating the carbon footprints they find within their community. Students can then upload the images to a classroom website and write a blog entry about their observations. Experts on the topic of carbon footprinting can provide additional information or guide approaches to the topic. The classroom can be moved outside the school building and beyond the limits of the school day.

SOCIAL NETWORKS

A **social networking service** facilitates online connections and interactions of users based on shared backgrounds, interests, and experiences. Users are able to share ideas, messages, information, and multimedia with people in their network. Google+, Facebook, Twitter, and Tumblr are examples of social networks. Social networks offer ways for users to join others interested in similar topics or issues through community groups. Groups can be open to anyone with similar interests or can be set up as "closed" groups that require an invitation before an individual can join. Because "open" groups are shared across the Internet, information on these sites is available to anyone around the world.

ASSURE Classroom Case Study Reflection

Identify the types of Web 2.0 tools and social media that Vicki Davis has incorporated into her lesson. How have the students used these tools to support their learning?

FIGURE 6.4 Edmodo

As a teacher, you can create your own class social networking site.
Source: Reprinted by permission of Edmodo.

Some social networking sites limit the amount of text a user can use in each post, encouraging brief communications when exchanging information. For instance, Twitter, an online communication network for sharing current, up-to-the-minute status reports in very brief messages, limits posts, or "tweets," to 140 characters. In response to the concept of quick notes, such as instant messages, tweets, and other social networking resources, users have created a type of shorthand to communicate their ideas without wasting letters. For example, a user would type the letter u for the word *you,* the numeral 2 for the word *to,* or BRB for *be right back.* You need to help your students know when it is appropriate to use the shortcuts and when they need to use formal writing skills.

Many schools restrict access to social networking sites within the building setting, which may mean that even if you create an educational application, you may not be able to use it with your students in the school. However, the 21st century student has become very comfortable with these kinds of resources, and it is important to consider how they might be useful in educational settings. Many students already have their own social network accounts, using them only for social interactions. You may have your own page as well, although you may want to consider the type of information and photos you place on your pages as they can potentially be viewed by students, parents, administrators, and school board members. You may want to learn about the educational uses of these types of resources to capitalize on the popularity of their use. You should be cautious in "friending" your students, so you may wish to establish two accounts, one for your own personal use with limited access, and one for a more professional use with a broader access. Some education sites are starting to mirror social networking resources but are restricted to classroom use only (Figure 6.4) as a means of better ensuring a safe environment for students.

Edmodo is a social learning platform that is frequently used as a social network connecting teachers, students, and parents within a class, school, or district. Edmodo can be used to post assignments, create polls for student responses, share audio and video clips, create learning groups, post a quiz, and share a calendar of events and assignment deadlines. Students can submit assignments and teachers can grade and annotate the assignments directly within Edmodo.

ISSUES

Whenever working with students online, you need to consider two important social–ethical issues: security and student interactions.

Security. Students need to understand they are not to give out personal information online, such as their last names, phone numbers, addresses, or other information. On occasion, there have been incidents in which students have been contacted or even harmed by unscrupulous individuals. Your role as teacher is to encourage students to give their school's address for correspondence *if* they need to provide such information. Also, as an educator, you must have parental permission to post children's photos and written work, such as essays, poems, and artistic creations, on the Web. You can learn more about online security issues through the Center for Education and Research in Information Assurance and Security (CERIAS) (www.cerias.purdue.edu).

Monitoring Student Use. When students are working in cybersettings, they need to engage in positive and appropriate interactions with others. As their teacher, you will need to guide your students in using appropriate behavior with others. It is important for you to help your students understand how to use clear and situation-specific language in their communications. For example, if the students are exchanging text messages, they will find abbreviations or word shortcuts to be effective, while in an email to an adult or an organization, they will want to use complete sentences.

ASSURE Classroom Case Study Reflection

Consider how Vicki Davis ensures that her students use technology appropriately. How has she guided students to remember to exhibit appropriate online behavior?

One issue that has become serious and needs your monitoring and intervention is cyberbullying. Cyberbullying can range from annoying an individual online to far more dangerous situations, if not handled properly. The Cyberbullying Research Center (www.cyberbullying.us) offers information about the problem, research, and suggestions for dealing with the issue at hand. Also, they provide examples of actual incidents and contact information for seeking assistance. The blog provides a means for discussion among professionals related to the examples and other issues regarding cyberbullying.

Integrating Web 2.0 and Social Media with Learning

In the classroom there are a number of ways that Web 2.0 tools and social media can support learning. Your role is to find the best means of optimizing the learning opportunities for your students using these types of resources (see **Selection Rubric: Web 2.0 and Social Media**).

Lisa Zawilinski (2009) describes how one teacher organized a blog for her fifth-grade students to support their reading activities. After giving her students prompts about books they were reading, encouraging them to reflect on the stories and in turn demonstrate their reading comprehension, her students began to ask if they could post some of their original work, such

TECHNOLOGY FOR ALL LEARNERS

Web 2.0 and Social Media

Students may have difficulty expressing themselves in class due to limited language skills from a learning disability or because their first language is not English. They frequently tend to be quiet or not participate in class or group discussions. Gifted learners may want more challenges for their own learning. There are many resources for helping all students access information to increase their learning.

Audio podcasts allow students to hear the teacher's instruction after class so that they can review the information, follow directions that might have been presented, or prepare for a test about the material covered in class. Video podcasts provide visual information, along with the audio, to help students follow along using multiple modes of learning. These tools may help learners who benefit from seeing visual depictions of concepts or strategies to be applied. It is also helpful for students who may need to review a process more than once to gain the full benefit of the demonstration.

When writing is a challenge for students, a wiki or word processing web app can be a way to let them improve their skills in sharing information with classmates or other audiences. These tools allow everyone to offer and exchange ideas. It also allows others to provide ideas about how to express those ideas in writing, thus influencing writing skills.

Challenging students with a wide range of skills and abilities is often difficult. By using collaborative social networking tools, such as the MIT New Literacies Project, gifted students can share their work with other students around the world. These types of exchanges provide students with opportunities to express themselves and to learn from others.

as poems or reactions to books they were independently reading. The teacher recognized an opportunity for expanding students' use of the blog format, allowing her to guide them in their exploration of literature.

Mashups are another way to support students' learning. For example, if you are working on estimation in math, you can have your students estimate the walking distance between home and school. Once they have guessed the distance, they can visit Gmaps Pedometer to get the actual measured distance (Branzburg, 2009). For a geography or science class, you can link to a site that provides information about the location and scale of any **earthquake** worldwide for the past seven days. You can guide students to compare that data with geology information they have on global fault lines and plate tectonics.

Social networking is a way for students to connect with others engaged in social studies inquiry. As part of a unit about your state, you might have students collect information using online resources. You can have them post their bookmarks of sites visited to Diigo to share links with others in the class. With Diigo, access to their bookmarks can be limited to members of your class. Or, if you know another teacher whose students are also studying the state, you could arrange for them to exchange links to extend the study of both groups of students. The exchange offers students opportunities to gather additional information and learn more about the content while seeing examples of how to find additional resources. To expand the idea of working collaboratively, you can create a wiki in which students collaborate on a report that can be shared with other students, parents, or the school board.

Advantages

- *Portable*. Information can be accessed and used anywhere on personal devices such as laptops, computer tablets, and cell phones.

- *Easy to produce*. The new types of technologies allow anyone to be able to prepare materials such as podcasts or online videos.

- *Authentic audience*. When developing literacy and communication skills, interactive tools such as blogs and wikis offer opportunities to reach readers beyond the classroom who can provide valuable feedback.

- *Connectedness*. Communication among students is facilitated, encouraging collaboration.

TAKING A LOOK AT TECHNOLOGY INTEGRATION

Web Tools and Social Media

Insects

When Ms. Paszotta's kindergartners were starting their study of insects, she wanted to capitalize on the school's philosophy of integrating arts and technology into their learning experiences. And, when talking with Ms. Mullins, a fourth-grade teacher, she learned that the fourth graders were studying insects as well. The two teachers collaborated on their lessons and decided on the culminating activity in which students worked together to create a mashup about what they learned.

The kindergarteners selected an insect to study. They worked with a fourth-grade partner to investigate the insect and to prepare a short presentation about what they learned together. The kindergarteners drew masks of their selected insects and their fourth-grade partner worked with them to prepare an introduction about the insect to be included in the mashup.

Student pairs worked to create short videos about their insects. With the aid of the technology teacher, they uploaded their videos to the school's website, embedded them into their mashups, and shared their resources with other elementary children throughout the district.

- *Social awareness*. Students become more sensitive to others through social networking sites where they have access to information about each other.
- *Free*. Many Web 2.0 tools are available for educational uses at no charge.

Limitations

- *Require sophisticated hardware*. Some interactive Web 2.0 tools require hardware capabilities not available on less expensive mobile technology models.
- *Quality of messages*. Because they are easy to produce and free, many types of Web 2.0 postings are of poor quality and not well prepared.
- *Credibility*. Just because it appears on the Web does not make it an authentic or authoritative source. Web 2.0 tools make it very easy to post information that may be inaccurate.
- *Safety issues*. Because of the open nature of the resources, it is essential that users understand the need for caution and concern when sharing personal information.

Innovations on the Horizon

SEMANTIC-AWARE APPLICATIONS

Using a current search engine like Google, you type in a keyword and may get a large number of hits. Semantic-aware applications actually work with your computer to help it "understand" what you want to know and guide the search for an answer that addresses the question you've posed. Rather than searching on a group of keywords, the computer makes connections based on working with your input to focus on what you wish to know. In this totally new way to engage in Internet searches, your computer recognizes the meaning of the word or question you've provided, even using images instead of words for some of the information pulled from various sites, and will gather the information you seek quickly. It makes browsing through multiple pages a thing of the past.

Semantic technology is making it much easier to pose questions and locate answers, saving you valuable time. Your computer understands more about you and tries to make the work of searching easier, helping you be more efficient and successful in a wide range of Internet activities such as searching and sharing your knowledge with others. Your computer could also learn to connect dates, places, and people and use that information to keep your calendar, places of interest, and contacts list up-to-date without having to do it yourself. Semantic-aware applications are making it easier to find and connect information, making learning and discovering new information much easier for everyone who has access to the Internet.

Summary

Cyberlearning opportunities continue to expand. More resources are available to students and teachers to enhance and extend classroom activities through Web 2.0 tools and social media. Teachers are no longer limited to the materials they have in their classrooms or in the school media center, but rather can access resources from around the world. Teachers can provide students with experiences that help them use the Internet and social media as sources of information, tools of collaboration, and avenues to express their creativity. Students can reach out to other students and experts to exchange ideas. Cyberlearning has opened classrooms to a wealth of information around the world through the Internet and social media!

ASSURE   Lesson Plan

This ASSURE Classroom Case Study is based on a lesson that integrates Web 2.0 resources. Ms. Vicki Davis collaborates with her ninth-grade students to create lessons for seventh graders in a virtual world.

This ASSURE Lesson Plan describes the instructional planning used by Vicki Davis, a ninth-grade teacher who wanted her students to develop lesson plans for seventh graders with whom they connected virtually. To address this challenge, Ms. Davis collaborated with her students to create these lessons. Below is Vicki Davis's ASSURE lesson plan for the project.

Vicki Davis
Ninth Grade
Topic: Web 2.0

Analyze Learners

General Characteristics. The students in Vicki Davis's high school class are primarily rural students with a variety of interests in technology. They are fairly equally distributed with regard to gender and range in age from 13 to 15 years old. Student reading ability is at or above grade level, although there are several students with diagnosed learning disabilities in the class. Student behavior problems are minimal.

Entry Competencies. The students are, in general, able to do the following:

- Demonstrate competency in keyboarding, document editing, and general computer skills.
- Prepare written materials, such as narratives, for the lessons they are going to teach to the seventh-grade students, including wiki and blog entries.
- Use Web 2.0 software to participate in blogs and wikis and to develop and interact in virtual world settings (primarily using OpenSim) with their own avatars.

Learning Styles. Vicki's students learn best when engaged in activities that are relevant and include lively discussions of meaningful topics. Her students vary in comfort level when speaking with the seventh graders, but are very comfortable in the virtual world created for

their class to help the younger students learn about "digital citizenship" and Internet safety. Vicki guides her students through their use of technology, building on their prior experiences and skills. When working in groups, her style of coaching facilitates their teamwork abilities.

State Standards and Objectives

Curriculum Standards. The following Common Core Standards for Technology and Career Education are addressed in this lesson: (2) Communicate thoughts, ideas, information, and messages in writing and technologically create documents: Students collaborate using blogs, wikis, and preparation of instruction for younger students; (5) Organize ideas and communicate orally in clear, concise, and courteous manner: Students convey their ideas within group discussions and in presentations; and (8) Implement a plan of action making modifications as needed to achieve stated objectives: Students arrange their presentations to ensure that the seventh-graders are able to learn the important elements of digital citizenship and Internet safety.

Technology Standards. *National Educational Technology Standards for Students 1—Creativity and Innovation:* Students use Web 2.0 tools to demonstrate creative thinking, construct knowledge, and develop innovative products and processes; *4—Critical Thinking, Problem Solving, and Decision Making:* Students use technology to plan and conduct research, manage projects, solve problems, and make decisions; and *5—Digital Citizenship:* Students understand human, cultural, and societal issues related to technology and practice legal and ethical behavior.

Learning Objectives. The learning objectives for this lesson are as follows:

1. Develop virtual worlds that engage students in scenarios in which they apply digital citizenship and safety guidelines.

2. Select appropriate technology tools to accomplish team objectives.

3. Participate in authentic research and use appropriate attribution for ideas.

4. Communicate strategies for using Web 2.0 tools to solve problems.
5. Write avatar scripts that demonstrate knowledge of digital citizenship and safety.

Select Strategies

Vicki Davis selects teacher- and student-centered strategies to plan the lesson for seventh graders. The teacher-centered strategies involve engaging the students in discussion through questions and feedback that lead to additional ideas. The student-centered strategies consist of students initiating design ideas for the lessons they plan to develop for the seventh graders and utilizing Web 2.0 tools to share information and create interesting learning experiences.

Select Resources

This lesson involves students' work with computers and Web 2.0 software to post their ideas to a wiki and a blog. They also use software to develop a virtual world environment that will serve the younger students' learning needs. Vicki applies the following guidelines to assess the appropriateness of her technology and media selections:

- *Alignment with standards, outcomes, and objectives.* The Web 2.0 tools provide the necessary support for Vicki Davis's students to meet the learning objectives.
- *Accurate and current information.* Students use both text-based and Internet resources to conduct their research on digital citizenship and safety.
- *Age-appropriate language.* Ms. Davis's students consider how to instruct the seventh graders about virtual worlds, digital citizenship, and safety in language that will help them understand the concepts in the lessons.
- *Interest level and engagement.* The ninth-grade students are excited about sharing their knowledge of digital citizenship and safety with the seventh graders through their virtual world environment. They are very engaged with developing their lessons to help the younger students gain skills in navigating virtual worlds and learning about digital citizenship and safety.
- *Technical quality.* The technical quality of the Web 2.0 tools allow the students to engage in a variety of online interactions and to facilitate their communications beyond the school day and setting.

- *Ease of use.* The Web 2.0 tools are fairly easy for high school students to understand, especially as they are using them regularly in their learning.
- *Bias free.* Web 2.0 tools are bias free.
- *User guide and directions.* The online help features of some Web 2.0 tools are moderately easy for students to use. Students most frequently ask each other or use the help option within the software for assistance with technical difficulties.

Select Materials

Vicki Davis provides her students with a number of types of Web 2.0 tools to use for their interactions, research, and design ideas.

Utilize Resources

Preview Resources. Vicki Davis previews the Web 2.0 software to ensure that it has the features needed for her students to be successful. She previews selected technology resources to ensure students can use them in the school setting, as well as making certain the tools will meet their needs.

Prepare Resources. Vicki prepares starter questions for the group discussion following the presentation the ninth graders completed for the seventh graders.

Prepare the Environment. Vicki tests the lab computers and ensures that the software needed is accessible from each computer. She also tests the capability of the technology to connect the lab classroom to the nearby school media center.

Prepare the Learners. Students in Vicki's class have been involved in group discussions previously, and learner preparation therefore primarily focuses on the topics to be covered during the live lesson and follow-up discussion.

Provide the Learning Experience. The learning experience occurs in three formats: live presentation to a group of seventh-grade students, interactions within the discussion following the presentation, and their online discussions on the blog and wiki for this project.

Require Learner Participation

Student Practice Activities. The students in Vicki Davis's class use computers, the virtual world they created, and Web 2.0 software to prepare for and participate in the presentation to the seventh-grade students. Her students use information from their observations and discussion to generate ideas to improve their next presentation and to develop a series of lessons about virtual worlds, digital citizenship, and safety. During the discussion, students practice and test their knowledge and skills by asking and answering student-created questions. They post their ideas to the class blog for further exploration and discussion beyond the class period. Furthermore, they work collaboratively on the class wiki in the planning and design of their instruction for seventh-graders on digital citizenship and Internet safety.

Feedback. Vicki provides continuous feedback as students participate in their discussion and guides them in their decisions on the best ways to interact with the seventh-grade students. She encourages them to provide feedback to each other through their online discussions.

Evaluate and Revise

Assessment of Learner Achievement. Vicki reviews the discussion notes posted to the wiki. She examines the materials that are prepared for the school blog and looks at the materials her students have developed for their next seventh-grade lesson. She also reviews the video that the students have located to see whether it is appropriate for the seventh graders. Vicki uses rubrics to assess both student ability to apply technology for creativity and their communication skills by evaluating student comments and their posted notes. She also uses a rubric to assess the accuracy of the digital citizenship and student safety information included in the virtual world scripts prepared by the ninth graders.

Evaluation of Strategies and Resources. Vicki evaluates the effectiveness of the lesson strategies, talking about the process with the students in her class. Evaluation of the technology and media involves examining the functionality of the Web 2.0 software and the virtual world environment created by her students.

Revision. The evaluation results revealed that student interactions could benefit from assigning students to work in design pairs to increase interactions and information exchange. Furthermore, teacher notes and edits of student work on the wiki provided improved documentation of the lesson. Another revision that emerged from the evaluation results was to limit teacher-directed questions to encourage more student-to-student discussion.

Professional Development

DEMONSTRATING PROFESSIONAL KNOWLEDGE

1. Define cyberlearning and provide an example of a classroom application.
2. Identify three Web 2.0 and social media resources and demonstrate an example of how they might assist learning.
3. Explain why social networking issues are important for the classroom.
4. Identify two social-ethical issues and why they are important in working with students.

DEMONSTRATING PROFESSIONAL SKILLS

1. Prepare a 10-minute presentation on how you might use one of the Web 2.0 tools in your teaching (ISTE NETS-T 5.A).
2. Locate resources online that provide guidance for ensuring student safety when working with Web 2.0 tools (ISTE NETS-T 4.C).
3. Locate and critique a lesson plan that describes an actual use of Web 2.0 tools (ISTE NETS-T 5.C).

BUILDING YOUR PROFESSIONAL PORTFOLIO

- *Creating My Lesson.* Using the ASSURE model, design a lesson for one of the case studies presented in the list in Appendix A or use a scenario of your own design. Incorporate into your lesson a Web 2.0 tool that will facilitate student learning. Carefully describe the audience, the objectives, and all the other elements of the ASSURE model. Be certain to match your intended outcomes to state or national curriculum and technology standards for your content area.
- *Enhancing My Lesson.* Using the lesson you created in the previous activity, consider how to meet the needs of students with varying abilities. What adaptations are needed to keep advanced learners actively engaged while helping students who struggle with reading?

What changes are needed to ensure students transfer the knowledge and skills to other learning situations? You might look for additional Web 2.0 resources to enhance the lesson. How can you integrate additional use of technology and media into the lesson?

- *Reflecting on My Lesson.* Reflect on the process you have used in the design of your lesson and your efforts at enhancing that lesson to meet student needs within your class. How did information from this chapter about Web 2.0 tools influence your lesson design decisions? In what ways did the technology and media you selected for your lesson enhance the learning opportunities for your students?

Suggested Resources

PRINT RESOURCES

Jenkins, H. (2009). *Confronting the challenges of participatory culture: Media education for the 21st century.* Boston, MA: MIT.

Johnson, L., Adams Becker, S., Cummins, M., Estrada, V., Freeman, A., & Ludgate, H. (2013). *NMC horizon report: 2013 K–12 edition.* Austin, TX: The New Media Consortium.

Kidd, T., & Chen, I. (2009). *Wired for learning: An educator's guide to Web 2.0.* Charlotte, NC: Information Age.

Lanclos, P. (2008). *Weaving Web 2.0 tools into the classroom.* Eugene, OR: Visions Technology in Education.

Paine, S. (2009, May). Profile. *T.H.E. Journal.* Retrieved from http://thejournal.com/articles/2009/05/01/profile--steven-paine.aspx

Richardson, W. (2009). *Blogs, wikis, podcasts, and other powerful web tools for classrooms* (2nd ed.). Thousand Oaks, CA: Corwin.

Solomon, G., & Scrum, L. (2007). *Web 2.0: New tools, new schools.* Eugene, OR: ISTE.

Vossen, G., & Hagemann, S. (2007). *Unleashing Web 2.0: From concepts to creativity.* Burlington, MA: Morgan Kaufmann.

WEB RESOURCES

Web 2.0: Cool Tools for Schools
http://cooltoolsforschools.wikispaces.com
This site offers many types of Web 2.0 tools that teachers have used in their classrooms. Organized by category, such as presentation tools, and by content areas like math and reading, a number of resources are suggested for classroom use.

International Society for Technology in Education
http://iste.org
ISTE is an association focused on improving education through the use of technology in learning, teaching, and administration. ISTE members include teachers, administrators, computer coordinators, information resource managers, and educational technology specialists.

eSchool News
http:///eschoolnews.com
This site offers a convenient way to keep up-to-date electronically with what is going on with technology in schools.

Educause Learning Initiative
http://educause.edu/eli
The Educause Learning Initiative provides information about new directions in technology and how it might be used to facilitate learning. Each spring the organization publishes the Horizon Report, which provides insights into short-, middle-, and long-range technology trends.

Project New Media Literacies
http://newmedialiteracies.org
The MIT New Media Literacies project explores ways to help young people understand the social skills and cultural competencies they need to become participants in a global world.

SELECTION RUBRIC   Web 2.0 and Social Media

Complete an evaluation and add it to your professional development portfolio using the Selection Rubric for Web 2.0 and Social Media.

Search Terms

_____

_____

_____

Title _____

Source/Location _____

©Date _____ Cost _____ Length _____ Minutes _____

Primary User(s) _____

Subject Area _____ Grade Level _____

Instructional Strategies _____

Brief Description

Standards/Outcomes/Objectives

Prerequisites (e.g., prior knowledge, reading ability, vocabulary level)

Strengths

Limitations

Special Features

Name _____ **Date** _____

Rating Area	High Quality	Medium Quality	Low Quality
Alignment with standards, outcomes, and objectives	Standard/outcome/objective addressed and use of technology should enhance student learning.	Standard/outcome/objective partially addressed and use of technology may enhance student learning.	Standard/outcome/objective not addressed and use of technology will likely not enhance student learning.
Accurate and current information	Information correct and does not contain material that is out of date.	Information correct but does contain material that is out of date.	Information is not correct and does contain material that is out of date.
Age-appropriate language	Language used is age appropriate and vocabulary is understandable.	Language used is nearly age appropriate and some vocabulary is above/below student age.	Language used is not age appropriate and vocabulary is clearly inappropriate for student age.
Interest level and engagement	Topic presented so that students are likely to be interested and actively engaged in learning.	Topic presented to interest students most of the time and engage most in learning.	Topic presented so as not to interest students and not engage them in learning.
Technical quality	The material represents best available technology and media.	The material represents technology and media that are good quality, although there are some problems.	The material represents technology and media that are not well prepared and are of very poor quality.
Ease of use (user may be student or teacher)	Material follows easy-to-use patterns with nothing to confuse the user.	Material follows patterns that are easy to follow most of the time, with a few things to confuse the user.	Material follows no patterns and most of the time the user is very confused.
Bias free	There is no evidence of objectionable bias or advertising.	There is little evidence of bias or advertising.	There is much evidence of bias or advertising.
User guide and directions	The user guide is an excellent resource for use in a lesson. Directions should help teachers and students use the material.	The user guide is good resource for use in a lesson. Directions may help teachers and students use the material.	The user guide is poor resource for use in a lesson. Directions do not help teachers and students use the material.
Reading level	Most students can use the web tools to create original pieces that represent learning.	Some students can use the web tools to start original pieces that begin to show their learning.	Most students cannot use the web tools to create original pieces that represent their learning.
Fosters collaboration	The material is presented at an appropriate level so that most students can share information.	The material is presented at a level so that some students can share information.	The material is presented at a level so that few students can share information.
Clarity of organization	The material is presented in such a way that most students are able to use the information.	The material is presented in such a way that some students are able to use the information.	The material is presented in such a way that few students are able to use the information.

Recommended for Classroom Use: _____ Yes _____ No

Ideas for Classroom Use: _____

_____

Achieving Learning at a Distance

Knowledge Outcomes

This chapter addresses ISTE NETS-T 1, 2, and 3.

1. Define distance learning.

2. State a rationale for the use of distance learning at the elementary, middle, and secondary education levels.

3. Explain how audio and video can facilitate distance learning.

4. Describe the characteristics of local area networks (LANs), wide area networks (WANs), intranets, and wireless networks.

5. Discuss five Internet netiquette guidelines for users.

6. Select an example of a copyright concern and explain why it is an important issue.

Goal

Describe distance education and how it can facilitate student learning.

O ne of the greatest advantages offered by modern electronic technology is the ability to instruct without the teacher's direct presence in the classroom. That is, we can both **time shift** our instruction—experience it at some time after the live lesson—and **place shift** our instruction—experience it at some place away from the live teacher (Figure 7.1). The book was the first invention that made it possible to time shift and place shift instruction, a use that continues to the present day.

For more than a century, people in all parts of the world have been able to participate in guided independent study through correspondence courses via the traditional mail system. Learners receive printed lessons, do written assignments, send them to the remote instructor, and get feedback. However, today's technologies now make it possible to experience place-shifted instruction with a stunning array of auditory and visual stimuli that far exceed print-based materials and extend the experience with a rich range of interaction, not only with the instructor but also with other learners. This chapter introduces the foundation of distance-learning concepts and provides general information about delivering instruction at a distance.

As a teacher, you need to be aware of the variety of options discussed in this chapter for facilitating instruction at a distance. Distance education encompasses a broad array of learning opportunities incorporating a selection of technologies to promote learning. You need to be able to select the best technology and media to support your students' learning. You can use the suggestions in this chapter to help you prepare to guide your students who are learning at a distance.

Learning at a Distance

Distance learning has become the popular term to describe learning via telecommunications. The term **telecommunications** embraces a variety of technology and media configurations, including audio, video, and

FIGURE 7.1 Types of Distance Education

Synchronous (Same time-different location)		Blended (Mix of time and location)		Asynchronous (Different time-different location)

Students can use online resources to interact with other students and teachers throughout the district, across the country, and around the world.

text-based resources. What they all have in common is implied in the Greek root word *tele,* which means "at a distance" or "far off"; that is, they are systems for communicating over a distance. As we explore the broad topic of distance learning, we will focus on student learning. Desmond Keegan (1980) identified key elements of a formal definition of distance education, which have not changed with the advent of newer technologies for delivery:

- Physical separation of learners from the teacher
- Organized instructional program
- Telecommunications technology
- Two-way communication

The emphasis on student learning is as important in a distance education setting as it is in a traditional classroom. Successful instructional strategies apply to the same degree in distance settings as they do in the regular classroom. Regardless of the technology used, from live video interactions to text-based discussions, an instructional telecommunication system must perform certain functions to be effective.

It is necessary for you to think about the instructional setting in a new light. Your classroom is now a series of "rooms" connected electronically. Your role may shift to that of facilitator of the learning rather than directly leading the class. You must also keep a watchful eye on the class to be sure no one is falling behind.

With the latest technological advances, your students can become more engaged in learning through interactions, yet it remains your responsibility to organize the instructional experience to encourage interactivity (Simonson, Smaldino, Albright, & Zvacek, 2012). Students, for their part, need to know how to use the distance education technology to communicate with you and with each other using proper communication etiquette.

As you look at these elements of distance education, you begin to see that the 21st century standards and NETS-T relate to the type of knowledge and skill you will need to bring to learning experiences within a distance learning setting. You will need to be prepared to engage your students by:

- Facilitating learning experiences that engage your students
- Modeling and promoting learning and responsibility for independent and collaborative work
- Engaging learners in active participation with you and with each other

The teacher should guide students in their viewing of video information.

When teaching at a distance, many issues need to be considered. Teachers have learned that it involves more than simply taking an existing lesson and teaching it online. There are many aspects that need to be adjusted or changed. You will need to organize and sequence content as it relates to outcomes, know what resources are available to your students, know what experiences your students have had with the distance learning system being used, and know what students need to do to ensure quality learning experiences (Dabbagh & Bannan-Ritland, 2005). These are all essential for you to consider when you are engaging your students in learning experiences, whether they are **blended,** where some of the time your students are in the classroom with you and

Distance Learning

In 2002, Congress revised the distance learning aspects of the copyright law by passing the TEACH Act. It extended fair use into the digital world and acknowledged that the boundaries of teaching space extend beyond the walls of a classroom. The act allows greater liberty to teachers in their use of materials in an online environment, permitting the display and performance of nearly all types of materials (visuals, sculpture, art, music, video, etc.) meeting the following conditions:

- The transmission is an integral part of a systematic, ongoing instructional activity mediated by an instructor.
- The transmission is directly related to and of material assistance in the teaching of content.
- The transmission is solely for and limited to students officially enrolled in the course.
- The teacher informs students that materials used may be subject to copyright protection.
- The institution employs measures to prevent retention of the materials in accessible form by the students for longer than the duration of the course.
- The institution employs measures that limit the transmission of the material to students enrolled in the course and precludes unauthorized student retention and/or redistribution to the extent technologically feasible.

- In order to facilitate digital transmissions, the TEACH Act permits scanning of some materials, but only if the material is not already available in digital form.

Certain specific restrictions are spelled out for use of copyrighted material in distance education:

- There is a time limit on use, comparable to the time the materials would be used in a face-to-face class. One may not continue to use the copyrighted materials beyond the duration of the semester the course is offered nor may the materials be used during another semester without prior permission.
- Teachers may not transmit textbooks, printed materials, or other media (including CDs and DVDs) that are typically purchased or acquired by students.
- Off-air recordings may not be altered from their original content. They may not be combined or merged (physically or electronically) to constitute teaching anthologies or compilations.

For more information, visit the Technology, Education, and Copyright Harmonization (TEACH) Act (2002) website at www.ala.org/washoff/teach.html.

For general information on Copyright, see Chapter 1. Suggested resources (print and web links) on copyright appear at the end of Chapter 1.

other times they are at a distance, or **online,** where your students are always at a distance, even though you might have scheduled meeting times.

One element often overlooked in distance learning is the access students have to resource materials. If you wish to have your students engaging in research or working together in a problem-solving or collaborative activity, it is critical that they have access to related materials, for example, books in the media center or Internet resources. You may need to change particular types of hands-on activities or make special arrangements for materials to be sent to your students. Your students at a distance location should not be at a learning disadvantage because of limited resources. You can work closely with your school library media specialist to ensure that your students have equal access to the materials essential for the learning experience. Although the Web has a wealth of materials, there are still some courses in which resources for students are not readily available on the Web or copyright issues do not allow using the Web to provide those resources. Your school library media specialist should be aware of the copyright issues and be able to help you provide access to materials.

STRATEGIES AND APPROACHES

The emphasis on student learning, whether in a teacher-led or student-centered environment, is as important in a distance education setting as it is in a traditional classroom. Regardless of the technology used or whether the lesson takes place in actual time by computer conferencing or through time-delayed interactions, an instructional telecommunication system must perform certain functions to be effective:

- *Information presentation.* A standard element for any lesson is presentation of information involving not only teacher-led strategies, but also procedures within student-centered approaches. Common examples include the following:

  - *Teacher presentation and demonstration, such as a prepared video on how to complete a specific task that students can view on their own.* In a blended learning setting, you could assign the instructional video in preparation for the hands-on class activities when your students meet in class.

  - *Student presentation or small-group work, which might be a small group of students who report their solution to a case study they investigate.* Your students can lead a topic discussion with the rest of the class and, as facilitator, you can provide support and guidance while they prepare their questions or discussion points.

  - *Class resources (e.g., handouts, correspondence, study materials), like a set of articles you have put on e-reserve with the school's library media center.* Your students can use these materials to provide them with the background they need for a live "chat" or illustrations that will help them see the images about the topic within an audio teleconference.

  - *Live or recorded voice, music, and other sounds.* For example, you might have an author or content expert prepare a podcast about why she wrote the story, to which your students can listen before they have an online discussion with that person.

  - *Full-motion images (video, CD, DVD), which could be archived news video for students to use in their study of historical events.* Your students can create their own video to share an idea with the rest of the class or as a means to demonstrate to you that they have learned the concept you are assessing.

- *Practice with feedback.* We know that the most learning takes place when learners are participating actively and mentally processing the material. Teachers induce activity in various ways, such as the following:

  - *Question-and-answer activities (carried out during or after the lesson).* You will want your questions to engage your students at a critical thinking level of inquiry. You can help your students improve their ability to think critically and creatively through additional questions you might provide following the instruction. Your students can generate questions they can use with an expert or to prepare for an in-depth inquiry into a topic.

  - *Discussion activities (during the class or as homework).* You will want your discussions to be engaging and allow your students to bring in additional information from resources they have located. In an online discussion, you can observe the discussion and add comments or redirect your students as the discussion proceeds.

  - *Testing.* A test can help your students recognize areas where they need to delve into the topic more to understand the details of the issue. Or, a test can help you assess the level of understanding your students have about the topic. By seeing how they are doing with the content, you can make adjustments in your instruction and help them see where they need to focus.

  - *Structured group activities (e.g., role-playing or games).* When you design online activities, you want to be certain that everyone understands what is expected of him or her. Keeping the instructions clear will help your students get started. Your observations of their progress will help you guide them when necessary.

  - *Group projects.* You can facilitate learning by bringing students together in groups to complete designated tasks or projects. At times you might let them form their own groups, other times you might organize the groups based on what you have learned about them. You can make yourself part of each group to check their progress, helping them in their work by adding comments as they work together.

- *Peer tutoring.* Your students can help each other to understand concepts and, in the process, learn the information better themselves. You can observe the tutoring and see how well students are learning the material.

- *Access to learning resources.* Lessons and courses are usually structured with the assumption that learners will spend time outside class working individually or in small groups with the material, doing homework, projects, papers, and the like. You will need to be certain your students can get to the resources in order for them to be successful in their learning experiences. External learning resources include the following:

  - *Text materials (e.g., textbooks, supplementary readings, worksheets).* Text materials are assets in any learning experience, so that your students will have the information to help guide them in their learning. In an online instructional setting, providing additional readings or worksheets will help your students as they gain confidence in working independently.

  - *Audiovisual materials (e.g., CDs, DVDs, podcasts, online resources).* Similar to printed materials, these materials support students' learning experiences. For example, you could have the author of the textbook provide a short video presentation of the book at the beginning of the learning experience.

  - *Web-based resources (e.g., for online searches).* You can find quite an array of web-based materials for your students to use. Some webpages are interactive, which give your students additional learning experiences. Other web resources contain detailed up-to-date information that supplements your instruction.

  - *Kits (e.g., for laboratory experiments or to examine specimens of real objects).* Subjects such as science are complicated without the necessary hands-on experiences. Providing your students with the appropriate materials to use for an experiment or the specimen to examine closely provides your students with the opportunity to gain in-depth knowledge of the topic.

  - *Library materials (e.g., original source documents).* It is essential for you to consider your students' access to library materials. You want to be certain that all your students will have the ability to find the materials that will assist them in completing tasks and assignments. Federal Resources for Educational Excellence (**www.free1.ed.gov**) provides a wealth of information from a number of public agencies at no cost.

As in a regular classroom, various technology, media, and materials can be employed in a distance learning setting (Figure 7.2). Each of the various telecommunication systems used in distance learning has strengths and limitations. The characteristics of the systems are discussed at greater length in the following sections of this chapter.

TYPES OF TECHNOLOGY RESOURCES

There are an assortment of distance learning resources used to support student learning: audio, video, and text-based resources, which we will describe briefly for you. All three types of resources can be used both **synchronously**, when all the participants are together at the same time, and **asynchronously**, when the participants are not working on the activities at the same time. When using any of these resources, you should

FIGURE 7.2 **Examples of Media Used in Distance Education**

Audio	Video	Text
Audio teleconference	Television	Bulletin board posting
Podcasting	Vidcasting	Correspondence (email/mail)
Audio recordings (tape or digital)	Online video	Blog/wiki

consider copyright issues, which you can read more about in the "Copyright Concerns" feature in this chapter.

Audio-based Technology. Audio has a rich history of facilitating instruction at a distance. Radio was one of the first technologies used to deliver education remotely. Although not used much today in the United States, there are still instructional applications of radio in some international settings, often in rural areas where Internet connections are very limited resources.

The key to successful use of audio in instruction is to consider what resources are available to students at various locations and to be aware that sometimes audio may be sufficient to convey the learning experience. To use audio as a viable option for delivery of information, resources such as podcasts can be available to students for individual use or a conference call can be established among members of a class as means for two-way communication.

An **audio teleconference**—a live, interactive conversation using telephone lines, satellites, or the Internet—connects people at different locations via audio. One issue associated with relying only on audio transmissions is the lack of visual information. However, audio can be supplemented by providing visual information such as handouts that can be attached to emails, or a PowerPoint presentation provided within a course management tool such as Blackboard, Edmodo, or Moodle.

Video-based Technology. Similar to audio, video has been available in many formats for distance education use for years. There are two primary types of video transmissions. **One-way video** is when the visual and auditory information is delivered to learners with limited opportunities for immediate connections with the teacher or source of the information. You might prepare a presentation using PowerPoint or Prezi to send to your students and then engage with them in an online chat at a different time. Or, you might have your students watch a National Geographic special on earthquakes and have them prepare a paper on what they learned. In both cases, the information is provided with little exchange between the students and the source of the information at the time of the presentation. And, because it is one-way, the students do not have to view the video at the same time or in the same location. In the example of the PowerPoint presentation, students can view it when they have time. For the television special, your students might be at home watching it with family.

Videoconferencing can be designed so that the teacher selects the image to be shown to all the students during the discussion.

Two-way video is when visual and auditory information are exchanged across the system between learners and the teacher synchronously. This is also referred to as **videoconferencing.** Two-way video is often preferred, since everyone can see each other and the interactions among the participants are easier and more immediate. When learners are new to distance learning experiences, two-way video makes it easier to become familiar with learning in a setting where the teacher and students are separated. You might decide that your students will benefit from engaging with the author of a novel they are reading. You can help them prepare by guiding them to think about what they would like to know about the author and more specifically about the book and the characters. At the time of the exchange, your students can prompt the author with their questions and share their views of the book. Because everyone can see and hear each other, the experience is enriched for all the participants. Or, you might want to share the instruction of a topic with a colleague from another region of the state. Together you plan your session, you bring the classes together in the two-way video setting, and you offer a new learning experience for all your students.

Text-based Technology. Text-based technology is instruction delivered electronically using computer-based, or online, media. For online learning, students need to access the Internet to obtain the materials through a network. However, online learning involves not just accessing information (e.g., locating webpages), but also assisting learners with specific outcomes (e.g., meeting objectives). In addition to delivering instruction via online resources, the teacher can monitor performance and report learner progress.

The uses of online learning in education are increasing. Your students no longer need to rely only on textbooks; they now have access to educational materials located far beyond the walls of the school building. You and your students can obtain information housed in many distant, physically inaccessible libraries around the world! Resources once beyond the dreams of all but the most affluent are readily available to everyone.

You and your students can enhance classroom learning by accessing information from an array of sources (databases, libraries, special interest groups) and by communicating via computer with other students or with experts in a particular field of study and exchanging data. Activities such as the Monarch Butterfly Journey North conducted by the Annenberg Foundation **(www.learner.org/jnorth/monarch)** and the GeoBee Challenge of the National Geographic Society **(www.nationalgeographic.com/geobee)** make it possible for your students to reap the benefits of connecting to a national network of students, teachers, and scientists to investigate a variety of topics.

Your students can also access electronic documents to enrich their study. Students can actively participate because online learning provides an interactive learning environment. Your students can hyperlink digital information to their papers and projects, making them "living" documents connected to other segments of their work or to additional documents or visual resources.

Because computers have the ability to deliver information in any medium (including text, video, and audio recordings of voice and music), the computer has become a boundless library. Your students are able to communicate instantly with text, picture, voice, data, and two-way audio/video, and the resulting interactions are changing the roles of both students and teachers. You can now be separated geographically from your students, and students can learn from other students in classrooms all over the world.

You might recognize that the content to be studied is very complex, but you feel that you don't need to meet daily with your students. You schedule specific class times during the week. For the other times during the week, you prepare activities online for your students to complete between class meetings. You will want to be certain to engage your students in challenging online learning experiences or collaborative experiences, such as small-group work, to facilitate their learning. You could use the non-class time for your students to learn about aspects of the topic online and use the class time when they are together for active hands-on activities where your students apply their knowledge. You might be teaching a topic that allows your students to complete their learning in an authentic setting. For some of the time, you meet with your students online via video or audio or engage in a text-based discussion. And, part of the time, your students are engaged in an authentic activity in a setting in which you can observe them at a distance, communicate with the person supervising them, and connect classroom knowledge with the actual application. Your role is to facilitate their active learning during that face-to-face time and to connect their knowledge with applications.

CRITICAL ISSUES

There are many important issues associated with distance learning, especially when using the Internet. They include security, monitoring student use, acceptable use policies, and netiquette.

ASSURE Classroom Case Study Reflection

Review the ASSURE Classroom Case Study and video at the beginning of the chapter. Explain how distance learning technology is helping Mr. Chun's students learn history. How does Mr. Chun support learning through the use of information presentation, practice with feedback, and access to learning resources?

Online Learning

Frequently, unauthorized copies of copyrighted works are posted on a website without the knowledge of the copyright owner. Recently the authors found the ASSURE model on five websites without attribution to its source. The casual observer would assume it was developed by the organization on whose website it was found. Instead, each of the cases involved a serious violation of copyright law!

Observe the following guidelines for online use of copyrighted materials:

- Contrary to popular opinion, *all* material on the Internet is copyrighted unless stated otherwise. It is copyrighted even if it does *not* display the copyright symbol.
- Email is considered an original work, fixed in a tangible medium of expression, that is covered by copyright. It can legally be read, but not legally forwarded or copied for instructional purposes, except under fair use. You can make one copy for your personal use. It is recommended that you not forward any email without permission, in consideration of both copyright and the Privacy Act. However, you may quote excerpts and report the "gist" of the message. For example, if a teacher has sent you an original poem, which is automatically copyrighted, and you forward it to a friend, then you have definitely violated *both* copyright law and the Privacy Act (adapted from Becker, 2003).
- Downloading an article from a newspaper's website, making copies, and distributing them to your students prior to a class discussion on the topic is permissible following the current photocopying guidelines, which permit making multiple copies for classroom use. The exception would be individually bylined, copyrighted articles, or articles from a source specifically designed for the educational market (e.g., *Scholastic Magazine*). Such articles *cannot* be copied legally for class distribution (adapted from Becker, 2003).
- You cannot post students' essays, poems, or other works on the school website unless you have permission of the students and their parents or guardians.
- Always link to the home page rather than a location within a website. In general, linking to another website is not viewed as a copyright infringement. However, it does offer the potential of becoming a copyright issue. If the link takes the user to the body of an author's work, and the initial website does not inform users they are being taken to another site, this may falsely give the impression that one is still on a page within the original website being viewed, thereby not giving credit to the linked site (Becker, 2003).
- Downloading and/or file sharing of video, audio, and other works is considered copyright infringement unless authorized by the copyright law or the owner of the work.

Educators should treat copyrighted materials from the Internet the same way they do print formats. Because the copyright law is still muddled, the best guideline is to always obtain permission. It is usually not that difficult. When in doubt, ask!

For additional information regarding copyright, refer to the "Copyright Concerns: Copyright Law" section in Chapter 1.

Security. Your students should be instructed not to give out information such as their phone numbers, addresses, or other personal information over the Internet. Students have been contacted and even harmed by unscrupulous individuals. It may be wise for your students to give their school's address for correspondence if they need to provide such information. Also, you must have parental permission to post children's photos and written work, such as essays, poems, and artistic creations, on the Web.

The Center for Education and Research in Information Assurance and Security (CERIAS) focuses on multidisciplinary research and education about information security. The organization is concerned with supporting educators on issues of privacy, ethics, and management of information. Exploring issues such as confidentiality of student records, privacy of information, and protection of students while they work online are important considerations. This organization provides guidelines for educators to establish policies within their schools to protect students, teachers, and the school community (contact them at **www.cerias.purdue.edu**).

Any time your students encounter an inappropriate contact while working online, they should inform you quickly. Your school should have a policy in place about addressing such an interaction. You will want to spend some time with your students to understand what it means to be bullied or approached by someone. Just as you would discuss such actions that might happen on school grounds or on the way to school, you will want to ensure your students understand cyberbullying and cyberstalking.

Monitoring Student Use. Teachers and parents must monitor students' Internet use to ensure that their behavior is appropriate and to discourage them from exploring inappropriate material either deliberately or accidentally. The amount and level of monitoring is often based on the age of the students—younger students *may* need more monitoring than older students. Your final decisions about monitoring should be made in conjunction with parents and school administrators. Also, if one of your students encounters information or visuals that are inappropriate, that student should feel comfortable letting you know about it. Software can assist with monitoring student access to information. For example, Snapture software allows you to prevent students from going to sites that are "off limits." The software makes it possible for you to "copy" sites and save them on the local computer hard drive; in this way, students simulate visiting the Web but are not actually connected.

Close supervision is essential. There is no organization or agency controlling activity on all computer networks. It is important for you to work with your students' parents to understand their responsibilities regarding student access to information outside the school setting. Control is in the hands of individuals; consequently, students may access questionable materials. Schools and libraries are required to have an Internet filtering system installed on their networks. Software such as NetNanny or Content Barrier is available for home use to prohibit access to topics specified by a parent.

Acceptable Use Policy. Agreements among students, parents/guardians, and the school administration outlining what is considered proper use of the Internet by all parties involved, called **acceptable use policies (AUPs),** have been developed by most schools. Check to see if your school has such a policy.

The policy usually includes a statement that the school will do what it can to control access to inappropriate information, that students will accept responsibility for not accessing such information, and that parents understand the possibility that children may access such information in spite of the school's efforts. All parties sign the document agreeing that they have read and will abide by the policy. Most states' departments of education have generated resources to assist educators in developing AUPs for their schools. For additional information on this topic, go to the Web Resources at the end of this chapter.

Netiquette. There are informal rules for appropriate behavior on the Internet. If the Internet is the information superhighway, these are the rules of the road. Referred to as **netiquette,** the following rules apply to email, texting, and to other interactions on the Web:

- Keep your message short and simple. Try to limit your message to one screen. Think before you write. Make it brief, descriptive, and to the point.
- Identify yourself as the sender somewhere in the communication, including your name and school address. Not all Internet addresses clearly identify the sender.
- Double check the address or URL before sending a message.
- When replying to a message, include the pertinent portions of the original message.
- Don't write anything you would not want somebody other than the receiver to read. Email can be intercepted or forwarded.
- Check spelling, grammar, and punctuation. Use lowercase letters except for proper names and beginnings of sentences. When texting, use common conventions where appropriate.
- Be sensitive to others. Treat other people with respect and courtesy, especially in reference to social, cultural, and ethnic differences.

- Don't use sarcasm. It often falls flat and doesn't come across as you intended.
- Be careful with humor. It is a double-edged sword. The reader doesn't have the benefit of your facial expression, body language, or tone of voice. You can use **emoticons** or email body language, such as ;) for a wink or :(for a frown, but this type of humor doesn't communicate as well as being there.
- Cooperate and share. Consider yourself a guest on the system just as if you were a guest in someone's home. Make an effort to share only pertinent information. In exchange for help and information you receive, be willing to answer questions and to share your resources.
- Carefully consider copyright. Just because something can be copied electronically doesn't mean it should be distributed without permission. Unless stated otherwise, *all* material on the Internet is copyrighted (see "Copyright Concerns" in this chapter).
- Be alert for obscenity. Laws governing obscenity apply to messages on the Internet. Moreover, even material that is not deemed legally obscene may still be inappropriate for school-age children!

Advantages of Distance Learning

- *Variety of media.* Distance learning is a versatile means of delivering information to learners around the world with a variety of media, including text, audio, graphics, animation, video, and downloadable software.
- *Up-to-date information.* Until recently, students were limited to the resources in their school buildings. Now, however, with the ability to connect to resources in the community and around the world, students can access current information.
- *Idea exchange.* Students can engage in "conversation" with experts in specific fields of study. Special speakers who can augment a class discussion or provide access to an area of study help students advance their learning.
- *Convenient communication.* Students in various locations can share ideas. They can "speak" to each other at different times and respond at their own convenience, based on the electronic record of their exchanges.
- *Interactive.* All participants get the same message, and the same interactivity in talking to the instructor or the other learners.
- *Extra/advanced resources.* Distance learning expands the opportunities for smaller schools, as well as for individuals participating in home schooling. Students who need additional challenges in their study or have moved beyond what is available in their school can access extra coursework that allows them to continue to advance in their learning.
- *Remediation/course recovery.* Distance learning expands the opportunities for students who are in need of supplementary instruction. Students who have fallen behind due to illness or other factors can enroll in distance education courses to continue their education.

Limitations of Distance Learning

- *Inappropriate material.* One concern is that some of the topics, especially on the Internet, are *not* appropriate for students. For example, tobacco and alcohol ads appear on the Internet along with games and music kids enjoy. Students can find their way, innocently enough, into topics that are inappropriate or into unsafe environments.
- *Copyright.* Because information is so readily accessible, it is easy for an individual to quickly download a file and illegally appropriate it. Thus, students may turn in a paper or project that is "cut and pasted" and is not their own work.
- *Finding information.* It is estimated that several thousand new websites are added to the Internet every day. Because this growth makes finding information more difficult, teachers

need to work with the school media specialist to help students learn effective search strategies. To assist in information retrieval, several commercial companies and universities provide search engines that follow web links to return results matching your query.

- *Support.* Without good technical support and thoughtful management, distance learning can be frustrating for the learner and the teacher. The teacher may have designed quality instruction, but if the technology is not working properly, the learner will find it difficult to access the information. It would be beneficial to have technical support as part of the delivery options for students at a distance.

- *Lack of quality control.* Students need to be critical thinkers and readers who know how to evaluate information. Everything posted on the Internet is not fact. Anybody can post anything on the Web, including unsubstantiated, erroneous, or untruthful information.

- *Cost.* It is expensive to establish a quality distance learning program. For the learner, many of the costs for Internet access are not apparent. To be effective, a program requires a large-capacity computer connected to the Internet for a file server. The design of the instruction requires not only the instructor's knowledge of content, but also the hardware and software for delivery and the technical support that is necessary to ensure success.

- *Intimidation.* Lack of experience with this type of communication technology may make some learners less willing to participate.

- *Limited experience using the systems.* Many teachers and students are unfamiliar with interactive learning systems.

Integrating Distance Resources into Learning

Distance learning options continue to expand, from whole courses or programs to enhanced classroom activities, as does the amount of information about topics of interest.

VIRTUAL PUBLIC SCHOOLS

A growing number of **virtual public schools (VPS)** using the Internet for delivery of instruction offer courses or whole programs of study (Wood, 2005). The VPS are typically offered as state-level initiatives in which students can access courses that might not be available to them at their local schools or take advanced placement classes from other high schools or from colleges and universities anywhere in the world. It is possible to obtain a high school or college diploma without ever setting foot in a classroom. Many software applications (e.g., WebCT, Blackboard) provide both ease of access to the instruction and resources for the instructor and students for successful study online.

The following issues need to be addressed by anyone wishing to venture into this area of academic study:

- Credentials of the institution offering the degree
- Quality and rigor of the courses
- Costs associated with online courses, such as equipment requirements, online charges, and tuition

CONNECTING WITH EMAIL

Text communication between individuals through **electronic mail (email)** can be integrated into lessons and used by students to gather information from and ask questions of individuals beyond the school walls (e.g., other students and experts). For example, during a unit on

TECHNOLOGY FOR ALL LEARNERS

Distance Learning Resources

Students in our classrooms have a variety of learning needs. The following examples show ways that your learners can use distance learning resources to help them with their learning.

For students who have visual disabilities or difficulty reading information on a webpage, various design guidelines can be helpful. When including graphics or images, text descriptions can be a resource. For example, along with the image of a feline, add the word *cat* nearby. Avoid using complex tables with many columns. Computer text readers read across one entire line at a time instead of reading each column separately. On hyperlinks, use meaningful terms rather than a graphic or "click here" link that tells nothing about the link. Additional information is available at the World Wide Web Consortium (W3C) Accessibility Initiative (**www.w3.org**). Bobby (**www.cast.org/ bobby**) is a site that will analyze webpages for accessibility to people with disabilities.

Young students who would like to learn more about using the Internet safely can join WoogiWorld (**www.woogiworld.com**). Through games and activities, students are guided through protocols that advise them about being safe when engaging in pursuits on the Internet. Each child must have parental permission to use the site before the child is allowed full access to all the resources. Parents are given information about their child's user name, password, and types of activities available.

Students who wish to advance their knowledge and be challenged in their thinking can use the Internet in a variety of ways. A Different Place (**www.adifferentplace.org**) provides students with activities and challenging studies in a variety of math, science, and language arts topics. In addition, there are resources for teachers and parents who wish to engage students.

weather, your students can gather weather data (temperatures, rainfall, and wind direction) from students in other geographic areas. They can also request weather maps from the local TV meteorologist, which can be sent as attachments to email, or use the NOAA website for recent satellite photos (Figure 7.3). Experts from the National Weather Service can be contacted for the answers to specific questions. Of course, you should always make any necessary arrangements in advance.

Your students can also use email to gather information for individual projects. For example, middle school students investigating careers can contact individuals in those professions for answers to their questions. The products of the students' investigation can be job reports to be shared with the class either as oral presentations or written documents.

One growing use of electronic learning at the PK–12 level promotes writing skills by connecting students with electronic pen pals or "key pals." For example, one teacher connected her elementary students with students in a language arts methods class at a university across the state (see "Taking a Look at Technology Integration: Key Pals"). Her students exchanged email in which the university teacher candidates helped the younger ones with their writing. Both groups benefited from this experience. The younger students learned ways to improve their writing, and the college teacher candidates learned about working with children. This is an example of how mentors can be linked with students to help them learn about a variety of topics.

Systems have also been set up that allow students from different countries, even those speaking different languages, to learn about each other's cultures through computer-mediated communications. To address any language barriers, the computer can be set up to provide language translations.

FIGURE 7.3 NOAA

Source: www.noaa.gov

Your students can participate in projects conducted with classes in other locations, allowing them to plan and produce projects collaboratively. Examples include sharing local history with students in other geographic locations and collaborating with students in different classes to solve complex mathematical problems.

TAKING A LOOK AT TECHNOLOGY INTEGRATION

Key Pals

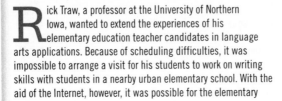 Rick Traw, a professor at the University of Northern Iowa, wanted to extend the experiences of his elementary education teacher candidates in language arts applications. Because of scheduling difficulties, it was impossible to arrange a visit for his students to work on writing skills with students in a nearby urban elementary school. With the aid of the Internet, however, it was possible for the elementary students to send their stories to their university "key pals" for review. The children had an exciting new audience for their writing, and the university teacher candidates had an opportunity to learn about working with emerging writers. Dr. Traw and the classroom teacher provided guidance to the college teacher candidates in techniques for assisting the young children with their writing.

INTEGRATING WEBQUESTS

Although students can access a rich array of information on the Web, their searches often use random or low-level thinking skills. With **WebQuests** you can help your students access the Web effectively for gathering information in student-centered learning activities within the classroom (Dodge, 1999). Developed by Bernie Dodge at San Diego State University, WebQuests have been a longtime teacher favorite for infusing Internet resources into the school's curriculum to make a **hybrid,** or mixed, learning environment. A WebQuest is an inquiry-oriented simulation activity designed with specific learning outcomes in mind, in which some or all of the information that students interact with comes from resources on the Internet. Students follow a series of steps to gather information meaningful to the task:

1. *Introduction.* A scenario points to key issues or concepts to prepare the students to ask questions.
2. *Task.* Students identify issues or problems and form questions for the WebQuest.
3. *Process.* In groups, students assume roles and begin to identify the procedures they will follow to gather information to answer their questions.
4. *Sources.* Resources that will be investigated in the WebQuest are identified by the teacher and students. This is one area where the teacher helps to provide the links to websites and to ensure students have access to other support materials.
5. *Conclusion.* This is the end of the WebQuest, but it invites students to continue to investigate issues or problems. WebQuests often end with an evaluation of the process students used, along with benchmarks for achievement.

WebQuests can be applied to many types of lessons and information sources:

- Monitoring current events for social studies
- Science activities, such as tracking weather and studying space probes to other planets
- Databases of information for expository writing assignments
- Mathematics puzzles, which require logical thinking
- Discussion groups with online exchange of information
- Job banks and résumé services for practice in job-seeking activities

TAKING A LOOK AT TECHNOLOGY INTEGRATION

WebQuest

Sherri Wright wanted to give her fifth graders a chance to practice their literacy, technology, and 21st century learning skills. Because of the daily schedule, it was difficult for her to develop a series of social studies units, but her idea was to engage her students in their inquiry into social studies topics. She decided a set of WebQuests was the way to make it possible for her students to investigate important concepts and give them opportunities to practice their skills. With the students, she generated a set of what, how, and why questions. These questions served as the foundation for her students' inquiry. She gave the students four topics: slavery, the Revolutionary War, the Louisiana Purchase, and the moon mission. Her students decided which of the topics to study, thus forming their collaborative groups. Ms. Wright and the school's library media specialist provided the students with print and Internet resources to investigate their topic. During the 4-week period, Ms. Wright met with her student groups to discuss their progress and to help guide them in their search for information. At the end of the 4 weeks, each group presented to their classmates the results of their inquiry, using Prezi and handouts. Their presentations had to be interactive and engaging for the rest of the class with activities and questions. Because they were so successful in their inquiry, the students asked if they could "show off" to their parents and repeat their presentations for them. In addition, Ms. Wright required her students to complete a set of reflection questions that focused on their collaboration, communication, inquiry and literacy skills, and their use of technology.

CONNECTING WITH COMPUTER CONFERENCING

You can establish opportunities for your students to learn from experts or to engage in collaborative activities with other students in a variety of settings. An example of the depth of this type of experience is the STEM Teen Read program at Northern Illinois University that brings middle school students together to explore the science in the young adult science fiction literature they are reading. The project brings together middle-school students who are interested in exploring the science behind the stories they are reading. The author of the novel and experts in the science used in the story are brought together electronically with the students to discuss the story and the ethics behind the issues within the novel. You can engage your students in studies of literature, mathematics, social sciences, and the arts through similar types of activities.

CONNECTING WITH PARENTS

Communications with parents can be enhanced if they have Internet access. You can send general information to the parents of your students or specific information or questions can be addressed to an individual student's parents or guardians. Class webpages can inform parents of homework assignments, parent meetings, or materials needed for a special project. For those parents without Internet access, you will need to employ written correspondence or use the telephone.

CONNECTING WITH OTHER TEACHERS

You can also use email to share ideas with other teachers in your content area or who teach the same grade level. Lesson plans can be sent as attachments or placed on the school's or district's server. Questions can be asked of an individual teacher or a group of teachers (e.g., all physics teachers in a state). Another means for electronic sharing of ideas is a **blog,** which looks a lot like an online discussion board. Blogs written by experts can provide teachers and students with access to information. Teachers can also assist students in developing personal blogs to enhance their ability to exchange ideas. One word of caution when beginning this type

TAKING A LOOK AT TECHNOLOGY INTEGRATION

GLOBE

Networking Students, Teachers, and Scientists

The GLOBE program (**www.globe.gov**) is a program that uses technology to promote scientific inquiry and environmentalism. To participate, students send scientific data they collect over the Internet to the GLOBE network. In return, the class receives information about the data they sent, as well as how those data fit into the larger global picture. Students from over 100 countries participate in GLOBE projects.

Professionals from many disciplines participate and use collected GLOBE data to advance scientific knowledge of environmental issues. For example, scientists use the valuable student-collected data to research global changes. Students benefit as well, learning about data collection, scientific protocols, and databases, in addition to opportunities to chat with scientists and other experts worldwide.

of electronic community: As stated throughout this book, you need to prepare your students regarding their online safety, advising them not to reveal personal information in any communication. In addition, your school's acceptable use policy will also assist you in ensuring your students will engage in ethical use of the online resources.

CONNECTING WITH COMMUNITIES

A number of cities have created websites that involve a broad cross section of the community, including schools, businesses, local government, and social agencies. This is another example of how the artificial wall between the classroom and the world beyond is dissolving, making it possible for students and teachers to access information and people from every imaginable source (see "Taking a Look at Technology Integration: GLOBE"). You can take your students on a virtual field trip to the local zoo or botanical garden. They can meet with a specialist in waste management as part of their study of their carbon footprint. You will want to explore your community and region to identify resources that will blend in to your curriculum.

Also, many museums and zoos are creating online "tours" of their exhibits. Your students can visit the Guggenheim and view the collections while learning more about the artists. They can visit the Natural History Museum or the Smithsonian National Zoological Park and participate in activities designed to help them learn. In addition, an increasing number of online journals and magazines are being published, either as supplements to existing print versions or as entirely new efforts. Moreover, most major publishers have put their catalogs on the Web, making it easy to locate and order books, software, and other products. Many publishers are willing to make their actual products available online, usually as trial packages that "dissolve" within a certain period of time (usually 30 days). However, the continuing prevalence of illegal copying and distribution of materials makes some publishers wary of providing complete and unlimited access to software and files.

COURSE CONNECTIONS

School districts or schools often purchase or develop instructional modules that can be sent over a restricted school-only network. This method of delivery is used to provide students with remediation or to enhance learning opportunities with the latest version of materials. Updating these materials is relatively easy because the core set of digital material can be electronically modified and made immediately available, whereas in the past, revisions often required

Classroom Case Study Reflection

▶ Review the ASSURE Classroom Case Study and video at the beginning of the chapter. What kinds of learning experiences can Mr. Chun offer his students? How can he capitalize on the types of learning opportunities to ensure all his students have access to the information?

shipping printed materials or computer disks to schools. Electronic learning provides flexibility to students as well because they may study materials at any time and at any location. Students can also take tests over the intranet. Once the answers are in the database, they are scored and the results are made available immediately to students and the teacher. Online learning is very useful when learners are geographically dispersed and instruction is updated frequently.

Network Resources

It is common knowledge that computers can be used to connect students to people and resources outside of the classroom. Once you connect computers in ways that enable people to communicate and share information, you have a **network.** Networks connect schools, homes, libraries, organizations, and businesses so that students, families, and professionals can access or share information and instruction instantly in several ways.

TYPES OF NETWORKS

LAN. The simplest of all networks is a **local area network (LAN),** which connects computers within a limited area, normally a classroom, building, or laboratory. These networks connect individual computers to one another to permit exchange of files and other resources (Figure 7.4).

A LAN relies on a centralized computer called a **file server** that "serves" all the other computers connected to it. A computer lab is often itself a LAN because all the computers

FIGURE 7.4 Typical Local Area Network (LAN)

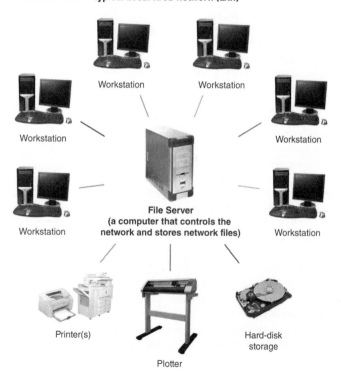

Workstation · Workstation · Workstation · Workstation · Workstation · Workstation

File Server
(a computer that controls the network and stores network files)

Printer(s) · Plotter · Hard-disk storage

in the lab are connected to a single file server, usually tucked away in a closet or other out-of-the-way space. Whole buildings can also be connected to a local area network, usually with a single computer that is located in the office or media center, which serves as the school's file server. Through a LAN, all of the classrooms in a school can have access to the school's collection of software. Many schools also allow teachers and students to save their computer work in personalized folders on the server, which is very useful when multiple students use one computer. It also allows teachers access to their materials, such as a PowerPoint presentations, while in the computer lab.

Within a school, LANs can also reduce a technology coordinator's workload, which might otherwise include installing programs, inventorying software, and other such tasks. Coordinators can then spend more time working with teachers and students rather than with machines and software. For example, the media center can store its catalog of materials on the file server, giving teachers and students easy access to the information available on a certain topic.

WAN. Networks that extend beyond the walls of a room or building are called **wide area networks (WANs)**. A campus or district-wide network connecting all buildings via a cable or fiber system is one such example. In this arrangement, the buildings are linked to a centralized computer that serves as the host for all the software used in common. Even though a WAN can connect computers over a wide geographic area (across a city, state, or even a country), it is most often used for smaller configurations, such as connecting the buildings within a school system.

As the name implies, a **wireless network** connects computers without wire. Instead it relies on radio frequency, microwave, or infrared technology that depends on a base station for connection to the network. Such networks use transmitters placed inside the room, throughout the building, or across a campus area and operate in the same manner as hardwired networks. Some cities have installed wireless networks in their downtown areas. Wireless networks omit the need for cabling, which can be costly to install, particularly in older buildings. Computers are no longer bound to workstations. Laptops may be used anywhere within the room, building, or campus area and still have access to the Internet.

Intranet. A special type of network called an **intranet** is used internally by a school or organization. It is a proprietary or closed network that connects multiple sites across the state, within the country, or around the world. Systems connected to an intranet are private and accessible only by individuals within a given school or organization.

Intranets provide internal networks for schools. Intranets are a way of increasing communication, collaboration, and information dissemination within schools where divisions, departments, and workgroups might each use a different **computer platform** (hardware and operating system), or where users work in geographically distant locations. Even though an intranet may be connected to a larger network (the Internet, for example), a software package called a **firewall** prevents external users from accessing the internal network, while allowing internal users to access external networks (Figure 7.5).

FIGURE 7.5   Firewalls: A firewall protects an internal network (intranet) from external users but allows internal users to access external networks (Internet).

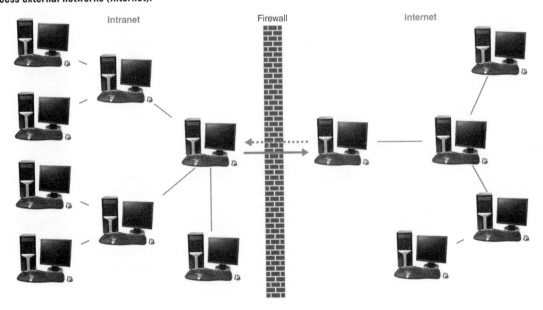

FIGURE 7.6   Internet Service Providers

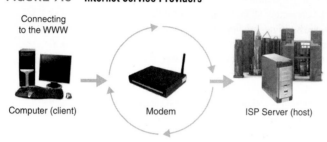

Connecting
to the WWW

Computer (client)   Modem   ISP Server (host)

Internet. The **Internet** is a global interconnection of computer networks with a broad collection of millions of computer networks serving billions of people around the world. Any individual on the Internet can communicate with anyone else on the Internet. Users can access any information, regardless of the type of computer they have, because of standard protocols that allow all computers to communicate with each other. Most information is shared without charge except for whatever access fee is required to maintain an account with an **Internet service provider (ISP).** Many schools provide Internet access to teachers and students at no charge.

Both telephone companies and television cable companies provide high-speed access to the Internet. **Integrated services digital network (ISDN)** lines provide speeds up to five times that of regular phone lines. A **digital subscriber line (DSL)** provides even faster access—up to 30 times that of a standard phone line. TV cable companies also offer high-speed service through a **cable modem.** All of these access services are popular with the home consumer (Figure 7.6).

Special communication software connects the computer to a telecommunication service. When you make a connection to the Internet, you enlist the help of four communication services: your computer, the ISP, the server (host computer), and the telecommunications network (communication software and a modem). Your computer (the client) runs the communications software. Your modem and communications software provide an open path between your computer and your ISP. The ISP provides you a link to the Internet.

Many educational and commercial organizations' networks are developing connections to the Internet called **gateways** or **portals,** designed to provide access to many Internet services. The maze of connections is largely "transparent" to the user. Users just log on to their computer (enter the computer system, often with a special password for privacy), connect to their networking service or ISP, and begin to exchange information.

Complicating information retrieval is the fact that the Internet does not operate hierarchically. There are no comprehensive directory trees or indexes for Internet resources. There is no Library of Congress cataloging scheme or Dewey Decimal system. You can consider the Internet a library where every shelf is labeled "Miscellaneous." Finding one interesting service or item of information is no guarantee that you're on the right track to others. In fact, most of the Internet's resources are in little cul-de-sacs on the network, not linked in any predictable way to other, similar resources. To find information on the Internet you must use **search engines,** programs that identify websites containing user-entered keywords or phrases (see "Examples of Media: Search Engines for Kids").

THE WORLD WIDE WEB

The **World Wide Web (the Web)** is a network of networks that allows you to access, view, and maintain documents that can include text, data, sound, and video. It is not separate from the Internet. Instead, it rides on top of the Internet, in the same way that an application such as PowerPoint runs on top of an operating system such as Windows.

The Web is a series of communications protocols between client and server. These protocols enable access to documents stored on computers throughout the Internet while allowing links to other documents on other computers. The Web protocol **hypertext transfer protocol (HTTP)** ensures compatibility before transferring information contained in documents called **webpages.** Each individual collection of pages is called a **website,** which users access by entering its address or **uniform resource locator (URL)** into a browser (see the list of websites at the

Search Engines for Kids

Askkids.com

This is a student version of Ask.com that uses age-appropriate content, filtering, and search terms to help kids narrow their searches by asking questions.

Kidsclick.org

Librarians created this site to help students conduct searches. Main topic menus and helpful links make it a kid-friendly search engine.

Kids.Yahoo.com

The student version of Yahoo! includes sites preselected for young people ages 7 to 12 that present information in a colorful, interactive way. Teachers have been asked to review identified sites, and there is a parent page designed to share information about Internet safety and offer suggestions for ways to help children gain value from using the Internet.

To research this media, pick a selection rubric to evaluate the media and determine which one would work with your lesson plans.

end of this chapter). The URL incorporates the name of the host computer (server), the domain, the directory on the server, and the title of the webpage (actual filename). Navigation within and among webpages relies on hypertext links that, when selected, move users to another location on the same page, another website on the same host computer, or to a different computer on the Web.

To use the Web for online learning, webpages have to be designed and written, and a host computer must be available to house them. Universities and large companies are usually directly connected to the Internet and run the necessary web-hosting (server) software. A popular resource in online distance learning, the **Course Management Tool (CMT),** is software designed to make it easier for the teacher to use the resources that are part of the system, such as the discussion board, test options, and grade book. When using a CMT program such as Blackboard or Moodle, the teacher can concentrate on the instruction and not have to be concerned with computer programming issues.

EVALUATING WEB RESOURCES

There are so many resources available for students and learners on the Web that it can be difficult to determine which are the best to support learning. A selection rubric (see **Selection Rubric: Web Resources**) has been provided at the end of this chapter to guide you in identifying websites that will benefit your professional development or support your students' learning. You can even ask students to use the rubric to evaluate sites they find while exploring new resources for their learning experiences.

Innovations on the Horizon

AUGMENTED REALITY

Augmented reality (AR) has been available for some time in engineering systems to blend virtual data—documents, media, live action—with the real world to enhance the information we perceive with our senses. With the advent of wireless mobile devices such as smart phones, AR can now combine real-world data with virtual data. Using the GPS capability of a smart phone and AR software, the user can capture an image and "augment" or enhance knowledge about that image with additional information from the Internet superimposed onto it. For example, while on a field trip to a nearby city, students can photograph a building and then obtain information from the Internet about it while they view the image. Rather than just being devices for interacting socially, their smart phones become learning tools that can easily bring them information when it is most useful. By also adding 3-D views to images they take with their mobile phones, images "pop out" of the page, giving students new views of real-world objects.

Summary

Learning at a distance is not new. Text, audio, and video resources have been used for many years in distance teaching settings. As the technologies have advanced, these capabilities have been incorporated into more learning opportunities for students. One major advantage of access to a variety of technology assets is that teachers can augment student study and bring additional resources into the classroom. The blending of the regular classroom and distance learning resources has made it possible for students of all ability levels to enjoy an enhanced educational experience.

Distance learning opportunities continue to expand and extend classroom activities. Teachers are no longer limited to the materials in their classrooms or in the school media center; they can now access resources from around the world. They can provide their students with experiences such as WebQuests that help them learn to use the Internet as a source of information. Students can reach out to other students and to experts for exchanges of ideas. The Internet has opened classrooms to a wealth of information around the world!

ASSURE Lesson Plan

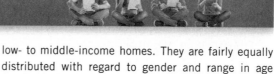

This ASSURE Classroom Case Study is based on the lesson Mr. Chun created for his high school social studies class in collaboration with another teacher in New Hampshire. The video shows Mr. Chun implementing the lesson with his students.

Mr. Chun wants his students to review their state's history and to consider the current status of the state. He plans to use the interactive distance learning resources to provide his students with opportunities to meet with high school students in New Hampshire who are engaged in a similar lesson.

Analyze Learners

General Characteristics. The students in Jimmy Chun's high school class are primarily Hawaiian and from low- to middle-income homes. They are fairly equally distributed with regard to gender and range in age from 15 to 17 years old. Student reading ability is at or above grade level. Student behavior problems are minimal.

Entry Competencies. The students are, in general, able to do the following:

- Conduct online research
- Use Blackboard software to participate in discussion boards and exchange digital documents

Learning Styles. Jimmy Chun's students learn best when engaged in activities that are relevant and include lively discussions of meaningful topics. His students vary in comfort level with speaking to students in the distance education (New Hampshire) class. Some students prefer live audio to using the text-based discussion boards.

State Standards and Objectives

Curriculum Standards. *National Council for the Social Studies, III. People, Places, and Environments:* Social studies programs should include experiences that provide for the study of people, places, and environments, so that the learner can describe and assess ways that historical events have been influenced by, and have influenced, physical and human geographic factors in local, regional, national, and global settings.

Technology Standards. *National Educational Technology Standards for Students 4—Technology Communications Tools:* Students use telecommunications to collaborate, publish, and interact with peers, experts, and other audiences; *5—Technology Research Tools:* Students use technology to locate, evaluate, and collect information from a variety of sources.

Learning Objectives.

1. Using content from conducting Internet and library research of pre-1770 U.S. history regarding Hawaiian and New Hampshire culture, religion, government, economy, and social structure, the students will write questions and give written responses during an online discussion.

2. Using the questions and information gained during discussion board dialog, the students will ask New Hampshire students questions regarding their pre-1770 society with respect to culture, religion, government, economy, and social structure.

3. Using the information gained during discussion board dialog and personal knowledge, the students will answer questions posed by the New Hampshire students regarding Hawaiian pre-1770 society with respect to culture, religion, government, economy, and social structure.

Select Strategies, Technology, Media, and Materials

Select Strategies. Jimmy Chun selects teacher- and student-centered strategies for the pre-1770 U.S. history lesson. The teacher-centered strategies involve providing a detailed description of the lesson objectives and how students should prepare for the video teleconference with New Hampshire students. Mr. Chun also provides feedback to his students as they complete their work. The student-centered strategies consist of students' Internet research on the pre-1770 history of both their states, posting their questions on the discussion board, and participating in the two-way audio/video distance education teleconference with the New Hampshire students.

Select Technology and Media. This lesson involves student use of computers, distance education equipment, and Blackboard software to post to the discussion board and exchange documents. Mr. Chun applies the following guidelines to assess the appropriateness of his technology and media selections:

- *Alignment with standards, outcomes, and objectives.* The Internet sites, Blackboard software, and distance education video teleconference provide the necessary support for Jimmy Chun's students to meet the learning objectives.

- *Accurate and current information.* Students use both text-based and Internet resources to conduct their research on pre-1770 U.S. history.

- *Age-appropriate language.* Mr. Chun has his students access websites that are appropriate for high school students. When needed, he provides assistance for student use of Blackboard.

- *Interest level and engagement.* The Hawaiian and New Hampshire students are very excited to "meet" and discuss important pre-1770 U.S. history and current topics of interest to them on the discussion boards and during the live two-way audio/video sessions.

- *Technical quality.* The technical quality of the two-way audio/video interactions is consistent with current standards in that the video is slightly delayed. Discussion board interactions and Internet searches have consistently high technical quality due to high-speed access at both schools.

- *Ease of use.* Blackboard requires initial training and support but is fairly easy for high school students to use after basic skills training.

- *Bias free.* Students find multiple references for their research to better ensure the content is bias free. Blackboard software is bias free.

- *User guide and directions.* The online help features of Blackboard are moderately easy for students to use. Students most frequently ask each other or Mr. Chun for assistance with technical difficulties.

Select Materials. Jimmy Chun provided a list of Internet sites for students to reference when conducting online research on pre-1770 U.S. history.

Utilize Technology, Media, and Materials

Preview the Technology, Media, and Materials. Jimmy Chun previews Blackboard software to ensure it has the features needed for the lesson. He previews selected resources to verify that students can find Internet and text-based information on pre-1770 U.S. history. He also previews the video teleconferencing system to make certain students will be able to see and hear each other.

Prepare the Technology, Media, and Materials. Mr. Chun prepares an assignment sheet that describes the lesson requirements and criteria that will be used to assess the final student products. He adds starter questions to the Blackboard discussion area.

Prepare the Environment. Jimmy Chun tests the Internet connections on the lab computers and ensures that Blackboard is accessible from each computer. He also tests the distance education equipment by connecting to the classroom in New Hampshire and practicing with the cameras, microphones, and lighting.

Prepare the Learners. Students in Mr. Chun's class have conducted Internet research and have participated in previous video teleconferences with the students in New Hampshire. Therefore, learner preparation primarily focuses on the topics to be covered on the discussion board and during the live session.

Provide the Learning Experience. The learning experience occurs in two distance education formats: text-based exchanges via discussion boards and live two-way audio/video interactions between the Hawaiian and New Hampshire students.

Require Learner Participation

Student Practice Activities. The students in Jimmy Chun's class use computers, the Internet, and Blackboard software to prepare for and participate in the online discussions of pre-1770 U.S. history of Hawaii and New Hampshire. The students apply information from their research and discussion board topics to generate questions to ask during the live video teleconference. During the live session, students practice and test their knowledge by asking and answering student-created questions.

Feedback. Jimmy Chun provides continuous feedback as students conduct their research, participate in discussion boards, and interact with students from New Hampshire.

Evaluate and Revise

Assessment of Learner Achievement. Mr. Chun reviews the discussion board posts of each individual student to assess knowledge of pre-1770 Hawaiian and New Hampshire society. He also reviews recordings of the video teleconference to assess student oral responses to questions asked by the New Hampshire students. Mr. Chun assesses student ability to use technology for communication and research by evaluating student Blackboard posts.

Evaluation of Strategies, Technology, and Media. Mr. Chun evaluates the effectiveness of the lesson strategies, talking about the process with the New Hampshire teacher and students and with the students in his class. Evaluation of the technology and media involves examining the functionality of the Blackboard software, the Internet browser, and the two-way audio/video distance education session.

Revision. The evaluation results revealed that student interactions could benefit from arranging students in cross-state pairs to increase interactions and information exchange. Another revision that emerged from the evaluation results was to limit teacher input during the live two-way audio/video sessions to encourage more student-to-student discussion.

DEMONSTRATING PROFESSIONAL KNOWLEDGE

1. Define distance learning.
2. Why use distance learning for elementary, middle-level, and secondary education?
3. Explain how audio and video facilitate distance learning.
4. Describe the characteristics LAN, WAN, intranet, and wireless networks.
5. Discuss five Internet netiquette guidelines for users.
6. Identify one copyright concern issue and explain why it is important.

DEMONSTRATING PROFESSIONAL SKILLS

1. Interview a teacher who regularly uses audio or television for distance learning in the classroom. Prepare a brief written or recorded report addressing the objectives covered, techniques utilized, and problems encountered. An example might be elementary students using a two-way audio/video system to investigate a community issue (ISTE NETS-T 1.B, 3.C).
2. Develop a lesson incorporating a WebQuest to engage learners. What changes did you need to make in the design of the lesson to incorporate the WebQuest?

What Internet safety issues have to be confronted? What learner skills and assessment considerations do you need to address when including a WebQuest in a lesson (ISTE NETS-T 1.B, 2.A, 2.C, 3.D, 4.A, 4.B)?
3. Develop an Internet acceptable use policy for your school (either where you attended or where you teach) (ISTE NETS-T 4.A, 4.C).
4. Observe or participate in a class taught at a distance. Describe how the teacher and students interact with each other. Also, describe the types and uses of media within the lesson (ISTE NETS-T 1.D, 3.C).

BUILDING YOUR PROFESSIONAL PORTFOLIO

- *Creating My Lesson.* Using the ASSURE model, design a lesson for a scenario from Appendix A or use a scenario of your own design. Apply one of the instructional strategies described in Chapter 4 and information from this chapter related to incorporating distance education and online learning into your instructional setting. Be sure to include information about the audience, the objectives, and all other elements of the ASSURE model. Be certain to match your intended outcomes to state or national learning standards for your content area (ISTE NETS-T 2.A, 2.B, 2.C).
- *Enhancing My Lesson.* Using the lesson you've designed in the previous activity, consider your audience again. Assume that some of your students have special needs, such as physical or learning impediments. Also assume that several students are identified as gifted. How will you change your lesson design to ensure that these students are recognized

and supported to allow them to succeed in your classroom? Also consider the options available to your students at a distance related to resources and technology. How might that affect your lesson design (ISTE NETS-T 2.A, 2.B, 2.C)?
- *Reflecting on My Lesson.* Reflect on the process of designing your lesson and your efforts at enhancing that lesson to meet student needs in your class. What have you learned about matching audience, content, instructional strategy, and materials? What could you have done to better develop your students' higher-order thinking or creativity skills or to engage them more deeply in active learning at a distance? In what ways did the strategies you selected for your lesson enhance learning opportunities for your students? What considerations do you need to better address when planning another lesson for a distance setting (ISTE NETS-T 5.C)?

Suggested Resources

PRINT RESOURCES

Conrad, R. M., & Donaldson, J. A. (2004). *Engaging the online learner: Activities and resources for creative instruction.* San Francisco, CA: Jossey-Bass.

Lipinski, T. A. (2005). *Copyright law and the distance education classroom: Working within the information infrastructure.* Lanham, MD: Scarecrow Press.

Moore, M. G., & Anderson, W. G. (2008). *Handbook of distance education* (2nd ed.). Mahwah, NJ: Lawrence Erlbaum.

Palloff, R. M., & Pratt, K. (2007). *Building online learning communities: Effective strategies for the virtual classroom.* San Francisco, CA: Jossey-Bass.

Shank, P. (2007). *Online learning idea book: 95 proven ways to enhance technology-based and blended learning.* San Francisco, CA: John Wiley & Sons.

Simonson, M., Smaldino, S. E., Albright, M. J., & Zvacek, S. (2012). *Teaching and learning at a distance: Foundations of distance education* (4th ed.). Upper Saddle River, NJ: Merrill/Prentice Hall.

WEB RESOURCES

Creative Commons

www.creativecommons.org

Creative Commons is a nonprofit organization to share and use through the use of free legal tools. They provide a simple, standardized way for you to give the public permission to share and use the web-based materials you develop. Creative Commons licenses are not an alternative to copyright, but they give you the tools to modify the copyright terms for your work.

The Adventures of Cyberbee

www.cyberbee.com

This site is filled with helpful ideas and activities for using the Internet in education.

CNN Interactive

www.cnn.com

CNN is an up-to-the-minute source for world news and information about weather, sports, science, technology, show business, and health.

Public Broadcasting Service (PBS)

www.pbs.org

A nonprofit consortium of the nation's public television stations, PBS makes noncommercial television available to the public. Its website includes resources related to quality programs and services for educators and parents.

San Diego Zoo and Wild Animal Park

www.sandiegozoo.org

This site provides a virtual tour of the San Diego Zoo and includes information about the zoo, its inhabitants, and endangered species.

Sesame Workshop

www.sesameworkshop.org

A nonprofit educational organization that creates entertaining and educational radio and television programming, the Sesame Workshop focuses on providing learning opportunities for children, while assisting teachers, day-care providers, and parents in developing quality learning experiences and curricula in a variety of media formats.

SELECTION RUBRIC   Web Resources

Complete and save the following interactive evaluation to reference when selecting web resources to integrate into lessons.

Search Terms

_____

_____

_____

Title _____

Source/Location _____

©Date _____   Cost _____

Primary User(s)

Subject Area _____   Grade Level _____

_____ Student

Learning Experiences _____

_____ Teacher

Brief Description

Standards/Outcomes/Objectives

Prerequisites (e.g., prior knowledge, reading ability, vocabulary level)

Strengths

Limitations

Special Features

Name _____   **Date** _____

Rating Area	High Quality	Medium Quality	Low Quality
Alignment with standards, outcomes, and objectives	Standards/outcomes/objectives addressed and use of web resource should enhance student learning.	Standards/outcomes/ objectives partially addressed and use of web resource may enhance student learning.	Standards/outcomes/objectives not addressed and use of web resource will likely not enhance student learning.
Accurate and current information	Information is correct and does not contain material that is out of date.	Information is correct, but does contain material that is out of date.	Information is not correct and does contain material that is out of date.
Age-appropriate language	Language used is age appropriate and vocabulary is understandable.	Language used is nearly age appropriate and some vocabulary is above/below student age.	Language used is not age appropriate and vocabulary is clearly inappropriate for student age.
Interest level and engagement	Topic is presented so that students are likely to be interested and actively engaged in learning.	Topic is presented to interest students most of the time and engage most students in learning.	Topic presented so as not to interest students and not engage them in learning.
Technical quality	The material represents the best technology and media.	The material represents technology and media that are good quality, although they may not be best available.	The material represents technology and media that are not well prepared and are of very poor quality.
Ease of use (student or teacher)	Material follows easy-to-use patterns with nothing to confuse the user.	Material follows patterns that are easy to follow most of the time, with a few things to confuse the user.	Material follows no patterns and most of the time the user is very confused.
Bias free	There is no evidence of objectionable bias or advertising.	There is little evidence of bias or advertising.	There is much evidence of bias or advertising.
User guide and directions	The user guide is an excellent resource for use in a lesson. Directions should help teachers and students use the material.	The user guide is good resource for use in a lesson. Directions may help teachers and students use the material.	The user guide is poor resource for use in a lesson. Directions do not help teachers and students use the material.
Clear directions	Navigation is logical and pages are well organized.	Navigation is logical for main use, but can be confusing.	Navigation is not logical and pages are not well organized.
Stimulates creativity	Use of web resources gives students many opportunities to engage in new learning experiences.	Use of web resources gives students some opportunities to engage in new learning experiences.	Use of web resources gives students few opportunities to engage in new learning experiences.
Visual design	The web resource is designed with appropriate use of graphics and text to ensure student understanding.	The web resource is designed with graphics and text that are of average quality.	The web resource is designed with graphics and text that are of poor quality and distract students from understanding.
Quality of links	The web resource links facilitate navigating the material and finding additional information.	The web resource links are not easy to navigate and make it difficult to find additional information.	The web resource links make it very difficult to navigate the material and to find additional information.

Recommended for Classroom Use: _____ Yes _____ No

Ideas for Classroom Use: _____

_____

CHAPTER

8

Enhancing Learning with Audio and Video

Knowledge Outcomes

This chapter addresses ISTE NETS-T 2.

1. Compare and contrast audio and video literacy.

2. Describe how audio enhances learning when listening skills are improved.

3. Explain how audio use in the classroom can involve teachers and students.

4. Select an audio resource and describe the advantages of integrating it into a lesson.

5. Explain how video can enhance students' cognitive, affective, psychomotor, and interpersonal learning.

6. List and describe how four types of educational video support student learning.

7. Explain how students benefit from producing video to demonstrate knowledge and skills.

Goal

Utilize a variety of audio and video materials to enhance PK–12 student learning.

ASSURE Classroom Case Study

This chapter's ASSURE Classroom Case Study describes the instructional planning used by Scott James, a fifth-grade teacher in a school with students coming from low- to middle-income homes. Mr. James realizes that students learn best when lessons reflect real-world situations. He has also seen increased student motivation and interest when computers are integrated into his lessons. Scott's school recently purchased a digital video camera and iMovie software for the lab computers. To take advantage of these resources, Scott designs a lesson on natural disasters that is multidisciplinary, incorporates the use of the new digital video camera, and builds his students' expository writing skills. During the lesson, student pairs create digital videos of natural disaster "news broadcasts" they have scripted. One student assumes the role of news anchor, while the other is the on-the-scene news reporter.

The ASSURE Classroom Case Study video for this chapter explores how Scott engages students in the use of digital audio and video and discusses the benefits, limitations, and suggestions for using audio and video to achieve 21st century learning environments. Throughout the chapter, you will find reflection questions to relate the chapter content to the ASSURE Classroom Case Study. At the end of the chapter, you will be challenged to develop your own ASSURE lesson that incorporates use of these strategies and resources for a topic and grade level of your choice.

 Watch Mr. James and his class as they develop videos of natural disasters.

T oday's PK–12 students are experiencing an explosion of enhanced learning through the use of audio and video resources. At the click of a mouse, teachers can select from a vast array of online podcasts and videos to support and enrich instructional experiences. In addition, audio and video production equipment is rapidly becoming the next technological wave in PK–12 schools (Carter, 2010). Thus, students can use these tools to demonstrate their knowledge and skills with media, which reflect a depth of understanding and application beyond written text. In this chapter, we explore the characteristics and effective uses of audio and video in learning.

Students need audio and video literacy skills to gain educational benefits from today's readily available resources.

Audio and Video Literacy

"No longer is it enough to be able to read the printed word; children, youth, and adults, too, need the ability to critically interpret the powerful images of a multimedia culture" (Thoman & Jolls, 2004, p. 18). Audio and video literacy are key factors required of today's students to interpret and produce multimedia. **Audio literacy** requires attentive listening and deciphering important message components to connect with prior knowledge, as well as to produce meaningful audio communication. **Video literacy** encompasses the knowledge and skills needed to "consume" or meaningfully view video, as well as to produce video to demonstrate knowledge and skills. Following are information and examples to build students' audio and video literacy knowledge and skills critical for success in the 21st century.

Enhancing Learning with Audio

If you examine a typical day in most PK–12 classrooms, a large portion of the day involves the delivery of auditory information. This can be teacher to student, student to student, digital resource to student, or in a variety of other formats. However, delivery of information doesn't automatically enhance learning, as seen when examining the differences between hearing and listening.

HEARING AND LISTENING

At the risk of oversimplification, hearing is a physiological process, whereas listening is a psychological process. Physiologically, **hearing** is a process in which sound waves entering the outer ear are transmitted to the eardrum, converted into mechanical vibrations in the middle ear, and changed in the inner ear into electrical impulses that travel to the brain. The psychological process of **listening** begins with someone's awareness of and attention to sounds or speech patterns **(encoding)**, proceeds through identification and recognition of specific auditory signals **(decoding)**, and ends in comprehension **(understanding)**.

Hearing and listening are important to the communication and learning processes. The quality of the prepared message is affected by the ability of the teacher to articulate the message clearly and logically and in a way that addresses the diverse needs of students. Below are five recommendations to better ensure students are able to learn from audio resources.

First, the volume of the sound should not be too low or too high. If too low, students may have trouble picking up the meaning with any accuracy. If too high, students may actually stop listening to the offending sounds.

Second, a sound that is sustained monotonously, such as the droning voice of a teacher, may trigger **auditory fatigue**, a process that is physiological as well as psychological. That is, the neural mechanisms transmitting the sound to the brain literally become fatigued from carrying the same load over and over. In addition, your conscious awareness of the noise is diminished because it is "old news" and no longer of interest. The brain has a remarkable capacity for filtering out sounds to which it doesn't want or need to attend.

Third, you may have students in your class whose ability to hear may be temporarily or permanently impaired. For example, when students have colds or allergies, their ability to hear in a noisy classroom may be reduced. Even a small difference in hearing acuity can cause students to have difficulty discriminating among words and phrases, thus increasing the potential for confusion. And, with the trend toward including students with significant loss of hearing acuity in regular classrooms, teachers need to adjust or individualize instruction to ensure students clearly hear and understand the information. Potential solutions include relocating the student to the front of the classroom or adding noise dampening devices, such as drapes and carpeting. Another strategy is to use a sound field amplification system (see "On the Horizon" at the end of the chapter). Such a system consists of the teacher wearing a wireless microphone and having several small speakers located throughout the classroom. These systems have been shown to help children who have colds, those with disorders that might affect their learning, and those for whom English is a second language (Crandell, Smaldino, & Flexer, 2005; Kollie, 2013).

Fourth, the message can also be affected by the learners' listening skills or lack of them. Students must be able to direct and sustain concentration on a message. They must have the skill to think ahead while receiving the message. We think faster than we hear, just as we think faster than we read or write. Use this time differential to organize and internalize the information so students can comprehend it.

ASSURE Classroom Case Study Reflection

Audio

Review the ASSURE video and reflect on what strategies Scott might use to guide his students to think about both the encoding and decoding of their natural disaster report messages.

Audio

We have students in our classrooms with a variety of learning needs. Here are some examples of ways you can arrange to use audio resources to support learning.

- *Audio for hearing-impaired learners.* The most familiar technique to assist hearing-impaired learners is closed-captioning for television and video programs. Multimedia presentations and audio materials on the Web use this feature as well. Captioning is often available with media as an option that needs to be selected. You will also find most media available today offer this option for your students. This technology is also useful for students who are learning a second language, those listening to content in a noisy environment, and students learning to read who need additional practice.
- *Audio for all learners.* Some students enjoy listening to stories and will often benefit from reading along with an audio recording of a book. Students who select books beyond their regular reading levels also benefit from the audio presentation of the story. The audio book option allows students to practice their vocabulary and enhance their reading experiences as part of their independent reading.
- *Audio for English language learners.* When working with English language learners, the addition of audio cues can help them understand the text that they are reading.

- *Audio for advanced learners.* Students who wish to challenge their learning experiences can delve deeper into history by using audio to explore famous speeches or to enhance their experience of a particular time period. For example, students who wish to explore the speeches of Martin Luther King to develop a presentation for their classmates on his themes and timeline might listen to his speeches and incorporate audio clips into their PowerPoint presentation for the class.

Fifth, communication can break down because the learner lacks the experiential and/or contextual background to internalize and thus comprehend the message. As their teacher, it is important that you use familiar vocabulary and language patterns that your students understand.

DEVELOPING LISTENING SKILLS

Until recently, much attention in formal education was given to reading and writing, a little was given to speaking, and essentially none was given to listening. Now, however, educators recognize listening as a skill that, like all skills, can be improved with practice. You can use a number of techniques to improve student listening abilities:

- *Guide listening.* To guide their listening, give students some objectives or questions beforehand. Start with short passages and one or two objectives. Then gradually increase the length of the passage and the number and complexity of the objectives or questions.
- *Give directions.* Prepare audio directions for students to follow when completing a class assignment. When giving directions orally, observe the "say it only once" rule so that students place value on both your and their time and their incentive to listen is reinforced. You can examine student work products to determine the need to revise the directions if common mistakes occur.

- *Ask students to listen for main ideas, details, or inferences.* Keeping the age level of your students in mind, you can present an oral passage. You can read a story and ask primary students to draw a picture about what happened. Ask students to listen for the main idea and then write it down. You can also use this technique when you want students to draw details and inferences from the passage.

- *Use context in listening.* Younger students can learn to distinguish meanings in an auditory context by listening to sentences with words missing and then supplying the appropriate words.

- *Analyze the structure of a presentation.* Ask students to outline an oral presentation. You can then determine how well they were able to discern the main ideas and to identify the subtopics.

- *Distinguish between relevant and irrelevant information.* After listening to an oral presentation of information, ask students to identify the main idea and then rate (from most to least relevant) all other presented ideas. A simpler technique for elementary students is to have them identify irrelevant words in sentences or irrelevant sentences in paragraphs.

Audio literacy is recognized as a 21st century skill needed to ensure that communication informs, instructs, and motivates learners. In addition to content knowledge, you need to provide opportunities for students to develop listening skills in order to take full advantage of audio used to enhance learning.

Audio in the Classroom

Audio adds a dimension to classroom environments that expands and deepens students' learning experiences. Imagine your students listening to Abraham Lincoln presenting his inaugural address, Einstein explaining relativity, Ernest Hemingway reading a passage from one of his novels, or Picasso interpreting one of his paintings. Also imagine a third-grade student being recorded as she reads a story for her digital portfolio, then comparing that recording with stories she recorded in first and second grade.

Using audio in the classroom offers advantages, but it also has limitations to consider when planning integration of audio into your instruction. You will discover that both teachers and students can use various types of audio to enhance learning opportunities, and you will discover ideas for accessing and producing audio.

Advantages of Audio

- *Readily available, simple to use, and portable.* Most students have been using CD and MP3 players since they were young. These types of players are easy to operate. Audio players are portable and can even be used in the field. Portable audio devices are also ideal for home study; many students already have their own players.

- *Inexpensive.* Once the storage devices and equipment have been purchased, there is no additional cost because the storage devices are erasable and reusable. Many MP3 files are available on the Internet for free or at low cost.

- *Reproducible.* You can duplicate digital files when using the appropriate software and equipment. You can easily duplicate audio materials in whatever quantities you need, for use in the classroom, in the media center, and at home. Remember to observe copyright guidelines.

- *Stimulating.* Audio media can provide a stimulating alternative to reading and listening to the teacher. Audio can enhance text messages through the addition of dramatic voice intonations and sound effects. With a little imagination, you and your students can create very versatile audio recordings.

Audio

LibriVox

http://librivox.org

Librivox provides a collection of public domain audiobooks available in titles ranging from classics, short stories, and poetry. The collection is based on voluntary submissions of audio media, but the entries must be public domain to be entered. Over 12 languages are available, providing native speakers reading familiar books.

Audio Theatre Production Kit

www.balancepublishing.com

Students can create their own audio theatre productions. The kit contains two versions of a script, one with altered vocabulary to meet the needs of below-grade readers, the second for grade-level and above-grade-level readers. In addition, there is a CD with background music and sound effects. Students, working together, record their production to be shared with others. They

develop technical skills, as well as work collaboratively in the production. It is a motivating way to help students with their reading and vocabulary competencies.

A Kid's-Eye View of the Environment

http://www.michaelmishmusic.com/kid%27s_eye_view.html

Michael Mish based this series of songs on his many visits to schools in southern California to talk to children about the environment. He found them to be more aware and concerned about environmental problems than he expected. Mish took the topics that the children were most concerned about (e.g., recycling, water and air pollution, and the greenhouse effect) and put them to music. The songs are engaging, with sing-along choruses. The messages should get primary-age children talking about making this a safer, cleaner world.

Source: Link reprinted by permission of Michael Mish, Owner Michael Mish Music.

- *Provides oral message.* Students who have limited reading ability can learn from audio media. Students can listen and follow along with visual and text material. In addition, they can replay portions of the audio material as often as needed to understand it.

- *Provides current information.* Web-based audio often consists of broadcasts of live speeches, presentations, or performances.

- *Supports second language learning.* Audio resources are excellent for teaching second languages because they not only allow students to hear words pronounced by native speakers, but they also allow them to record their own pronunciations for comparison.

- *Easy to store.* MP3 files can be stored on a computer hard drive, USB drive, or MP3 player.

Limitations of Audio

- *Copyright concerns.* Commercially produced audio can easily be duplicated, which might lead to copyright violations.

- *Doesn't monitor attention.* Some students have difficulty studying independently, so when they listen to recorded audio their attention may wander. They may hear the recorded message but not listen attentively and comprehend. Teachers can readily detect when students are drifting away from teacher-directed learning, but an audio player cannot do this.

- *Difficulty in pacing.* Determining the appropriate pace for presenting information can be difficult if your students have a range of attention spans, abilities, and experiential backgrounds.

- *Fixed content.* The content of audio media presentation segments is fixed, even though it is possible to hear a recorded segment again or select a different section.

INTEGRATION OF AUDIO

The uses of audio are limited only by the imaginations of you and your students, as it can be used in all phases of instruction—from introduction of a topic to evaluation of student learning. As seen in the "When to Use Audio" box, integration of audio resources can

Audio

Use audio when student learning will be enhanced by ...	Examples
Text being read	High school students with limited reading ability listen to a recording of a Shakespeare sonnet being read.
Listening to key political speeches	Middle school students prepare for a debate by listening to podcasts of speeches given by candidates for mayor of their city.
Recording impressions	Students create a digital journal of their learning by recording weekly impressions of the most important things they learned.
Easy access to verbal examples	Students use the noun menu of a Spanish-language CD to listen to new vocabulary pronounced by a Spanish-language speaker.
Listening to an author-read story	As a story is being projected on a screen, elementary students listen to a recording of the author as she reads the story that is streamed from a children's storybook website.
Hearing the sounds of nature	Intermediate-grade students use a bird website to practice identifying the sounds of different birds from their local area to prepare for a nature trail field trip.
Listening to an expert	Students in an art class listen to a recording of a successful photographer sharing tips for taking balanced photos.
Listening to current events	A high school social studies class listens to Internet radio broadcast of a United Nations General Assembly opening session.
Recording personal reading	Elementary students create a digital reading journal that contains yearly recordings of the students reading a favorite story.

enhance learning of all students. Multiple levels of higher-order thinking are required for students, working individually or in groups, to create their own recordings. In addition, these activities provide opportunities for students to express their innovative and artistic abilities. Also important, foundational knowledge and skills can be reinforced for students with learning disabilities through the use of digital recordings to go back and repeat segments of instruction as often as necessary because the recorder-playback capability is a very patient tutor.

HOW TEACHERS CAN USE AUDIO

Teachers can prepare their own recordings or use commercially available or free digital recordings to supplement instruction. For example, a second-grade teacher can record directions for students to create sentences with word cards or provide skills practice, such as pronunciation of new vocabulary or a foreign language. A teacher of ninth-grade students with learning difficulties, but average intelligence, can provide instruction on how to listen to lectures, speeches, and other oral presentations. The students practice their listening skills with CDs of recorded stories, poetry, and speeches.

A middle school teacher downloads an audio file to play with the sound system of her classroom for the 20 minutes she needs to set up her classroom for the school day. After a few seconds of music, the song fades as the narrator says, "What's new in classroom management techniques? Today we are going to explore together three techniques that will enhance your

Audio

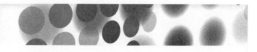

Poet Laureate

One day a tenth-grade English teacher was listening to NPR on his way to school. That morning the show "All Things Considered" had an interview with the poet laureate of the United States, who was explaining his "favorite poem project." Essentially, he traveled all over the United States randomly asking people, from schoolteachers to welders, to read and discuss their favorite poem while he recorded their responses on audiotape. He created an extensive library of people and poems. This teacher got the idea to adapt this project for his classes. The students loved it! The teacher was surprised not only by the emotional oral interpretations they submitted, but also by the depth of analysis portrayed in their short discussions of the poems. Low-achieving students were successful in the learning experience.

Source: Reprinted by permission of Matt Rose

classroom skills." The recording converts the classroom work setting into a learning environment, thereby making efficient use of the teacher's time for professional development.

An often-overlooked use of audio materials is for evaluating student attainment of lesson objectives. For example, you may prerecord test questions for members of the class to use individually. You may ask students to identify the composer of a particular piece of music. Students in social studies classes could listen to excerpted speech passages and be asked to identify the historical speaker and the relevance of the speech. Testing and evaluating in the audio mode is especially appropriate when teaching and learning have also been in audio mode.

HOW STUDENTS CAN USE AUDIO

Students can use audio in multiple ways. A popular project in social studies classes is the recording of **oral histories.** The students interview local citizens regarding the history of their community. This project serves the dual purpose of informing students and residents about local history as well as collecting and preserving information that might otherwise be lost.

Audio recordings are an excellent way for students to prepare book reviews. The recordings can be posted on a classroom or library website. These recorded reviews can be used to encourage other students to consider their options before selecting books to read.

Students learn from recording oral history.

Students can also use mobile devices to record information gleaned from a field trip. Upon returning to the classroom, students can play back the recording for discussion and review. Many museums, observatories, and other public exhibit areas now supply visitors with prerecorded messages about various items on display, which may, with permission, be downloaded or rerecorded for playback in the classroom.

Another use is for students to record themselves reciting a poem, presenting a speech, performing music, and so on. They can then listen to the recording privately or have the performance critiqued by the teacher or other students. Many small-group projects can include recorded reports for presentation to the rest of the class. These recordings can become part of each student's electronic portfolio.

A primary student at a learning center listens to her favorite storybook. She follows along in the book to associate letter combinations with sounds. The technique encourages reading and promotes literacy.

The elementary class performs daily physical exercises to a recording of music and exercise instructions. The teacher hopes the experience will promote lifelong good health through daily exercise and proper diet, which she also teaches.

Students love to hear and tell stories. Stories can be entertaining and informative. Storytelling is an important skill to develop in students of all ages. The goal should be teaching students to express ideas through verbal communication. Students can use Audacity, a free open source software program, to prepare the recordings with special sound effects or elements of music to enhance their presentations. Students also could use an audio interview with a special "guest" as a part of their presentation.

Individual students use a keyboard connected to a computer to "compose" their own music. They can "see" the music on the screen and hear what they have composed through headphones to keep them from disturbing other students in the room. They then write stories around the music or sounds they have created.

ACCESSING AUDIO

Digital audio files for consumer use are typically encoded in MP3 format, which transfers and plays on most digital audio devices. Popular ways of accessing MP3 digital audio files are streaming, podcasts, and Internet radio via a digital player.

Streaming Audio. **Streaming audio** files are sent in packets to the user, giving you an opportunity to listen to portions of a file as it is being downloaded. Streamed MP3 files are available to anyone who has access to the Internet. The software your computer needs to play MP3 audio files, like Windows Media Player and iTunes, is free and typically comes installed on most mobile devices and computers.

Podcasting. **Podcasts** (from the words "iPod" and "broadcasting") are recorded audio files in MP3 format that are distributed over the Internet. These audio files can be sent automatically to "subscribers" and stored for listening at their convenience. Podcast Alley (**www.podcastalley .com**) provides a variety of audio resources to support student learning. With podcasting software, students and teachers can create their own newscasts or documentaries and have subscribers download and listen to them on their computers or portable audio devices. Podcasting offers teachers and students remarkable opportunities for their voices to be heard in their local communities or around the world. One could think of podcasting as blogging without writing or as a way for every class to have its own radio station.

Internet Radio. **Internet radio** uses the Internet to offer online radio stations consisting of a variety of programming—music, sports, science, weather, and local, national, and world news.

Audio—Music

The use of music is the most highly regulated activity in the realm of copyright law. It is also heavily policed and enforced by the music industry!

Permitted copying of music includes the following:

- For academic uses other than performances, teachers and students may make copies of up to 10 percent of a musical work, provided the excerpt does not comprise a part of the whole that would constitute a performable unit such as a section, movement, or aria.
- Single copies of a recording of student performances may be made for rehearsal purposes or evaluation.
- Single copies of a recording, such as a CD or cassette, of copyrighted music may be made from a recording owned by a school or teacher for the purpose of constructing aural exercises or assessments.

The following are not allowed:

- Compiling a collection of recordings.
- Making copies of printed music scores. Additional copies must be purchased or duplication rights must be negotiated.
- Making an arrangement of a copyrighted musical work without permission of the copyright holder. This falls into the category of creating a derivative work.
- Performing a musical work publicly without the copyright owner's permission.

- Copying music from a website. You must also pay for the use of music you download from the Internet. The copyright owners of sound recordings have rights set forth in the Digital Performance Right in Sound Recordings Act of 1995 and the Digital Millennium Copyright Act of 1998. These laws give sound recording copyright owners rights to online performances of their recordings.

Internet transmissions may involve the reproduction and distribution of musical works and the copying of a copyrighted musical work or sound recording onto your server or hard drive (as when you load the file containing the work). Unauthorized copying constitutes exploitation of the reproduction rights. You must contact the copyright owner of the sound recording (usually the distributor) for authorization to copy the sound recording onto your server or hard drive. Some Internet sites advertise music free from copyright. You are wise to check out sites that offer music files, as it is better to ask than to be caught with illegal copies of music.

The landmark litigation between the music industry and the Napster online music sharing service in early 2000 is a prototypical example of efforts to ensure that copyright holders receive proper remuneration for all commercial transactions involving their work.

For general information on copyright, see the "Copyright Concerns: Copyright Law" section in Chapter 1.

Live and recorded programming from around the world can enhance language, social studies, science, and current events lessons. Any Internet-connected device can play Internet radio stations. Visit InternetRadio (**www.internet-radio.com**) for an extensive list of stations.

A **portable digital audio player** enables users to take their audio files with them. It is also called a "portable digital music player" because most people today use them to play music. One example is the Apple iPod. It fits into the user's hand or pocket and can store thousands of songs or sound files. The files are transferred wirelessly from the Internet or by connecting the device to a computer.

PRODUCING AUDIO

Portable digital recorders are easy-to-use devices that allow students to dictate notes, practice foreign languages, conduct interviews, record bird songs, or any other sounds needed for educational experiences. Specialized software enables students to add music and sound effects to their digital creations. It is important to follow copyright guidelines when working with music, as seen in the "Copyright Concerns" box. Two examples are musical instrument digital interface (MIDI) and digital synthesizer software.

Musical Instrument Digital Interface. **Musical instrument digital interface (MIDI)** enables MIDI-equipped instruments to interact with synthesizer software to compose music. MIDI not only transmits which notes are played, but also the length of time and velocity or intensity with which they are played. This technology allows students to create music by focusing on musical ideas rather than the mechanics of playing an instrument or learning musical notation. The technology is relatively inexpensive and can be plugged into most computers. Gardner (2006) identifies "musical/rhythmic" as one of his nine aspects of intelligence. MIDI technology can be used to develop this aspect of intelligence.

MIDI technology allows students to create music as easily as word processing facilitates writing. Rather than using conventional musical notation, this technology uses lines of sound on a grid whose height corresponds to pitch and whose length corresponds to duration.

MIDI and music composition software like Apple's GarageBand (**www.apple.com/ilife/garageband**) provide creative learning opportunities for students. All this is required is a keyboard, an interface, and a software program.

Synthesizer Software. Students use synthesizer software, or *softsynth,* to create original music, radio programs, and other materials to demonstrate their learning. Features of the software give student productions a professional polish. For example, creating podcasts using digital synthesizer software puts your students in the control room of their own full-featured radio station. The software includes sound effects and jingles from an audio library. An example of this software is Acoustica's Mixcraft (**www.acoustica.com/mixcraft).** Students can browse and select from sound effects including sounds of people, animals, and machines. They can then drag these sounds into their podcast to sync up with their vocal track.

Enhancing Learning with Video

The presence of video, or entertainment media in the form of television, DVDs, and video games, in a child's daily life is growing dramatically. A Kaiser Family Foundation survey (2010) revealed that 8- to 18-year-olds spent approximately 53 hours per week using entertainment media. Thus, teachers can build on this predisposition by integrating the viewing or producing of video into instruction.

It is important to understand the attributes of video regarding the manipulation of time and space and how these impact student learning. Also important is the role of video in four domains of learning: cognitive, affective, psychomotor, and interpersonal.

SPECIAL ATTRIBUTES OF VIDEOS

Because most of us think of video as a medium designed to produce a realistic image of the world around us, we tend to forget that a basic attribute of video is the ability to manipulate temporal and spatial perspectives. Manipulation of time and space, use of animation, and other video conventions not only serve dramatic and creative ends, but they also have important implications for instruction.

Manipulation of Time. Video permits us to increase or decrease the amount of time required to observe an event. For example, it would take a very long time for students to actually witness a highway being constructed, but a carefully edited video of the different activities that go into building a highway recreates the essentials of such an event in a few minutes. We can also remove segments of time. For example, you are familiar with the type of sequence in which a scene fades out and then fades in the next day. Time has been taken out of the sequence, but we accept that the night has passed even though we did not experience it in real time.

Compression of Time. Video can compress the time it takes to observe an event. A flower can appear to open before our eyes, or stars can streak across the nighttime sky. This technique, known as **time lapse,** has important instructional uses. For example, the process of a chrysalis turning into a butterfly is too slow for easy classroom observation. However, through time-lapse videography, the butterfly can emerge from the chrysalis in a matter of minutes.

Expansion of Time. Time can also be expanded by video through a technique called **slow motion.** Some events occur too fast to be seen by the naked eye. By photographing such events at extremely high speeds and then projecting the images at normal speed, we can observe what is happening. For example, a frog catches an insect too rapidly for the human eye to observe, but high-speed videography can slow down the motion so that we can observe the process.

Manipulation of Space. Video allows us to view phenomena in both macrocosm and microcosm—that is, at extremely close range or from a vast distance. Your students can view the earth from a space shuttle (macro view) and, at the other extreme, observe cell division under a microscope (micro view). Live TV allows our students to observe two events occurring simultaneously but many miles apart using split screen. This technique is often used in news events where one reporter is located in the station while one is live on the scene, often in a different country.

Animation. Time and space can also be manipulated by animation. This technique takes advantage of **persistence of vision** to give motion to otherwise inanimate objects. There are various techniques for achieving **animation,** but basically it is made up of a series of photographs, drawings, or computer images of small displacements of objects or images. With the continuing evolution of computer software that can manipulate visual images, we are experiencing a rediscovery of the art of animation through video. Computer-generated animation sequences are being used more and more in instructional video programs to depict complex or rapid processes in simplified form.

VIDEO AND THE DOMAINS OF LEARNING

The multifaceted nature of videos makes them an excellent educational resource to expand student learning in the four major domains: cognitive, affective, psychomotor, and interpersonal.

Cognitive Domain. In the cognitive domain, learners can observe dramatic recreations of historical events and actual recordings of more recent events. Color, sound, and motion make personalities come to life. Video can enhance the textbook by showing processes, relationships, and techniques. Students can read books in conjunction with viewing videos. You may have students read before viewing as an introduction to the topic, or use the video to interest students in reading about the topic.

Affective Domain. When there is an element of emotion or the desire for affective learning, video usually works well. Role models and dramatic messages on video can influence attitudes. Because of their great potential for emotional impact, video can be useful in shaping personal and social attitudes. Documentary programs have often been found to have a measurable impact on student attitudes. Documentaries made during the Great Depression, for example, bring the hardships of that era to students who have never known hard times. Cultural understanding can be developed through viewing video depicting people from all parts of the globe.

Psychomotor Domain. Video is great for showing processes involving the use of motor skills. For example, there is a short educational video called *Colonial Cooper* that shows how an 18th-century artisan made a barrel at Colonial Williamsburg. Demonstrations of psychomotor skills are often more easily seen through media than in real life. If you are teaching a step-by-step process with a DVD, you can show it in real time, use fast-forward for an overview, stop the action for careful study, or move forward one frame at a time. Recording student performances enables learners to observe their own performances and receive feedback from peers, teachers, or others.

Interpersonal Domain. By viewing a video program together, a diverse group of learners can build a common base of experience as a catalyst for discussion. When students are learning interpersonal skills, such as dealing with conflict resolution or peer relationships, they observe the behavior of others on video for demonstration and analysis. Students then practice their interpersonal skills before a camera, watch themselves, and receive feedback from peers and teachers. Role-play vignettes can be analyzed to determine what happened and to ask the learners what they would do next. You can use open-ended dramatizations to present unresolved confrontations to your students, and then challenge them to identify various solutions.

ASSURE Classroom Case Study Reflection

Video

Review the ASSURE video and reflect on the following questions. How can Scott James use video to develop the cognitive, affective, interpersonal, and psychomotor skills of his fifth-grade students? Which of the four domains are reinforced during student creation and editing of the natural disaster videos? In what ways did the lesson activities reinforce learning?

Video in the Classroom

Videos can be an excellent addition to classroom instruction, but you must consider its advantages and limitations. Video can be used in all instructional environments with whole classes, small groups, and individual students. Videos are available on almost any topic for all types of learners in all the domains of instruction—cognitive, affective, psychomotor, and interpersonal. They can take the learner almost anywhere and extend students' interests beyond the walls of the classroom. Objects too large to bring into the classroom, as well as those too small to see with the naked eye, can be studied. Events too dangerous to observe, such as an eclipse of the sun, are studied safely. The time and expense of a field trip can be avoided, as many companies and national parks provide video tours to observe assembly lines, services, and the features of nature. It is important for you, as a teacher, to know the types of video available and how to locate and evaluate them. You also need guidelines for viewing and producing videos.

Advantages of Video

- *Motion*. Moving images have an obvious advantage over still visuals in portraying concepts and processes in which motion is essential to learning (such as Newton's Laws of Motion, erosion, metamorphosis).

- *Risk-free observation*. Video allows learners to observe phenomena that might be too dangerous to view directly, such as an eclipse of the sun, a volcanic eruption, or warfare.

- *Dramatization*. Dramatic recreations bring historical events and personalities to life. They allow students to observe and analyze human interactions.

- *Affective learning.* Because of its great potential for emotional impact, video can be useful in shaping personal and social attitudes such as "going green." Documentary and propaganda videos have often been found to have a measurable impact on audience attitudes.

- *Problem solving.* Open-ended dramatizations are frequently used to present unresolved situations, such as a growing homeless population in the United States, leaving it to the students to discuss various ways of dealing with the problem.

- *Cultural understanding.* Seeing depictions of everyday life in other societies helps develop an appreciation for other cultures. The genre of ethnographic video serves this purpose, as seen in *The Hunters, The Tribe That Hides from Man, The Nuer,* and *River of Sand.*

- *Establishing commonality.* By viewing video programs together, a dissimilar group of students can build a common base of experience to effectively discuss an issue.

Limitations of Video

- *Fixed pace.* Although videos can be stopped for discussion, this is not usually done during group showings. Because the program runs at a fixed pace, some students may fall behind while others are waiting impatiently for the next point.

- *Talking head.* Many videos, especially local productions, consist mostly of headshots of people talking. Video is not a great oral medium—it is a visual medium. Use audio recordings for strictly verbal messages.

- *Still phenomena.* Although video is advantageous for concepts that involve motion, it may be unsuitable for other topics for which detailed study of a single visual is involved (e.g., a map, a wiring diagram, or an organization chart).

- *Misinterpretation.* Documentaries and dramatizations often present a complex or sophisticated treatment of an issue. A scene intended as satire might be taken literally by a young or naive student. The thoughts of a main character may be interpreted as the attitudes and values of the producer.

- *Abstract, nonvisual instruction.* Video is poor at presenting abstract, nonvisual information. The preferred medium for words alone is text. Philosophy and mathematics do not lend themselves well to video unless the specific concepts discussed lend themselves to illustration using historical footage, graphic representation, or stylized imagery.

TECHNOLOGY FOR ALL LEARNERS

Adapting Video

Video offers different options for meeting the needs of diverse learners.

- *Video technology for hearing impaired.* Captioning is readily available on TV and other video formats as a way to assist students with learning disabilities and hearing impairments. Captioning consists of text at the bottom of the viewing area. The text provides students the opportunity to read what others are hearing through the audio channel of the video.

- *Video technology for visually impaired.* A technique called descriptive video is available to students who have visual impairments. A soft-spoken voice describes the scenes that are on the video. The visually impaired student then is able to hear the description and grasp the idea of what is being presented visually. This service is available for many TV programs and instructional videos. For more information see "The Development of the Descriptive Video Services" by Cronin and King (2007), available at the National Center to Improve Practice in Special Education through Technology, Media, and Materials (www2.edc.org/NCIP/library/v&c/cronin.htm).

- *Video technology for gifted students.* Gifted students can be challenged to explore videos for higher-order concepts, generate questions for further research, or present summary points to share in groups of mixed ability students. In addition, students gifted with different aspects of video production can provide peer tutoring to build the skills of all students.

INTEGRATION OF VIDEO

We are now teaching a video generation. Consequently, the use and creation of video can greatly enhance student learning. As emphasized in the ASSURE model, student viewing or production of videos should directly support achievement of the lesson objectives and build video literacy knowledge and skills.

One approach is to strategically integrate segments of video that align with the lesson. Keep in mind that students have grown up with TV programs that utilize short segments rather than 30-minute programs. Like many shows, *Sesame Street* changes topics every few minutes. Many educational videos are available as segments that are a few minutes in length, in order to provide you maximum flexibility to promote learning specifically related to student needs.

Also important is the adaptation of lessons to meet the special needs of students. Video-based courses with multiple sound tracks can be aimed at different types of learners. Text can be displayed in multiple languages and used to subtitle or annotate video content. DVDs can be navigated by title, chapter, track, or time stamp for quick navigation. Quick Response (QR) codes are often added to text materials to access specific video segments on a DVD. Some DVDs offer the ability to view an object from different angles selected by the viewers, with up to nine different camera angles selected in real time during playback.

There are multiple benefits for integrating student production of video into instruction. Understandably, increased student engagement and motivation are at the top of the list because is it is fun to create videos. Additional benefits include the use of higher-order skills to solve authentic, ill-defined problems through the collaborative production of a video that demonstrates a solution for a real audience (Schuck & Kearney, 2008). Student creation of video also aligns and supports achievement of the six NETS-S and builds real-world skills required for 21st century careers. For example, benefits of video production include:

- Dramatization of student stories, songs, and poems
- Immediate feedback to improve performance
- Skills training (e.g., how to use digital science probes)
- Interpersonal techniques (e.g., how to work cooperatively)
- Student documentaries of school or neighborhood issues
- Preservation of local folklore
- Demonstrations of science experiments and safety drills
- Replays of field trips for in-class follow up

When planning lessons, keep in mind the prominent features of video that will help to enhance student learning. These include the ability to depict motion, show processes, offer risk-free observations, provide dramatizations, and support skill learning. Videos also portray scenarios to build affective learning, introduce open-ended problem-solving vignettes, and develop cultural understanding and establish commonality. See "When to Use Video" for examples of each guideline.

TYPES OF EDUCATIONAL VIDEOS

Although there are vast numbers of commercially produced educational videos appropriate for use in PK–12 classes, most videos can be grouped into four common types: documentary, dramatization, video storytelling, and virtual field trips.

Documentary. Video is the primary medium for documenting actual or reenactments of events and bringing them into the classroom. The documentary deals with fact, not fiction or fictionalized versions of fact. Documentaries attempt to depict essentially true stories about real

Video

Use video when student learning will be enhanced by ...	Example
Motion	High school students watch video clips of various chemical reactions to determine the environmental impact of using gasoline engines.
Processes	Elementary students watch a video that shows each step of the recycling process to learn how aluminum cans are recycled.
Risk-free observation	Middle school students view a video of a Hawaiian volcano eruption.
Dramatization	Elementary children watch a video showing the evolution of transportation.
Skill learning	Art students in a middle school view a video that shows step-by-step techniques used to draw shadows.
Affective learning	Kindergarten students watch a video to better understand the feelings and challenges of children with disabilities.
Problem solving	Middle school students in an interdisciplinary gifted class view documentaries explaining the overpopulation concerns of some large U.S. cities, and then discuss possible solutions.
Cultural understanding and establishing commonality	High school students in a school with a growing population of English language learners from multiple ethnic backgrounds view videos that highlight the commonalities between ethnicities.

situations and people. Many nonprofit organizations, such as the Public Broadcasting System (PBS), regularly produce significant documentaries available at PBS Video **(http://video.pbs .org).** For example, the video *To the Ends of the Earth* allows students to "experience" the story of a perilous sea voyage based on William Golding's novel of the same name. *The Civil War* miniseries is a documentary of a critical period in U.S. history. Programs such as *Nova* and National Geographic specials offer outstanding documentaries on science, culture, and nature, many of which are available for viewing on the Internet. Virtually all television documentaries are available for purchase.

Dramatization. Video has the power to hold your students spellbound as a drama unfolds before their eyes. Literature classics available on video, such as *Anne of Green Gables, Hamlet,* and *Moby Dick,* expand student learning opportunities as they compare and contrast the differences between the text and video. Historical fiction, such as *Shogun* and *War and Peace,* use a combination of fiction and facts to dramatize historical events. Dramatization is also an excellent venue to build positive student character and attitudes concerning such areas as multiculturalism, disabilities, self-esteem, and working cooperatively.

Video Storytelling. From childhood, we have learned to love to hear and tell stories because they are entertaining and informative. Stories can be incorporated into instruction through videos, such as the online "Real-Life Stories" of teenagers involved with Internet safety issues such as cyberbullying (NCMEC, 2013). Storytelling is an important skill to develop in students of all ages. Video storytelling allows students to be creative while developing their visual literacy skills, writing skills, and video production skills. The goal is to teach students to express ideas,

TAKING A LOOK AT TECHNOLOGY INTEGRATION:

Video

Bridges to Understanding

Bridges to Understanding (**www.bridgesweb.org**) is an international nonprofit organization that provides a website for student-created video stories. The Bridges mission is for students to use "digital technology and the art of storytelling to empower and unite youth worldwide, to enhance cross-cultural understanding, and to build global citizenship." Bridges offers several student opportunities, such as the Bridges Ambassador Program, Global Citizens Program, Passport Program, and Discovery Program. Teacher training workshops and curriculum for integrating digital video storytelling into classroom instruction are also offered.

concepts, and understandings through stories. In the process, students can both teach and learn from each other. See "Taking a Look at Technology Integration: Video" for additional information on video storytelling.

Virtual Field Trips Videos can take students to places they might not be able to go otherwise. You can take your students to the Amazon rainforest, the jungles of New Guinea, or the Galapagos Islands. Students can also go on a virtual tour of the Egyptian pyramids, the Great Wall of China, or the Acropolis in Athens, Greece. Videos enhance and build upon knowledge gained from reading textbooks, Internet descriptions, or listening to presentations.

LOCATING AND EVALUATING VIDEO

As seen, there are many types of video for use in PK–12 instruction. The first step to integrating these useful resources is to locate videos that are directly aligned with and support achievement of your lesson objectives and that are in a format appropriate for your video viewing equipment. The second step is to evaluate the selected video to ensure that it *actually* aligns to your objectives and will meet the needs of your students.

Locating Videos. In most educational settings, teachers have access to numerous educational videos from a variety of sources. Common digital video formats include DVD, Blu-ray discs, computer-based video, and Internet-based video.

DVD. A digital videodisc (DVD) is a medium offering digital storage and playback of full-motion video. The disc is the same physical size as an audio CD but can hold hours of video with high-quality soundtracks. Like CDs, DVDs have instant random access and are durable, play in slow motion, and provide superior sound and picture quality.

Blu-ray discs. **Blu-ray discs** (also known as BD) store high-definition video, games, and other data on discs the same size as a standard DVD. Although the BD is the same size as standard DVDs and CDs, they store almost ten times more data than a DVD. The name comes from the blue laser used to read the disc. A BD cannot be viewed on a DVD player, but DVDs can be viewed on a Blu-ray player.

Computer-based video. Students can prepare video reports, class presentations, and digital portfolios on computers. Using video sequences or images from materials they have recorded or from DVDs, they can use video editing software such as iMovie or Movie Maker to manipulate the images and sounds similar to manipulation of information in word processing or presentation software. For example, students can use a multimedia approach when creating an oral report. Students begin by researching a topic using books, databases, videos, CDs, and other media. Relevant content is "captured" on video, edited, and student narration is added before presenting the final report. Remember that copyright laws also apply to the use of video created by others. For additional information regarding copyright, refer to the "Copyright Concerns: Copyright Law" section in chapter 1. Digital videos are also an important component in computer-based student portfolios because the videos capture actual student reflections and performance over time. This enables the students, teachers, and others to follow student progress through the archived videos.

Internet video. Many websites now offer Internet broadcasts of events or activities at their site, including newsworthy stories, scientific activities, and cultural presentations. Some of the broadcasts are live and others are recorded. Live web cams can take students to a museum, a national park, zoo, historical landmark, or an aquarium to observe activities in real time. See Monterey Bay Aquarium **(www.montereybayaquarium.org)** for a variety of live web cams. These Internet broadcasts use compressed video or streaming video (explained below).

Compressed video. Compressed video saves data space by recording only the moving or changing parts of each frame. The parts of the picture that are not changing are not recorded; hence, less data are needed to reproduce the image, resulting in smaller video files. Compressed video is used to transmit video over the Internet.

Streaming video. Video also can be delivered over the Internet using streaming video. *Streaming* means that the file doesn't have to be completely downloaded before it starts playing. Instead, as soon as the user clicks on a link that contains streaming video, the content begins to play. The video content is actually downloading to the user's computer in a series of small information packets that arrive shortly before the viewer sees the material. Any video materials can be delivered over the Internet using the streaming technique. The content is not stored on your computer. It "flows" into your active memory, is displayed (or played), and then is erased.

Sources of educational videos. School districts for more than one million teachers provide online access to a multitude of digital media, including educational videos, through a subscription to *Discovery Education* (http://www.discoveryeducation.com/). The Internet also offers vast educational video options, with most being freely available for classroom viewing. For example, the Teaching Channel is a nonprofit organization described as a "video showcase—on the Internet and TV—of inspiring and effective teaching practices in America's schools" (Teaching Channel, 2013). School library media specialists are also a key resource for locating videos owned by the school, district, or regional resource center. They also assist with locating other providers of sponsored videos, as discussed below.

Private companies, associations, and government agencies sponsor videos for a variety of reasons. Private companies may make videos to promote their products or to enhance their public image. Associations and government agencies sponsor videos to promote causes, such as better health habits, conservation of natural resources, and proper use of park and recreation areas. Many of these sponsored videos are worthwhile instructional materials that have the advantage of being free or inexpensive. A certain amount of caution, however, is called for in using sponsored videos for instructional purposes. Some privately produced materials may be too flagrantly self-serving. Or, they may deal with products not suitable for instructional settings, for example, the manufacturing of alcoholic beverages or cigarettes. Some association and government materials may contain a sizable dose of propaganda or special pleading for favorite causes. When properly evaluated, many sponsored videos can be valuable additions to

MEDIA SAMPLES

Video

Freedom Fighters

www.nestlearning.com/freedom-fighters-pack_p311288.aspx

The Freedom Fighters four-pack highlights four women seen as heroes who caused a change in the social order of their time in history. Included are animated stories of Harriet Tubman, Helen Keller, Joan of Arc, and Pocahontas.

Math...Who Needs It?

www.fasestore.org/Math-Who-Needs-It-DVD-p/mwni.htm

This video is aimed at parents and their kids. It gives a perspective on the rewards and opportunities open to anyone with good math skills. It challenges myths about math, pokes fun at society's misconceptions of the subject, and provokes viewers to think and talk about math in a more positive way.

The Supreme Court

www.ambrosevideo.com/items.cfm?id=1217

A winner of eight prestigious awards, including the 2008 Parents' Choice Gold Award, this four-part video series about the Supreme Court is appropriate for high school history and social studies classes. The videos use archival footage, interviews with the justices, and digital graphics to explore and personalize the history and impact of the Supreme Court.

One Woman, One Vote

www.pbs.org/wgbh/americanexperience/films/OneWomanOneVote

Witness the 70-year struggle for women's suffrage, from fledgling alliances to a sophisticated mass movement. This video documents the history of the women's suffrage movement from the Seneca Falls Convention in 1848, when Elizabeth Cady Stanton demanded the right for women to vote, to the last battle for passage of the 19th Amendment in 1920.

---

classroom instruction. The LearnZillion (**http://learnzillion.com**) site provides numerous high-quality common core resources developed by leading teachers across the nation.

Evaluating Video After you have located some potentially useful videos, use an evaluation tool to assess alignment with your lesson. A good appraisal form is brief enough not to be intimidating but complete enough to help teachers choose materials that will enhance student learning. In some cases, the evaluation results help justify the purchase or rental of specific titles.

The **Selection Rubric: Videos** includes the most commonly used criteria, particularly those that have research-based evidence of effectiveness. The specific areas of importance for evaluating video are pacing and the use of cognitive learning aids, such as an overview, cues, and a summary. Cues are features that help point learners to important aspects of the video, such as a flashing arrow pointing to parts of a flower as each is being presented. Evaluating videos also provides you the opportunity to make notes for class discussion of the key topics and areas that need further explanation or emphasis to enhance student learning.

VIEWING AND PRODUCING VIDEO

After locating and evaluating video for instructional use, it is important to prepare your students to view the video. Similarly, students need preparation before viewing or producing video to demonstrate their learning.

Viewing Video. Students have several options for viewing educational videos, including whole-class viewing with a digital projector or a large-screen television monitor, computers, and mobile devices such as netbooks, iPads, and iPhones. When teaching students to

Video

Review the ASSURE video and reflect on the following questions. How does Scott James use script writing to support student learning? In what ways does Scott engage students in the production of digital video? What role does Scott play during video production?

"critically" view video, you can guide the viewing process by asking questions that require students to think critically about core concepts (Jolls, 2008). For example: Why do you think this video was created? Who is the intended audience for this video and why? What would you do differently to enhance the purpose of the message and why?

Producing Video. The core concepts also help students increase video literacy knowledge and skills through **videography,** or the creation of video. Producing video requires students to engage in the higher-order thinking skills of planning a video that will "tell the story," recording key scenes and editing the content to ensure the intended message is shared. Throughout the production process, students should be encouraged to reflect on their work to ensure the product aligns with the intended purpose and engages the audience with a compelling message (Jolls, 2008).

PLANNING

As with all media production, preproduction planning is necessary. Actively involve students in planning videos they are to produce. This planning involves storyboarding, scripting, and planning for recording, editing, and revising their video productions. To provide each student with a variety of experiences, involve them in rotating roles of writers, editors, camera operators, and on-camera talent. Students begin the process of video production by creating a series of storyboards to facilitate planning and production of video. The storyboards include a rough sketch of the scene, script, and any notes for the camera operator, such as "zoom in for close-up of object." Graphic organizer software, such as Kidspiration and Inspiration, or multiple free software programs provide useful tools for creating storyboards. When a group of students are cooperatively involved in designing a video, storyboarding is particularly helpful to organize and represent multiple viewpoints.

RECORDING

Hand-held cameras usually come with a built in microphone. This microphone has an automatic level control that adjusts the volume to keep the sound at an audible level; in other words, the camera hears as well as sees. The problem is that these microphones amplify all sounds within their range, including shuffling feet, coughing, street noises, and equipment noise, along with the sounds you want. You may therefore want to bypass the built-in microphone by plugging in a separate microphone better suited to your particular purpose. The lavaliere, or neck mike, is a good choice when recording a single speaker. It can be clipped to a shirt or dress, hung around the neck, or even hidden under lightweight clothing. A desk stand may be used to hold a microphone for a speaker or several discussants seated at a table. For situations in which there is unwanted background noise or the speaker is moving, a highly directional microphone is best.

EDITING

Digital video editing refers to the means by which video can be taken apart and put back together using a computer and editing software. Some digital camcorders have no videotape, while others use specialized videotape to record in a digital mode. After shooting video, you can watch it on the camera's built-in LCD monitor or connect the camcorder to a TV or computer to view the footage or to transfer the file to the computer. The transferred video

The Copyright Act of 1976 did not cover educational uses of video recordings of copyrighted broadcasts. A negotiating committee composed of representatives from industry, education, and government agreed on a set of guidelines for video recording of broadcasts for educational use. The following guidelines apply only to nonprofit educational institutions.

You may do the following:

- Ask your media/technology specialist to record the program, if you lack the equipment or expertise. The request to record must come from a teacher.
- Retain the recording of a broadcast (including cable transmission) for a period of 45 calendar days, after which you must erase the program.
- Use the recording in class once per class during the first 10 school days of the 45 calendar days, and a second time if instruction needs to be reinforced.
- Have professional staff view the program several times for evaluation purposes during the full 45-day period.
- Make a limited number of copies to meet legitimate needs, but you must erase these copies when erasing the original recording.
- Use only a part of the program if instructional needs warrant.
- Enter into a licensing agreement with the copyright holder to continue use of the program.

You may *not* do the following:

- Record premium cable services, such as HBO, without express written permission.
- Alter the original content of the program.
- Exclude the copyright notice on the program.
- Record a program in anticipation of use.
- Retain the program, and any copies, after 45 days.

Remember that these guidelines are not part of the copyright act but are rather an agreement between producers and educators. You should accept them as guidelines in good faith.

For general information on copyright, see the "Copyright Concerns: Copyright Law" section in Chapter 1.

file is then edited using standard editing software, such as Apple's iMovie or Windows Movie Maker. The editing software provides tools not only to delete and rearrange content, but also to add titles, music, photos, and special transitions. There are several methods for storing video on a computer. One format is QuickTime, for use with Mac and Windows operating systems. Many applications, such as Compton's Multimedia Encyclopedia, incorporate QuickTime "movies." Remember, you and your students must follow copyright guidelines when producing video.

Innovations on the Horizon

CLASSROOM VOICE AMPLIFICATION SYSTEMS

The 21st century classroom is moving to an audio technology system that optimizes the listening environment for all students. A lightweight wireless teacher's microphone links to a set of speakers strategically placed around the classroom. The end result is a quality listening setting that helps engage students and supports student learning and performance (Kollie, 2013).

Using voice activation solutions for the amplification, the system only raises the volume level of the teacher's voice slightly above the ambient room noise. In a noisy classroom, when it is often hard to hear the teacher, his or her voice is amplified just a little, but enough that it is easier for students to hear. In addition, there is evidence that all students benefit from the amplified sound, including those with hearing problems and learning disabilities, those for whom English is their second language, and even those students who have no identified learning difficulty (Crandell, Smaldino, & Flexer, 2005). To see an example, visit the Lightspeed (**www .lightspeed-tek.com**) site.

VIDEO: 3-D PRODUCTION COMES TO SCHOOLS

The advent of 3-D technology is seen in today's movies, TV shows, and state-of-the-art class-rooms. Teachers now have multiple resources available for viewing with a 3-D projection system. Going beyond these systems is an emerging innovation in PK-12 schools, portable 3-D cameras, which are available at prices starting below $100. The 3-D cameras consist of two HD cameras combined to record and synchronize 3-D video. Some systems combine the two cameras in one device, while others use a frame to hold two cameras set to record from slightly different viewpoints to achieve 3-D images. Specialized software is used to edit the footage into a 3-D video that is viewed with a 3-D player or on a computer equipped to view 3-D videos. Viewing requires 3-D glasses. Engaging students in the creation of 3-D videos will not only increase their motivation to learn, but also require their use of higher-order thinking to plan, record, and edit a video that meaningfully uses the third dimension to enhance the message.

Summary

This chapter discussed ways to enhance learning with audio and video and placed key emphasis on the chapter's knowledge outcomes.

- *Compare and contrast audio and video literacy.* Audio literacy requires attentive listening and deciphering of messages to identify what is meaningful and important to learning and connecting it with prior knowledge. Video literacy requires meaningful viewing or produc-tion of video that results in increased knowledge and skills.

- *Describe how audio enhances learning when listening skills are improved.* Audio can enhance learning when teachers use the following techniques to improve listening skills: guide listening; give directions; ask students to listen for main ideas, details, or inferences; use context in listening; analyze the structure of a presentation; and distinguish between relevant and irrelevant information.

- *Explain how audio use in the classroom can involve teachers and students.* Both teachers and students can use various types of audio to enhance learning opportunities. Teachers can prepare their own recordings or use commercially available or free digital recordings to supplement instruction. Students can record oral histories, book reviews, field trip notes, personal recitations of poems or other works, small group performances, and other class-room activities that involve audio content.

- *Select an audio resource and describe the advantages of integrating it into a lesson.* When selecting the resource, determine whether you will use streamed video, a podcast, Internet radio, or a self-produced audio recording and determine how the resource will enhance learning. For example, advantages for integrating an audio resource into a lesson for second-language learners, could include uses native language narrators, audio readily available, inexpensive, reproducible, and interesting to the selected age group.

- *Explain how video can enhance student cognitive, affective, psychomotor, and interpersonal learning.* Video can enhance cognitive learning by showing processes, relationships, and techniques. Affective learning is enhanced when video shapes personal, social, and cultural attitudes. Demonstrations of psychomotor skills are often more easily seen through video than in real life through the use of fast forward, stop action, and slow motion. By viewing a video program together, a diverse group of learners can build a common base of experience as a catalyst for discussion.

- *List and describe how the four types of educational video support student learning.* Documentaries attempt to depict essentially true stories about real situations and people. Dramatization enables students to compare and contrast the differences between a book and video of the same story, as well as to build positive student attitudes concerning such areas as multiculturalism, disabilities, self-esteem, and working cooperatively. Video storytelling develops visual literacy skills, writing skills, and video production skills. Virtual field trips enhance and build upon knowledge gained from reading textbooks, Internet descriptions, or listening to lectures.

- *Explain how students benefit from producing video to demonstrate knowledge and skills.* The key benefits of student video production are increased engagement and motivation and use of higher-order and collaboration skills to solve authentic, ill-defined problems in a video that demonstrates a solution for a real audience.

ASSURE Lesson Plan

The Classroom Case Study for this chapter is based on an interdisciplinary fifth-grade lesson created by Scott James. The video shows Scott James implementing the lesson in his fifth-grade classroom and providing his insights for achieving successful use of student-created video.

This ASSURE Lesson Plan describes the instructional planning used by Scott James, a fifth-grade teacher, to create an interdisciplinary lesson that incorporates student creation of digital videos. Mr. James wants to increase student awareness of natural disasters while increasing their expository writing skills. To address this challenge, student pairs select a natural disaster of their choice and conduct online and library research for their selected topic of interest. Students use this information to write a script and storyboards for their digital video news broadcasts. Below is Scott James's ASSURE lesson plan for the natural disaster news broadcast lesson.

Scott James
Fifth Grade
Topic: Natural Disasters

Analyze Learners

General Characteristics. The students in Scott James's fifth-grade class are of mixed ethnicities and from low- to middle-income homes. They are fairly equally distributed with regard to gender and are either 9 or 10 years old. Student reading ability ranges from below to above grade level. Student behavior problems increase when completing traditional seatwork.

Entry Competencies. The students are, in general, able to do the following:

- Conduct online research
- Use iMovie software to edit digital video

Learning Styles. Scott's students learn best when engaged in activities that are relevant to the content and for which they can self-select topics. His students' interest and motivation increase when they use technology. The students vary greatly in their comfort level with speaking and acting for the digital video news broadcasts. Differences are also seen with regard to use of graphics and sound; some students use a traditional approach, while others use a creative and fun method for the final products.

State Standards and Objectives

Curriculum Standards. *National Council of Teachers of English, Curriculum Standard 4*: Students adjust their use of spoken, written, and visual language (e.g., conventions, style, vocabulary) to communicate effectively with a variety of audiences and for different purposes; *National Science Education Standards for 5–8: Earth and Space Science*: Structure of the Earth System: Global patterns of atmospheric movement influence local weather. Oceans have a major effect on climate, because water in the oceans holds a large amount of heat; *Common Core State Standards, ELA Literacy, Grade 5.3*: Write narratives to develop real or imagined experiences or events using effective technique, descriptive details, and clear event sequences.

Technology Standards. *National Educational Technology Standards for Students 1:* Creativity and Innovation: Students demonstrate creative thinking, construct knowledge, and develop innovative products and processes using technology.

Learning Objectives. The learning objectives for this lesson are as follows:

1. Using content from Internet and library research on a student-selected natural disaster, the fifth-grade students will write a script for a news anchor and an on-the-scene reporter.

2. Using the student-written scripts, the students will create storyboards that include segments for a news anchor and an on-the-scene reporter and meet the lesson criteria for storyboards.

3. Using their student-created storyboards and scripts, each student records his or her portion (news anchor or on-the-scene reporter) of the news broadcasts with digital video.

4. Using the digital video of their news broadcast, students will use iMovie to produce a final edit of their news broadcast that meets the lesson criteria.

Select Strategies

Scott James selects teacher- and student-centered strategies for the natural disaster lesson. The teacher-centered strategies involve providing a detailed description of the lesson objectives and how the student pairs will conduct their research and create their news broadcasts. The student-centered strategies include

conducting Internet and library research, writing scripts, developing storyboards, and planning, recording, and editing their news broadcast video.

Select Resources

This lesson involves student use of computers, a digital camcorder, microphones, a green screen, and iMovie to edit their natural disaster videos. Scott uses the following guidelines to assess his technology and media selections:

- *Align to standards, outcomes, and objectives.* The library, Internet sites, and iMovie software provide the necessary tools for students to meet the learning objectives.
- *Accurate and current information.* Students use text-based and Internet resources to conduct their research on natural disasters.
- *Age-appropriate language.* Students use websites and books that are appropriate for fifth-grade students. Scott provides assistance and job aids for student use of iMovie.
- *Interest level and engagement.* Students choose a natural disaster of interest to them and create a personalized news broadcast, which increases student interest and engagement.
- *Technical quality.* Both the Internet sites and iMovie have high technical quality.
- *Ease of use.* Student use of iMovie requires initial training and support, but is fairly easy for fifth-grade students to use after basic skills training.
- *Bias free.* Students use multiple references for their research to better ensure use of bias free content. iMovie software is bias free.
- *User guide and directions.* The online help features of iMovie are not very easy for fifth-grade students to use. Therefore, students most frequently ask each other or Scott for assistance with technical difficulties.

Utilize Resources

Preview Resources. Scott selects and previews the "kid-friendly" Internet sites, library materials, and iMovie software to ensure they have the needed features.

Prepare Resources. Scott prepares an assignment sheet that describes the lesson requirements and criteria used to assess the final student products.

Prepare the Environment. Scott tests the Internet connections on the lab computers and ensures that iMovie is installed on each one. He also tests the digital video camera to ensure that it is working and downloads to the computers.

Prepare the Learners. The students have experience with Internet research and iMovie, thus the lesson begins with an overview of technical skills and an introduction to natural disasters.

Provide the Learning Experience. Scott guides student learning during video production and presentation of final videos to the class.

Require Learner Participation

Student Practice Activities. The students in Scott James's class use computers, the Internet, library materials, and iMovie to complete their natural disaster news broadcasts. Student pairs select a natural disaster and then conduct Internet and library research to find information about the topic. The students use this information to write the news anchor and on-the-scene reporter scripts and storyboards. Digital video is then recorded during students' presentations of their news broadcasts, and students use iMovie to create final cuts of their videos, which are presented to the class.

Feedback. Scott James provides continuous feedback as students conduct their research, write their scripts, create storyboards, edit videos, and present their news broadcasts.

Evaluate and Revise

Assessment of Learner Achievement. Scott assesses learner achievement in two ways. First is demonstration of content knowledge, as seen in student scripts, storyboards, and iMovie presentations. The second is demonstration of technology skills, which is assessed according to the assignment criteria as stated in the learning objectives.

Evaluation of Strategies and Resources. Scott evaluates the lesson strategies through continuous communication with the students. He also examines student products to determine whether the strategies were effective. Evaluation of the technology and media involves noting technical problems that occur during the lesson. This involves examining the functionality of the various software applications, Internet and library resources, and the digital camcorder.

Revision. After reviewing the evaluation results from the lesson implementation, Scott concludes that the lesson worked well, with one minor exception. He thought three weeks was too much time to devote to the designated standards and objectives. Therefore, he revised the lesson by borrowing digital video cameras from a regional media center to decrease the time needed to record all students.

Professional Development

DEMONSTRATING PROFESSIONAL KNOWLEDGE

1. Compare and contrast audio and video literacy.
2. Describe how audio enhances learning when listening skills are improved.
3. Explain how audio in the classroom can involve teacher and student use.
4. Select an audio resource and describe the advantages of integrating the audio into a lesson.
5. Explain how video can enhance student cognitive, affective, psychomotor, and interpersonal learning.
6. List and describe how the four types of educational video support student learning.
7. Explain how students benefit from producing video to demonstrate knowledge and skills.

DEMONSTRATING PROFESSIONAL SKILLS

1. Obtain commercially prepared audio materials and appraise them using the **Selection Rubric: Audio Materials**. Analyze the rubric findings and write an argument presenting the pros and cons for classroom use of each audio resource (ISTE NETS-T 2.A).

2. Develop a short oral history of your school or organization by interviewing people who have been associated with it for a long time. Edit your interviews into a five-minute presentation (ISTE NETS-T 3.C).

3. Use an audio format to collect your thoughts and ideas about what it means to use technology in your teaching. Listen to your narration after a few entries. What have you learned about your ideas? How does keeping your ideas on audio impact your collection of reflections? Would you consider your audio materials to be a variation of a written journal? Why or why not (ISTE NETS-T 5.C)?

4. Preview a video and appraise it using the **Selection Rubric: Videos**. Analyze the rubric findings and write an argument presenting the pros and cons for classroom use of the video material (ISTE NETS-T 2.A, C).

5. Identify one video for each learning domain and describe the cognitive, affective, psychomotor, or interpersonal objectives that are addressed in the video (ISTE NETS-T 2.A).

6. Create a digital video to support and enhance a topic you teach as a way to model creative and innovative thinking to your students (ISTE NETS-T 1 A).

BUILDING YOUR PROFESSIONAL PORTFOLIO

- *Creating My Lesson.* Using the ASSURE model, design a lesson for a scenario from Appendix A or use a scenario of your own design. Use an instructional strategy that you believe to be appropriate for your lesson and information from this chapter related to incorporating audio and/or video into your instructional setting. Be sure to include information about the audience, the objectives, and all other elements of the ASSURE model (ISTE NETS-T 2.A).

- *Enhancing My Lesson.* Enhance the lesson you created in the previous activity by describing how you would meet the diverse needs of learners. Specifically, describe additional strategies you would include for advanced students who already possess most of the knowledge and skills targeted in your lesson plan. Also, describe strategies and resources you could integrate to assist students entering the lesson who have not met the lesson prerequisites. Describe other types of technology and media that could be integrated into the instructional strategies (ISTE NETS-T 2.B; 2.C; 3.D; 5.C).

- *Reflecting on My Lesson.* Write a reflection describing the lesson you created and on how you enhanced the lesson. Also reflect on the process you used and what you have learned about matching audience, content, strategies, technology, media, and materials. Address the following in your reflection: What audio and video materials were used and in what ways do the media enhance the learning experiences of your students? What could be done to better develop your students' higher-order thinking or creativity skills? Justify why you proposed changes (ISTE NETS-T 5.C).

Suggested Resources

PRINT RESOURCES

Abrams, A., & Hoerger, D. (2009). *Award winning digital video projects for the classroom.* Eugene, OR: Visions Technology in Education.

Boyle, E. A., Rosenberg, M. S., Connelly, V. J., Washburn, S. G., Brinckerhoff, L. C., & Banerjee, M. (2003). Effects of audio texts on the acquisition of secondary-level content by students with mild disabilities. *Learning Disability Quarterly, 26*(3), 203–214.

Chenail, R. J. (2008). YouTube as a qualitative research asset: Reviewing user generated videos as learning resources. *The Weekly Qualitative Report, 1*(4), 18–24.

Farkas, B. G. (2006). *Secrets of podcasting* (2nd ed.). Berkeley, CA: Peachpit Press.

McDrury, J., & Alterio, M. (2003). *Learning through storytelling: Using reflection and experience to improve learning.* London: Kogan Page.

Schmeidler, E., & Kirchner, C. (2001). Adding audio description: Does it make a difference? *Journal of Visual Impairment and Blindness, 95*(4), 197–212.

Theodoskis, N. (2009). *The director in the classroom: How filmmaking inspires learning* (Version 2.0). British Columbia: Author.

Watson, L. (2010). *Teach yourself visually: Digital video.* New York, NY: Wiley.

WEB RESOURCES

Audio

NPR Podcast Directory

www.npr.org/rss/podcast/podcast_directory.php

The National Public Radio (NPR) partners with over 50 radio stations and producers to provide podcasts on topics such as art and life, economy, opinion, politics, pop culture, the world, and many more. The organization of the podcasts is by topic, title, or provider.

Multimedia Seeds: Exploring Audio and Visual Collection Use

http://eduscapes.com/seeds/different.html

The site provides hints for using audio and visuals for learning. Whether you're a school media specialist working with teachers and children or a teacher working with students, there are many ways to assist them in the effective use of audio and video media.

Sound Learning

http://soundlearning.publicradio.org

Sound Learning offers connections between Minnesota Public Radio programming and current academic standards, a technical guide to help you access audio files, and suggestions for effective learning strategies.

Video

Library Video Company

http://libraryvideo.com

A distributor of educational videos, DVDs, and audio books to schools nationwide, the company stocks over 18,000 titles covering a diverse range of topics for all ages and grade levels. Each program has been carefully reviewed and selected for content that is appropriate for the classroom setting.

neoK12

www.neok12.com

This site provides a collection of free online educational videos, lessons, games, Web 2.0 tools, and quizzes for K–12 students. Topic areas include physical, life, earth, and space science, social studies, math, English, and the human body. The American Library Association recognized neoK12 as one of its "Great Web Sites for Kids 2009."

TED: Ideas Worth Spreading

www.ted.com

TED is a small nonprofit organization devoted to "Ideas Worth Spreading" regarding Technology, Entertainment, Design (TED). The award-winning site has a collection of more than 500 free talks from the world's most fascinating thinkers and doers, who are challenged to give the talk of their lives (in 18 minutes). All of the talks feature closed captions in English, and many feature subtitles in various languages. These videos are released under a Creative Commons license, so they can be freely shared and reposted.

SELECTION RUBRIC   Audio Materials

Complete and save the following interactive evaluation to reference when selecting audio materials to integrate into lessons.

Search Terms

_____

_____

Format

Title _____

Source/Location _____

©Date _____ Cost _____ Length _____ Minutes _____

Subject Area _____ Grade Level _____

Instructional Strategies _____

_____ Compact Disc

_____ Internet Audio

_____ Podcast

_____ Digital Audio

Brief Description

Standards/Outcomes/Objectives

Prerequisites (e.g., prior knowledge, reading ability, vocabulary level)

Strengths

Limitations

Special Features

Name _____ Date _____

Rating Area	High Quality	Medium Quality	Low Quality
Alignment with standards, outcomes, and objectives	Standard/outcome/objective addressed and use of audio should enhance student learning.	Standard/outcome/objective partially addressed and use of audio may enhance student learning.	Standard/outcome/objective not addressed and use of audio will likely not enhance student learning.
Accurate and current information	Information is correct and does not contain material that is out of date.	Information is correct but does contain material that is out of date.	Information is not correct and does contain material that is out of date.
Age-appropriate language	Language used is age appropriate and vocabulary is understandable.	Language used is nearly age appropriate and some vocabulary is above/below student age.	Language used is not age appropriate and vocabulary is clearly inappropriate for student age.
Interest level and engagement	Topic presented so that students are likely to be interested and actively engaged in learning.	Topic presented to interest students most of the time and engage most in learning.	Topic presented so as not to interest students and not engage them in learning.
Technical quality	The material represents best available technology and media.	The material represents technology and media that are good quality, although there are some problems.	The material represents technology and media that are not well prepared and are of very poor quality.
Ease of use (user may be student or teacher)	Material follows easy-to-use patterns with nothing to confuse the user.	Material follows patterns that are easy to follow most of the time, with a few things to confuse the user.	Material follows no patterns and most of the time the user is very confused.
Bias free	There is no evidence of objectionable bias or advertising.	There is little evidence of bias or advertising.	There is much evidence of bias or advertising.
User guide and directions	The user guide is an excellent resource for use in a lesson. Directions should help students use the material.	The user guide is a good resource for use in a lesson. Directions may help students use the material.	The user guide is a poor resource for use in a lesson. Directions do not help students use the material.
Appropriate pacing	The audio material is presented so most students can understand and process the information.	The audio material is presented so some students start to understand and process the information.	The audio material is presented so most students cannot understand and process the information.
Use of cognitive learning aids (overviews, cues, summary)	The audio material is well organized and uses cognitive learning aids.	The audio material is fairly well organized and uses some cognitive learning aids.	The audio material is not well organized and does not use cognitive learning aids.

Recommended for Classroom Use: _____ Yes _____ No

Ideas for Classroom Use: _____

_____

SELECTION RUBRIC   Videos

Complete and save the following interactive evaluation to reference when selecting audio materials to integrate into lessons.

Search Terms

_____

_____

_____

Format

Title _____ _____ DVD

Source/Location _____ _____ Blu-ray

©Date _____ Cost _____ Length _____ minutes _____ _____ Computer-based

Subject Area _____ Grade Level _____ _____ Internet

Instructional Strategies _____ _____ Compressed

_____ Streaming

Brief Description

Standards/Outcomes/Objectives

Prerequisites (e.g., prior knowledge, reading ability, vocabulary level)

Strengths

Limitations

Special Features

Name _____ **Date** _____

Rating Area	High Quality	Medium Quality	Low Quality
Alignment with standards, outcomes, and objectives	Standard/outcome/objective addressed and use of video should enhance student learning.	Standard/outcome/objective partially addressed and use of video may enhance student learning.	Standard/outcome/objective not addressed and use of video will likely not enhance student learning.
Accurate and current information	Information is correct and does not contain material that is out of date.	Information is correct but does contain material that is out of date.	Information is not correct and does contain material that is out of date.
Age-appropriate language	Language used is age appropriate and vocabulary is understandable.	Language used is nearly age appropriate and some vocabulary is above/below student age.	Language used is not age appropriate and vocabulary is clearly inappropriate for student age.
Interest level and engagement	Topic presented so that students are likely to be interested and actively engaged in learning.	Topic presented to interest students most of the time and engage them in learning.	Topic presented so as not to interest students and not engage them in learning.
Technical quality	The material represents best available media.	The material represents media that are good quality, although there are some problems.	The material represents media that are not well prepared and are of very poor quality.
Ease of use (user may be student or teacher)	Material follows easy to use patterns with nothing to confuse the user.	Material follows patterns that are easy to follow most of the time, with a few things to confuse the user.	Material follows no patterns and most of the time the user is very confused.
Bias free	There is no evidence of objectionable bias or advertising.	There is little evidence of bias or advertising.	There is much evidence of bias or advertising.
User guide and directions	The user guide is excellent resource for use in a lesson. Directions should help students use the material.	The user guide is good resource for use in a lesson. Directions may help students use the material.	The user guide is poor resource for use in a lesson. Directions do not help students use the material.
Appropriate pacing	The video material is presented so most students can understand and process the information.	The video material is presented so some students start to understand and process the information.	The video material is presented so most students cannot understand and process the information.
Use of cognitive learning aids (overviews, cues, summary)	The video material is well organized and uses cognitive learning aids.	The video material is fairly well organized and uses some cognitive learning aids.	The video material is not well organized and does not use cognitive learning aids.

Recommended for Classroom Use: _____ Yes   _____ No

Ideas for Classroom Use: _____

_____

Enhancing Learning with Text and Visuals

Knowledge Outcomes

This chapter addresses ISTE NETS-T 2 and 3.

1. Compare and contrast text and visual literacy.

2. Select a text resource and describe the advantages of integrating it into a lesson.

3. Describe variables that affect how a learner interprets or decodes a visual.

4. Provide an example visual for each of the seven purposes of visuals, and explain how the visual fulfills the intended purpose.

5. List and describe how the six categories of visuals support student learning.

Goal

Discuss the various types and uses of text and visuals and the general principles for creating and using text and visuals to enhance student learning.

Mrs. Roman, a third-grade teacher, noted that her students' test scores indicated they were having problems visualizing geometric forms. She especially noted that they had problems with mentally converting a two-dimensional picture on a test into a three-dimensional image that it represented. She spoke with Mrs. Edlund, the art teacher, to seek ways of helping her students understand visualization of ideas. Mrs. Edlund also wanted to find ways to use art to assess learning due to the school's interest in using art and technology in the learning process. She was trying to find a way to bring technology into the art classroom. Both teachers have noted that the children have difficulty thinking about their learning and expressing themselves.

Please view the ASSURE Classroom Case Study video for this chapter to explore how Mrs. Roman works with the art teacher, Mrs. Edlund, to seek ways of using art and technology to help her students understand the visualization of geometric concepts. Throughout the chapter, you will find reflection questions related to the chapter content and the ASSURE Classroom Case Study. At the end of the chapter, you will be challenged to develop your own ASSURE lesson that uses text and visuals for a topic and grade level of your choice.

 Watch Mrs. Roman and Mrs. Edlund and their class as they develop artwork to demonstrate geometric concepts.

In this chapter we will explore the selection and use of text and visuals for learning. Even though these resources are commonly used, the actual benefit to student learning is dependent upon the teacher's ability to choose or create effective materials that build students' text and visual literacy knowledge and skills.

Effective design and use of text and visuals require you, as a teacher, to understand the advantages, limitations, and strategies needed to integrate text and visuals into your instruction. You will need to understand the variables that affect how learners interpret text and visuals, how text and visuals enhance learning, and key strategies for you and your students to create meaningful text and visual resources.

Text Literacy

Rowe (2012) advocates that today's student must be able to locate, understand, and use informational text to fully participate in our society. These skills are foundational components of **text literacy.** There are two aspects to a student becoming literate in the use of text as part of the learning process. One aspect is that of comprehending text, or the ability to understand and evaluate the message. The other is producing text, which is the ability to synthesize and write about what they read or experience. In both cases, text literacy skills develop over time and the technology and media you use as a teacher can help to address these abilities (Handsfield, Dean, & Cielocha, 2009).

COMPREHENDING TEXT

As a teacher, you will not only be responsible for locating literary and informational text resources that support and enhance student learning and achievement of learning outcomes, but you will also need to ensure students comprehend the intended message of the resources.

The International Reading Association CCSS Committee (2012) offers three recommendations for teachers to increase student comprehension:

1. Engage students in closely and critically reading high-quality texts.
2. Teach research-proven reading comprehension strategies using gradual release of responsibility approaches.
3. Guide students to apply strategies when reading particularly challenging texts. (p. 2)

In addition, it is important for students to engage in opportunities to steadily increase their level of understanding when reading complex informational text. Thus, you should assist students in "making an increasing number of connections among ideas and between texts, considering a wider range of textual evidence, and becoming more sensitive to inconsistencies, ambiguities, and poor reasoning in texts" (NGA Center & CCSS, 2010, p. 8). These skills will also better enable students to create or produce text that meaningfully demonstrates their learning.

PRODUCING TEXT

Most students begin producing simple forms of text during early primary grades and continue communicating with text throughout their years of education and while in the workforce. As a teacher, you will be challenged to prepare your students to produce text that meets three primary goals that are components of most curriculum standards: (1) *to persuade,* in order to change the reader's point of view or affect the reader's action; (2) *to explain,* in order to expand the reader's understanding; and (3) *to convey experience,* real or imagined, in order to communicate individual and imagined experience to others (NAGB, 2010, p. 3). States and school districts frequently require the use of a specific writing process. Common steps in a writing process are prewriting, drafting, revising, editing, and publishing. Revising and editing can be repeated, as needed, to produce a quality product.

As technology is increasingly available at school and home, text materials created by students are often in a digitial format. Most commonly, text is produced with word processing software that easily supports revisions such as changing font styles, moving text, adding features such as bullets, and inserting images, charts, and hyperlinks to online resources. Students also produce digital text materials in programs such as presentation software, graphic organizers, blogs, wikis, and discussion boards.

Text in the Classroom

Text is everywhere in students' learning experiences. Students encounter text through print and digital materials such as textbooks, fiction and nonfiction books, newspapers, booklets, pamphlets, magazines, study guides, manuals, and worksheets, as well as word-processed documents prepared by students and teachers. Text materials are divided into two primary types, **literary** and **informational.** Examples of literary text include stories, dramas, poetry, and myths, whereas informational texts include textbooks and other nonfiction resources. The Common Core State Standards **(www.corestandards.org)** (CCSS) for English Languare Arts (ELA) and Literacy in History/Social Studies, Science, and Technical Subjects emphasize that "to build a foundation for college and career readiness, students must read widely and deeply from among a broad range of high-quality, increasingly challenging literary and informational texts" (NGA Center & CCSS, 2010, p. 10). However, as students progress in grades, a greater emphasis is placed on consuming and producing informational texts. The foundation for this shift is found in "extensive research establishing the need for college and career ready students to be proficient in reading complex informational text independently in a variety of content areas" (NGA Center & CCSS, 2010, p. 4). This increased emphasis is also seen on the 2009 National Assessment of Educational Progress (NAEP) Reading Framework that includes equal distribution of literary and informational passages on the grade 4 assessment, but shifts to 30% literary and 70% informational passages on the grade 12 assessment (National Assessment Governing Board, 2008).

Advantages of Text

- *Availability.* Text materials are readily available on a variety of topics and in many different formats.
- *Flexibility.* They are adaptable to many purposes and may be used in any environment.
- *Portability.* Most text materials in print form or viewed with a mobile device are easily carried from place to place.
- *User friendly.* Properly designed text materials are easy to use, not requiring special effort to "navigate" through them.
- *Personalization.* Digitized text often includes tools to personalize content to reader preferences, such as adding highlights, bookmarks, comments, links to associated resources, or modifying font size and color to improve readability.

Limitations of Text

- *Reading level.* The major limitation of text materials is that they are written at a certain reading level that may not align with all students in your class.
- *Vocabulary.* Some textbooks introduce a large number of vocabulary terms and concepts in a short amount of space. Readers sometimes lack the prerequisite knowledge to comprehend the vocabulary and terminology.
- *One-way presentation.* Since most text materials are not interactive, they tend to be used in a passive way, often without comprehension.
- *Curriculum determination.* Sometimes textbooks dictate the curriculum rather than being used to support the curriculum. Textbooks are often selected to accommodate the curriculum guidelines of particular states or provinces rather than specific needs in local school districts.
- *Cursory appraisal.* Selection committees might not examine textbooks carefully. Sometimes textbooks are chosen by the "five-minute thumb test"—whatever catches the reviewer's eye while thumbing through the textbook.

INTEGRATION OF TEXT

As described above, the most common types of text materials are literary and informational. These are integrated into lessons through reading and project-based assignments in which the text materials are shared during class discussions, in student products, and on assessments. Lessons frequently integrate student use of supplementary text materials on a specific topic not covered in their textbook. Check with your school's information specialist to identify print materials in the library media center and to locate digital resources aligned to your lesson stanards and objectives.

As a teacher, you will want to consider all types of text-based materials available to enhance your lessons, keeping in mind the limitations mentioned above as well as student literacy levels. It is important to assess the reading ability of each student and work with a special education coordinator to identify needs of students with learning disabilities. See "Technology for All Learners: Text for information" on text readers and digital books. Another important step

Text

Text Readers and Digital Books

Students who are poor readers because of dyslexia and other learning disabilities find that their reading is slow, inaccurate, and boring. They frequently have to reread passages, struggle to decode unfamiliar words, and suffer from fatigue and stress. And, gifted learners often find the text materials in the classroom too simple or boring to challenge them. There are many resources for helping students access information in print formats within the classroom.

- Audio or digital books allow instant access to any page, chapter, or subheading with the touch of a button. To listen, students need a portable media player equipped to play the books, or a multimedia computer with a CD drive and specialized software. The Kindle, an electronic book device, provides a text-based means to manipulate the reading materials.

- Students with visual impairments or severe learning disabilities have access to thousands of digital books available for download or on CD from Recording for the Blind and Dyslexic (www.rfbd.org). A collection of over 6,000 digitally recorded educational titles, including books from the Harry Potter series, have been added to the nonprofit organization's collection of 91,000 accessible textbooks.

- Kurzweil (**www.kurzweiledu.com**), a text-to-speech program, provides students with a multimedia approach by presenting printed or electronic text with additional visual and audible cues. It can also "read" the Internet.

is to evaluate the reading materials in your classroom. You will find the **Selection Rubric: Text Materials** at the end of this chapter a helpful tool for this evaluation process.

Visual Literacy

Visual literacy refers to the learned ability to interpret visual messages accurately and to create such messages. Visual literacy can be developed through two major approaches: helping learners to interpret, or **decode,** visuals proficiently by practicing visual analysis skills, and helping learners to create, or **encode,** visuals to express themselves and communicate with others.

INTERPRETING VISUALS

Seeing a visual does not automatically ensure that one will learn from it. Learners must be guided toward correct decoding or interpeting of visuals. One aspect of visual literacy, then, is the skill of interpreting and creating meaning from visuals.

Many variables affect how a learner decodes a visual. Young children tend to interpret images more literally than do older children. Very young children have been shown to have difficulty discriminating between realistic images and the objects they depict (DeLoache, 2005). Prior to the age of 12, children tend to interpret visuals section by section rather than as a whole. In reporting what they see in a picture, they are likely to single out specific elements within the scene. Students who are older, however, tend to summarize the whole scene and report a conclusion about the meaning of the picture.

In teaching, we must keep in mind that the act of decoding visuals may be affected by the viewer's cultural background. Different cultural groups may perceive visual materials in different ways. For example, let's say your instruction includes visuals depicting scenes typical of the home and community life of inner-city children. It is almost certain that students who live in the inner city will decode these visuals differently than will students whose cultural backgrounds do not include firsthand knowledge of inner-city living.

Visual Literacy

Visuals inundate today's students, so their ability to read, understand, create, analyze, and learn from the persuasiveness of visuals has become more important than ever. Recent research has highlighted the value of using and creating visuals as learning tools for students. Technology plays a critical role in visual media design, development, and production, which all utilize critical thinking and problem-solving skills that enhance students' abilities to learn. Students exhibit their learning, share their work with global students, and gain the skills and competencies required to succeed in an increasingly visual world. Visual literacy development has been embedded within education programs throughout the United States and in many other countries to introduce students to the concepts and skills related to interpreting visuals and communicating visually. In these programs, teachers are encouraged to think visually and to focus students' attention on the visual aspects of printed and digitally available materials, including textbooks and storybooks. Therefore, these programs are designed for children from preschool through high school and college and encompass both encoding and decoding visual information in all media. Visual literacy has now become well accepted as an important aspect of the curriculum at all levels of education, and is best developed when embedded within content areas, with activities and assessment that are related to local, state, or national learning standards. The International Visual Literacy Association (IVLA) is an organization established for professionals involved in visual literacy.

Programs in public schools involve students in critical viewing activities and media production projects with the aim of meeting standards in technology, while achieving content standards in subject areas such as language, literacy, social studies, and science. For example, students examine materials with a focus on how elements within each medium, such as color, perspective, design, or pacing can affect the impact of visual messages. Art prints and museum websites such as the National Gallery or the Library of Congress and many others support this analysis. Teachers are encouraged to consider students' visual learning styles in selecting materials, and the importance of visuals in developing multimodal skills and assisting second language learners is emphasized. In many districts, students are engaged in learning and in using technology appropriately to create poster campaigns, design new products and advertising, examine their television viewing habits, analyze commercial messages, and digitally report the results of their research. They produce and share digital movies, create websites, and produce photo exhibits and other media to both extend their learning and share their knowledge with the global society to which they belong.

Source: Reprinted by permission of Rhonda Robinson.

In selecting visuals, teachers have to make appropriate choices between the sorts of visuals that are preferred and those that are most effective, as students do not necessarily learn best from the kinds of pictures they prefer. Most learners prefer colored visuals to black-and-white visuals. However, there is no significant difference in the amount of learning except when color is related to the content to be learned. Most learners also prefer photographs to line drawings, even though in many situations line drawings may communicate better. In addition, learners may prefer realistic visuals to abstract representations, yet teachers must strike a balance between the two to achieve their instructional purposes. Young learners prefer simple visuals and older students prefer more complex ones, but simpler visuals are usually more effective, whatever the age group.

CREATING VISUALS

Another aspect of visual literacy is student creation of visual presentations. Just as writing can spur reading, producing visuals can be a highly effective way of promoting visual understanding. You should encourage students to generate reports that include carefully selected or created images that transmit their message. Remind students to follow copyright guidelines in all these activities.

One skill that students need when creating visuals is that of sequencing. Reading specialists have long known that the ability to *sequence*—that is, to arrange ideas in logical order—is an extremely important factor in verbal literacy, especially in the ability to communicate in

Visuals

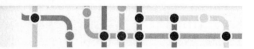

The following guidelines address use of visuals by teachers and students.

You are permitted to use:

- One illustration per book, periodical, or newspaper
- One diagram, chart, or picture from a single source
- One visual per source for presentation visuals (PowerPoint slides, overhead transparencies, etc.)

You are *not* permitted to use:

- Reproductions of copyrighted cartoon characters

For general information on copyright, see the "Copyright Concerns: Copyright Law" section in Chapter 1.

---

writing. Students may need practice in arranging visuals into a logical sequence, which is a learned skill, like the verbal sequencing in reading and writing. For this reason, it is important to emphasize student activities that call for arranging visuals. The sequential nature of digital presentations such as those created in PowerPoint assists students in acquiring this skill.

Visuals in the Classroom

Visuals are an integral component of instruction and learning. This section discusses the advantages, limitations, and integration of visuals in the classroom and information regarding the purpose of visuals and categories of visuals, as well as guidelines for viewing, creating, and capturing visuals.

Advantages of Visuals

- *Readily available*. Visuals are pervasive. They are in textbooks, computer programs, and most instructional materials.

- *Range of materials*. Visuals cover the complete range of curriculum areas and grade levels.

- *Ease of preparation*. You can easily prepare your own visuals and visual displays as described in this chapter.

- *Inexpensive*. Visuals are available at little cost. Many are free.

- *Simplification of complex ideas*. Visuals help to simplify even the most complex content and relationships. As the old adage goes, "A picture is worth a thousand words!"

- *Ease of use*. Visuals are very easy to use. Even young children can effectively use them for presentation of ideas.

- *Interactivity*. Visuals are ideal for "what if" displays of spreadsheet data or brainstorming activities using such software as Inspiration. This becomes an interactive medium when viewers' decisions or ideas are fed into the program and the outcome is displayed on the screen.

- *All students have equal view*. Visuals permit everyone to have an equal opportunity to easily view the same material at the same time.

Limitations of Visuals

- *Two-dimensional*. Visuals are two-dimensional and show only one view of the object or scene. Using multiple views or software that provides a three-dimensional perspective to images can compensate for this limitation.

- *Too many words on one visual.* Some people put too many words on one visual. Limit the number of words on each.
- *Bulky hardware.* Visual displays often require a large monitor, which is bulky, heavy, and cumbersome to move without a cart, or a digital projector, which requires a computer and a screen on which to project. You cannot use projected digital displays without a monitor or digital projector.
- *Expense.* Although prices steadily decrease, many teachers may not have the funds to purchase high-quality digital cameras, scanners, and projectors. Lower-priced equipment may lack the capability to meet your instructional needs.

INTEGRATION OF VISUALS

Every teacher can integrate visuals effectively to promote learning. Visuals are useful in a wide variety of instructional situations. Applications may be found in all curriculum areas at all grade levels. Here are some examples:

- *Art.* Illustrate the use of color to evoke emotions; demonstrate what happens when two colors are combined; show examples of art from various cultures and periods.
- *Consumer and family science.* Use a document camera to view sewing patterns, textiles, and recipes. Individuals create digital portfolios of various furniture styles and room layouts.
- *Foreign language.* Students examine images and texts related to their study of German; the teacher assigns small groups of students to study different Spanish-speaking countries. Each small group works collaboratively to prepare a presentation, with drawings and charts, to share with the class. They use pictures to help present their information.
- *Health.* Study the need for a healthy diet to support growing bodies. Some posters and other visual materials can be obtained by the teacher from local sources. The students put together a display of visuals showing various foods, along with additional visual materials to explain the significance of the foods that were selected.
- *Language arts.* Demonstrate examples of plagiarism by showing a visual of two texts. Elementary-level books have colorful visuals accompanying the story to motivate young readers. A teacher can show a print illustrating a rural scene and asks each student to write a short story related to the visual.
- *Library skills.* Show a floor plan of the layout of the school media center as part of library orientation; illustrate how to use library computers to locate a book.
- *Mathematics.* The algebra textbook contains a graph showing the relationship between the values of x and y in an equation. A teacher can demonstrate how to measure the distance between any two points on a map via a yardstick on an interactive whiteboard.
- *Music.* Show a staff with notes arranged in three-part harmony, with different colored notes for each part. Students can study pictures of various types of instruments.
- *Physical education.* The instructor uses still pictures of the warm-up exercises to remind each student of the body positions and sequence. Various basketball plays are illustrated.
- *Science.* Before solving a problem, each student is required to visualize the physics problem by drawing a diagram that shows the relationship among the known qualities and the unknown value. Students view animals of the world from a CD as they prepare to present a play for the PTA depicting endangered species. Visuals can be used to demonstrate the stages of volcanic eruptions.
- *Social studies.* Compare typical living conditions of children from various countries around the world. Students can study battles and timelines for a war. The class can "tour" local historical sites.

Visuals

Use visuals when student learning will be enhanced by...	Examples
Simplifying complex concepts	A high school teacher uses a genetics chart to show dominant and recessive traits. Students take digital photos of each classmate and classify them into genetic groups (e.g., attached ear lobes, curly hair, eye color).
	Middle school students select and assemble photos into a PowerPoint presentation that represents their concept of freedom.
Seeing relationships	Early childhood students study historical photos from the 1800s that show children in their homes to identify similarities and differences with their current home lives.
	A high school history teacher projects a spreadsheet chart showing population growth in their local community over the past 100 years. She has students predict changes over the next 100 years, and then shows the predicted changes on the chart by changing the numerical values of various cells.
Depicting processes	Elementary students in social studies build a model Alaskan igloo while using a disposable camera to create a photo journal of the building process.
	An ESL elementary teacher projects an interactive bilingual (English/Spanish) chart showing the life of a seed.
Stimulating interest	When introducing Shakespeare to middle school students, the teacher begins the lesson by using study prints showing different scenes of a Shakespearean play to stimulate interest in the topic.
	When studying cultural backgrounds, each elementary student uses the document camera to share a drawing of her or his ethnic history.
Encouraging creativity	Students work in pairs to create their own political cartoons of an historical event.
	Middle school student pairs write original math word problems shared via a digital projector so the problem can be solved as a whole group activity led by the teacher.

- *Vocational/technical.* A guest speaker from a local manufacturing company provides a photographic tour for students without traveling to and walking through the plant. Blueprints can be projected for group study.

PURPOSES OF VISUALS

Visuals can serve a multitude of purposes in the classroom. They can make abstract ideas more concrete, motivate your students, help direct their attention to important concepts, assist in recalling prior learning, and, most importantly, reduce the effort required to learn.

Provide a Concrete Referent for Ideas. Words don't look or sound like the thing they stand for; instead, visuals are **iconic**—that is, they have some resemblance to the concrete thing they represent (see Figure 9.1). Just like icons on a computer screen are used to represent the hard drive, your Internet browser, or the trash bin, visuals serve as a more easily remembered link to the original idea. In the classroom, a teacher uses visuals to help students more easily remember the content being taught. For instance, a geometry teacher may bring in a bag of grocery items to teach shapes (e.g., orange = sphere, can = cylinder).

FIGURE 9.1   The Concrete-Abstract Continuum

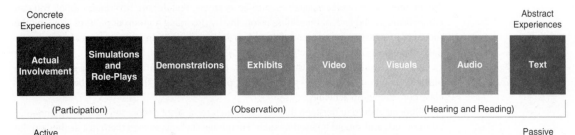

Source: Adapted from Paul Saettler, *The Evolution of American Educational Technology*. Copyright © 2004 Information Age Publishing. Reprinted by permission.

Make Abstract Ideas Concrete. Teachers use multiple methods to help make abstract ideas concrete. These include using photographs of people voting to represent freedom, a series of connected beads to show a model of DNA, or a diagram of word endings to assist beginning readers. It is also useful for students to select visuals to represent abstract ideas and then provide a rationale for their selection choice.

Motivate Learners. Interest enhances motivation. Visuals can increase interest in a lesson and motivate learners by attracting and holding their attention, thus generating engagement in the learning process. Visuals draw on the learners' personal interests to make the instruction relevant. For example, when teaching a history lesson, show "then" and "now" photos, such as buttons used before zippers, crank telephones before cell phones, or butter churns before margarine tubs.

Direct Attention. Use a visual pointer to draw the learner's attention and thinking to relevant parts of a visual. Visual pointers may be color, words, arrows, icons, shading, and animation. Use these signals to focus attention to important points within complex visual content.

Repeat Information. When visuals accompany spoken or written information, they present that information in a different modality, giving some learners a chance to comprehend visually what they might miss in verbal or text format (Paivio, 1971).

Recall Prior Learning. Visuals can be used to activate prior knowledge stored in long-term memory and to summarize the content from a lesson. These same visuals can be used at the beginning of the next lesson to remind the learners of what should have been learned.

Reduce Learning Effort. Visuals can simplify information that is difficult to understand. Diagrams can make it easy to store and retrieve such information. They can also serve an organizing function by illustrating the relationships among elements, as in flowcharts or timelines. Often, content can be communicated more easily and effectively with visuals (Mayer & Moreno, 2003). As a teacher, you want to convey your message in such a way that students expend little effort making sense out of what they are seeing and are free to use most of their mental effort for understanding the message itself.

TYPES OF VISUALS

Let's explore six types of visuals commonly used to support student learning: photos, drawings, charts, graphs, posters, and cartoons.

Photos. Photos are representations of people, places, and things. They are readily available on the Internet and in books, magazines, and newspapers. Pictures are two-dimensional. You can compensate for the lack of three-dimensionality by providing a group of pictures showing the same object or scene from several different angles or positions. In addition, a series of sequential still pictures can suggest motion.

You may use photos in a variety of ways. Photos of local architecture, for example, can illustrate a unit on architectural styles. Digital pictures taken on field trips can be valuable for classroom follow-up activities.

Students should understand that textbook pictures are not decorations but are intended to be study aids and should be used as such. Encourage students to read them just as they do the printed words. You should teach skills for decoding pictures and motivate learners to use them for study purposes. The quality and quantity of illustrations are, of course, important factors in textbook and media choice.

Drawings. Drawings, sketches, and diagrams employ the graphic arrangement of lines to represent persons, places, things, and concepts. Drawings are readily found in text materials. You can use them in all phases of instruction, from introduction of the topic through evaluation.

Teacher-made drawings can be effective aids to learning. You can sketch on a whiteboard to illustrate specific aspects of your instruction. For example, you may quickly and easily draw stick figures and arrows to show motion in an otherwise static representation.

You and your students can use software programs for layout, design, and illustration. Examples of these programs are Tux Paint (**www.tuxpaint.org**), iDraw (**www.indeeo.com/idraw**), and Draw in OpenOffice (**www.openoffice.us.com**). Most computer graphics software programs come with a wide variety of fonts and clip-art images and can manipulate visuals in every imaginable way. Most word processing and presentation software comes with basic drawing tools and some enhanced tools, such as Microsoft's SmartArt.

Charts. **Charts** are visual representations of abstract relationships such as chronologies, quantities, and hierarchies. They appear frequently as tables and flowcharts. They are also presented in the form of organization charts, classification charts (e.g., the periodic table), and timelines (see Figure 9.2).

A chart should have a clear, well-defined instructional purpose. In general, it should express only one major concept or concept relationships. A well-designed chart should communicate its message primarily through the visual channel. The verbal material should supplement the visual, not the reverse. If you have a lot of information to convey, develop a series of simple charts rather than a single complex one.

Graphs. **Graphs** provide a visual representation of numerical data. They also illustrate relationships among units of data and trends in data. Data can be interpreted more quickly in graph form than in tabular form. Graphs are also more visually interesting than tables. There are four major types of graphs: bar, pictorial, circle, and line (see Figure 9.3). The type you choose to use will depend largely on the complexity of the information you wish to present and the graph-interpretation skills of your students.

Numerous computer software programs, typically spreadsheet software such as OpenOffice Calc or Microsoft Excel, make it easy to produce professional-looking graphs. Enter your data into the spreadsheet and with just a few clicks of the mouse, the software depicts a variety of graphs as the types are selected from a pull-down menu. This features enables students to identify the graph that best displays findings for the targeted solution.

Posters. Posters incorporate visual combinations of images, lines, color, and words. They are intended to capture and hold the viewer's attention at least long enough to communicate a

FIGURE 9.2   Types of Charts: It is important to understand which type of chart is best for conveying information to your students.

Organization charts show the structure or chain of command in an organization such as a company, corporation, civic group, or government department. Usually they deal with the interrelationships of personnel or departments.

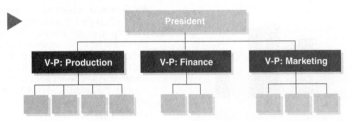

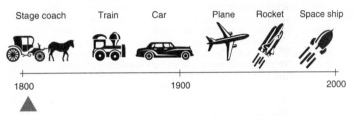

Timelines illustrate chronological relationships between events. They are most often used to show historical events in sequence or the relationships of famous people and these events. Pictures or drawings can be added to the time line to illustrate important concepts. Timelines are very helpful for summarizing a series of events.

Classification charts are similar to organization charts but are used chiefly to classify or categorize objects, events, or species. A common type of classification chart is one showing the taxonomy of animals and plants according to natural characteristics. The Food Guide Pyramid uses colors to organize foods into groups and to represent the proportions of these groups in a healthy diet.

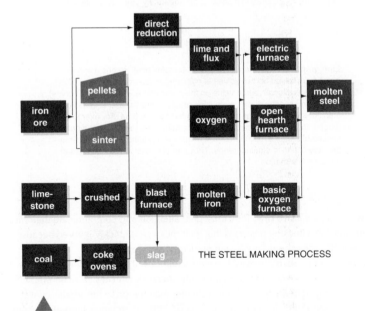

THE STEEL MAKING PROCESS

Flowcharts, or process charts, show a sequence, a procedure, or, as the name implies, the flow of a process. Flowcharts show how different activities, ingredients, or procedures are interrelated.

Import Percentages

	Wheat	Cotton	Steel	Oil
USA	0	0	20	35
England	65	95	35	10
France	15	95	30	90
Japan	85	15	0	95
Brazil	0	0	20	70

Tabular charts, or tables, contain numerical information, or data. They are also convenient for showing time information when the data are presented in columns, as in timetables for railroads and airlines.

FIGURE 9.3   Types of Graphs: It is important to understand which type of graph is best for conveying information to your students.

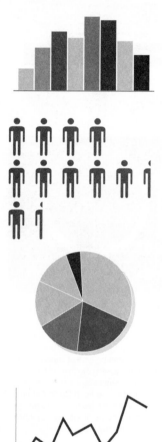

Bar graphs are easy to read and can be used with all students. The height of the bar is the measure of the quantity being represented. The width of all bars should be the same to avoid confusion. A single bar can be divided to show parts of a whole. It is best to limit the quantities being compared to eight or less; otherwise the graph becomes cluttered and confusing. The bar graph is particularly appropriate for comparing similar items at different times or different items at the same time; for example, the height of one plant over time or the heights of several students at any given time. The bar graph shows variation in only one dimension.

Pictorial graphs are an alternate form of the bar graph in which numerical units are represented by a simple drawing. Pictorial graphs are visually interesting and appeal to a wide audience, especially young students. However, they are slightly more difficult to read than bar graphs. Since pictorial symbols are used to represent a specific quantity, partial symbols are used to depict fractional quantities. To help avoid confusion in such cases, print values below or to the right of each line of figures.

Circle (or pie) graphs are relatively easy to interpret. In this type of graph, a circle or "pie" is divided into segments, each representing a part or percentage of the whole. One typical use of the circle graph is to depict tax-dollar allocations. The combined segments of a circle graph should, of course, equal 100 percent. Areas of special interest can be highlighted by illustrating a piece of pie separately from the whole.

Line graphs are the most precise and complex of all graphs. Line graphs are based on two scales at right angles. Each point has a value on the vertical scale and a value on the horizontal scale. Lines (or curves) are drawn to connect the points. Line graphs show variations in two dimensions, or how two or more factors change over time. For example, a graph can show the relation between pressure and temperature when the volume of a gas is held constant. Because line graphs are precise, they are very useful in plotting trends. They can also help simplify a mass of complex information.

brief message, usually a persuasive one. They must grab attention and communicate their message quickly. One drawback in using posters is that their message is quickly ignored because of familiarity. Consequently, they should not be left on display for too long.

Posters can be effective in numerous learning situations. They can stimulate interest in a new topic, announce a special event, or promote social skills. They may be employed for motivation—attracting students to a school recycling meeting or to the media center, or encouraging them to read more. In industrial education courses, science laboratories, and other situations where danger may be involved, posters can remind people of safety tips. Posters can also promote good health practices such as not using drugs and avoiding junk food (see Figure 9.4).

You may obtain posters from a variety of sources, including commercial companies, airlines, travel agencies, government departments, and professional organizations. You can make your own posters with colored markers, computer printouts, and devices that print poster-sized pages.

Cartoons. Cartoons are line drawings that are rough caricatures of real or fictional people, animals, and events. They appear in a variety of print media—newspapers, periodicals, textbooks—and range from comic strips intended primarily to entertain to drawings intended to make important social or political comments. Humor and satire are mainstays of the cartoonist's skill.

Cartoons are easily and quickly read and appeal to children of all ages. The best of them contain wisdom as well as wit. You can often use them to make or reinforce a point of instruction. Appreciation and interpretation, however, may depend on the experience and sophistication of the learner. Be sure the cartoons you use for instructional purposes are within the experiential and intellectual range of your students.

An additional option is for students to create cartoons with free online software, such as ToonDoo (**www.ToonDoo.com**). The software provides an array of characters, settings, and props for students to assemble into a cartoon that depicts the assigned message. ToonDoo also provides "A Teacher's Guide to ToonDoo" to help you utilize the software to engage students For example, students can create a cartoon representing ideas on recycling, global warming, historical events, current events, or story lines from a book.

FIGURE 9.4   Poster: Posters catch the eye to convey a single message.

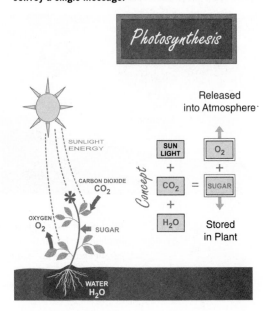

CATEGORIES OF VISUALS

The visual selected for a particular situation should depend on the learning task. Visuals can be subdivided into six categories: realistic, analogical, organizational, relational, transformational, and interpretive (Clark & Lyons, 2004).

Realistic. Realistic visuals show the actual object under study. They can translate abstract ideas into a more realistic format. They allow instruction to move from the level of abstract (verbal) symbols on the concrete–abstract continuum (refer to Figure 9.1) to a more concrete (visual) level. For example, the color photograph of a covered wagon in Figure 9.5 is a realistic visual. Using natural colors can heighten the degree of realism. No representation, of course, is totally realistic. The real object or event will always have aspects that cannot be captured pictorially, even in a three-dimensional, color motion picture.

FIGURE 9.5   Photographs as Realistic Visuals: Photographs, illustrations, graphics, and words represent a continuum of realism for different kinds of symbols.

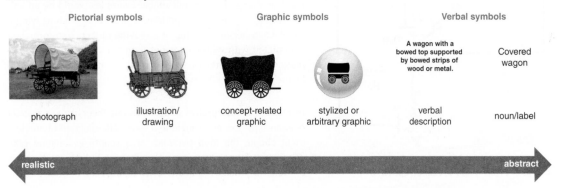

FIGURE 9.6 Movement Indicators: Arrows in the water cycle image depict movement.

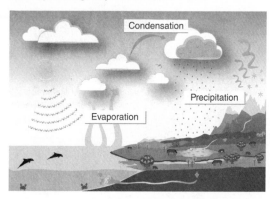

FIGURE 9.7 Transformational Visuals: An active posture, as in the drawing on the left, communicates movement more reliably than arbitrary graphic conventions such as speed lines, as in the drawing on the right.

Analogical. **Analogical** visuals convey a concept or topic by showing something else and implying a similarity. Teaching about electricity flow by showing water flowing in a series of parallel pipes is an example of using analogic visuals. An analogy for white blood cells fighting off infection might be an army attacking a stronghold. An early study by Newby, Ertmer, and Stepich (1995) showed that student learning of biological concepts benefited from the use of visual analogies. Such visuals help learners interpret new information in light of prior knowledge and thereby facilitate learning.

FIGURE 9.8 Interpretive Visual: An evacuation plan is an example of an interpretive visual.

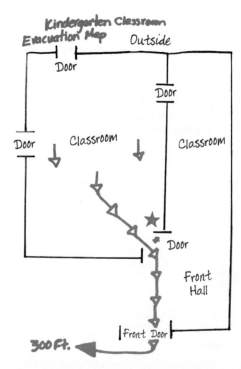

Source: Annie Pickert/Pearson, Pearson Education

Organizational. **Organizational** visuals show the qualitative relationships among various elements. Common examples include classification charts, timelines, flowcharts, and maps discussed in the Types of Visuals section of this chapter. These graphic organizers can show relationships among the main points or concepts in textual material. This type of visual helps communicate the organization of the content.

Relational. **Relational** visuals communicate quantitative relationships. Examples include bar charts, pictorial graphs, pie charts, and line graphs (see the "Types of Visuals" section).

Transformational. **Transformational** visuals illustrate movement or change in time and space. Examples would be an animated diagram of how to perform a procedure such as tying a shoelace, a person running, or a moving object. Transformation is depicted with with movement indicators as seen in the animation of the water cycle (Figure 9.6) and line drawings in Figure 9.7.

Interpretive. **Interpretive** visuals illustrate theoretical or abstract relationships. Examples include a schematic diagram of an electrical circuit, the food pyramid, or a school evacuation plan (Figure 9.8). Interpretive visuals help learners build mental models of events or processes that are invisible, abstract, or both.

Visuals

Presentation Software

Teachers can do several things to make presentations more accessible for students with visual impairments, including converting text to Braille. Another approach is to increase the interaction between teacher and students during and immediately after the presentation. Increasing verbalization and descriptions of the text and images increase the probability of visually impaired students' comprehension and retention. This really applies to all students!

Students who are developing new mathematical concepts may find the additional visuals prove to be very helpful. The ability to connect the components of a subject, such as mathematics with visuals, helps students make their own mental images and thus helps them understand the concepts being taught. For these students, such things as graphs, line drawings, or charts might be beneficial for them to recall essential information during an assessment.

Putting ideas into visual forms is a great way to challenge students who are ready to move beyond more traditional formats in demonstrating their learning. Asking students to prepare visuals in the form of drawings, charts, or graphics may allow them the flexibility to express their knowledge in unique and interesting ways.

VIEWING VISUALS

There are many ways to view visuals in a classroom. Still images may be enlarged and displayed on a screen. Such projection may be achieved by sending images from a computer or document camera to a digital projector or television monitor. Common classroom display surfaces for viewing visuals include whiteboards, interactive whiteboards, bulletin boards, cloth boards, magnetic boards, and flip charts.

Presentation Software. Presentation software provides a format for displaying computer-based visuals with a digital projector. The most widely known presentation software is PowerPoint. Students, as well as teachers, can use templates to produce very professional-looking presentations. These packages allow you to include text; draw pictures; produce tables, diagrams, and graphs; import digital photos and video clips; include audio; and create animation. Students, as well as teachers, can make digital presentations with little training on the software itself. Most software includes "Getting Started" tutorials and Help menus to assist you and your students.

Presentation software allows you to generate handouts for your students. From one to nine slides can be put on each sheet of paper. The software also allows you to create note pages that contain only three slides per page and include blank lines next to each slide. With this format, students take notes on the handouts, rather than frantically copying down both what is on the slides and what you say.

Document Camera Projection. The **document camera** is a video camera mounted on a copy stand, pointed downward at documents, flat pictures, graphics, or small objects (such as

ASSURE Classroom Case Study Reflection

▶ Review the ASSURE video and identify how the use of visuals helps students learn about visualizing three-dimensional geometric forms. How might Mrs. Roman use visuals to help her students better understand how to visualize three-dimensional geometric forms in a two-dimensional plane? What types of visuals might be most effective and why?

ASSURE Classroom Case Study Reflection

▶ Review the ASSURE video and consider the benefits of Mrs. Roman using PowerPoint when teaching her students math concepts. What strategies can Mrs. Roman use to have students explain their ideas? How might Mrs. Edlund use PowerPoint as part of her art lessons? What can she do to have children connect what they are learning in art class with their math lessons?

The teacher or students can use document cameras to project large images of hands-on demonstrations or small objects.

coins). The image may be shown with a digital projector or a large-screen television monitor within the room, or it may be transmitted to distant sites via web conferencing or telecommunications technology. Any sort of visual can be placed on the stage, and you can manipulate the material or write on paper placed on the stage.

One alternative to the copy stand version of a document camera is the computer flex camera, such as the Video Flex camera from Ken-A-Vision, which is designed for use in face-to-face classrooms as well as telecommunications. This camera can be connected to the television monitor, digital projector, or computer and used in a similar way as the document camera. The advantage to using this type of camera is that it is smaller and less expensive.

Printed Visuals. The simplist use of visuals is to look at a visual in a book, on the wall, or held by the teacher. Printed visuals are easy to use because they do not require any equipment. They are relatively inexpensive; in fact, many can be obtained at no cost. They can be used in many ways at all levels of instruction and in all disciplines.

CREATING VISUALS

Planning is an important component of creating visuals. Graphic organizers and presentation software are excellent for using planning techniques such as storyboarding and concept mapping. It is also helpful to understnd methods such as lettering techniques and how to create simple drawings, sketches, or cartoons. Techniques for creating presentation graphics are also important when creating visuals.

Planning Tools. If you or your students are designing a *series* of visuals—such as a series of computer screens, a set of PowerPoint slides, or a video sequence—**storyboarding** is a handy strategy for planning. This technique, borrowed from film and video production, allows you to creatively arrange and rearrange a whole sequence of thumbnail sketches. In storyboarding, you place on a card or piece of paper a sketch or some other simple representation of the visual and text you plan to use. If the series will include narration, this would also be included on the storyboard, along with production notes that link the visuals to the narration. After developing a series of such cards, place them in rough sequence on a flat surface or on a storyboard holder (Figure 9.9).

Index cards are commonly used for storyboarding because they are durable, inexpensive, and available in a variety of colors and sizes. Self-sticking, removable notes have become popular because they will stick to anything—cardboard, desks, walls, whiteboards, bulletin boards, and so on.

Divide the individual storyboard cards into areas to accommodate the text or narration and the production notes (Figure 9.10). The exact format of the storyboard card should fit your needs and purposes. Design a card that facilitates your work if the existing or recommended format is not suitable. You can make a simple sketch, write a short description of the desired visual on the card, use digital photographs, or use visuals cut from magazines.

Inspiration (**www.inspiration.com),** while not designed for storyboarding, may be used to help you and your

students organize ideas. Inspiration is a software package that facilitates brainstorming, concept mapping, and planning. It creates a visual diagram of the ideas generated by an individual or group. Use the program to create overviews, presentation visuals, and flowcharts. Once the group's thoughts have been visualized, Inspiration easily converts from the concept map into a word processing outline. You and your students can use the software to map concepts. Inspiration allows students to easily couple the images with the text, and move their ideas around the computer screen, allowing them to get their information organized.

For younger students (PK–5), Kidspiration can promote visual thinking and learning. It is designed to help younger students develop their thinking, visualizing, and concept mapping skills. Even the youngest students can brainstorm ideas with words and visuals using Kidspiration. They can learn to organize and categorize information visually. They can explore new ideas with thought webs and visual mapping.

FIGURE 9.10   **Storyboard Cards: The storyboard card contains places for the visual, production notes, and the narration.**

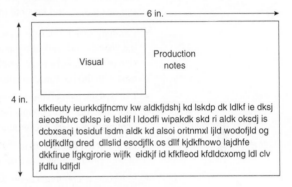

Lettering Techniques. A variety of lettering techniques can be used for visuals. The simplest is freehand lettering with felt-tip markers, which come in an array of colors and sizes. Precut letters are available in stationery and office supply stores. The letters are easy to use because most come with an adhesive backing; however, they are rather expensive. Large, neat letters or other shapes can be cut quickly from construction paper with scissors. Letter-cutting devices from Ellison (**www.ellisoneducation.com**) are available in many schools or can be purchased in major hobby and scrapbook supply stores. Letters of the alphabet in die form are mounted into a cutter to produce one or many copies of each letter from colored construction paper.

Drawing, Sketching, and Cartooning. One often-overlooked source of visuals is *you*. You don't have to be an artist to draw. There are some basic guidelines and many how-to books that can help you communicate effectively using drawing, sketching, and cartooning. With a little practice, you may be surprised by how well you can draw. Simple drawings can enhance whiteboard presentations, class handouts, and bulletin boards.

Clip Art. Clip art is prepared visual images (drawings and digital pictures) that can be inserted into a variety of digital documents and presentations. The size and placement of the image can be modified to meet your needs. Recently there has been an explosion in copyright-free visuals available primarily through the Web and software collections.

Designing Visuals with Computers. You and your students can use drawing programs for layout and design, as well as for drawing and illustrating. Most computer graphics programs come with hundreds or even thousands of typefaces and clip-art images and can manipulate visuals in every imaginable way. Examples of these programs are KidPix 3D **(www.mackiev .com/kidpix)**, FreshPaint, and Adobe Illustrator. The visuals created with these programs can be projected using a computer and digital projector, or printed as a paper copies.

Creating Presentation Graphics. With presentation graphics software, such as Microsoft's PowerPoint and Apple's Keynote, even users without specialized graphics training can create attractive graphic displays in a form suitable for professional presentation. You select a visual style from a menu, specify the desired type of layout (e.g., outline, bulleted list, graph, chart, or combination), then just type in your message where directed by the program. The program automatically selects legible type fonts and sizes and organizes the pictures and text into a clean visual layout.

Guidelines for preparing presentation graphics using software such as Prezi **(www.prezi .com),** PowerPoint, and Keynote include the following:

- *Carefully select font type, size, and color.* Arial is a *sans serif* font (a font that does not have the "hands and feet" at the ends of the letters) and is easy to read (see Figure 9.11). A font size of 24 points or larger ensures readability. The text color should provide adequate contrast with the background color. Use upper- and lowercase letters where appropriate.

- *Use a plain, light-colored background.* Busy "wallpaper" backgrounds can be distracting to your students. Most people find that dark text on a light background is easier to read than light text on a dark background.

- *Center or left justify titles at the top of the slide.* To help your students follow the organization of your presentation, use a descriptive title or subtitle at the top of each slide.

- *Use concise communication.* Keep the number of words on a slide to an absolute minimum. The "6 × 6 rule" recommends no more than six words per line and no more than six lines. If you need more words, use a second slide.

- *Use master slides to establish a consistent visual and text format.* Master slides allow you to place text of a specific font on each page, and visuals to be repeated in the same position on every slide.

- *Minimize "bells and whistles."* You should create a presentation with substantive content rather than a lot of pizzazz. The overuse of eye-catching features is distracting and often annoying to students. Don't use it just because the software has it!

- *Use appropriate graphics.* Avoid stock images that are inappropriate and irrelevant to your content. Select or create graphics that effectively communicate your message.

- *Use consistent transitions.* Transitions—the way one slide changes to the next—should be consistent throughout your presentation. Do not use random transitions and avoid "noise" (audio effects) with transitions.

- *Use simple "builds."* Build effects are how bulleted text or graphics are introduced within a single slide. Avoid build effects, like "swirling" (where new text spins onto the slide), that can divert student attention. Watching the effect often takes longer than reading the new text.

- *Carefully use animation to support the instructional message rather than to add a dramatic element to your presentation.* For example, components of a model can be added as each is discussed, such as adding one layer at a time to the food pyramid or adding planets in order of their distance from the sun.

- *Minimize the use of sound.* Use sound only if it enhances your presentation. Screeching tires and cash register sounds quickly become distracting.
- *Use footers to identify slides.* Footers allow you to annotate the bottoms of slides with your name, your affiliation, the presentation topic, and/or date prepared or presented.

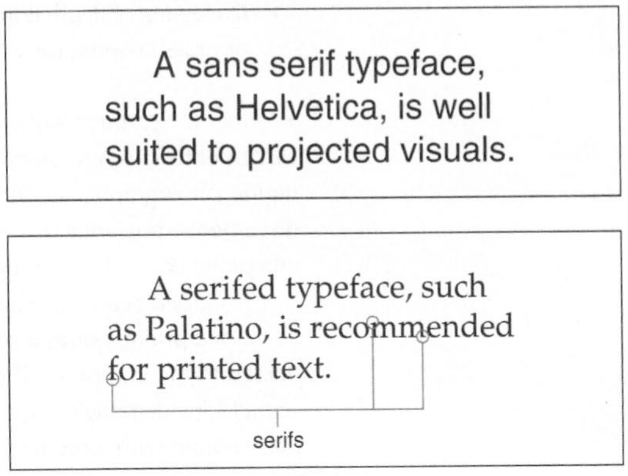

CAPTURING VISUALS

Digital imaging allows users to capture, edit, display, and share still and video images. The technology of digital cameras and scanners makes the process of capturing visuals easy for both teachers and students. Users may send images to other digital devices, store them on computers, or share them through the Internet.

Photography. Digital cameras convert light energy to digital data, which is stored in a small digital recorder such as a removable memory card that can store hundreds of photos. You may immediately view your images on a small monitor. Digital cameras allows you to see the picture before you take it and after it has been "captured." You can delete images you don't want and reshoot on the spot until you get exactly what you want .

Printing the digital images is quick and easy with a color printer or photo printer. You can use your computer to print the images, or you can make copies of the photo without using a computer. Photo printers make copies directly from the data on the memory card. Copies of digital photos can be made without degradation in quality and the colors resist fading over time.

You can download images to a computer for manipulation and can store them on a computer hard drive, flash drive, or a photo CD. It is important to recognize the need for caution when digitally editing or modifying images, as there are possibilities of misrepresentation. With the advanced capabilities of computer tools, a computer user could alter an image in a way that might distort reality and present a false message to the reader or that might violate a copyright holder's rights in regard to the original image. For more information about copyright, refer to the "Copyright Concerns: Copyright Law" section in Chapter 1.

Whether you are recording the things you see on a field trip, creating a photo essay, shooting an historical subject, or developing an instructional picture sequence, a few guidelines can make your photographs more effective.

- Include all elements that are helpful in communicating your ideas.
- Eliminate extraneous elements, such as distracting backgrounds.
- Include size indicators (e.g., a car, a person, a hand, a coin) in the picture if the size of the main object of interest is not apparent.
- Divide the picture area in thirds both vertically and horizontally. The center of interest should be near one of the intersections of the lines. This is called the "rule of thirds." Don't cramp the important part of the image near the edge of the picture.

FIGURE 9.11   **Font Types: Styles of type should be selected to suit their purpose.**

A sans serif typeface, such as Helvetica, is well suited to projected visuals.

A serifed typeface, such as Palatino, is recommended for printed text.

serifs

ASSURE Classroom Case Study Reflection

Review the ASSURE video to see how digital images are used to help the children with their visualization of math concepts. What could Mrs. Edlund do with the school's digital cameras to further expand students' knowledge of math concepts?

- When making how-to documents, take the picture from the viewpoint of the learner, not the observer.

- If a feeling of depth is important, use foreground objects (e.g., blossom-covered tree branches or moss-covered rocks) to frame the main subject.

Scanners. Scanners work with computers to transfer existing paper-based visual images, such as student drawings, storyboards, or images, into digitized computer graphic files. As with digital photographs, students may quickly incorporate scanned images into word processing documents, presentations, webpages, and other digital products. The scanned images can be enhanced or modified using the appropriate software.

A *flatbed scanner,* which functions similar to a photocopy machine, is often included in all-in-one printers or as a separate piece of classroom or computer lab equipment, and is connected to the computer. The user places the image face down on the glass surface and selects scan. Many of today's scanners allow you to scan text documents in a way that allows the contet to be edited with word processing software.

Innovations on the Horizon

MAKING THE CLASSROOM COME ALIVE WITH 3-D IMAGES

Classrooms are coming alive with 3-D images in lessons! Three-dimensional projectors are beginning to make their way into schools. Nothing captures the attention of students like 3-D. Both still and moving images are more compelling in 3-D. These projectors allow your students to "walk" thorough famous architectural structures of the past, present, or future. The projectors actually produce two images on the screen at the same time—one for the left eye and one for the right eye. The viewer uses 3-D glasses that combine the two images into create an amazing 3-D effect. The same technology has been used in movie theatres. Now it is moving to the schools.

Summary

This chapter discussed ways to enhance learning with text and visuals by emphasizing the chapter's knowledge outcomes.

Compare and contrast text and visual literacy. Text literacy is the ability to gather, comprehend, and evaluate the message and to synthesize and to write about what you read or experience, whereas visual literacy is the learned ability to interpret visual messages accurately and to create such messages.

Select a text resource and describe the advantages of integrating it into a lesson. When selecting text resources, determine how the resource will be an advantage to student learning. For example, is the text readily available, does it offer flexibility to adapt to student needs, is it user friendly, and if the resource is digital, does it offer personalization tools?

Describe variables that affect how a learner interprets or decodes a visual. When selecting visuals, teachers should consider these variables to ensure students effectively interpret the visuals:

- Prior to the age of 12, children tend to interpret visuals section by section, whereas older students tend to summarize the whole scene.

- Cultural groups may perceive visual materials in different ways.

- Young learners prefer simple visuals and older students prefer more complex ones, but simpler visuals are usually more effective, whatever the age group.

Provide an example visual for each of the seven purposes of visuals; explain how the visual fulfills the intended purpose. The seven key purposes of visuals presented in this chapter are to (1) provide a concrete referent for ideas; (2) make abstract ideas concrete; (3) motivate learners; (4) direct attention; (5) repeat information; (6) recall prior learning; and (7) reduce learning effort.

List and describe how the six categories of visuals support student learning. The six categories of visuals, and how they support learning, are as follows: (1) *Realistic* visuals show the actual object under study; (2) *analogical* visuals convey a concept or topic by showing something else and implying a similarity; (3) *organizational* visuals show the qualitative relationships among various elements; (4) *relational* visuals communicate quantitative relationships; (5) *transformational* visuals illustrate movement or change in time and space; and (6) *interpretive* visuals illustrate theoretical or abstract relationships.

ASSURE Lesson Plan

▶ *The ASSURE Classroom Case Study for this chapter is based on an interdisciplinary third-grade lesson created by Mrs. Roman and Mrs. Edlund. The video shows the teachers implementing the lesson in the classroom and provides their insights for achieving successful use of student-created digital portfolios.*

The ASSURE Lesson Plan describes the instructional planning used by Mrs. Roman, a third-grade teacher, and Mrs. Edlund, an art teacher. The two teachers found they had similar needs in terms of helping the third-grade students learn visual concepts associated with geometry. They shared their concerns and found ways of helping the students learn through the use of digital images and electronic portfolios.

Mrs. Roman and Mrs. Edlund
Third-Grade Mathematics and Art
Topic: Visual Concepts

Analyze Learners

General Characteristics. The students consist of 23 third graders who have recently completed state tests to assess their mathematics knowledge and skills. Because the school is new, they have not had many opportunities to know each other prior to this year. Some come from the same neighborhood, while others are from surrounding small communities. All of the students like to play at recess and enjoy movies and video games. Many of the boys are interested in sports, especially baseball. Most of the girls are interested in reading and watching television.

Entry Competencies. A number of the children have scored well on their earlier tests in mathematics. There are a few who are struggling with some of the basic mathematics skills they have yet to master. The students have demonstrated difficulty in understanding the concepts of three-dimensional images when shown them on paper. They have difficulty with the concept of how to visualize this type of image. Their recent test scores reflect this problem.

Learning Styles. The class members display a range of learning styles. Most of them have visual and spatial skills and good math abilities. The children enjoy drawing and look forward to art classes, as they find they can express their ideas with a variety of materials.

State Standards and Objectives

Curriculum Standards. *National Council for Teachers of Mathematics, Standard 3*: Geometry and Spatial Sense.

Analyze characteristics and properties of two- and three-dimensional geometric objects; *National Standards for Arts Education, Content Standard 5:* Reflecting upon and assessing the characteristics and merits of their work and the work of others.

Technology Standards. *National Educational Technology Standards for Students (#3) Technology Productivity Tools:* Students use technology tools to enhance learning, increase productivity, and promote creativity.

Learning Objectives. The objectives for this lesson are as follows:

1. Given art materials, the students will demonstrate their ability to build three-dimensional objects by cutting and shaping construction paper into three shapes: cylinder, cone, and box.

2. Given drawing materials, the students will draw on paper their three-dimensional objects, employing conventions learned in art class.

3. Given drawing materials, students will draw a picture of the playground, using the art conventions for showing dimension.

4. Given a digital camera and PowerPoint software, the students will create an e-portfolio of their art, reflecting on what they have learned.

Select Strategies

Mrs. Roman decided that it would be best to try to work with Mrs. Edlund, the art teacher, to find ways of helping her students with their ability to make the connection between the two-dimensional picture and the three-dimensional object. She liked the idea of having another way of demonstrating student learning through the use of an e-portfolio, something Mrs. Edlund has been hoping to develop with her students. Together they decided to use several different approaches to instructing students. Mrs. Roman planned to combine direct instruction with some hands-on experiences with the math manipulatives that are available with the textbook. Mrs. Edlund led the children through a process of selecting their art for a portfolio, which, because of the school's focus on art and technology, could be an electronic portfolio (e-portfolio). She demonstrated the use of the digital camera, showed students how to load their pictures into the computer, and helped them learn PowerPoint so they could create their e-portfolios. To help the children with their reflections about their art and the connections to their classroom knowledge, she guided them through thoughtful questions.

Select Resources

This lesson involves student use of computers, digital cameras, Photoshop, and PowerPoint software to create their electronic portfolios. Mrs. Edlund chooses to use laptop computers from the portable laptop cart. She decided to use PowerPoint as the software for the e-portfolio because it was available on the laptops as well as the classroom computers. She felt that the program provided enough flexibility that the children would be able to build their e-portfolios without having to learn a complex program. And, she knew that they would be able to keep adding to their portfolios as they progressed through school because PowerPoint would be available to them through high school.

She uses the following guidelines to assess the appropriateness of her technology and media selections:

- *Alignment with standards, outcomes, and objectives.* The digital cameras allow students to capture their art pieces for inclusion in their portfolios. Photoshop and PowerPoint software provide the necessary tools the students need to create the portfolios as described in the learning objectives.

- *Accurate and current information.* Students are working with art that they created, so it is current. Internet information is not used, so accuracy is not of concern for this lesson.

- *Age-appropriate language.* Photoshop and PowerPoint menus are written at a level that requires initial training for third-grade students and ongoing support during use.

- *Interest level and engagement.* The combined use of student-created artwork, Photoshop, and PowerPoint provides students the opportunity to create personalized electronic portfolios that demonstrate their reflections and talents in a creative fashion.

- *Technical quality.* The digital camera, Photoshop, and PowerPoint have superior technical quality.

- *Ease of use.* After basic skills training, the third-grade students are able to use the digital camera, Photoshop, and PowerPoint software.

- *Bias free.* Photoshop and PowerPoint are bias free.

- *User guide and directions.* The online help features of Photoshop and PowerPoint are too sophisticated for use by third-grade students. Therefore, Mrs. Edlund provided ongoing support and directions to her students.

Mrs. Edlund decided to have students work with clay to create three-dimensional objects. Then she showed the students how to draw their clay objects on paper, demonstrating the art conventions that show depth. She decided to see if they could apply that knowledge by taking the children out to the playground to have them draw the area. Mrs. Edlund determined that the children were making the connections between their art and their classroom experiences. She decided that it would be best for the children to build art portfolios as a way to demonstrate their learning and to capture points in time with their art achievement.

Utilize Resources

Preview Resources. Mrs. Edlund previews the digital camera features and the Photoshop and PowerPoint software to ensure they have the features needed for students to create electronic portfolios of their artwork.

Prepare Resources. Mrs. Edlund checks the digital camera to ensure it is working, and ensures the laptop cart is reserved. She gathers the student artwork folders and reviews the content to ensure they are complete.

Prepare the Environment. Mrs. Edlund sets up the digital camera for still shots and ensures that the digital photos download from the camera to the computer. She tests all computers to ensure that Photoshop and PowerPoint are loaded and functional. She sets out the student collections of artwork.

Prepare the Learners. Students in Mrs. Edlund's class are shown how to take digital photos of their artwork, how to use Photoshop to crop the photos, and how to use PowerPoint to create the electronic portfolios.

Provide the Learning Experience. Mrs. Edlund wants to make the process easy for the third-grade students, so she focuses on having them use the traditional art materials first. By letting them create their images in art class, she can guide them in their thinking about the content associated with their classroom mathematics

lessons, as well as mastery of art. She wants to incorporate technology into their art and feels that the idea of an e-portfolio will accomplish that end.

Require Learner Participation

Student Practice Activities. The children learned to use various art media to demonstrate their understanding of the concepts they were learning in both their math classroom and art classes. They learned to use the digital camera, making certain their photos were of high quality to ensure the essence of their art was captured in the picture. They learned to use the computer to upload their pictures, crop and adjust the image on screen, and save their pictures to the school's server. The children learned the basics of PowerPoint and then began to explore ways to use the software to demonstrate their achievements.

Feedback. Mrs. Edlund provided ongoing guidance while the children were writing their reflections into their e-portfolios. Through this feedback, the students were able to develop an understanding of reflecting on their ideas and began to separate those pieces of their art that represented their current views.

Evaluate and Revise

Assessment of Learner Achievement. Mrs. Edlund and Mrs. Roman met to look at what the children had done in their artwork. They determined that the children were able to connect their classroom mathematics study with their art. Further, the e-portfolio was a way for them to demonstrate their understanding of the concepts in a meaningful way. Both Mrs. Roman and Mrs. Edlund felt that the children had learned to be more reflective in their approach to learning.

Evaluation of Strategies and Resources. Both teachers felt that the e-portfolio experience was valuable for the children and would be a viable assessment approach in the future.

Revision. Both teachers looked at the approaches to the lessons they taught and considered ways to extend their collaboration between the classroom and the art room. They also explored ways to assess learning beyond the traditional testing approaches.

Professional Development

DEMONSTRATING PROFESSIONAL KNOWLEDGE

1. Compare and contrast text and visual literacy.
2. Select a text resource and describe the advantages of integrating it into a lesson.
3. Describe variables that affect how a learner interprets or decodes a visual.
4. Provide an example visual for each of the seven purposes of visuals, and explain how the visual fulfills the intended purpose.
5. List and describe how the six categories of visuals support student learning.

DEMONSTRATING PROFESSIONAL SKILLS

1. Preview three text resources you would use when teaching and appraise each one using the **Selection Rubric: Text Materials**. Analyze the rubric findings and write an argument presenting the pros and cons for classroom use of each text resource (ISTE NETS-T 2.A, C).
2. Design a series of instructional images for a lesson. Attach a description of the students, objectives, and features that help achieve the lesson objectives (ISTE NETS-T 2.A).
3. Locate six visuals that you believe would be useful in your own teaching and evaluate them using the **Selection Rubric: Visual Materials**. Analyze the rubric findings and write an argument presenting the pros and cons for classroom use of each text resource (ISTE NETS-T 2.A, C).
4. Create one graph (line, bar, circle, or pictorial) and one chart (organization, classification, timeline, tabular, or flow) for a topic you might teach. Use the **Selection Rubric: Visual Materials** as a guideline (ISTE NETS-T 3.C).

BUILDING YOUR PROFESSIONAL PORTFOLIO

- *Creating My Lesson.* Using the ASSURE model, design a lesson that uses text and visuals for learning. Select the lesson topic from a scenario in Appendix A inside the back cover, or use a scenario of your own design. Use instructional strategies that you believe to be appropriate for your lesson and information from this chapter related to using text and visuals for learning. Be sure to include a description of the students, the objectives, and all other elements of the ASSURE model (ISTE NETS-T 2.A, 3.A).
- *Enhancing My Lesson.* Enhance the lesson you created in the previous activity by describing how you would meet the diverse needs of learners and how you would integrate different types of technology. Specifically, describe additional strategies you would include for students who already possess the knowledge and skills targeted in your lesson plan. Also describe strategies, technology, media, and materials you could integrate to assist students entering the lesson who have not met the lesson prerequisites (ISTE NETS-T 2.D, 3.D, 5.D).
- *Reflecting on My Lesson.* Reflect on the lesson you created and describe how you enhanced the lesson. Also reflect on the process you used and what you have learned about matching students, content, strategies, technology, media, and materials. Address the following in your reflection: What visuals were used? How can the visuals enhance the learning experiences of your students? If you were to redesign your lesson, what text and/or visuals would you select and why (ISTE NETS-T 4.C, 6.B)?

Suggested Resources

PRINT RESOURCES

Frey, N., & Fisher, D. (2008). *Teaching visual literacy: Using comic books, graphic novels, anime, cartoons, and more to develop comprehension and thinking skills.* Thousand Oaks, CA: Corwin Press.

Gangwer, T. (2009). *Visual impact, visual teaching: Using images to strengthen learning* (2nd ed.). Thousand Oaks, CA: Corwin Press.

Lidwell, W., Holden, K., & Butler, J. (2010). *Universal principles of design*. Beverly, MA: Rockport Publishers.

Lohr, L. L. (2007). *Creating graphics for learning and performance: Lessons in visual literacy* (2nd ed.). Upper Saddle River, NJ: Prentice Hall.

Luckner, J., Bowen, S., & Carter, K. (2001). Visual teaching strategies for students who are deaf or hard of hearing. *Teaching Exceptional Children, 33*(3), 38–44.

Newby, T. J., Stepich, D., Lehman, J., & Russell, J. D. (2011). *Education technology for teaching and learning* (4th ed.). Upper Saddle River, NJ: Merrill/ Prentice Hall.

Rasinski, T., & Padak, N. (2012). *Research to practice: Text considerations in literacy teaching and learning*. Ohio Literacy Research Center. Retrieved March 22, 2013, from http://literacy.kent.edu/Oasis/Pubs/0200-14.htm

Stafford, T. (2010). *Teaching visual literacy in the primary classroom: Comic books, film, television, and picture narratives*. New York, NY: Routledge.

Walling, D. R. (2005). *Visual knowing: Connecting art and ideas across the curriculum*. Thousand Oaks, CA: Corwin Press.

Woolner, P., Clark, J., Hall, E., Tiplady, L., Thomas, U., & Wall, K. (2010). Pictures are necessary but not sufficient: Using a range of visual methods to engage users about school design. *Learning Environments Research, 13*(1), 1–22.

WEB RESOURCES

Text

Common Core Writing in Action

www.literacyta.com/common-core-standards/writing

The Common Core Writing in Action website provides a variety of classroom resources focused on building the writing literacy skills of students. The resources organized by (1) text types and purposes, (2) production and distribution of writing, (3) research to build and present knowledge, and (4) range of writing.

ReadWriteThink

www.readwritethink.org/classroom-resources

The ReadWriteThink site is provided by the International Reading Association (IRA) and the National Council of Teachers of English (NCTE). The classroom resources on this site include lesson plans, student interactives, mobile apps, calendar activities, and printouts. Lesson plans and activities are aligned with NCTE Standards and the Common Core State Standards (CCSS), when applicable.

Primary Literacy Framework: Text Types

www.teachfind.com/national-strategies/primary-framework-literacy-text-types

This site provides an overview of text types for three genres: narrative, nonfiction, and poetry. The overview for each text type includes a table containing the generic structure, language features, and knowledge for the writer. Information is provided for six years of primary education.

Visuals

International Visual Literacy Association

www.ivla.org

The International Visual Literacy Association (IVLA) is a not-for-profit association of researchers, educators, and artists dedicated to the principles of visual literacy.

Inspiration and Kidspiration software

www.inspiration.com

Inspiration is a tool students use to plan, research, and complete projects. With the integrated diagram and outline views, they create graphic organizers and expand topics into writing. This combination encourages learning in multiple modes. Kidspiration supports visual thinking techniques, enabling students to easily create and update graphic organizers, concept maps, idea maps, and other visuals.

PowerPoint software

www.microsoft.com

PowerPoint Viewer lets the user view full-featured presentations created in PowerPoint. This viewer also supports opening password-protected Microsoft PowerPoint presentations.

Kodak website

www.kodak.com

The Kodak website provides the user with information about digital cameras, printers, accessories, and more. It also includes a section on taking great pictures.

SELECTION RUBRIC   Text Materials

Complete and save the following interactive evaluation to reference when selecting text materials to integrate into lessons.

Search Terms

_____

_____

_____

Format (Digital or Print)

_____ Textbook

_____ Novel/Story Book

_____ Periodical

_____ Other

_____

Title _____

Source/Location _____

©Date _____ Cost _____ Length _____ Minutes _____

Subject Area _____ Grade Level _____

Instructional Strategies _____

Brief Description

Standards/Outcomes/Objectives

Prerequisites (e.g., prior knowledge, reading ability, vocabulary level)

Strengths

Limitations

Special Features

Name _____ Date _____

Rating Area	High Quality	Medium Quality	Low Quality
Alignment with standards, outcomes, and objectives	Standard/outcome/objective addressed and use of audio should enhance student learning.	Standard/outcome/objective partially addressed and use of audio may enhance student learning.	Standard/outcome/objective not addressed and use of audio will likely not enhance student learning.
Accurate and current information	Information is correct and does not contain material that is out of date.	Information is correct but does contain material that is out of date.	Information is not correct and does contain material that is out of date.
Age-appropriate language	Language used is age appropriate and vocabulary is understandable.	Language used is nearly age appropriate and some vocabulary is above/below student age.	Language used is not age appropriate and vocabulary is clearly inappropriate for student age.
Interest level and engagement	Topic presented so that students are likely to be interested and actively engaged in learning.	Topic presented to interest students most of the time and engage most in learning.	Topic presented so as not to interest students and not engage them in learning.
Technical quality	The material represents best available technology and media.	The material represents technology and media that are good quality, although there are some problems.	The material represents technology and media that are not well prepared and are of very poor quality.
Ease of use (user may be student or teacher)	Material follows easy-to-use patterns with nothing to confuse the user.	Material follows patterns that are easy to follow most of the time, with a few things to confuse the user.	Material follows no patterns and most of the time the user is very confused.
Bias free	There is no evidence of objectionable bias or advertising.	There is little evidence of bias or advertising.	There is much evidence of bias or advertising.
User guide and directions	The user guide is an excellent resource for use in a lesson. Directions should help students use the material.	The user guide is a good resource for use in a lesson. Directions may help students use the material.	The user guide is a poor resource for use in a lesson. Directions do not help students use the material.
Reading level	Most students can use the software to create original pieces that represent learning.	Some students can use the software to start original pieces that begin to show their learning.	Most students cannot use the software to create original pieces that represent their learning.
Fosters collaboration	The material is presented at an appropriate reading level so that most students can understand the information.	The material is presented at a reading level so that some students can understand the information.	The material is presented at a reading level so that few students can understand the information.
Clarity of organization	The material is presented in such a way that most students are able to use the information.	The material is presented in such a way that some students are able to use the information.	The material is presented in such a way that few students are able to use the information.

Recommended for Classroom Use: _____ Yes _____ No

Ideas for Classroom Use: _____

_____

SELECTION RUBRIC   Visual Materials

Complete and save the following interactive evaluation to reference when selecting visual materials to integrate into lessons.

Search Terms

_____

_____

_____

Format (Digital or Print)

_____ Still Picture

_____ Drawing/Cartoon

_____ Chart/Graph

_____ Poster

_____ Other

_____

Title _____

Source/Location _____

©Date _____ Cost _____ Length _____ Minutes _____

Subject Area _____ Grade Level _____

Instructional Strategies _____

Brief Description

Standards/Outcomes/Objectives

Prerequisites (e.g., prior knowledge, reading ability, vocabulary level)

Strengths

Limitations

Special Features

Name _____   Date _____

Rating Area	High Quality	Medium Quality	Low Quality
Alignment with standards, outcomes, and objectives	Standard/outcome/objective addressed and use of audio should enhance student learning.	Standard/outcome/objective partially addressed and use of audio may enhance student learning.	Standard/outcome/objective not addressed and use of audio will likely not enhance student learning.
Accurate and current information	Information is correct and does not contain material that is out of date.	Information is correct but does contain material that is out of date.	Information is not correct and does contain material that is out of date.
Age-appropriate language	Language used is age appropriate and vocabulary is understandable.	Language used is nearly age appropriate and some vocabulary is above/below student age.	Language used is not age appropriate and vocabulary is clearly inappropriate for student age.
Interest level and engagement	Topic presented so that students are likely to be interested and actively engaged in learning.	Topic presented to interest students most of the time and engage most in learning.	Topic presented so as not to interest students and not engage them in learning.
Technical quality	The material represents best available technology and media.	The material represents technology and media that are good quality, although there are some problems.	The material represents technology and media that are not well prepared and are of very poor quality.
Ease of use (student or teacher)	Material follows easy-to-use patterns with nothing to confuse the user.	Material follows patterns that are easy to follow most of the time, with a few things to confuse the user.	Material follows no patterns and most of the time the user is very confused.
Bias free	There is no evidence of bias or advertising.	There is little evidence of bias or advertising.	There is much evidence of bias or advertising.
User guide and directions	The user guide is an excellent resource for use in a lesson. Directions should help students use the material.	The user guide is a good resource for use in a lesson. Directions may help students use the material.	The user guide is a poor resource for use in a lesson. Directions do not help students use the material.
Legibility for use (size and clarity)	The visual is presented so that most students can see and understand the information.	The visual is presented so that some students can see and understand the information.	The visual is presented so that most students cannot see and understand the information.
Simplicity (clear, unified design)	The visual is well organized; students are able to understand the information.	The visual is fairly well organized; students are mostly able to understand the information.	The visual is poorly organized; students are unable to understand the information.
Appropriate use of color	Colors are appropriate and enhance the learning potential.	Colors are somewhat appropriate and may enhance the learning potential.	Colors are not appropriate and do not enhance the learning potential.
Communicates clearly and effectively	The visual communicates clearly and effectively.	Visual communicates somewhat clearly and effectively.	Visual does not communicate clearly and effectively.
Visual appeal	The visual attracts the attention of most students.	The visual attracts the attention of some students.	The visual attracts the attention of few students.

Recommended for Classroom Use: _____ Yes _____ No

Ideas for Classroom Use: _____

_____

CHAPTER

10

Preparing for Tomorrow's Challenges

Knowledge Outcomes

This chapter addresses ISTE NETS-T 5.

1. Describe how the ASSURE model supports 21st century learning as described in the National Education Technology Plan.

2. Discuss the characteristics of a 21st century teacher who is technologically competent, is information literate, and maintains professional growth and engagement.

3. Compare components of a 21st century environment with regard to being a global classroom, connecting schools and homes, and offering online education.

4. Describe the types of technology grants available for 21st century learning and briefly describe the basic components included when writing a grant proposal.

Goal

Understanding factors influencing the advancement of 21st century teaching and learning.

Today's schools and teachers must be prepared to continually advance 21st century learning as our society transitions to innovative digital tools for work, communication, and entertainment. This advancement can be supported with use of the ASSURE model and technology-focused professional development to guide teacher implementation of 21st century learning environments. Technology grants can assist schools in increasing student access to cutting-edge technology and media that build 21st century knowledge and skills.

The ASSURE Model and 21st Century Learning

The ASSURE model is structured to help teachers achieve 21st century classrooms. By following the step-by-step ASSURE model, teachers receive the support and guidance to develop, implement, evaluate, and revise lessons that integrate technology to increase student learning and prepare them for future careers. The ASSURE model directly supports the following National Educational Technology Plan (NETP) foundational goal (USDOE, 2010):

> All learners will have engaging and empowering learning experiences both in and outside of school that prepare them to be active, creative, knowledgeable, and ethical participants in our globally networked society. (p. 9)

The first step in the ASSURE model, *analyze learners,* asks teachers to identify the needs of all learners to better ensure that they have the resources and individualized support to participate in learning experiences. The next four steps—*stating standards and objectives, selecting strategies, utilizing technology, media, and materials,* and *requiring learning participation*—help teachers to strategically plan and implement learning experiences that support deeper levels of learning (e.g., engaging, empowering, active, creative, and knowledgeable) (CCSS, 2013). The final ASSURE model step, *evaluate and revise,* involves assessment of both student progress and the instructional process to determine what worked well and what needs to be revised before implementing the lesson again. Application of the ASSURE model enables 21st century teachers to continually engage students in activities that increase 21st century knowledge and skills and better prepare them for successful careers.

21st Century Teachers

A teacher will always have the foundational responsibility of enabling students to learn. However, differences have been seen over time in *how* teachers accomplish this goal. The role of the 21st century teacher is still to improve student learning, but it requires the teacher to have broader capabilities than content knowledge and the ability to use pedagogy in the classroom. Teachers also need to be technologically competent and information literate.

TECHNOLOGICAL COMPETENCE

Most teachers have basic computer literacy skills, but often lack the understanding to apply those skills effectively to integrate technology into their instruction. Twenty-first century teachers need to go beyond computer literacy to attain **technological competence** (Morrison & Lowther, 2010). This means that teachers know the basics of computer literacy, but more importantly, also know how and when to use technology to enhance student learning. For example, technologically competent teachers seamlessly integrate rich multimedia experiences into classroom activities that engage students in meaningful learning. Teachers use digital assessment tools, such as e-portfolios that maintain PK–12 archives of student-created digital audio, video, and other documents in individual student portfolios. The teachers can individualize instruction with data collected from digital records of daily performance.

INFORMATION LITERACY

Twenty-first century teachers need to be highly capable with regard to **information literacy.** To prepare for a class, teachers need to locate materials from a variety of online sources and ensure the material is accurate, appropriate, easily accessible, and useable according to copyright guidelines. Teachers should model the information literacy skills for their students by demonstrating how to:

- Access information
- Verify data
- Appropriately acknowledge information sources
- Follow copyright regulations

Twenty-first century teachers should develop and maintain a classroom website to keep students and parents informed of learning expectations and activities and regularly communicate with parents through email and discussion boards. They also exemplify a willingness to explore and discover new technological capabilities that enhance and expand learning experiences. This involves an openness to learn from and ask students for their thoughts about applying innovative technologies to examine and solve real-world problems, thus better preparing students to demonstrate these abilities in their future careers. Teachers should regularly participate in reality-based experiences that use technology and media for learning.

TECHNOLOGY-FOCUSED PROFESSIONAL DEVELOPMENT

As with any profession, long-term and consistent professional development is necessary for teachers to maintain professional growth and to have a positive impact on student learning. The same is true for teacher professional development focused on effective use of technology, which consists of six components (ISTE, 2009):

1. Preservice technology training aligned to inservice expectations
2. Modeling of technology use by trainers and experienced teachers
3. Communities of practice
4. Professional engagement
5. School and district leadership in (and modeling of) technology use
6. Online learning (on both the type and topic of professional development) (p. 8)

The National Educational Technology Standards for Teachers (NETS-T) **(www.iste.org/ standards/nets-for-teachers)** describe classroom practices, lesson development, and professional expectations for 21st century teachers (ISTE NETS-T, 2008). The content and activities of technology-focused professional development (PD) should address the NETS-T through face-to-face or virtual sessions. Face-to-face and virtual sessions include:

- District or school-provided in-service vendor sessions
- Workshops or webinars at educational conferences
- Graduate coursework

Virtual PD also includes teacher communities of practice, which are groups of teachers with common interests who share best practices and solutions, and often join advocacy initiatives.

NETS-T 1: Facilitate and Inspire Student Learning and Creativity. Engage teachers in activities that demonstrate how new and innovative uses of technology and media can advance student learning and creativity in face-to-face and virtual environments. PD facilitators can achieve this goal by having teachers assume the role of students while they model a variety of ways to help, facilitate, and inspire learning during the hands-on activities. For example, teachers could have students use a site such as Glogster (**http://edu.glogster.com/what-is-glogster-edu**) to create interactive digital posters that demonstrate content and skills to be learned by their students.

NETS-T 2: Design and Develop Digital-Age Learning Experiences and Assessments. This standard requires teachers to participate in ongoing hands-on activities facilitated by technology coaches or similar PD staff. Teachers should design, develop, and evaluate authentic learning and assessment experiences that require students to use technology and media. The goals of the PD for teachers are to produce lessons that foster student achievement of learning objectives and to meet the NETS-S standards of technology implementation.

NETS-T 3: Model Digital-Age Work and Learning. As mentioned, it is important for 21st century teachers to be competent users of technology and media. To achieve this goal, many teachers will need PD to help them gain the knowledge and skills to apply digital solutions needed to model digital-age work and learning processes needed in a global and digital society. PD topics can include how to create and maintain a class website, use social networking tools, participate in webinars, and use digital tools to manage teacher responsibilities.

NETS-T 4: Promote and Model Digital Citizenship and Responsibility. For teachers to gain an understanding of the legal and ethical issues associated with digital citizenship, they need to be provided PD in which they study and practice applying copyright regulations, district acceptable use policies, and other generally acceptable guidelines such as netiquette rules offered by many different sources. Within these areas it is critical to prepare teachers with knowledge and tools to address digital issues such as cyberbullying and Internet safety for students.

NETS-T 5: Engage in Professional Growth and Leadership. It is important to provide teachers PD to demonstrate how to become lifelong learners and how to serve as leaders in the effective use of technology by modeling these skills in their schools, districts, and community. Teachers can also be introduced to technology and media associations and journals as additional options for achieving professional growth and engagement.

PROFESSIONAL ENGAGEMENT

The 21st century is an exciting time for teachers as the opportunities to expand teaching and learning are becoming more and more pervasive in formal and informal education each year. Associated with this growth are the increasing numbers of professional organizations that support educators interested in application of technology and media to improve learning.

Professional Organizations. Whether your interest is in instructional technology and media in general, or you intend to specialize in this area of education, it is important to be familiar with some of the major organizations dedicated to its advancement.

***Association for Educational Communications and Technology (AECT)* (www.aect.org).** AECT is an international organization representing educational technology professionals working in schools, colleges, and universities, as well as the corporate, government, and military sectors. Its mission is to provide leadership in educational communications and technology by linking professionals holding a common interest in the use of educational technology and its application to the learning process. AECT has 10 divisions designed around areas of special interest represented within the membership: design and development, distance learning, graduate student assembly, international, multimedia production, research and theory, school media and technology, systemic change, teacher education, and training and performance.

The association maintains an active publications program, including the journals *Tech Trends* and *Educational Technology Research and Development,* both published six times during the academic year, as well as a large number of books and videos. AECT sponsors an annual conference that features over 300 educational sessions and workshops focusing on how teachers are using new technologies and teaching methods in the classroom. It also hosts a summer professional development conference and a biannual research symposium.

***Association for the Advancement of Computing in Education (AACE)* (www.aace.org).** AACE is an international educational and professional organization dedicated to the advancement of the knowledge, theory, and quality of learning and teaching at all levels with information technology. AACE disseminates research and applications through publications and conferences. Journals published by AACE include *Journal of Computers in Mathematics and Science Teaching (JCMST), Journal of Interactive Learning Research (JILR), Journal of Educational Multimedia and Hypermedia (JEMH), Journal of Technology and Teacher Education (JTATE), AACE Journal (AACEJ),* and *Contemporary Issues in Technology & Teacher Education (CITE).*

***American Library Association (ALA)* (www.ala.org).** ALA is the largest library association in the world. Over 60,000 members represent all types of libraries—public, school, academic, state, and special libraries serving persons in government, commerce, the armed services, hospitals, prisons, and other institutions. The association has 11 divisions focusing on various types of libraries and services. The American Association of School Librarians (AASL), one of the divisions, holds national conferences focusing on the interests of school media specialists. AASL also publishes the *School Library Media Research,* which presents research that pertains to the uses of technology for instructional and informational purposes. Special issues have dealt with such themes as communications, technology, and facility design for learning environments that require a great deal of technology.

***Global SchoolNet Foundation (GSN)* (www.globalschoolnet.org).** Teachers founded the GSN with a mission to support 21st century learning through content-driven collaboration among teachers and students in order to improve the academic performance of students. GSN brings together online youth from 194 countries to explore community, cultural, and scientific issues that prepare them for the workforce and help them to become responsible and literate global citizens. Global SchoolNet's free membership program provides project-based learning support materials, resources, activities, lessons, and special offers from its partners.

***International Society for Technology in Education (ISTE)* (www.iste.org).** The mission of ISTE is to improve education through the use of technology in learning, teaching, and administration. ISTE members include teachers, administrators, computer coordinators, information resource managers, university faculty, and educational technology specialists. The organization maintains regional affiliate memberships to support and respond to grassroots efforts to improve the educational use of technology. Its support services and materials for educators include books, courseware, conferences, and a variety of publications.

ISTE publishes *Learning and Leading with Technology, Journal of Research on Computing in Education, Journal of Digital Learning in Teacher Education, ISTE Daily Leader, ISTE Update,* books, and courseware packages. Of particular interest to teachers is the *Leading and Learning with Technology* journal, which focuses on technology integration into PK–12 classrooms.

Many of the articles are written by teachers, sharing what they have accomplished using computers in their classrooms with children of all ages and abilities.

International Technology and Engineering Educators Association (ITEEA) (www.iteaconnect.org). ITEEA is the professional organization for technology, innovation, and design in engineering education. Its mission is to promote technological literacy by supporting the teaching of technology and promoting the professionalism of those engaged in this pursuit. ITEEA strengthens the profession through leadership, professional development, membership services, publications, and classroom activities.

ITEEA publishes two peer-reviewed scholarly journals, *Technology and Engineering Teacher* and the *Journal of Technology Education*. Another journal is *Children's Technology and Engineering* (CET). CET is a useful, interesting tool for K–6 teachers interested in technological literacy. ITEEA also provides the *Science, Technology, Engineering, and Mathematics (STEM) Connections,* a free online newsletter to keep teachers current on the latest STEM strategies and resources.

International Visual Literacy Association (IVLA) (www.ivla.org). IVLA is dedicated to exploring the concept of visual literacy—how we use visuals for communication and how we interpret these visuals. It is particularly concerned with the development of instructional materials designed to foster skills in interpreting visuals. The organization draws its members from a variety of disciplines and professions, including public schools, higher education, business and communication, professional artists, production specialists, and design specialists.

United States Distance Learning Association (USDLA) (www.usdla.org). USDLA promotes the development and application of distance learning for education and training. The 20,000 members and sponsors represent PK–12 education, higher education, continuing education, corporate training, telemedicine, and military and government training. The association has become a leading source of information and recommendations for government agencies, the U.S. Congress, industry, and those involved in the development of distance learning programs. USDLA has chapters in all 50 states. It is a sponsor of annual USDLA National Conferences and provides a variety of online resources. In addition, USDLA holds regular meetings with leaders of distance learning programs in Australia, Europe, India, Japan, and the United Kingdom.

State Organizations. Several of the national professional organizations have state and/or local affiliates (AECT, ALA, ISTE, USDLA). By joining one or more of these, you will quickly make contact with nearby professionals who share your particular interests. As a teacher, you will want to be active in at least one local or state organization in addition to active participation in at least one national organization. If you are a full-time student, you can join many organizations at a reduced rate.

Professional Journals. As shown previously, a key contribution of professional organizations in instructional technology and media is to publish journals of interest to their members. Various other print and electronic periodicals are targeted to educators interested in using educational technology and media. Electronic journals are quickly becoming the journals of choice because they provide teachers with current information that includes interactive links to additional information and they are a "green" solution. Examples of highly respected journals are listed here.

- *T.H.E. Journal* (**http://thejournal.com**) is dedicated to informing and educating PK–12 practitioners to improve and advance the learning process through the use of technology. It has over 90,000 subscribers to a variety of resources, including a monthly print and digital magazine, two websites, and five newsletters.

- *eSchool News* (**www.eschoolnews.com**), a print and online publication, provides "Technology News for Today's K–20 Educator" covering education technology in all its aspects—from legislation and litigation to case studies and new products. The newspaper has over 300,000 subscribers and the website has over 500,000 unique visitors each month.
- *Media and Methods* (**www.media-methods.com/**) highlights new software and hardware to assist schools with purchase decisions.
- *Tech & Learning* (**www.techlearning.com**) is a free online journal with practical PK–12 recommendations for resources and strategies to integrate digital technologies.

Through regular reading of educational technology journals, teachers can expand their professional knowledge and growth by staying informed of new technology and media that have positive impacts on student learning. Teachers can use this knowledge and growth to better create and implement a variety of 21st century learning environments.

21st Century Learning Environments

Twenty-first century learning environments go beyond the traditional classroom, which is dependent on the teacher and textbooks as the primary sources of information. These new environments expand into "global" classrooms. They also use technology for connecting schools and homes, and offering the choice of online education.

THE GLOBAL CLASSROOM

Our world, through the use of a complex satellite system, is connected with an invisible digital network that truly makes today's classrooms global. Students now learn from a multitude of resources that range from textbooks to live videoconferences with people geographically separated by thousands of miles. Teachers use resources such as ePals Global Community (**www.epals.com**), which has supported cross-cultural learning activities through connections among over 1 million teachers and their students in over 200 countries and territories. This site provides resources for teachers to collaboratively plan lessons with one or two teachers or engage their students in one of the many large interactive research projects involving children from around the globe.

The world is also opened to students through live, streamed video that begins playing before the entire file is downloaded from the Web. Students can see live shots from the South Pole, the streets of Vienna, Kenya game reserves, the Eiffel Tower, the Bavarian Forest, Mt. Fuji, a city market in Hong Kong, or the Smithsonian's National Air and Space Museum (**http://airandspace.si.edu/exhibitions/america-by-air/online/behindscenes/webcam.cfm**).

Many of these sites have user controls on the cameras so students can freely explore the distant site from multiple viewpoints. By visiting different countries through live video, such as EarthCam (**www.earthcam.com**), student awareness of differences in time is increased because the video may show the sun rising when it is afternoon in the student's classroom. Viewing the world "as it happens" opens student eyes to differences and similarities found in the world's cultures by seeing what people are wearing, driving, eating, and doing.

TECHNOLOGY CONNECTS SCHOOLS AND HOMES

As computers become increasingly popular in today's homes, teachers have greater opportunities to communicate with students and parents. Many teachers maintain class websites that contain teacher contact information, calendars, assignment sheets, parent notices, links to

Internet resources, and social networking tools to encourage ongoing communication. Class websites are often supported by a school or district server or by one of the free or inexpensive Web hosting services, such as Wikispaces Classroom **(www.wikispaces.com/content/teacher).**

Common links on teacher websites include basic skills practice, online demonstrations, or content-specific reference information. For example, PK–12 students can be directed to the National Library of Virtual Manipulatives **(http://nlvm.usu.edu)** to use interactive math tools to solve homework problems for numbers and operations, algebra, geometry, measurement, data analysis, and probability. The Internet also offers students help to complete their work. For example, over 10,000 students visit Discovery Education's B. J. Pinchbeck's Homework Helper **(http://school.discoveryeducation.com/homeworkhelp/bjpinchbeck/bjscience.html)** every day to "Ask BJ" questions about their homework and to use the "Homework Help" content area resources.

Another useful site is infoplease's Homework Center **(www.infoplease.com/homework)** that provides students access to resources categorized by subject area and skills (writing, research, speaking, listening, studying). The site also has links to searchable references (almanacs, atlas, dictionary, encyclopedia, and biographies), tools (conversion calculator, distance calculator), practice tools (math flash cards, spelling bee), and links to current events by year.

With this increased communication between school and home, it is possible to lengthen the time devoted to learning. Technology permits teachers to send homework and assignments over networks to homes. Parents, students, and teachers are able to interact about the assignment. Students can access their personal data files from home and also connect to instructional materials housed on the school's computer. However, as mentioned, teachers who assign technology-based homework need to assist underserved students to find alternative ways to access digital resources to ensure equitable learning opportunities.

THE CHOICE OF ONLINE EDUCATION

According to the 2013 International Association for PK–12 Online Learning (iNACOL) "Fast Facts about Online Learning" report, there has been explosive growth of online learning opportunities in PK–12 environments. Specifically, in 2011–2012, there were over 275,000 enrolled as full-time PK–12 online students as compared to only 50,000 students in 2000 (iNACOL, 2013). Additionally, 31 states had statewide full-time online schools.

Florida Virtual School (FLVS) **(www.flvs.net)** has grown from being the first state to offer an Internet-based high school in 1997 to a nationally recognized e-Learning model that more than doubled enrollment from 71,000 students in 2009 to 148,000 in 2012 (FLVS, 2012). FLVS is the only public school where funding is tied directly to student performance. FLVS offers online students multiple resources such as a virtual library, information sessions, student clubs, Facebook updates, and a tour of an online course for new users. Typically, statewide programs are free of cost to residents and often target students in rural, high-poverty, or low-performing schools.

Distance education opportunities are continually increasing as online learning bridges the gap of distance, poverty, and limited course offerings in small schools. States must recognize and support the distance education initiatives with policies and funding if future programs are to be sustainable and of high quality. The following five principles are recommended as "model legislation" for states offering PK–12 online learning (iNACOL, 2013):

1. Shift to competency-based education from seat time.

2. Increase access for each student and permit the entire continuum of student-centered, online, and blended learning.

3. Design outcomes-based accountability and funding incentives.

4. Increase access to excellent, effective teachers.

5. Provide room for innovation. (p. 1)

Overall, 21st century learning environments provide new opportunities for teachers to expand opportunities for student learning by creating "global classrooms." They also use technology and media to address the diverse needs of students, to improve communication with students and parents, and to explore online learning options to better meet the individual learning requirements of students.

Technology Grants for 21st Century Learning

Even though PK–12 access to technology is continually increasing, many teachers prefer to have a class set of computers rather than limiting student use to one or two days per week in the computer lab or bringing in a laptop cart. To solve this dilemma, districts, schools, and/or teachers apply for technology grants. These grants provide hardware, software, and very frequently require professional development to use the technology. Computers and other digital devices can also be acquired with grants focused on areas such as core content, social behavior improvement, and career training, if technology is integrated as a program component.

TYPES OF GRANTS

There are two basic types of technology grants: government grants funded at the federal, state, district, or school level, and organization grants from businesses and corporations or nonprofit organizations such as foundations, groups, or associations.

Government Grants. The U.S. Department of Education's Office of Educational Technology (US-DOE OET, 2013) and other departments offer several grant programs, as seen in the ED.gov Apply for a Grant site **(www.ed.gov/fund/grants-apply.html)**. The grants range from statewide funding for longitudinal data systems to program-specific initiatives such as funding to improve the provision of assistive technology for individuals with disabilities. Government grants can provide substantial funding, but frequently require the submission of a lengthy, detailed proposal and budget; collaborative partnerships between districts, universities, and community organizations; and matching funds from the districts and partners. Thus, federal grants are normally awarded to districts or regions rather than to schools or teachers. However, the U.S. General Services Administration of the Federal government sponsors the Computers for Learning (CFL) **(http://computersforlearning.gov)** program as a way to promote the reuse of government computers scheduled for replacement. The CFL program transfers excess computers and technology equipment to high-needs schools that complete the application and meet the program requirements.

Organization Grants. Grants from nongovernment organizations and foundations often involve a less extensive proposal process that is flexible enough to award funding to individual schools or teachers as well as to districts and collaborative partnerships. In addition, most schools can typically meet the requirements of grants sponsored by well-known organizations such as AT&T, the Kellogg Foundation, and Cisco Systems Virtual Schoolhouse. However, please note that some grants have a very targeted focus. For example, the Lockheed Martin Corporation Philanthropy only funds K–16 science, technology, engineering, and math initiatives in schools located in communities in which Lockheed Martin has employees.

Numerous websites provide lists of organizations that offer PK–12 technology grants. Examples include SchoolGrants **(http://k12grants.org)** and Top Teaching Resources **(www.top teachingresources.com)**. The Fund $ Raiser Cyberzone **(www.fundraiser.com)** offers fundraising ideas, such as silent auctions, raffles, and donations. For further examples, see "Technology Grant Resources" in the Suggested Resources the end of the chapter.

WRITING A GRANT PROPOSAL

Writing a successful grant proposal begins with a clear and structured process to describe how the funds will be used to achieve the overall purpose of the grant. It is critical to follow the specific guidelines in the Request for Proposal (RFP), as most proposals have a strict page limit and require information to be presented in a designated order. Many grants use an outline similar to the one presented here and in Figure 10.1.

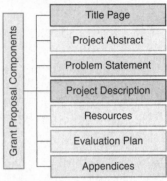

FIGURE 10.1   Grant Proposal Components: Technology and other types of grants typically have seven key components.

- *Title page.* Select a title that is concise and clearly states the intent of the project. Avoid the use of clever or cute titles. Include the funder name and the names of the key people involved with the project.

- *Project abstract.* Typically a one-page description of the project that includes overall goal/purpose, description of the project and how it will be implemented, who will benefit from the project, key staff, evaluation plans, overall costs, and timeline. Avoid overuse of academic jargon.

- *Statement of the problem.* The intent of this section is to convince the funder that your proposed project will benefit students. Your argument should be supported with data and research. It is important to include data about your current situation by providing information such as the student-to-computer ratio and a description of student and teacher needs. For example, will the project focus on students who are from low-income families, who are English language learners, or who have special learning needs, including providing advanced studies for gifted students? Show how your project will use research-based approaches to guarantee successful outcomes.

- *Project description.* The project description includes the goals and outcomes, target population, methods, project staff, and timeline.

  - *Goals and outcomes:* Begin this section with clearly stated goals and measurable outcomes that will be achieved at the end of the project.

  - *Target population:* Describe who will benefit from the project. Include descriptions of the students by grade level and subject areas that will be emphasized, and the teacher(s) who will implement the project.

  - *Methods:* Provide clear and concise descriptions of the methods that will be used to implement the project. How and what type of technology will be provided to the targeted population? How will teachers be prepared? How will the project change classroom practices and learning opportunities?

  - *Project staff:* Most grants designate the lead project staff as the principal investigator (PI) and secondary lead staff as co-PIs. Begin your list with the PI and co-PIs, then list other key staff: professional development facilitators, technology coaches, and technical assistants. It is not necessary to list those who provide accounting or secretarial support. Include names and a brief description of qualifications for the assigned roles of each staff member.

  - *Timeline:* Use a timeline to depict when each major activity will take place and the staff responsible for the activity. A table works well to display the information by using the following columns: date, activity, and person(s) responsible. It is sometimes helpful to outline how the project will continue beyond the grant period to demonstrate how you plan to sustain the project beyond the grant-funded time period.

- *Resources.* Describe the available resources that will be used to support the project (e.g., facilities, personnel, and equipment: printers, projectors, interactive whiteboards). Then describe resources that will be purchased with project funds. Include a rationale for each purchase.

- *Evaluation plan.* Provide a clear description of the methods and procedures for evaluating the degree to which the project goals and outcomes are met. Describe which participants will be included in the evaluation, the evaluation instruments to be used, how the results will be analyzed, and how the findings will be shared.
- *Appendices.* The RFP typically limits the appendices to specific types of content and number of pages. Common information in an appendix includes detailed descriptions of professional development models, example student work, data collection instruments, and staff curriculum vitas.

One way to improve technology grant proposals is to review past proposals submitted by your school or district, which often have descriptions of your student population and local setting that can be adapted for your proposal. It is also useful to review sample proposals (**www.k12grants.org**) submitted by other schools and districts, such as those provided by SchoolGrants.

Summary

This chapter discussed factors influencing the advancement of 21st century teaching and learning and placed key emphasis on the chapter's knowledge outcomes.

Describe how the ASSURE model supports 21st century learning as described in the National Education Technology Plan. By following the step-by-step ASSURE model, teachers receive the support and guidance to develop, implement, evaluate, and revise lessons that integrate technology to increase student learning and prepare them for future careers.

Discuss the characteristics of a 21st century teacher who is technologically competent, information literate, and maintains professional growth and engagement. A technologically competent teacher not only knows the basics of computer literacy, but also, more importantly, knows how and when to use technology to enhance student learning. An information literate teacher prepares for instruction by locating materials from a variety of online sources and ensuring the material is accurate, appropriate, easily accessible, and useable according to copyright guidelines. Twenty-first century teachers are lifelong learners who regularly participate in professional development and stay actively involved in technology and media associations, and stay informed by reading professional journals.

Compare components of a 21st century environment with regard to being a global classroom, connecting schools and homes, and offering online education. Complex satellite systems enable today's classrooms to be global by connecting with resources and people geographically separated by thousands of miles. Schools connect with homes through class websites that contain teacher contact information, calendars, assignment sheets, parent notices, links to Internet resources, and social networking tools to encourage ongoing communication. Online education opportunities are continually increasing as they bridge the gap of distance, poverty, and limited course offerings in small schools.

Describe the types of technology grants available for 21st century learning and briefly describe the basic components included when writing a grant proposal. There are two basic types of technology grants: government grants funded at the federal, state, district, or school level, and organization grants from businesses and corporations or nonprofit organizations such as foundations, groups, or associations. Writing a successful grant proposal begins with a clear and structured process to describe how the funds will be used to achieve the overall purpose of the grant. It is critical to follow the specific guidelines in the Request for Proposal (RFP), which typically requires information to include the following components: title page, project abstract, statement of problem, project description, resources, evaluation plan, and appendices.

Professional Development

DEMONSTRATING PROFESSIONAL KNOWLEDGE

1. Describe how the ASSURE model supports 21st century learning as described in the National Education Technology Plan.
2. Discuss the characteristics of a 21st century teacher who is technologically competent, information literate, and maintains professional growth and engagement.

3. Compare components of a 21st century environment with regard to being a global classroom, connecting schools and homes, and offering online education.
4. Describe the types of technology grants available for 21st century learning and briefly describe the basic components included when writing a grant proposal.

DEMONSTRATING PROFESSIONAL SKILLS

1. Review ASSURE lesson plans that you have developed or other technology integration lessons and describe how each lesson aligns with the NETP goals for learning and in what ways the lesson can be modified to address goals not included in the lesson (ISTE NETS-T 2.A and C).
2. Conduct a self-reflection to assess the ways in which you demonstrate technological competence and other traits of a 21st century teacher. Address the following questions in your self-assessment: What are your strengths and weaknesses in how you use technology to support your teaching? What are the strengths and weaknesses of how your students use technology and media to improve learning? How could you address the weaknesses (ISTE NETS-T 5.C)?

3. Interview two or more teachers who integrate various types of technology and media into their instruction to learn how the teachers create 21st century learning environments. In a three- to five-page paper, compare and contrast how each teacher uses technology to interact with parents, and what their thoughts are about using online learning as a learning option (ISTE NETS-T 5.C).
4. Analyze the technology needs of the school in which you work or would like to work and locate a grant that would help the school address the identified needs. Use the grant proposal outline to write a brief description of how you would write each section of the proposal (ISTE NETS-T 5.B).

BUILDING YOUR PROFESSIONAL PORTFOLIO

- *Enhancing My Portfolio.* Select a technology integration lesson from the Web, or one that you have developed. After citing the source of the lesson, analyze it according to topics discussed in this chapter. Specifically, take note how or if the lesson addresses 21st century learning by examining: (1) types of technology and media used to communicate outside the classroom, (2) types of technology skills required for the teacher and the student, (3) how the lesson could be improved if

grant funding provided students greater access to technology (ISTE NETS-T 4.B, 5.C).
- *Reflecting on My Learning.* Reflect on the need to advance to 21st century teaching, as described in this chapter, and write a description of how you think this need will impact your teaching. Explain what you think the most rewarding aspects of 21st century teaching will be and why. Explain what you think will be the most challenging aspects and why (ISTE NETS-T 2.A, 5.C).

Suggested Resources

PRINT RESOURCES

Orey, M., & Fortner, P. (2010) Graduate programs. In M. Orey, S. A. Jones, & R. M. Branch (Eds.), *Educational* *Media and Technology Yearbook* (Vol. 35, pp. 293–444). New York, NY: Springer.

Martin, G., & Ritz, J. (2012). Research needs for technology education. *Journal of Technology Education, 23*(2), 25–43.

New Media Consortium (NMC). (2013). *NMC Horizon Report: 2013 K–12 Education Edition.* Austin, TX: The New Media Consortium.

Reiser, R. A., & Dempsey, J. V. (2011). *Trends and issues in instructional design and technology* (3rd ed.). Upper Saddle River, NJ: Merrill/Prentice Hall.

Technology Grant News. (2010). *Winning at IT: Grant writing for technology grants.* New York, NY: Technology Grant News Publication.

WEB RESOURCES

Discovery Education
http://education.discovery.com
Through its public service initiatives, products, and partnerships, Discovery Education reaches over 90,000 schools across the United States, serving 1.5 million teachers and their 35 million students each year. The site provides free lesson plans, Kathy Schrock's Guide for Educators, Teaching Tools, Curriculum Center, Brain Boosters, clip art, Puzzlemaker, Science Fair Central, Discovery Student Adventures, and more.

Edutopia
www.edutopia.org
Edutopia is supported by the George Lucas Educational Foundation (GLEF). This site provides more than 100 video segments of classroom practices and expert interviews and free instructional modules that include articles, videos, blogs, PowerPoint presentations, discussion questions, and class activities. They draw from GLEF's archives of best practices and correlate with the NETS standards.

Eduscape
eduscapes.com
Eduscape was developed by Annette Lamb and Larry Johnson. This site includes multiple resources for teachers:

- 42eXplore, a weekly project section that contains multiple resources
- Multimedia Seeds, which contains ideas and resources to improve the use of multimedia
- Teacher Tap, a professional development resource that helps teacher address common technology integration questions
- Activate E-Journal, an online publication with articles aimed at developing technology-rich learning environments

National Center for Technology Innovation
www.nationaltechcenter.org
The National Center for Technology Innovation (NCTI), funded by the U.S. Office of Special Education Programs (OSEP), advances learning opportunities for individuals with disabilities by fostering technology innovation. The website provides resources and information to promote partnerships for the development of tools and applications by developers, manufacturers, producers, publishers, and researchers.

Study Guides and Strategies
www.studygs.net
This is a public service site developed by Joseph Landsberger that provides study guides and strategies for multiple topics.

Example topics are time management, problem solving, learning, learning with others, studying, classroom participation, online learning communication, thinking, memorizing, reading, research, project management, presenting projects, writing basics, taking tests, math, science and technology, and the teaching corner.

Creating Class Websites
TeacherWeb
http://teacherWeb.com
A popular site that for a nominal yearly fee provides teachers a wide variety of tools to create an interactive class website. Sample tools include pages to post announcements, homework, links, teacher information, calendar, frequently asked questions, WebQuests, and teacher-created interactive tests.

Assign-a-Day
http://assignaday.4teachers.org
A free site hosted by "4Teachers" that has an easy to personalize calendar for teachers to post homework assignments.

School Rack
www.schoolrack.com
An easy to use site that allows teachers to quickly set up a site that offers posting of digital files, assignments, parent notices, and more.

Technology Grant Resources
Funding Your Technology Dreams
http://www.cpsb.org//site/default.aspx?PageID=501
Multiple listings of ongoing sources of technology grants, funding opportunities, and creative solutions to obtain technology resources for your class. The site also includes resources to help write grants.

SchoolGrants
www.school-grants.org
This site contains variety of information and resources on grant writing, grant opportunities, and sample grant proposals. Also provided are newsletters and an index of links, including one for technology resources.

Teacher Tap: Grants and Grant Writing
www.eduscapes.com/tap/topic94.htm
This website provides professional development resources for teachers and librarians focused on grant resources starting points, exploring grant possibilities, getting started, identifying the need and your solution, goal setting, and writing a grant proposal.

Appendix: Lesson Scenarios

Scenario	Content	Students	Goal
Mr. Wilson wants his preschool children to have a better understanding of the weather cycles.	Weather/seasons	Preschool-aged children, 4–5 years old, with little instruction in weather patterns	At the end of the lesson, the children will have a general understanding of the seasons and the weather patterns associated with them.
Mrs. Harris plans to introduce the concept of simple addition to her K–1 class.	Mathematics	Students, 5–6 years old, with knowledge of number concepts	At the end of the lesson, the students will be able to complete simple addition problems with sums less than 10.
Mr. Martinez wants to reinforce his students' understanding of prepositions.	Language arts	Elementary students, 7–8 years old, who are building their vocabulary skills	At the end of the lesson, students will be able to place graphics in the location specified in given prepositions.
Ms. Eller's class expresses interest in the states surrounding their own.	U.S. geography	Students, 8–9 years old, with limited knowledge of the influence of geography on states' development	At the end of the lesson, the students will be able to identify the geographic factors that influence the states' economic, social, and political histories.
Mr. Cheon wants to introduce his students to art forms made from natural stone.	Art	Intermediate grade students, 9–10 years old, who have limited knowledge about using stone for artwork	At the end of the lesson, the students will be able to identify several types of artwork that are created with natural stone.
Ms. Chinn wants to introduce her students to the concept of life cycles by studying the life cycle of a frog.	Life science	Students, 11–12 years old, with strong physical science and limited biological science background	At the end of the lesson, the students will be able to identify the stages in the life cycle of the frog and be able to describe the relationships among the stages in the development of the frog.
Mr. Heller's class is interested in issues related to health, especially those identified in eating a balanced diet.	Nutrition	Middle school/junior high students, 13–14 years old, with knowledge of the Food Guide Pyramid	At the end of the lesson, the students will be able to select a balanced menu covering three meals per day for one week.
Ms. Galloway has decided to collaborate with the world history teacher's lesson on World War II by introducing her students to the literature of the period.	World literature	High school, college-bound students, 16–17 years old, who have an interest in reading and exploring period literature	At the end of the lesson, students will be able to discuss the relationship between international events during World War II and the literature produced in that period.
Mr. Wasileski's high school English class is ready to learn how to write a research paper.	English writing	High school students who have limited experience writing a research paper	At the end of the lesson, students will be able to write a paper that includes appropriate use of references, following the pattern of introduction, research questions, analysis, and conclusions.

A

Acceptable use policy (AUP) An agreement among students, parents/guardians, and school administrators regarding appropriate use of the Internet.

Affective domain The domain of human learning that involves changes in interests, attitudes, and values and the development of appreciation.

Alt-tag Alternative textual descriptions to provide brief descriptions of graphics or images.

Analogical visuals Visuals that convey a concept or topic by showing something else and implying a similarity.

Animation A technique in which the artist gives motion to still images by creating and juxtaposing a series of pictures with small, incremental changes from one to the next.

Applications Games, simulations, tutorials, problem-solving programs, productivity software, and graphic software programs.

Asynchronous Not at the same time.

Asynchronous setting A distance learning setup in which the teacher and students are not together at the same time.

Audio literacy Understanding the role of hearing and listening in learning.

Audio teleconference A teleconference involving transmission of voices only. The voices are amplified at each end by a speaker system.

Auditory fatigue The process by which attention to a sound gradually decreases because of the monotony of the sound.

Augmented reality (AR) Combining real-world data with virtual data.

Authentic assessment Evaluation that is usually performance based and that requires students to demonstrate their learning in a natural context.

B

Behaviorism A theory that equates learning with changes in observable behavior. With this theory, there is no speculating about mental events that may mediate learning.

Benchmarks Standards against which students are tested.

Bit An acronym for binary digit, the smallest unit of digital information. The bit can be thought of as a 1 or a 0 representing a circuit on or off, respectively.

Blended instruction A combination of e-learning with live, face-to-face instruction.

Blended learning The result of instruction that is a combination of e-learning and live, face-to-face instruction.

Blog Web log serving as a publicly accessible personal journal for an individual.

Blu-ray disc (BD) A medium that stores high-definition video, games, and other data. The disc is the same size as a standard DVD, but stores almost ten times more data than a DVD. The name comes from the blue laser used to read the disc.

Byte The number of bits required to store or represent one character of text (a letter or number); most commonly, but not always, it is made up of eight bits in various combinations of 0s and 1s.

C

Cable modem A television cable connection that provides very high speed access to the Internet.

Cartoon Line drawing that is a rough caricature of real or fictional people, animals, or events.

Central processing unit (CPU)   The core element of a computer that carries out all the calculations and controls the total system.

Chart   Visual representation of abstract relationships.

Classroom voice amplification system   Audio technology system that optimizes the listening environment for all students using a lightweight wireless teacher's microphone linked to a set of speakers strategically placed around the classroom.

Clip art   Prepared visual images (drawings and digital pictures) that can be inserted into digital documents and presentations.

Cloud computing   System in which applications are available through networked computers to distribute greater access to processing power and applications.

Cognitive domain   The domain of human learning involving intellectual skills, such as assimilation of information or knowledge.

Cognitivism   A theory according to which mental processes mediate learning and learning entails the construction or reshaping of mental schemata.

Collaborative   A sharing or cooperative nature of an experience.

Community of practice (CoP)   A group of educators from across the nation and around the world who have common goals and share ideas and resources.

Compressed video   Video images that have been processed to remove redundant information, thereby reducing the amount of bandwidth required to transmit them. Because only changes in the image are transmitted, movements appear jerky compared with full-motion video.

Computer-assisted instruction (CAI)   Instruction delivered directly to learners by allowing them to interact with lessons programmed into the computer system.

Computer conferencing   Connecting two or more computers together for textual and/or graphical information exchange.

Computer-managed instruction (CMI)   The use of a computer system to manage information about learner performance and learning resources and to then prescribe and control individual lessons.

Computer platform   Different types of computer operating systems, such as Mac OS, Unix, or Windows.

Configuration   A computer's specific combination of hardware components.

Constructivism   A theory that considers the engagement of students in meaningful experiences as the essence of learning.

Cooperative learning   An instructional configuration involving small groups of learners working together on learning tasks rather than competing as individuals.

Copyright   Regulations that describe the manner in which an original work can be used and copied. Copyright laws regulate the manner in which authors or artists can be reimbursed for their creative work.

Course management tool (CMT)   Software designed to make it easier for teachers to use resources in the distance learning system, such as the discussion board, test options, and grade book.

Cyberlearning   The use of Web 2.0 networked computing and communication technologies to support learning.

D

Decode   To comprehend information that is presented.

Digital fabricator   Three-dimensional printer or rapid prototyping machine, also known as a "fabber" (short for fabricator), that can build 3-D objects by carefully depositing materials drop by drop, layer by layer, using a geometric blueprint from a CAD program.

Digital subscriber line (DSL)   A telephone line that provides very high-speed access to the Internet.

Digital video editing Taking apart and putting back together video segments using a computer and associated software.

Diorama A static display employing a flat background and 3-D foreground to achieve a life-like effect.

Discovery A teaching strategy that proceeds as follows: immersion in a real or contrived problem situation, development of hypotheses, testing of hypotheses, and arrival at conclusion (the main point).

Discussion A teaching strategy involving the exchange of ideas and opinions.

Display An array of objects, visuals, and printed materials.

Distance learning An instructional situation in which students learn via telecommunications.

Documentary A video program that deals with fact, nonfiction, or fictionalized versions of fact.

Document camera A video camera mounted on a copy stand to show documents, pictures, graphics, and real objects to groups.

Drawing Graphic arrangement of lines to represent persons, places, things, and concepts.

Drill-and-practice A teaching strategy in which learners are led through a series of exercises or problems and given feedback.

E

Educational gaming A competitive environment in which learners follow prescribed rules as they strive to attain a challenging goal.

Electronic mail (email) Transmission of private messages over a computer network. Users can send mail to a single recipient or broadcast it to multiple users on the system.

Electronic portfolio (e-portfolio) A digital collection of student work that demonstrates progress in learning as shown in student self-reflections of the portfolio contents.

Emoticon An email symbol generated from punctuation marks.

Encode To visually express an idea to others.

Entry tests Assessments, both formal and informal, to determine whether students possess desired identified prerequisites.

Exhibit A display incorporating various media formats (e.g., realia, still pictures, models, graphics) into an integral whole intended for instructional purposes.

F

Fair use Basic criteria an educator can use to determine whether it is appropriate to use copyrighted materials in a classroom setting.

Feedback (learner) Information provided to the learner regarding correctness of performance and suggestions for improvement.

File server In local area networks, a station dedicated to providing file and mass data storage services to the other stations on the network.

Firewall Intranet software that prevents external users from accessing a proprietary network, while allowing internal users access to external networks.

Flash drive USB minidrive, a form of removable storage device that allows the user to store files outside the computer; also called a jump drive.

G

Gateway A computer that interconnects and makes translations between two different types of networks. Also called a portal.

GB See Gigabyte.

Gigabyte (GB) Approximately 1 million bytes, or 1,000 megabytes.

Graph Visual representation of numerical data.

H

Hardware   The mechanical and electronic components that make up a computer; the physical equipment that makes up a computer system, and, by extension, the term that refers to any audiovisual equipment.

Hearing   A physiological process in which sound waves entering the outer ear are transmitted to the eardrum, converted into mechanical vibrations in the middle ear, and changed in the inner ear to nerve impulses that travel to the brain.

HTTP   See Hypertext transfer protocol.

Hybrid   A mixed learning environment that combines Internet resources (i.e., WebQuests) with traditional classroom curriculum.

Hybrid instruction   See Blended instruction.

Hypertext transfer protocol (HTTP)   The web protocol that ensures compatibility before transferring information.

I

Iconic   Any referent that resembles the thing it represents.

ILS   See Integrated learning system.

Informal learning   An instructional setting that provides students with opportunities to learn from experiences outside of the classroom.

Information   Knowledge, facts, news, comments, and content as presented in memos, lectures, textbooks, or websites.

Informational text   Nonfiction text materials including textbooks.

Information literacy   The ability to use a range of critical thinking and problem-solving skills to effectively participate in today's society.

Input device   Hardware that transmits information to the computer, for example, a keyboard and mouse.

Instruction   Deliberate arrangement of experience(s) to help learners achieve a desirable change in performance; the management of learning, which in education is primarily the function of the teacher.

Instructional material   Specific items used within a lesson that influence student learning.

Instructional technology   Hardware, software, and/or processes to facilitate learning.

Integrated learning system (ILS)   A set of interrelated computer-based lessons organized to match the curriculum standards.

Integrated services digital network (ISDN)   A network that provides high-speed access to the Internet using digital communication.

Internet   A global interconnection of computer networks with a broad collection of millions of computer networks serving billions of people around the world.

Internet radio   A system used for broadcasting online programs over the Internet.

Internet service provider (ISP)   A company that provides account holders with access to the Internet for a fee.

Internet video   Internet broadcasts of events or activities on a website using compressed video or video streaming; some broadcasts are live and others are recorded.

Interpersonal domain   The domain of learning that involves interaction among people and the ability to relate effectively with others.

Interpretive visuals   Visuals that illustrate theoretical or abstract relationships.

Intranet   A proprietary or closed internal network that connects multiple sites across the state, within the country, or around the world; systems connected to an intranet are private and accessible only by individuals within a given school or organization.

K

KB   See Kilobyte.

Kilobyte (KB or K)   Approximately 1,000 bytes; more precisely, 1,024 bytes.

L

Learning center   A self-contained environment designed to promote individual or small-group learning around a specific task.

Learning communities   Student and teacher use of electronic connectedness to share ideas, engage in inquiry, and search for additional information.

Learning style   A cluster of psychological traits that determine how a person perceives, interacts with, and responds emotionally to learning environments.

Listening   A psychological process that begins with someone's awareness of and attention to sounds or speech patterns, proceeds through identification and recognition of specific auditory signals, and ends in comprehension.

Literary   Fictional text materials including stories, dramas, poetries, and myths.

Local area network (LAN)   A simple network that connects individual computers to one another within a limited area—normally a classroom, building, or laboratory—to permit the exchange of files and other resources.

Log-on   The process of entering a specific username and password to access online materials.

M

Manipulative   Object that can be viewed and handled in a learning setting.

Mashups   Websites that bring together content from a variety of resources, creating resources that are new and different from the original sources, for example, online news media sites.

MB   See Megabyte.

Media   See Medium.

Media centers   School facilities that offer traditional library reading resources as well as a variety of information technology assets.

Media format   The physical form in which a message is incorporated and displayed; examples include whiteboards, webpages, PowerPoint or Prezi slides, CD, DVDs, and computer multimedia.

Media literacy   The ability to interpret and produce a wide variety of media, including text, audio, visuals, and video, which are often combined to form multimedia.

Medium   A means of communication. Derived from the Latin medium ("between"), the term refers to anything that carries information between a source and a receiver. Plural: media.

Megabyte (MB or M)   Basic unit of measurement of mass storage.

Metacognition   Knowledge of and thinking about one's own thinking process.

Mobile app   Software application designed for mobile devices that enable many of these devices to take photos and short video, email, surf the Web, play games, provide location-based services (GPS), and use calendars and other personal management tools.

Mobile assessment tool   Mobile computing resource that enables teachers to record student assessment data directly into a mobile device that transfers the data to a computer for report generation.

Mobile technology   Portable technology such as smart phones, portable music players, tablet computers, e-readers, and other handheld technologies.

Mock-up   Representation of a complex device or process.

Model   A 3-D representation of a real object; it may be larger, smaller, or the same size as the thing represented.

Multiple intelligences   Theory developed by Howard Gardner that suggests humans have multiple methods of learning: verbal/linguistic (language), logical/mathematical (scientific/quantitative), visual/spatial, musical/rhythmic, body/kinesthetic (dancing/athletics), interpersonal (understanding other people), intrapersonal (understanding oneself), naturalist, and existentialist.

Musical instrument digital interface (MIDI)   Technology that allows students to create music by focusing on musical ideas rather than the mechanics of playing an instrument or learning musical notation.

N

National Education Technology Standards for Students (NETS-S)   A document that specifically outlines expectations for student use of technology to guide their learning.

Netiquette   Guidelines relating to email and other interactions on the Web.

Network   A communication system linking two or more computers.

O

One-way video   Video transmission in which visual and auditory information is delivered to learners with limited opportunities for immediate connections with the teacher or source of the information.

Online learning   The result of instruction that is delivered electronically using computer-based media.

Open source   Websites that offer free productivity suites (e.g., word processing, spreadsheets, presentation software).

Operating system   Software that functions as the computer's interface with the user.

Oral history   Historical documentation of a time, place, or event by means of recording the spoken recollections of participants in those events.

Organizational visuals   Visuals that show the qualitative relationships among various elements.

Output device   Hardware that displays the information from a computer to the user, for example, a monitor or digital projector.

P

Persistence of vision   The psychophysiological phenomenon that occurs when an image falls on the retina of the eye and is conveyed to the brain via the optic nerve. The brain continues to "see" the image for a fraction of a second after the image is cut off.

Personal response system   Handheld wireless devices (similar to TV remotes) used to collect and graphically display student answers to teacher questions.

Photos   Two-dimensional representations of people, places, and things.

Pin boards   Online websites that enable users to organize photos, videos, and other information onto digital boards by lesson, unit, grade level, or subject area.

Place-shift   Experiencing instruction at some place away from the live teacher.

Podcast   Internet-distributed multimedia file formatted for direct download to mobile devices.

Podcasting   Distribution of recorded audio files in MP3 format over the Internet.

Portable digital audio player   Device that allows users to take digital audio files with them, such as an Apple iPod.

Portal   See Gateway.

Poster   A visual combination of images, lines, color, and words.

Practice   Learner participation that increases the probability of learning.

Prerequisites   Competencies that learners must possess to benefit from instruction.

Presentation   An instructional strategy in which a source tells, dramatizes, or disseminates information to learners.

Presentation software   Computer software used to create attractive graphic displays without specialized production skills and to display visuals with a digital projector.

Pretest   A test administered before teaching a lesson to identify students who need remediation prior to lesson implementation and also to identify those who have already mastered what you plan to teach.

Problem-based learning   A process in which students actively seek solutions to structured or ill-structured problems situated in the real world.

Problem-solving skills   Reaching a solution to a novel problem using higher-order thinking skills such as defining the problem, considering alternatives, and using logical reasoning.

Productivity tools   Web applications that allow users to create and edit documents online while collaborating in real time with other users. Examples include web apps for word processing, slideshows and presentations, spreadsheets, note taking, concept maps, and calendars.

R

RAM   See Random access memory.

Random access memory (RAM)   The flexible part of computer memory. The particular program or set of data being manipulated by the user is temporarily stored in RAM, then erased to make way for the next program.

Read-only memory (ROM)   Control instructions that have been "wired" permanently into the memory of a computer. Usually stores instructions that the computer will need constantly, such as the programming language(s) and internal monitoring functions.

Realistic visuals   Visuals that show the actual object under study.

Real object   Not a model or simulation but an example of an actual object used in instruction.

Relational visuals   Visuals that communicate quantitative relationships.

Removable storage device   High-capacity portable computer storage unit that allows the user to store information and move it from one computer to another.

Response to Intervention   A program of assessment and appropriate instructional assistance in schools.

ROM   See Read-only memory.

S

Scaffold   To build on prior knowledge as part of the learning process.

Scanner   A computer device that converts an image on a piece of paper into an electronic form that can be stored in a computer file.

School media center   An area of the school where a variety of media are organized and made available to students and teachers.

Search engine   A program that identifies Internet sites that contain user-identified keywords or phrases.

Semantic-aware application   Application that works with a user's computer to help it "understand" what the user wants to know and guides the search for an answer that addresses the question the user has posed.

Simulation   An abstraction or simplification of some real-life situation or process.

Slow motion   High-speed videography that slows down a motion so that we can observe the process.

Social bookmarking   Online service that enables users to organize, store, manage, and search for bookmarked resources online and provides users with links to online resources they want to remember and share.

Social media   Mobile and web-based applications that enable users to interact, collaborate, co-create, share, and publish information, ideas, and multimedia.

Social networking service   Website that facilitates online connections and interactions of users based on shared backgrounds, interests, and experiences. Users are able to share ideas, messages, information, and multimedia with people in their network.

Social psychology   The study of the effects of the social organization of the classroom on learning.

Standardized tests State-wide tests that are administered in a consistent manner and using the same scoring procedures. These are used to identify student learning that is meeting or exceeding state standards and to determine where there is a need for improvement.

Storyboarding An audiovisual production and planning technique in which sketches of the proposed visuals and verbal messages are put on individual cards or into a computer program; the items are then arranged into the desired sequence on a display surface.

Streaming Transmission method by which an audio file itself stays on a network server, but the file is available to listeners on an audio device.

Streaming audio Audio sent in packets to allow listening to portions of a file before all portions are downloaded.

Streaming video A video file downloaded from the Internet that starts playing before it is completely downloaded.

Student-centered strategies A type of learning experience in which the learners are involved in the direction of the experience.

Synchronously Distance learning when all the participants are together at the same time.

Synchronous setting A learning situation where the teacher and the student are together at the same time, for example, a face-to-face classroom or real-time video conferencing.

Synthesizer software Computer software used to create original music, radio programs, and other materials to demonstrate student learning; also called softsynth.

T

TB See Terabyte.

Teacher-centered strategies A type of learning experience in which the teacher directs the learners in the experience.

Technological competence Knowing not only the basics of computer literacy, but also how and when to use technology to enhance student learning.

Technology (1) A process of devising reliable and repeatable solutions to tasks. (2) The hardware and software (i.e., the products) that result from the application of technological processes. (3) A mix of process and product, used in instances where the context refers to the combination of technological processes and resultant products or where the process is inseparable from the product.

Technology lab A room set apart from regular classrooms and furnished with multiple computers, usually established in schools that do not have computers in individual classrooms.

Technology literacy Students' abilities to engage in the use of technology to support their learning and show competency in six key areas: creativity and innovation; communication and collaboration; research and information fluency; critical thinking, problem solving, and decision making; digital citizenship; and technology operations and concept.

Telecommunications A means for communicating over a distance; specifically, any arrangement for transmitting voice and data in the form of coded signals through an electronic medium.

Terabyte (TB) Approximately 1 million megabytes.

Text literacy The ability to use text as a means to gather information or to communicate.

Time lapse Videography that compresses the time it takes to observe an event.

Time-shift Experiencing instruction at some time after the live lesson.

Transformational visuals Visuals that illustrate movement or change in time and space.

Tutorial A teaching strategy in which content is presented, questions are posed, responses are given, and feedback is provided.

Two-way video Video transmission where visual and auditory information are exchanged across the system between learners and the teacher synchronously; also referred to as videoconferencing.

U

Understanding   The final step in the listening process that involves comprehension of auditory signals.

Uniform resource locator (URL)   The address for an Internet site or World Wide Web page containing the protocol type, the domain, the directory, and the name of the site or page.

URL   See Uniform resource locator.

USB (universal serial bus)   A hardware interface technology that allows the user to connect a device without having to restart the computer.

V

Video conferencing   Distance teaching using the computer and classroom cameras to both see and hear your students at a distance.

Videography   The creation of video.

Video literacy   The knowledge and skills needed to understand and evaluate video messages and to create video that appropriately achieves the intended outcomes.

Virtual field trip   A type of field trip in which the students do not leave the classroom setting; instead they use media to provide the experience of "being there."

Virtual public schools (VPS)   State-level initiatives that use the Internet for delivery of instruction and that offer courses or whole programs of study that students can access, including courses that might not be available to them at their local schools or advanced placement classes from other high schools or from colleges and universities anywhere in the world.

Visual literacy   The learned ability to interpret visual messages accurately and to create such messages.

W

WAN   See Wide area network.

Web   See World Wide Web.

Web application   Browser technology used as a client to accomplish one or more tasks over a network, for example, webmail.

Webpages   Documents that make up the World Wide Web. See also Website.

WebQuest   A set of steps that provide guidance when seeking information about a simulated problem.

Website   A collection of webpages available on the Internet that provides information about products, services, events, materials, and so forth.

Web 2.0   Available online resources that provide students with many types of learning opportunities beyond simple information access.

Wide area network (WAN)   A communications network that covers a large geographic area, such as a state or country.

Wiki   A web-based document subject to edit by any of its users.

Wireless network   Computers connected by radio frequency, microwave, or infrared technology instead of wires.

Word cloud   A visual representation of text-based data used to convey concepts, key vocabulary, significant events, ideas from brainstorming, and much more; also called a tag cloud.

World wide web (the Web)   A graphical environment on computer networks that allows you to access, view, and maintain documents that can include text, data, sound, graphics, and video.

Becker, G. H. (2003). *Copyright: A guide to information and resources* (3rd ed.). Lake Mary, FL: Gary H. Becker.

Bergmann, J., & Sams, A. (2012). *Flip your classroom: Reach every student in every class every day.* Washington, DC: International Society for Technology Education.

Black, P., & William, O. (1998). Assessment and classroom learning. *Assessment in Education, 5*(1), 7–73.

Bloom, B., & Krathwohl, D. (1984). *Taxonomy of educational objectives, Handbook 1: Cognitive domain.* New York: Addison-Wesley.

Bloom, B. S., Engelhart, M. D., Furst, E. J., Hill, W. H., & Krathwohl, D. R. (Eds.). (1956). *Taxonomy of educational objectives: The classification of educational goals. Handbook 1: Cognitive domain.* New York, NY: David McKay.

Bowes, K. A., D'Onofrio, A., & Marker, E. S. (2006). Assessing technology integration: Its validity and value for classroom practice and teacher accountability. *Australasian Journal of Educational Technology, 22*(4), 439–454.

Bransford, J., Brown, A., & Cocking, R. (Eds.). (2000). *How people learn: Brain, mind, experience, and school.* Washington, DC: National Academic Press.

Branzburg, J. (2006, May). *Use Google Maps mashups in K-12 education.* Retrieved from http://www.techlearning.com/departments/0040/use-google-maps-mashups-in-k-12-education/43534

Calkins, L., Ehrenworth, M., & Lehman, C. (2012). *Pathways to the common core: Accelerating achievement.* Portsmouth, NH: Heinemann.

Carter, D. (2010, May). Ed-tech officials: Video will make schools more "efficient." *eSchool News.* Retrieved May 14, 2010, from http://www.eschoolnews.com/2010/05/05/ed-tech-officials-video-will-make-schools-more-efficient/2/?_login=cb81edbc3b?_login=cb81edbc3b

Center for Applied Special Technology (CAST). (2013). *Universal design for learning.* Retrieved March 5, 2013, from http://www.cast.org/about/index.html

Churches, A. (2008). Bloom's Taxonomy blooms digitally. *Tech & Learning, 1.* Retrieved September 24, 2013, from http://www.techlearning.com/studies-in-ed-tech/0020/blooms-taxonomy-blooms-digitally/44988.

Clark, R. C., & Lyons, C. (2004). *Graphics for learning.* San Francisco, CA: Pfeiffer.

Common Core State Standards (CCSS). (2010). *Common Core State Standards.* Retrieved May 19, 2013, from http://www.corestandards.org

Common Core State Standards (CCSS). (2013). *Common Core State Standards.* Retrieved March 5, 2013, from http://www.corestandards.org

Cooper, C., & Varma, V. (Eds.). (1997). *Processes in individual differences.* London: Routledge.

Crandell, C. C., Smaldino, J. J., & Flexer, C. (2005). *Sound field amplification: Applications to speech perception and classroom acoustics* (2nd ed.). Clifton Park, NY: Thompson/Delmar Learning.

Dale, E. (1969). *Audio-visual methods in teaching* (3rd ed.). New York, NY: Holt, Rinehart, & Winston.

Debbagh, N., & Bannan-Ritland, B. (2005). *Online learning: Concepts, strategies, and application.* Upper Saddle River, NJ: Pearson.

DeLoache, J. S. (2005). Mindful of symbols. *Scientific American, 33*(3), 73–77.

Dick, W., Carey, L., & Carey, J. O. (2014). *The systematic design of instruction* (8th ed.). Boston, MA: Allyn & Bacon.

Dodge, B. (1999). *The WebQuest page.* Retrieved from http://wequest.org

Driscoll, M. P. (2005). *Psychology of learning for instruction* (3rd ed.). Boston, MA: Allyn & Bacon.

Florida Virtual Schools (FLVS). (2012). *Florida Virtual School stakeholder surveys executive summary: 2011–2012.* Retrieved May 18, 2013, from flvs.net/areas/aboutus/Annual%20Evaluations/Exec2012.pdf

Flynn, J., & Russell, J. (2008). Personal response systems: Is success in learning just a click away? *Educational Technology, 48*(6), 20–23.

Gagné, R. M. (1985). *The conditions of learning* (4th ed.). New York, NY: Holt, Rinehart & Winston.

Gagné, R. M., Wager, W. W., Golas, K., & Keller, J.M. (2004). *Principles of instructional design* (5th ed.). Beverly, MA: Wadsworth Publishing.

Gardner, H. (2006). *Multiple intelligences: New horizons.* New York, NY: Basic Books.

Gardner, H. (2011). *Frames of mind: The theory of multiple intelligences.* New York, NY: Basic Books.

Gee, J. (2005). Good video games and good learning. *Phi Kappa Phi Forum, 85*(2), 33–37.

Glass, G., Welner, K., & Bathon, J. (2011, October). *Online K–12 schooling in the U.S.* National Education Policy Center. Retrieved November 23, 2012, from http://nepc.colorado.edu/publication/online-k-12-schooling

Gronlund, N. E. (2009). *Writing instructional objectives for teaching and assessment* (8th ed.). Upper Saddle River, NJ: Merrill/Prentice Hall.

Handsfield, L. J., Dean, T. R., & Cielocha, K. M. (2009). Becoming critical consumers and producers of text: Web 1.0 and Web 2.0. *The Reading Teacher, 63*(1), 40–50.

Hertz, M. B. (2012, July). The flipped classroom: Pro and con. *Edutopia*. Retrieved November 23, 2012, from http://www.edutopia.org/blog/flipped-classroom-pro-and-con-mary-beth-hertz

Huitt, W. G., Monetti, D. M., & Hummel, J. H. (2009). Direct approach to instruction. In C. Reigeluth & A. Carr-Chellman (Eds.), *Instructional-design theories and models: Building a common knowledge base* (Vol. III, pp. 73–97). New York: Routledge.

International Association for K–12 Online Learning (iNACOL). (2013, February). *Fast facts about online learning.* Retrieved May 19, 2013, from http://www.inacol.org/cms/wp-content/uploads/2013/04/iNACOL_FastFacts_Feb2013.pdf

International Society for Technology in Education (ISTE). (1998). *National Educational Technology Standards (NETS) for Students.* Retrieved August 21, 2009, from http://www.iste.org/Content/NavigationMenu/NETS/ForStudents/1998Standards/NETS_for_Students_1998.htm

International Society for Technology in Education (ISTE). (2007). *National Educational Technology Standards for Students (NETS-S)* (2nd ed.). Eugene, OR: Author.

International Society for Technology in Education (ISTE). (2008). *National Educational Technology Standards for Teachers (NETS-T).* Eugene, OR: Author.

International Society for Technology in Education (ISTE). (2009a). *ISTE policy brief: Technology and teacher quality—the indelible link.* Retrieved May 19, 2013, from http://www.computerexplorers.com/parents-download/Teacher-Quality-Brief.pdf

International Society for Technology in Education (ISTE). (2009b). *National Educational Technology Standards for Students (NETS-S).* Eugene, OR: Author.

International Society for Technology in Education (ISTE). (2012a). *National Educational Technology Standards (NETS) for Students.* Retrieved March 5, 2013, from http://cnets.iste.org/students/index.html

International Society for Technology in Education (ISTE). (2012b). *National Educational Technology Standards (NETS) for Teachers.* Retrieved March 5, 2013, from http://www.iste.org/Content/NavigationMenu/NETS/ForTeachers/NETS_for_Teachers.htm

Jenkins, H. (2009). *Confronting the challenges of participatory culture: Media education for the 21st century.* Boston, MA: MIT.

Johnson, D. W., & Johnson, R. T. (1999). *Learning together and alone: Cooperative, competitive, and individualistic learning.* Boston, MA: Allyn & Bacon.

Johnson, L., Adams Becker, S., Cummins, M., Estrada, V., Freeman, A., & Ludgate, H. (2013). *NMC horizon report: 2013 K–12 edition.* Austin, TX: The New Media Consortium.

Jolls, T. (2008). *Literacy for the 21st century: An overview and orientation guide to media literacy education.* Retrieved May 11, 2010, from http://www.medialit.org/reading_room/article540.html

Jonassen, D. H., Howland, J., Marra, R., & Crismond, D. (2008). *Meaningful learning with technology* (3rd ed.). Upper Saddle River, NJ: Pearson/Merrill/Prentice Hall.

Jonassen, D. H., Howland, J., Moore, J., & Marra, R. M. (2003). *Learning to solve problems with technology: A constructivist perspective.* Upper Saddle River, NJ: Merrill/Prentice Hall.

Kaiser Family Foundation. (2010). *Generation M2: Media in the lives of 8- to 18-year-olds.* Retrieved March 12, 2013, from http://www.kff.org/entmedia/upload/8010.pdf

Keller, J. M. (2010). *Motivational design for learning and performance: The ARCS model approach.* New York, NY: Springer Science + Business Media.

Kidd, T., & Chen, I. (2009). *Wired for learning: An educator's guide to Web 2.0.* Charlotte, NC: Information Age.

Kollie, E. (2013). Classroom amplification systems allow teachers to be heard. *School Planning and Management.* Retrieved March 12, 2013, from http://www.peterli.com/spm/resources/articles/archive.php?article_id=1230

Lehman, B. A. (1998) *The conference on fair use: Final report to the commissioner on the conclusion of the conference on fair use.* Retrieved September 24, 2013, from http://www.uspto.gov/web/offices/dcom/olia/confu/confurep.pdf

Livingston, G. (2011, February 9). *Latinos and digital technology.* Retrieved November 6, 2012, from http://pewresearch.org/pubs/1887/latinos-digital-technology-internet-broadband-cell-phone-use

Mager, R. F. (1997). *Preparing instructional objectives: A critical tool in the development of effective instruction* (3rd ed.). Atlanta, GA: The Center for Effective Performance.

Marzano, R. J., & Heflebower, T. (2012). *Teaching and assessing 21st century skills: The classroom strategies series.* Bloomington, IN: Marzano Research Laboratory.

Marzano, R. J., Pickering, D. J., & Heflebower, T. (2011). *The highly engaged classroom: The classroom strategies series.* Bloomington, IN: Marzano Research Lab.

Mayer, R. E., & Moreno, R. (2003). Nine ways to reduce cognitive load in multimedia learning. *Educational Psychologist, 38*(1), 43–52.

Morrison, G. R., & Lowther, D. L. (2010). *Integrating computer technology into the classroom* (4th ed.). Upper Saddle River, NJ: Merrill/Prentice Hall.

National Assessment Governing Board. (2008). *Reading framework for the 2009 National Assessment of Educational Progress.* Washington, DC: U.S. Government Printing Office.

National Assessment Governing Board. (2010). *Writing framework for the 2011 National Assessment of Educational Progress.* Washington, DC: U.S. Government Printing Office.

National Center for Missing & Exploited Children (NCMEC). (2013). *Netsnartz workshop.* Retrieved March 12, 2013, from http://www.netsmartz.org/RealLifeStories

National Governors Association Center for Best Practices (NGA Center) & Council of Chief State School Officers (CCSSO). (2010). *Common Core State Standards, English Language Arts.* Retrieved March 26, 2013, from http://www.corestandards.org/assets/CCSSI_ELA%20Standards.pdf

Nelson, T. A. (1992). *Metacognition.* Boston, MA: Allyn & Bacon.

Newby, T. I., Ertmer, P. A., & Stepich, D. A. (1995). Instructional analogies and the learning of concepts. *Educational Technology Research and Development, 43*(1), 5–18.

Newby, T. J., Stepich, D. A., Lehman, J. D., & Russell, J. D. (2010). *Educational technology for teaching and learning* (4th ed.). Upper Saddle River, NJ: Merrill/Prentice Hall.

Nielsen Company. (2012, January 22). *Led by Facebook, Twitter, global time spent on social media sites up 82% year over year.* Retrieved March 8, 2012, from http://blog.nielsen.com/nielsenwire/global/led-by-facebook-twitter-global-time-spent-on-social-media-sites-up-82-year-over-year

Paine, S. (2009, May). Profile. *T.H.E. Journal.* Retrieved from http://thejournal.com/articles/2009/05/01/profile--steven-paine.aspx

Paivio, A. (1971). *Imagery and verbal processes.* New York, NY: Holt, Rinehart & Winston.

Papert, S. (1993a). *The children's machine: Rethinking school in the age of the computer.* New York, NY: Basic Books.

Papert, S. (1993b). *Mindstorms: Children, computers, and powerful ideas.* New York, NY: Basic Books.

Partnership for 21st Century Learning. (2011). *Framework for 21st century learning.* Retrieved March 5, 2013, from http://www.21stcenturyskills.org/index.php?option=com_content&task=view&id=254&Itemid=119

Partnership for 21st Century Skills. (n.d.). *Learning for the 21st century: Report and mile guide for 21st century skills.* Retrieved October 2, 2008, from http://www.21stcenturyskills.org

Pfaffman, J. (2007). It's time to consider open source software. *TechTrends, 51*(3), 38-43.

Prensky, M. (2006, December/January). Adopt and adapt: 21st century schools need 21st century technology. *Edutopia,* 43–45.

Richardson, W. (2009). *Blogs, wikis, podcasts, and other powerful web tools for classrooms* (2nd ed.). Thousand Oaks, CA: Corwin.

Robertson, K. (2008). *Preparing ELLs to be 21st-century learners.* Retrieved February 15, 2010, from http://www.colorincolorado.org/article/21431

Rowe, S. S. (2012). A new kind of currency: Informational text literacy in elementary school. *National Association of School Psychologists. Communiqué.* Retrieved March 26, 2013, from http://www.readperiodicals.com/201201/2576109791.html#b

Schuck, S., & Kearney, M. (2008). Classroom-based use of two educational technologies: A sociocultural perspective. *Contemporary Issues in Technology and Teacher Education, 8*(4). Retrieved May 15, 2010, from http://www.citejournal.org/vol8/iss4/currentpractice/article2.cfm

Shaffer, D., Shaffer, K., Squire, R., & Gee, J. (2005). Video games and the future of learning. *Phi Delta Kappan, 87*(2), 105–111.

Simonson, M., Smaldino, S., Albright, M., & Zvacek, S. (2012). *Teaching and learning at a distance: Foundations of distance education* (5th ed.). Upper Saddle River, NJ: Pearson.

Slavin, R. E. (1989–1990). Research on cooperative learning: Consensus and controversy. *Educational Leadership, 47*(4), 52–54.

Smutny, J. F., & von Fremd, S. E. (2009). *Igniting creativity in gifted learners, K–6: Strategies for every teacher.* Thousand Oaks, CA: Corwin Press.

Solomon, G., & Scrum, L. (2007). *Web 2.0: New tools, new schools.* Eugene, OR: ISTE.

Stepien, W. J. (1999). Corsortium for problem based learning—Northern Illinois University. [Ebola problem no longer available.] Accessed June 6, 2010, from http://ed.fnal.gov/trc_new/tutorial

Teaching Channel. (2013). *Great teaching inspiring classrooms: About us.* Retrieved March 12, 2013, from https://www.teachingchannel.org/about-us

Thoman, E., & Jolls, T. (2004). Media literacy: A national priority for a changing world. *American Behavioral Scientist, 48*(1), 18–29.

U.S. Department of Education (USDOE). (2010). *National Education Technology Plan (NETP).* Retrieved May 18, 2013, from http://www.ed.gov/technology/netp-2010

U.S. Department of Education Office of Educational Technology (US-DOE OET). (2013). *Educational technology grants.* Retrieved May 14, 2013, from http://www.ed.gov/edblogs/technology/grants

Usher, A., & Kober, N. (2012). *Student motivation: An overlooked piece of school reform.* Retrieved December 2, 2012, from http://www.cep-dc.org/displayDocument.cfm?DocumentID=405

Vossen, G., & Hagemann, S. (2007). *Unleashing Web 2.0: From concepts to creativity.* Burlington, MA: Morgan Kaufmann Publishers.

Wagner, T. (2008). *The global achievement gap: Why even our best schools don't teach the new survival skills our children need—and what we can do about it.* New York, NY: Basic Books.

Warschauer, M. (2010, October). New reports on technology in U.S. schools: The changing divide. *Papyus News.* Retrieved November 25, 2012, from http://papyrusnews.com/2010/10/26/new-reports-on-technology-in-us-schools-the-changing-divide

Weinstein, P. (2005). Assessments unplugged. *Technology and Learning, 25*(6), 8–12.

Wikipedia. (2009). *Digital literacy.* Retrieved February 19, 2013, from http://en.wikipedia.org/wiki/Digital_literacy

Wood, C. (2005, April/May). Highschool.com: Online learning comes of age. *Edutopia,* 32–37.

Zawilinski, I. (2009). HOT blogging: A framework for blogging to promote higher order thinking. *The Reading Teacher, 62*(8), 650–661.

MP3 format, 165
Multi-device classroom, 103
Multimedia product rubric, 33
Multiple intelligences, 28
Multiple means of action, 17
Multiple means of engagement, 17
Multiple means of representation, 17
Music, visuals in, 195
Musical instrument digital interface (MIDI), 166–167
Musical/rhythmic, 167

National Assessment of Educational Progress (NAEP) Reading Framework, 191
National Educational Technology Plan (NETP), 219
National Educational Technology Standards for Students (NETS-S), 11, 27, 28–29, 38, 41, 42, 44, 52, 53–54, 171, 221
National Educational Technology Standards for Teachers (NETS-T), 9, 27, 38, 132, 220–221
National Geographic Society, 81, 136, 137, 172
National Instructional Materials Accessibility Standard (NIMAS), 17
National Library of Virtual Manipulatives, 225
National Medical Association, 83
National/state curriculum standards, 14
National Weather Service, 142
Netbooks, 10, 175
Netiquette, 139–140
Network, defined, 146
Network resources, 146–149
 evaluating web resources, 149
 types of, 146–148
 World Wide Web, 148–149
New Tech Network, 27
Nielsen Company, 11
NOAA, 142
Nonstructured informal study, 80–81

Ohm's Law, 29, 56
One-way video, 136
One Woman, One Vote (video), 175
Online education, choice of, 225–226
Online learning, 133, 138. See also Distance learning
Online office tools, 116–118
OpenOffice, 81
OpenOffice Calc, 198

Open source materials, 84. See also Free and inexpensive materials
Open source websites, 81
Operating system, 99
Oragnization charts, 198, 199
Organizational visuals, 202
Organization grants, 226
Output devices, 101

Papert, 93, 94
Parents, connecting with, 144
Participation of learners, in ASSURE model, 52–55
 feedback, 55
 practice, 52, 53–54, 55
Peer tutoring, in distance learning, 135
Performance checklist, 30
Persistence of vision, 168
Personal response systems (PRS), 7
Photos and photography, 198, 201, 207–208
Physical education, visuals in, 195
Pictorial graphs, 198, 200
Pie graphs, 198, 200
Pin boards, 118
Place shift, 131
Planning tools, 204–205
Podcast Alley, 165
Podcasts, 11, 165
Portable digital audio (music) player, 166
Portals, 148
Portfolio, 32–34
 artifacts in, 33
 assessment, 32–33
 traditional vs. electronic, 33, 34
Posters, 198, 200
PowerPoint, 34, 71, 99, 146, 203, 204, 206–207
Practice, 52, 53–54, 55
 communication and collaboration, 53–54
 creativity and innovation, 53
 critical thinking, problem solving, and decision making, 54
 education software for, 54
 with feedback, 134–135
 media for, 54, 55
 research and information fluency, 54
Preparation of learners, in ASSURE model, 52
Prerequisites, 40
Presentation evaluation form, 57
Presentation graphics, creating, 206–207

Presentations, 64–66, 77, 96, 134
Presentation software, 203
Pretest, 40
Prezi presentation, 71, 118, 206–207
Printed visuals, 204
Privacy Act, 138
Problem-based learning, 71–73, 77
Problem solving, for practice, 54
Problem-solving skills, 73
Process-type behaviors, 30
Product creation, 30
Product evaluation checklist, 32
Productivity suites, 81
Productivity tools, 116–118
Product-rating checklist, 31
Professional development, technology-focused, 220–221
Professional Development sections, 17–18, 35–36, 60–61, 87–88, 108–109, 126–127, 153, 181–182, 212, 229
Professional engagement, 221–224
 professional journals, 223–224
 professional organizations, 221–223
 state organizations, 223
Professional journals, 223–224
Professional organizations, 221–223
 American Library Association, 222
 Association for Educational Communications and Technology, 221–222
 Association for the Advancement of Computing in Education, 222
 Global SchoolNet Foundation, 222
 International Society for Technology in Education, 222–223
 International Technology and Engineering Educators Association, 223
 International Visual Literacy Association, 223
 United States Distance Learning Association, 223
Psychomotor domain, 25–26, 167, 169
Public Broadcasting System (PBS), 172
Puzzles, 74

Question-and-answer activities, in distance learning, 134
Quick Response (QR) codes, 171
QuickTime, 177

Random access memory (RAM), 101
Rapid prototyping machines, 105
Rating scales, 31
Read-only memory (ROM), 101

Credits

Design Elements: Chapter openers and Technology for All Learners image: Julien Eichinger/Fotolia; ASSURE Classroom Case Study, A Model to Help ASSURE Learning, and ASSURE Lesson Plan image: Pojoslaw/Fotolia; Copyright Concerns image: Tovovan/Fotolia; Media Samples and Technology Resources image: Vladgrin/Fotolia; Taking a Look at Technology Integration image: Dimec/Shutterstock; When to Use image: Keo/Fotolia.

Chapter 1: p. 1: Paul Hill/Fotolia; p. 3: Elypse/Fotolia; p. 5: (Audio) Kokhanchikov/Fotolia, (People, teenagers) Michael Flippo/Fotolia, (Video, camcorder) Himmelssturm/Fotolia, (Manipulatives, blocks) JackF/Fotolia, (Text, children) Karin & Uwe Annas/Fotolia, (Video, filmstrip) Mickyso/Fotolia, (Visuals, hand drawing) Peshkova/Fotolia, (Visuals, anatomy) Adimas/Fotolia, (Text, tablet with book) Pixel & Création/Fotolia, (People, icons) Niroworld/Fotolia, (Manipulatives, puppy) EwaStudio/Fotolia, p. 6: Joseph Sweeney/Pearson Education; p. 7: Joseph Sweeney/Pearson Education; p. 8: Joseph Sweeney/Pearson Education; p. 10: (top) Joseph Sweeney/Pearson Education, (bottom) Temych/Fotolia; p. 13: Joseph Sweeney/Pearson Education.

Chapter 2: p. 20: Samuel Borges/Fotolia; p. 21: Joseph Sweeney/Pearson Education; p. 22: Joseph Sweeney/Pearson Education; p. 23: (top) Joseph Sweeney/Pearson Education, (bottom) Robert Kneschke/Fotolia; p. 27: Joseph Sweeney/Pearson Education; p. 29: Joseph Sweeney/Pearson Education.

Chapter 3: p. 37: Poulsons Photography/Fotolia; p. 39: Patrick White/Merrill Education/Pearson Education; p. 51: (top left, and bottom) Lori Whitley/Merrill Education/Pearson Education, (top right) Valerie Schultz/Merrill Education/Pearson Education; p. 52: Lori Whitley/Merrill Education/Pearson Education.

Chapter 4: p. 62: Andres Rodriguez/Fotolia; p. 66: Lori Whitley/Merrill Education/Pearson Education; p. 67: Joseph Sweeney/Pearson Education; p. 70: Joseph Sweeney/Pearson Education; p. 71: Joseph Sweeney/Pearson Education; p. 73: Joseph Sweeney/Pearson Education; p. 74: Katelyn Metzger/Merrill Education/Pearson Education; p. 78: Joseph Sweeney/Pearson Education.

Chapter 5: p. 91: Operafotografica/Fotolia; p. 93: Joseph Sweeney/Pearson Education.

Chapter 6: p. 112: Samuel Borges/Fotolia, p. 114: Joseph Sweeney/Pearson Education; p. 119: Joseph Sweeney/Pearson Education.

Chapter 7: p. 130: Paul Hill/Fotolia, p. 132: Joseph Sweeney/Pearson Education; p. 136: Joseph Sweeney/Pearson Education; p. 146: (Workstation and Printers) Dmitriy Melnikov/Fotolia, (Plotter) Supertrooper/Fotolia, (Hard-disk storage) Damir Fajic/Fotolia, (File Server) MarFot/Fotolia; p. 147: Dmitriy Melnikov/Fotolia; p. 148: (Computer) Dmitriy Melnikov/Fotolia, (ISP Server, buildings) Andres Rodriguez/Fotolia, (modem) Ekipaj/Fotolia, (ISP Server, computer) MarFot/Fotolia.

Chapter 8: p. 157: Andres Rodriguez/Fotolia; p. 158: Lori Whitley/Merrill Education/Pearson Education; p. 160: Lorraine Swanson/Fotolia; p. 164: Joseph Sweeney/Pearson Education.

Chapter 9: p. 188: Operafotografica/Fotolia; p. 199: (Stage coach) Kreatiw/Fotolia, (Train, Car, Plane, Rocket, Space ship) Bitter/Fotolia, (Classification chart) U.S. Dept. of Agriculture, p. 200: (Pictorial graphs) Alexghidan89/Fotolia; p. 201: (Poster) Greentree/Fotolia, (photograph) Stoonn/Fotolia, (illustration/drawing) Caraman/Fotolia, (concept-related graphic) HuHu Lin/Fotolia, (stylized or arbitrary graphic) Katerinarspb/Fotolia; p. 202: (water cycle) M and R photos/Fotolia; p. 204: Valerie Schultz/Merrill Education/Pearson Education; p. 205: Freehandz/Fotolia.

Chapter 10: p. 218: Poulsons Photography/Fotolia.